Pete Seeger in His Own Words

Nine Lives Musical Series

Edited by David Amram

Pete Seeger in His Own Words,
Pete Seeger, Selected and Edited by Rob Rosenthal and Sam Rosenthal

Woody's Road: Woody Guthrie's Letters Home, Drawings, Photos, and Other Unburied Treasures,
Mary Jo Guthrie Edgmon and Guy Logsdon

Upbeat: Nine Lives of a Musical Cat,
David Amram

Offbeat: Collaborating with Kerouac,
David Amram

Vibrations: A Memoir,
David Amram

Pete Seeger

---

in His Own Words

Pete Seeger

Selected and Edited by

Rob Rosenthal and Sam Rosenthal

Paradigm Publishers

Boulder • London

The majority of writings in this book are from Pete Seeger's archive and have not been published before. Grateful thanks to other publishers who granted permission to reprint some published writings, especially to *Sing Out!* for multiple articles. Credits appear with any reprinted article. Thanks also to publishers of the following lyrics:

"Last Night I had the Strangest Dream." Ed McCurdy   Almanac Music, Richmond Publishing © 1955.

"I've Got to Know." Woody Guthrie, words and music © Woody Guthrie Publications.

"This Land Is Your Land." Woody Guthrie, words and music © Woody Guthrie Publications.

Published in the United States by Paradigm Publishers, 5589 Arapahoe Avenue, Boulder, Colorado 80303 USA.

Paradigm Publishers is the trade name of Birkenkamp & Company, LLC, Dean Birkenkamp, President and Publisher.

Library of Congress Cataloging-in-Publication Data

Seeger, Pete, 1919–
   Pete Seeger in his own words / Pete Seeger, with Rob and Sam Rosenthal.
     p. cm.—(Nine lives musical series)
   Includes bibliographical references and index.
   ISBN 978-1-61205-218-2 (hardcover : alk. paper)
   1. Seeger, Pete, 1919– 2. Folk singers—United States—Biography.   I. Rosenthal, Rob, 1951–   II. Rosenthal, Sam.   III. Title.
   ML420.S445A3 2012
   782.42162'130092–dc23
   [B]   2012009746

Printed and bound in the United States of America on acid-free paper that meets the standards of the American National Standard for Permanence of Paper for Printed Library Materials.

Designed and Typeset by Straight Creek Bookmakers.

16 15 14 13 12
2 3 4 5

Contents

Social Movements in the United States

Beyond the United States

Part 4: Looking Back and Looking Forward

Editors' Note

Pete originally wanted to make changes that would reflect his evolv-
ing political understandings, such as changing "he" to "he or she,"
or "Negroes" or "Afro-Americans" to "African Americans." We felt it
was important to preserve the historical accuracy of the pieces; they
shouldn't reflect a political sensibility that was not part of the times
when Pete wrote a particular entry. Our compromise has been to leave
the pieces as originally written and include this note.

Foreword by David Amram

Pete Seeger in His Own Words is destined to become a classic for the ages.

Rob Rosenthal and Sam Rosenthal painstakingly selected from countless letters and articles in Pete Seeger's personal archive this collection of gems—most of which are now being published for the first time. Together these writings reveal the unique strength of character that has made Pete Seeger a blessing for American society. Pete has helped to create a better world ever since he left Harvard in 1938, traveling the ribbon of highway with Woody Guthrie to Oklahoma and Texas.

As with Hector Berlioz's classic memoir *Evenings with the Orchestra*, the letters of Mozart and Beethoven, Dizzy Gillespie's spirited *To Be or Not To Bop*, Woody Guthrie's *Bound for Glory*, and Bob Dylan's *Chronicles*, we enter worlds of music that few of us have experienced before. Pete encourages us to join him in celebrating these musical highlights, sharing what he has learned during his journeys in the same inclusive way that he brings us together every time he invites us to sing along.

Pete's articles about folk music are among the best ever written. His knowledge of the history of thousands of songs has always been legendary among musicians. Now a wider audience has the opportunity to see Pete as a historian of the music he plays, as well as a brilliant and incisive biographer of himself and others.

One of the book's highlights appears in a previously unpublished letter to be read by his grandchildren after his demise. Fortunately, Pete gave permission to publish it here to share his philosophy of politics. He describes the story of some of his forebearers, a group of dissenters, who arrived on these shores on a ship called the Mayflower. *Pete Seeger in his Own Words* details how this descendent of the settlers has become a voice for all Americans. On every page, his words ring as clear as his banjo playing.

For more than fifty years, I have been fortunate to know Pete and play music with him. I continue to marvel at his dedication to his ideals. A recent event sums up what he has always been like—and how he remains, at the age of ninety-three—an idealist in action.

After an energy-packed concert for the Clearwater organization in New York City in September 2011, Pete's grandson, Tao Rodriguez Seeger, invited us to march from the stage and walk through the aisles of the Symphony Space theater as if we were going to march back on-stage, the way musicians in New Orleans often end their concerts. But instead of walking back onstage, Pete led us on a march thirty-six blocks from West 95th Street to the Columbus Circle Fountain.

Arlo Guthrie joined Tao, Pete, and me as we left the theater to begin the march, where we were to give an impromptu concert at midnight in front of the water fountain at Columbus Circle for all the people who couldn't afford the gala concert at Symphony Space. As we left the theater, we were greeted by a mob of marchers and well-wishers who knew from someone's website about our plans. As we walked, Pete commented on how useful his two new canes were to make this walk, which he felt was an addition to his many marches for freedom over the years. We agreed it was a pleasure not to walk through clouds of tear gas, as we had done in some marches in Washington, DC, decades ago.

The police officers who escorted us were friendly and supportive, and some even sang along with us. Pete told me how happy he was to see marchers with picket signs from the United Auto Workers and other unions, as well as teachers' groups and hordes of young people, including participants in Occupy Wall Street.

Pete hoped the march and the spontaneous midnight concert would be a peaceful message to all New Yorkers to find their own way to help assure a future for our kids and restore a world where fairness and decency for everyone was celebrated. As a child he was taught that we have to care for our family, friends, and neighbors, and to strive to be compassionate toward one another. Equally important, while we had to champion our right to make our voices heard, we also were obliged to pay attention and give respect to those with whom we don't agree, because freedom of speech is the precious right of everyone.

Pete, now in his nineties, seemed as energetic as he was when I first saw him playing for Henry Wallace's 1948 presidential campaign. Marching beside him, it was all I could do to keep up with him. Suddenly, Pete bent over and scooped up a scrap of paper from the sidewalk. Folding it carefully, he placed it in his pocket and resumed marching. I looked down a moment later and saw a discarded popsicle stick. Inspired by Pete, I made a touch-your toes-calisthenics movement and scooped it up. Pete leaned over and whispered in my ear, "You may put it in my jacket pocket if you wish."

Pete's gesture reminded me of how littered the streets of New York once were, when Pete initiated his pioneering efforts with the *Clearwater* to clean up the Hudson River. It was an example of what all of us who know Pete have heard him say: "Think globally, act locally."

Pete Seeger in His Own Words is a treasure trove of stories told by Pete himself. His words ring true; he celebrates the unique beauty of our country, and he inspires people of every political persuasion to celebrate living together in harmony. In his own words, Pete Seeger calls on us all to join together to create a better world for our children.

Preface

I was asked to write a short last chapter to this book. But Rob and Sam said it would be better as a preface. So here 'tis.

Dear Reader:

For 30 years or more, I had put copies of letters, unfinished diaries, and miscellaneous essays in a filing cabinet and forgot about 'em. Then four years ago, a professor asked if he could look through them, perhaps reprint some. I said "sure" in my usual unthinking way.

Behold. The professor and his son have made a book. I'm now age 93. Whatever insights I've had and whatever mistakes I've made in my long life are now displayed. The inconsistencies, the contradictions are all here. All? Well, at least a lot of 'em, thanks to Rob and Sam.

Yes, thanks also to Dean Birkenkamp and the folks at Paradigm Publishers, you can now read them.

Now, I'll waste a little time to say that I found myself wanting to rewrite almost all of the pieces in this book. But Rob and Sam thought it best not to go down that road. What was, is.

> *To all of you I say, stay well.*[1] *Keep on,*
> *Old Pete Seeger*

---

1. "Arabs are proud that the whole world uses Arabic numerals. If you have your health, put down a number '1.' If you have a family put a '0' next to it. 10! If you have land, put another '0' next to that. 100! If you have a good reputation, 1,000! You got it all. But take away the 1, whatcha got? Three zeroes. (In a book around the year 1200 CE, an Italian mathematician, Fibonacci, urged people to stop wasting time dividing and multiplying with Roman numerals. Use Arabic numerals, said he!)" —P. S

Introduction

Pete Seeger, an Appreciation

Pete Seeger is quite arguably the most important American folksinger of the 20th century.

Pete—as he's invariably known to everyone—would hate almost everything about that sentence. He would take out his black pen and start editing, as is his wont. "I'm just one link in a chain," he'd say. "There are much better singers and writers than I, the people I learned from and still learn from [see chapter 3, entry 1]. Those are the important people to listen to."

"And why talk about 'American'? If there's anything I've learned in my travels all over the world, it's that people want to hear and learn about American folk songs, but they all have wonderful, vibrant traditions of their own [see chapter 12]. All this emphasis on one country— any one country—is foolish. We ought always to be thinking about the whole world" [see chapters 10, 11, and 20].

"I don't even know what you mean by 'folk singer' [see chapter 4]. The biggest mistake I ever made was letting people call me a folk singer, when all music is a mixture of all kinds of influences. Anyway, this whole emphasis on who's important and who's not—we're all important, and the artist no more than anyone else. The goal isn't to be an Important Artist, a star, separate from everyone else. The goal is to get *everyone* to be an artist, a singer, a participant [see chapter 14]. As my father said, 'Judge the musicality of a nation not by the presence of virtuosos, but by the general level of people who like to make music'" [see chapter 20, entry 2].

Well, all good points. What, then, makes a volume like this worth doing and worth reading? What has made Seeger important enough to the rest of us that we think his words worth pondering?

Seeger matters, first of all, because he has provided a model of an alternative way of being for musicians, for activists, for all those who want alternatives to the American Way of Life in the twentieth and twenty-first centuries. He and his wife Toshi have lived most of their adult lives on 17 acres overlooking the Hudson, where they built their first home, a log cabin, in the early 1950s, and where they continue to live in a modest one-bedroom home, often surrounded by their children and other members of their extended family. They tap the trees for maple syrup, split wood for their stoves, and attend local meetings and protests.

This is particularly striking given the privileged lives of most entertainment stars in the United States (and in many other places), a model Seeger has quite consciously rejected. He washes the dishes at home; he takes his turn cleaning up after the pot luck meetings. He has never sought a "career" in which personal advancement was the goal (although he's been quite happy to have made a living all these years doing something he loves). His alternative kind of career has instead proclaimed to others: it's possible to use your art for our collective good, not just for individual advancement. This has been an extremely powerful model for young artists, a way of thinking about what they're doing and what their aims should be that has rarely been offered elsewhere.

This commitment to the collective good is implicit in a second great contribution Seeger has made: his emphasis on the importance of participation by those normally thought of as "the audience." With his gently enthusiastic manner, carefully honed and recalibrated over the years, he encourages his audiences to join him in performance. For Seeger, the politics of the activity itself is its most important aspect; a musician encourages democracy by encouraging people to lift their voices in song. Solidarity and equality are not only stated, but also felt. In a 1998 interview with one of this book's editors, he said

> I'm singing a wide variety of songs, trying to touch base with these different kinds of people, get 'em involved, not just listening but singing. I think the act of singing is very important.... Even singing a sentimental old song can actually be a very political thing if people are singing together. It might be *You Are My Sunshine*. Because Black and White people are singing that together, getting a little harmony together, it becomes a very important thing.... When it first came out I was rather contemptuous of it—one more attempt of the ruling class to give us nice, pretty songs and forget about problems we should face up to. Well, now I see that it's not just the words of the song, but the singing of the song which is even more important.

Repeatedly, Seeger has expressed this as his primary goal: "It all boils down to what I would most like to do as a musician. Put songs on people's lips instead of just in their ears."

Seeger's importance as role model, committed to collective singing and collective struggle, has endured for over seventy years now, a span that's hard to fathom, and in this lies his third major contribution: he has served as a bridge between eras, struggles, and peoples. Seeger has always argued that movements for social justice, whatever their particular focus, must link up together: "You can't really solve the problem of poverty on earth unless you can also solve the problem of pollution on earth," he writes in "There Are No Old, Bold Pilots" [in chapter 20]. "And vice versa. My guess is we won't solve the problem of racism and sexism and a whole lot of other things until each of us, individually, realizes how much we depend on others—sometimes those near and dear to us, sometimes those faraway and unknown." Seeger was a visible, embodied link between the Old Left and the New Left, the labor movement and the civil rights movement, the civil rights movement and the movement against the war in Vietnam, the antiwar movement and the labor movement. He spoke of women's issues while he discussed the Israeli/Arab conflict; he raised questions of race while he supported the Cuban revolution. Issues of justice and freedom, he has insisted, are always intertwined, and our attempts to deal with such issues must always acknowledge these interconnections.

As a bridge between movements for so long, Seeger has also spanned the generations, consciously mentoring younger generations of musicians and activists and appealing to an audience—his coparticipants—that ranges in age far more than most "entertainers." Of course, his impact has been greatest among those who grew up at about the same time he did, but it's a legacy that has been handed down as well. The various celebrations of his work in the last decade—the *Seeger Sessions* concerts and album by Bruce Springsteen, the film biography *Pete Seeger: The Power of Song*, and other recent works—have introduced or reintroduced him to younger generations, in some cases rekindling buried memories of listening to his records being played by their parents when they were growing up. And the songs he has written and/or made famous—"Turn, Turn, Turn," "If I Had a Hammer," "Where Have All the Flowers Gone," "Little Boxes," and so on—have never faded from public consciousness nor artists' repertoire, with new versions constantly finding their way into popular and folk culture, making his work, if not always his name, familiar to successive generations.

As he has linked generations and struggles, Seeger has consciously, intentionally, relentlessly linked lands and cultures. He has travelled the world for well over sixty years, singing songs from the United States to and with audiences in other countries, but always also picking up songs in each country he visited and bringing these back home and around the globe. Some of these, like "Guantanamera," have become among his most readily recognized songs. At each stop, he has delighted in showing others what he feels to be authentic cultural products of the United States (as opposed to what he refers to as the "Coca-Cola" products of the society), but as he has done so, he has urged those who come to hear this music to also treasure their own culture, to resist being overwhelmed by the popular culture being beamed in from the dominant economic powers.

In this sense, he has been a repository of the traditions of many cultures. When he traveled to Spain after the fall of Franco and heard people singing revolutionary songs that had been banned there for the thirty-six years Franco was in power, he asked them, "Where did you learn those songs?" and they said, "From tapes of your records."[1]

He would demur: "You can sing [your own songs] better than anyone else," he tells us [in chapter 12, entry 9]. But this has not always been possible for all people. Censorship or social disapproval or disuse, and therefore loss of a tradition, have robbed different people at different times of their cultural heritage. His struggle against that loss—in general, and in specific cases of specific songs—is another of his important contributions.

In his dual identities as ambassador of U.S. folk culture and respectful collector of the cultures of other societies, Seeger has been adopted by widely disparate groups of people as one of their own. Several years ago, one of this book's editors gave a talk at a local arts center about the work we were doing with Seeger, accompanied by YouTube videos of groups across the world singing just one of his songs, "Where Have All the Flowers Gone?": Joan Baez at the 1994 Kennedy Center ceremony honoring Seeger; Earth Wind and Fire on their 1972 album *Last Days and Time*; children in a school chorus in Singapore on parents' night in 2006; Marlene Dietrich in a London concert in 1963; Pedro Capeto, a young man sitting on a plaza in Mexico with his guitar in 2007; Ase Kleveland, a Swedish/Norwegian singer, who later became the minister of culture in Norway, on a television show in 1963; Saint Peter's Church Chorus in Saskatchewan in 2008; The Tansads, an English punk band, in 2009; Gogliola Cinquetti, an Italian singer, in 1969; and Pete and his grandson Tao in Barcelona in 1993.

When we began working with Pete to assemble this book, he had only one request: "Don't make me out to be a saint. I'm no saint!" The writings to follow make that clear. We present not a saint but a man struggling with the complexities and conflicts of time and place, making good choices, making other choices he now regrets, seeking to understand what makes sense and what is right in a world of turbulence and confusion.

But that said, we answer the question of why create or read a book about Seeger by insisting that no matter the mistakes, no matter the confusion, no matter the obvious truth that his glory and his errors were not his alone, Seeger has lived a life of such impact—and lived it so honorably—that understanding how he navigated that life is important.

---

1. Hear this story on the song "Jarama Valley," on the album *Spain in My Heart* (Appleseed Records APRCD 1074, 2003).

Seeger would be the first to say that his approach to life was in large part a legacy from others, beginning with his parents, and in particular his father, Charles Seeger, whose radical democratic tendencies in politics and in music were cornerstones of Pete's understanding of the role of the citizen and the artist in modern society. His family—first the extended family he grew up in, and then the extended family he and Toshi created—has been central to his intellectual and emotional life and to his ability to live the kind of life he has lived. It's a truism among Seeger's friends that he "could not have been Pete" (as it's often expressed) without Toshi, who has functioned as manager, agent, and political consultant/confidante, all while doing the lion's share of raising the three children (and in a house that, for a time, lacked modern conveniences such as an indoor toilet). Seeger's musical mentors (including Alan Lomax, Leadbelly, and above all Woody Guthrie) and those with whom he grew to musical maturity (Lee Hays, Bess Lomax Hawes, Mill Lampbell, Sis Cunningham, Ronnie Gilbert, and many others) provided the education and inspiration Seeger's hungry mind and heart were more than ready to exploit. There were those like Woody who consciously strove to educate the young, idealistic, naïve Seeger in the ways of the world and the ways of the folk, but the truth is that Seeger was a sponge, soaking up new ideas and licks as fast as they came, convinced he had a date with destiny even as he despaired of ever amounting to anything [see chapter 2, entry 10].

If specific relationships were crucial to Seeger's growth, these occurred against the backdrop of a time and place that framed them in particular ways. Seeger came from an old genteel Yankee family, yet one that had largely lost its money. He went to boarding school as a scholarship student during the Depression, and then on to Harvard (until he dropped/flunked out) as massive unemployment, the rise of fascism, and the opening skirmishes of World War II emerged. The old Yankee values—honor, duty, fairness, self-reliance—confronted a world that seemed to have little to do with the world those values assumed; nonetheless, it was his interpretation of those very values in the context of that world in turmoil that led Seeger to position himself in ways some of his ancestors would hardly have understood, allying himself with an international working class against the power of the elite class from which he descended.

Coming of age in the late '30s, in New York, in the left-wing world that grew up around the Communist Party and other progressive groups—an environment that included not only political groupings but all variety of cultural initiatives tied to those groups—was a heady experience. In that ferment, Seeger helped form the Almanac Singers, in many ways the group that remains closest to Seeger's ideal: "We were a strange combination of people and we put out some good songs, and lived through exciting times," he recalled many years later in a piece written just for his fellow Almanacs [see chapter 2, entry 6]. "We participated in these exciting times.... We called ourselves Communists. Probably none of us agree even now exactly on the definition of Communism. But I don't think any of us are ashamed of what we did way back in the days of 1941 and '42."

The Popular Front policy of the Communist Party in the 1930s had already laid the groundwork for a political and cultural philosophy that encouraged alliances beyond the narrow confines of just the Left, a conflating of the radical class-struggle tenets of Marxism with the homegrown radical democratic tradition of Tom Paine, Jefferson, Lincoln, and Roosevelt. With the exception of the years of the Stalin-Hitler pact between August 1939 and June 1941 [see chapter 2, entry 6], it was entirely possible to be a dedicated leftist and still celebrate existing American society: "Communism is twentieth-century Americanism," Community Party leader Earl Browder had famously declared in 1935.

Against the background of these (shifting) theoretical and political concerns, the practical daily task was the building of industrial labor unions, and it was this task beyond any that preoccupied Seeger and his friends. The Almanacs' best-known album was called *Talking Union;* their famous, almost mythical, 1941 tour was designed to support organizing efforts of the newly emerging Congress of Industrial Organizations (CIO) [see chapter 2, entry 6]. In this critical period of Seeger's formation, if one objective summed up what he wanted to do, it was to build "a singing union movement."

A worldview that combined culture with politics and socialism with Americanism was relatively easy to sustain in the years of World War II. In the army, Seeger was able to serve his country and fight fascism at one and the same time. In the aftermath of the war, however, that conflation was no longer possible. As the cold war set in, anticommunism became a hysteria in the United States; Communists, Communist allies, and leftists and liberals of many stripes became subject to legal and economic sanctions. Seeger suffered being blacklisted for the next two decades, on the one hand a great economic hardship, but on the other (as Dick Flacks has argued[2] and Seeger himself has said), a narrowing of commercial opportunities that compelled him to further develop the very grassroots democratic approach that was implicit in the worldview he inherited from his father, visible in his work with the Almanacs before the war, and which came to be the epitome of what he stood for: singing *with* people rather than *to* people.

The blacklist was ongoing; similarly, the threat of going to prison for contempt of Congress for refusing to cooperate with investigations into Communist "subversion" by the House Un-American Activities

---

2. "Richard Flacks on Pete Seeger." www.truthdig.com/arts_culture/item/200090806_richard_flacks_on_ pete_seeger/, August 7, 2009.

Committee (HUAC) hung over his head for five years, from 1957 to 1962. But a single event, born of the same hysteria, may have marked Seeger more than either of these—the Peekskill riot of September 1949 [see chapter 5, entry 5]. His car and over a thousand other cars were stoned by right-wing anti-Communists as they left a performance, the lives of his family endangered; sixty years later, conversations with Seeger still tend to circle back to that night as pivotal, a first-hand look at what a world of fascism might really mean, a personal touchstone and reason for never giving up his political work.

Seeger and his family survived that day, survived the blacklist, survived the threat of imprisonment, and gradually the country caught up with him. As the great social movements of the 1960s and '70s changed the nation, Seeger emerged first as a hero to the younger generation of activists, and eventually, in large part due to his work starting a clean-up of the Hudson River [see chapter 8], to a broader, more mainstream population. Though to this day he encounters people who hate him for his past, who call him "Stalin's Songbird" and think he's a traitor to his country, he has achieved a level of respectability he could scarcely have imagined when he set out to become a political musician in the late 1930s. He's received, for example, the Presidential Medal of the Arts from Bill Clinton and a Lifetime Legends medal from the Library of Congress. Perhaps the crowning moment of this new status came when, supported by Bruce Springsteen and Tao Seeger, he performed at the 2008 Inaugural Concert for President Barack Obama. There, in the center of the spotlight, he sang Woody's greatest song, "This Land Is Your Land," including the long-suppressed verses that question private property and celebrate the radical democracy, the small "c" communism, in which he's always believed—a very sweet moment, earned by a lifetime of commitment.

We were asked to take on this project by Dean Birkenkamp of Paradigm Publishers in the spring of 2009. At the time, Dean spoke (with some slight reverence) of "The Barn" on Seeger's land in Beacon, New York, which, it was rumored, held all sorts of papers from Seeger's past. David Dunaway, author of the most authoritative of the Seeger biographies, *How Can I Keep From Singing?*, had already made use of many of those files, but Dean's idea, which he'd discussed the previous fall with Pete, was that a book could be created exclusively from Seeger's writings, drawing on his published writings and some of the many unpublished pieces that could be found in the file cabinets, cardboard boxes, and accordion folders to be found in The Barn and the loft office in Seeger's house. The published writings were fairly daunting in themselves—Seeger has written or cowritten more than thirty books (including songbooks), he contributed a regular column called "Johnny Appleseed, Jr." (later simply "Appleseeds") to *Sing Out!* magazine for over fifty years, and he has penned an astounding number of book forwards, articles for other journals, album liner notes, and so on. The unpublished materials, it turned out, were equally daunting: 70 years' worth of letters, notes to himself, diaries, lists, and so forth.

For a year and a half, we drove over to Seeger's house a few times a month, going through everything he had, reading it all piece by piece and scanning anything that seemed important. ("I believe you're going to know more about me than I do," Pete told us once, with a chuckle.) The thousands of letters, to and from him (he kept carbons from very early on), were particularly striking. Although we were only planning on using those from him (since this was a collection of *his* writings), it was hard not to be fascinated by the letters that he received. The collection embodied the Seegers' democratic perspective, with letters from former presidents lying in a folder next to letters from a fan, an inmate in a prison down the road, an activist in South Africa. The tone of many of the letter writers mirrors that perspective, an equation of all letters as equally important, equally familiar, even from those who don't know him personally. People send him their stories and songs and poetry; they feel like he's their personal friend. For many years, he and Toshi personally answered every one of these letters.

The letters that arrive are stunning in another way as well: many arrive from political activists, from all over the world, in all kinds of situations—in prison, in struggle, in defeat, in victory. One message appears over and over: "Thank you for your music! It's helped me bear the burdens and celebrate the joy of my struggle."

Once we had scanned everything we thought might be of use, we spent another year reading and re-reading it all, picking the pieces we thought most important and trying to form chapters around themes. As folksingers rework the old folk songs they interpret, Seeger uses and reuses his own ideas, refashioning them for different purposes and audiences, revising them until he feels satisfied with how they turn out. Thus, different versions of pieces often turned up in different forms, and in those cases, we chose the one that we felt best represented the theme he was developing.

Above all, our goal was to let Seeger's voice come through with as little interference from us as possible (and indeed, after this introduction you will hear very, very little from us again). We have edited only to maintain focus or clarify passages we thought hard to follow because of references that might be unrecognized by some readers, or because words were obviously missing, or to add or omit punctuation when we thought it made Seeger's intent clearer. We have signaled where we omitted more than a few words by adding an ellipsis. But by and large, we have presented these writings as Seeger originally wrote them. We have added explanatory footnotes when needed; explanatory footnotes written by Seeger (either at the time or in later readings) are followed by his initials and presented in quotation marks.

Our agreement with Pete was that he would be able to read everything we wanted to include and reject anything he didn't want to appear. True to his editor's nature, he did indeed read everything, commenting on many things, filling the margins of some readings with his suggested edits. But he did not ask us to remove a single entry.

"Don't make me out to be a saint" is what he told us, and we have held him to his word. Our intent in our selections has never been to beatify Seeger, or make him look good (or bad). Our goal has been to present the perspective of a fascinating man of our times, to trace his evolution as he struggled to make sense of a world in pain and the groups of people who wanted to make the world a better place. Our thanks to Pete, and to Toshi, Danny, Mika, and Tinya (son and daughters), for letting us try to do that.

Rob Rosenthal and Sam Rosenthal
Middletown, Connecticut, and New York City

Part 1
The Early Years:
1919~1947

1

Growing Up (1919–1934)

"My Family Background," 1957

Draft of letter to Paul Ross,[1] dated
May 10, 1957; found in Seeger files

Dear Paul,

You wanted some résumé of my family background and life, so I sit me down and try to organize a teeming memory.

First of all, like many people, I have spent much of my youth trying to forget my antecedents. I confess it. I tried to ignore them, to disparage them. I felt they were all upper-class, and I was trying to identify myself with the working people. Now, at the sage and sober age of 38 I have finally come around to assess them more objectively, to be grateful for their strength and character, for their making it possible for me to be alive on this world today, and to realize that a good honest streak of independency has run through them for as much of the last three hundred years as I know about.

Most of them seemed to be teachers, doctors, teachers, preachers, businessmen, teachers, artists, writers, or teachers. The generations seem shot through with pedagogues. In this century, both parents, several brothers, aunts, and uncles have all been teachers. Going back a few generations, we find several doctors, and more teachers. Back further, even a few soldiers, perhaps a lawyer, a hymn writer, and more teachers. Even old Elder Brewster on the Mayflower was as much a scholar as anything else. So: my hat off to them all, and the pursuit of knowledge. "Where men gather to seek truth, that spot is holy ground." Probably the most financially successful was old great grandpa Charlier,

---

1. Seeger's attorney who represented him during the blacklist years. See chapter 5.

3

whose select Institute was one of New York's most elegant a century ago. But then he was the only one also ever brought before a congressional committee and asked how come some rich men's sons were arranging bribes to congressmen for West Point applications. So maybe it's just as well most of them weren't too successful.

As for radicals, Lordy, the family seems shot through with them, too. In earlier centuries, this took the form of religious protest: Pilgrims, puritans—and I'm proud to see a lot of Quakers around, on both sides of the family (and now I find, in Toshi's family, too). Even great grandpa Charlier was the son of a French Huguenot preacher.

Later, the radicalism took a more political turn. Great-great grandpa Seeger got disgusted with Prussian tyranny, came to America and was an ardent Jeffersonian. Refused to teach any of his sons the German language even. Went around New England orating for the new Republican-Democratic party (in between making his living as a doctor). Another branch of the family were all fervent abolitionists about one generation later. Even the businessman I knew best, my grandfather, had the independence to quit his job in the local bank (Springfield, Mass.) and seek his fortune in Mexico. Made it, or at least got it. Lost a good deal of it, I'm told, when a partner defaulted and a firm went bankrupt. My grandfather spent many years of his life conscientiously paying off every single debt, although he was not legally required to do so.

The main radicals in the 20th Century seem to have been of an aesthetic bent. I won't mention the respectable relative who took me (at age 14) walking in the New York May Day parade. In those days, as the *New Yorker* magazine recently remarked, everyone was a social reformer. Sitting around the house without a job, it was the natural thing to do. I will mention my uncle Alan, whom I never knew. He was killed in 1914. He was a Shelley[2] type poet. I only found this out recently. As a kid, I was unable to make out his poetry. But now, upon reading it, I find lots of it very good. He was in the famous Harvard class of 1910, along with Lippman,[3] Broun,[4] and his friend John Reed.[5] My grandparents thought him a ne'er-do-well, because he then wouldn't settle down to the life of a respectable businessman. Instead he went to France, fell in love with the country and the people, and when the First World War broke out, enlisted in the Foreign Legion, and was the second American to be killed. He left behind a slim volume of verse, and some miscellaneous writings,

2. Percy Bysshe Shelley (1792–1822) was an English Romantic poet, known for combining elements of fantasy and reality in intensely personal poems.
3. Walter Lippmann (1889–1974) was a political commentator and journalist who co-founded *The New Republic* magazine.
4. Heywood Broun (1888–1939) was a journalist and the founder of a journalists' labor union, the American Newspaper Guild.
5. John Reed (1887–1920) was a journalist, war correspondent, and Communist activist, best known for *Ten Days That Shook the World,* his first-person account of the Russian Revolution in 1917.

to tell what a wonderful contribution he could have made, had he lived. As I say, I only recently appreciated this. When I (at age 6) was forced to read before the 2nd grade class (mispronouncing almost every word): "I have a rennn–dezzz–voozz with death ..." Poor Uncle Alan!

Oh, and in this century, miscellaneous other relatives experimented with Christian Science, yogism, nudism, advocated woman's suffrage, pacifism, vegetarianism, organic gardening, and one was part of the NY *Daily Worker*.[6] This might all add up to sound like a family full of crackpots, but believe me, they have all have all been well-thought-of members of their communities. It does all point up to a remarkable streak of independence and I, at age 38, take my hat off to it.

Me? I was born in 1919. Never had to go hungry, but witnessed a good deal of family penny pinching. Been at boarding school almost all my life, first starting at aged five. Went for five years to a small private progressive school in Connecticut, where I became a fervent disciple of Ernest Thompson Seton, the Canadian naturalist, whose descriptions of the primitive communist lives of the American Indian communities seemed ideal to me. Loved the woods and hills above all, till I was sixteen. Once argued that I wanted to be a hermit, live by myself on a mountainside, and let the sinful world go its way. (Cracks Toshi now: Yeah, but why ask your wife to do it too?)

"All Mixed Up," 2009

From *Where Have All the Flowers Gone,* Revised
Edition, W. W. Norton & Company, 2009

My mother was a good violinist.[7] My father was head of the music department at the University of California, Berkeley. But, he got radicalized by some fellow professors. In 1918 he was making speeches against imperialist war and got fired. Back east he got the great idea to take the music of Bach and Beethoven out to the countryside. He built one of America's first automobile trailers in his parents' barn in upstate New York. It looked more like a covered wagon, with a canvas top and [big wheels with] four solid rubber tires, pulled by a Model T Ford. It was to be kind of a one-family Chautauqua[8] tour.

---

6. *The Daily Worker* was the most important newspaper published by the Communist Party USA, beginning in 1924.
7. "Constance De Clyvver Edson (1886–1975) was ⅜ English descent, ¼ French, ¼ Irish, ⅛ Dutch. My father, Charles Louis Seeger (1886–1978), was ⅛ German and the rest English settlers in Massachusetts. So far as I know. One never knows what went on between the sheets. We're all distant cousins, all 7-plus billion of us. A grandfather and a great-grandmother played piano, another could rattle the bones, another loved to sing and dance, into her 70s." —P. S.
8. Chautauqua tours were touring lecture series, popular in the late nineteenth and early twentieth centuries in the United States. The tours were aimed at educating adults about issues of the day, usually catering to a Christian populist viewpoint.

But, roads in 1921 were mostly unpaved. The Tin Lizzie [slang for a Model T] pulled the trailer at an average speed of 20 to 25 miles an hour. My mother had to wash my diapers in an iron pot over an open fire. She finally said, "Charlie, this is not going to work." They returned to New York and got jobs teaching at the Institute of Musical Art (now Juilliard). It was a world of high ideals, long training, great discipline. But, early in life I learned that rules were made to be broken. Henry Cowell,[9] the modern composer, was a family friend. When I was six, I remember him playing the piano with his fists.

My mother had hoped that one of her children would play the violin. She bought miniature fiddles for my two older brothers. They rebelled. When I came along my father said, "Oh, let Peter enjoy himself." But she left musical instruments all around the house. I remember having fun at age four or five making a racket on Autoharp, pennywhistle, marimba, a pull-push accordion, a piano, a pump organ. All by ear.

At age eight I was given a ukulele. Started picking out chords, learning their names. At boarding school I learned popular tunes of the day. Silly words but clever rhymes. Plunk, plunk. My father was researching some of the few collections of folk music available in those days. I learned from him that there were often different versions of the same song. People changed words, melody, made up new verses. This was an important lesson: you can choose the version of the song you want to sing.

"A Laissez-faire Upbringing," 1972

From *The Incompleat Folksinger,* Simon and Schuster, 1972

I said I had a *laissez-faire* upbringing. I'm forever grateful for it. From age eight I was away at boarding school. It was the decade when the term "progressive education" first flowered. Our class would take up a "project" (ancient Egypt, the Middle Ages, etc.). We'd write a play about some event in those times, stage it and act in it. Shop class, English class, even math would be drawn into it. The main thing we all got from it: learning, real learning, is fun.

And summers at home we were forever building things. One summer it was model boats, another summer model airplanes. Music? We made music for the fun of it. My parents, bless them, decided to let me find out for myself what kind of music I liked.

---

9. Cowell (1897–1965), a composer and music theorist who studied under Charles Seeger while he was a member of the faculty at UC Berkeley, is among the most important American avant-garde composers of the twentieth century. In addition to his experiments in Western music, Cowell was a student of many other musics of the world, occasionally helping to compile and writing liner notes for Folkways releases in the world music genre.

I did get one strict lesson at school, which I'll not forget. At age fourteen I started a school newspaper, just for the hell of it.[10] It was in competition with the official school paper, which was dull, respectable, and always late. Mine was pure Free Enterprise, a mimeographed weekly; I gathered the news, typed it up, sold it for a nickel, and kept the money.

But after a few months I'd had my kicks and decided to quit it. The headmaster called me in. "Peter, I think you ought to continue the paper." He explained that the wealthy old woman who paid the school's deficit liked reading it; its informal tone made her feel closer to the school. Her journalist friends, the young Alsop brothers,[11] had complimented her on it.

I demurred. It's a lot of work, says I, and doesn't leave me as much free time as I'd like. But the headmaster was firm. "Better get your copy for next week's issue."

My favorite teacher sided with the headmaster. "You can't be a butterfly all your life, Peter." So for two more years I brought it out on schedule. Years later I discovered that this was why I got a complete scholarship to an otherwise rather expensive school. But just as valuable was what I learned in running the *Avon Weekly Newsletter*: typing, writing, editing, cartooning, and learning how to walk up to a stranger and try to ask the right questions. The goofs I made! Edna St. Vincent Millay[12] visited the school when we put on her play *Aria Da Capo*, an antiwar allegory. (With my hair in curls, I'd played the female lead—Avon was not co-ed).

The English teacher said I should take the opportunity to get an interview with her. "She's an important modern poet."

"What the heck will I ask her?"

"Don't be silly."

So I found myself seated awkwardly before this demure and beautiful woman, blurting out, "What do you think of Shakespeare?"

"I Would Like to Buy a Big Banjo," 1932

Letter to Constance de Clyver Edson Seeger from Avon Old Farms boarding school, Fall 1932; found in Seeger files

Dearest Mama,

I'm really awful mad at myself for not writing sooner, I'd put it off and put it off and put it off until I just had to.

---

10. "No. I hoped to make a few nickels." —P. S.

11. Joseph and Stewart Alsop, newspaper columnists who co-wrote a column for the *New York Herald Tribune* from 1945 to 1958, were natives of Avon, Connecticut, where Seeger's boarding school was located.

12. Millay (1892–1950) was a feminist playwright and poet whose works often addressed the horrors of war.

I'm getting along pretty well and am fitting in very well with every-thing. Did you get the card of my monthly marks? I got an "A", a "D", a few "Cs", and a "B". I'll try to pull 'em up because I know that they aren't very good.

I'm going to try and write one letter every day to somebody or other at least. Some time along now, pretty soon, there will be what is called a "long weekend" and if one wants to, one may come home for it. May I? I'll write as soon as I find out when it is.

If one gets on the Dean's list one may get an extra weekend home and so I'm going to try and get on it.

I think I'll start a diary. It would be terribly useful only I wouldn't know what to put in it. And then I'd put off writing something down that night and put it off till evening, the next morning, and so on.

I would like to buy a big banjo and play in the very little jazz band up here that has just been started. I have been practicing on one of the masters' banjos but it's awful awkward to keep borrowing it. It's not half so hard to play one as I thought and I've already learned about ten chords the last week and can read "B# dim." and play something that sounds okay and is technically correct. I'm having lots of fun. The music teacher said that he would go into Hartford with me and help me choose one from a pawn shop and I could use my allowance money to get it if it wasn't over nine dollars or so. Will you let me get one? Please.

Your loving son,
Peter

"I'd Like to Buy a Good Banjo," 1933

Letter to Constance De Clyver Edson Seeger from Avon Old Farms boarding school, Winter 1933; found in Seeger files

Dearest Mama,

How are you? Don't work too hard. I'm getting along quite well. My shoe-shining business is thriving, only now that there is so much snow on the ground, shoes get wet and then they don't take a shine.

I was wondering what I should do about my banjo, you see, being second hand, as it is, it will naturally cost quite a bit to repair it because small parts will be constantly falling apart or breaking. Only two days ago one of the pegs broke from long wear and I will have to buy a new one. Do you think that I should spend $15 or $20 of my savings in the bank to buy a good banjo with a nice tone and everything? I'd like to a lot and honestly I think that it would be worth it because I'm awfully interested in the banjo and I'd like to learn how to play it really well.

You know, so I can dance around on it the way some of the guys who play over the radio can.

Our orchestra is coming along very well and last night we played for supper. It made quite a hit. The only trouble is trying to get guys to harmonize and practice. (Y'know, these temperamental artists!) But we're having heaps of fun.

Give my love to everybody and please write me.

Peter

"On Awakening in Camp the Morning After a Snowfall," 1934

From *The Winged Beaver,* Avon Old Farms' literary magazine

Still, white trees,
Softly drawn on a blue sky,
Are weighted down
With the white ashes of
    Wahkonda's pipe,
Now he has finished smoking.

Only a murmur's heard,
Where once proud waters flowed.
A deer drinks at black waters,
Then bounds away.

Up! Up! Make the fire,
Chop the ice from the spring below!
Up! Up! And look at the world!
It's white in a foot of snow!

Still, white trees,
Softly drawn on a blue sky,
Are weighted down
With the white ashes of
    Wahkonda' s pipe,
Now he's finished smoking.

"Forbidden," 1934

Found in Seeger files

I saw a frightened child
Peering through a crack
Which looked out on the courtyard of the
    world.

His mind was full of wonder
Trying hard to comprehend
The forbidden, secret, good things that he
    saw.

But voices of guardians,
The secret, silent guardians,
Came floating down the hallway, and he fled

I saw him again
And he'd brought along a chisel,
Trying, trying, to see more clearly.
But once again the guardians,
The stealthy, ghostly guardians
Came gliding down the passageway.
Again he fled.

"That's forbidden."
"That's not right."
"Run and save yourself
Before you fall to Hell."

And then, very satisfied,
They walked slowly back
With their rusty, unused keys
In their mouths.

I've never seen him since,
For he's stayed
Where all good children should.
But he's dropped his chisel.
Let's pick it up.

"An Interview," 1935

From the *Avon Weekly Newsletter,* May 7, 1935

Ladies and Gentlemen: We here present to you an interview at last, a human interest episode, too.

Sunday afternoon while seeing Bill Worrall for some dope of the *Winged Beaver,* we were ignominiously cornered by those two athletic gentlemen, Messrs. Geyelin and Harriman. There was nothing to do about it; they wanted themselves interviewed, and had the upper hand, so the following conversation ensued:

Mr. H.–"Say, listen; we're getting pretty sore. Here I've been subscribing to your newssheet all year and you haven't had my name in once."

Mr. G.–"Well, the only time I get my name in is when I go to the infirmary, and that isn't very good publicity."

Etc. When we told them that all they needed was to do something and we would print it if possible, they obliged by relating achievements and heroic deeds known previously (as far as we can find out) to none but themselves, which unfortunately, we have now forgotten. (Apologies to Mr. H. and Mr. G.) But at last it ended:

"You can quote us on that, too."

"Crow Shooting," c. 1935

From the *Avon Weekly Newsletter*

Through the kindness of "Brooks," Baekeland's father, the school now has a very fine owl decoy and also a crow call. Commander Hunter and Mr. Thayer will soon rig up a place for the "Avon Owl" to roost, so that boys from a blind may be able to make him flap his wings and appear lifelike. The owl plus the crow call should attract many birds to the vicinity of the blinds, so that boys can shoot them. Crow shooting is an excellent sport, and has the advantage of killing a very undesirable bird. They (the crows) eat birds' eggs and are known to do away with a half grown chicken. Another black mark against them is the fact that they make sufficient noise to wake up those who do not sleep soundly in the morning. Boys interested in crow shooting should buy 5 cent shot and then see Commander Hunter.

2

Becoming a "Folk Singer"
(1935–1947)

"The American Folk Song Revival," 1963

Dated November 1963; found in Seeger files

When I was a child, it seemed to me that there were two kinds of music: "Good" music, like Bach and Beethoven, all of which came from Europe. And American popular songs which one could hear on the phonograph or radio. I liked to sing but the words of the "art songs" didn't seem very interesting. And the words of the "pop" songs were obviously pretty cheap and trivial.

Oh, there was one other kind of music: the kind of songs we were taught in school. Some of them weren't bad. But most had rather wishy-washy words, and sometimes downright silly words. I didn't know then, as I know now, that often a good folksong was spoiled when they put it into a school songbook: they took all the sex out of it, took all the protest out of it. In the schoolbooks these were called "folksongs," but frankly, they weren't very interesting to me or the other children. They were emasculated folksongs.

Then in 1935 I discovered folksongs with teeth. I was sixteen years old, and met some folklorists who had spent years collecting songs among the poorest of the working people of the country: Irish miners and railroad workers, Negro cotton farmers from the deep south, and among the most musical were the white settlers, "backwoodsmen," who had remained in isolated small mountain communities while the tides of "civilization" flowed around and past them.

I had never heard any of these songs before. 95 percent of Americans had not heard these songs. It was understandable. We Americans are an uprooted people. Our ancestors crossed an ocean. Then we were uprooted to go west in covered wagons. Worst of all, we then went to live among strangers in strange cities, working in factories and offices. We had, most of us, completely lost the rich heritages of folk music which our ancestors had possessed in various parts of Europe. So the average American, if he liked music, was told that he should learn the foreign "art" music. If he wanted something more American, he was stuck with the cheap popular music, which changed in fashion from year to year, as its promoters restlessly sought new ways of making money. (Do you know Oscar Wilde's definition of fashion? "A form of ugliness so unbearable it must be changed every few months.")

In the 1930s some of the younger folklorists such as Alan Lomax[1] said, "American folk music is too good to die out. Let's give it back to the folks, and see if it can grow and flourish again." And I seized upon it with enthusiasm. Here were songs with words full of all the richness and variety of life: love, hate, satire, protest against injustice. Fine poetry. Fine melodies that had stood the test of time. I said to myself, "These are great songs. Twice as good as anything that the Tin Pan Alley songwriters are writing. Ten times as good as anything Stephen Foster wrote. And it's American down to the core."

And I, born in New York City, started learning songs of Kentucky miners, Wisconsin lumberjacks, and Texas farmers. It appears I was just one of the first of thousands, perhaps hundreds of thousands of Americans from the city, who felt the same way.

"I Dropped Out of College," 2009

From *Where Have All the Flowers Gone,* Revised Edition, W. W. Norton & Company, 2009

I dropped out of college in 1938, aged 19. Got too interested in politics. Let my marks slip. Lost my scholarship. Family finances too low.

I'd run school newspapers for six years in boarding schools, so I looked for a job as a reporter on a newspaper. No luck. Studied watercolor painting for a short while. Spent a summer bicycling, camping, painting watercolor pictures of farmers' houses in return for food.

In the winter of 1939, I was a member of a young artists group in New York City. It was a branch of the Young Communist League. We met weekly, 25 to 50 of us, in a loft near 14th Street. Come spring I helped build a set of puppets. Come summer I joined three others giving puppet shows in the small towns of upstate New York. In August 20,000 dairy farmers went on strike against Bordens and Sheffields, the big companies that dictated the price of milk. Farmers were getting 2 cents a quart ($1 for a 48-qt. can), when milk was selling for 10–12 cents a quart in stores.

---

1. Lomax (1915–2002) was, with his father, John, among the most important early collectors of folk, country, blues, and other marginalized musics. See chapter 3.

Our puppet show went from strike meeting to strike meeting. I played the part of a cow who tells the farmer he's foolish not to get together with other farmers to demand a decent return for their labor. Between acts I sang "The Farmer Is the Man That Feeds Them All" in front of the stage. And it wasn't hard to change the 1920 cotton farmers' song, "Seven Cent Cotton and Forty Cent Meat, How in the World Can a Poor Man Eat," to sing it to dairy farmers as "One Dollar Milk and 40 Cent Meat." I also changed "Pretty Polly," a Kentucky ballad about seduction and murder, into "Mister Farmer," telling how they were seduced and cheated by the big-money boys.

Writing songs was a heady experience. The folk process was working for me. In the fall I was persuaded by Alan Lomax to quit looking for a job on a newspaper and come to Washington to help him go through stacks of old country music records looking for interesting songs.

And in February 1940 Woody Guthrie hitched from California to the New York Island, and my life was never the same again.

Woody must have liked my banjo picking, because everything else about me must have seemed pretty strange to him. I didn't drink or smoke or chase girls. He said to someone, "That Seeger guy is the youngest man I ever knew."

"This Young Fella, Pete," 1999

From *Hard Travelin': The Life and Legacy of Woody Guthrie,* Wesleyan University Press, 1999

In February [1946] Woody had written "This Land Is Your Land" as he hitchhiked across the nation. Some of his other well-known songs—"So Long, It's Been Good to Know You," "Pretty Boy Floyd," "Do Re Mi"— he had already written a few years before. Woody came to New York because Will Geer, who by this time was in New York playing the lead in the Broadway play *Tobacco Road,* had written Woody that he'd help find work for him. Will got the use of the theater for a midnight benefit concert for California farmworkers. In addition to Will, the evening also featured Burl Ives, Leadbelly, Josh White,[2] Earl Robinson,[3] Aunt Molly Jackson,[4] and the Golden Gate Quartet,[5] among others. I was allowed to sing one song on the program because my friend folklorist Alan Lomax insisted on it. I wasn't entirely welcome; it was a full program and there were a lot of dependable performers already part of it. But Alan said, "If you're asking me to be on it, you've got to have this young fella, Pete." So the director gave me one song to sing. I remember

2. White (1914–1969) was a folk singer and civil rights activist. He became among the first black musicians to gain mainstream success in the 1940s. White, who was a personal friend of Franklin and Eleanor Roosevelt, reached a career peak in the early 1950s on a goodwill tour of Europe. While he was in Europe, the FBI began investigating White's Communist affiliations, and he was subsequently blacklisted.

3. Earl Robinson (1910–1991) was a classical composer and a folksinger with whom Seeger collaborated on many recordings of labor songs.

walking out to the front of the stage and singing, very amateurishly, the outlaw ballad "John Hardy." I got a smattering of polite applause.

Woody was the star of the show. This midnight concert was a benefit for California agricultural workers, and there was Woody, a genuine Okie with a cowboy hat shoved back on his head. He'd tell a joke and sing a song, and then he'd tell another joke. He must have been onstage for twenty minutes, more than any other member of the cast. Backstage, he was still singing, so I got to accompany him with my banjo. We got well acquainted that night.

I was a very naïve, puritanical New Englander. It's a wonder Woody put up with me. But I was a pretty good banjo picker who also happened to have a good ear. I could find the right notes to accompany him anytime. I didn't try anything too fancy. Woody didn't like a lot of fancy chords, so I stuck to the chords he wanted.

"So Many Different Schemes in the Wind," 1940

Letter to his grandmother from the Division of Music at the Library of Congress, February 16, 1940; found in Seeger files

Dear Grandmother,

Note by the letterhead that I am now a man of position. I type out cards, and listen to and file phonograph records for my friend Alan Lomax, who is Librarian in charge of the Archive of American Folk-Song here. All in all, it is very interesting and enjoyable work.

Life down here is always full of a lot of talk. New projects, books, shows, trips, jobs, etc., etc. In a way, my position is that of lying in wait for some nice, juicy opportunity to float unsuspectingly by—one that I can capably swallow—then I jump out and grab it.

On March 3rd, in the theatre where Tobacco Road is given, the folk music program that was discussed last December will take place. It is much different from what was originally envisaged, and I have a good deal smaller part, but it is all for the best, and may lead to more programs of folk music in the future. I will be up in New York between now and then, helping to get things ready—I think and hope—and shall, I trust, see you.

---

4. Jackson (1880–1960) was a folk singer and activist, especially as a member of the United Mine Workers, for which she wrote many pro-union songs. Jackson and her songs were discovered in Kentucky in 1931, and she traveled to New York, where, along with raising money for union causes in Kentucky, she became a part of the New York City folk scene.
5. The Golden Gate Quartet was an all-black vocal gospel music group with a rotating membership. The Quartet achieved great fame in its time and sang at Franklin Delano Roosevelt's inauguration in 1941, the first black group to sing at a presidential inauguration.

I wish you would give my love to Elie and Anita,[6] and hand them this letter—as a matter of fact. I would like to know what they are doing these days.

I am living less on my own reputation, as I was in New York, and more on my friends and associates, whose influence pulls me up. March eighth I go to sing at a conference of the Progressive Education Association at the Mayflower Hotel. What do you think?! In a dress suit, I understand. I guess I'll borrow father's. About the same type of songs as I sung at the Earl Browder[7] meeting last fall, which you remember, but what a far cry it is! Well, we shall see what the future brings. I really don't know what to expect myself; there are so many different schemes in the wind.

You will be glad to know that I am eating and sleeping regularly.

The children[8] are thriving, as one's ears tell one. Peggy is becoming a little girl. And the youngest is learning to talk. Peggy and Mike are learning to play the piano—not by intention of their parents, especially, but because they have insisted on being allowed to poke out tunes. I have heard the first four measures of "Silent Night" played consecutively for fifty minutes by Peggy. Then a little later she was at it again for another half hour.

Well, my love to yourself and everyone.
Pete

"The Only Sensible Way to Travel," c. 1947

Early draft of a piece which eventually saw publication in *The Incompleat Folksinger,* Simon and Schuster, 1972; found in Seeger files

The first train I ever hitched a ride on was in [St. Joseph], Missouri. Up until that time I'd only hitch-hiked along the highways. Some professional hoboes assured me, however, that the only sensible way to travel was by freight. After lurking around the yards all night, I finally jumped on what I thought was the right train, only to find after an hour of switching back and forth that I had been shunted on a siding.

Later on, I got the right train, but when we finally pulled into Lincoln, Nebraska, where I was assured that I'd have to jump off before the

6. Elie Edson (~1882–1971), Seeger's uncle on his mother's side, and Anita Pollitzer (1894–1975), his wife. Edson was a press agent for theater actors, and Pollitzer was a women's rights activist who campaigned for women's suffrage in the early twentieth century.
7. Browder (1891–1973) served as General Secretary of the Communist Party USA from 1929 to 1945. He was a comparatively moderate leader and expressed support for Popular Front policies, embracing some facets of establishment politics, including Franklin Roosevelt's New Deal policies. Toward the end of World War II, he sought to establish the Communist Party USA as independent from Soviet influence, even declaring that Communism and capitalism were not mutually exclusive. These attitudes alienated many members of the Party, and Browder was removed from power and expelled from the Party in 1946.
8. Charles Seeger (1886–1979) and Constance de Clyver Edson (1886–1975), Pete Seeger's mother, divorced in 1927. In 1932, Charles married Ruth Porter Crawford

yard bulls came around to check the cars, in my inexperience I broke my banjo when jumping off. This really put me in a spot, since it was the only way I had to make a living. I hocked a small camera I had for a five-dollar guitar, and started playing in saloons. In about three days I was able to get the camera out of hock and continued west, exploring one new city after another.

In Butte, Montana, I told some members of the local miners union that I knew some miners' songs, and they asked me to sing at the next union meeting. I had planned to catch a freight train east at nine o'clock, and as the agenda grew long, I became afraid I wouldn't be able to make it. I heard the train whistle down at the foot of a hill, and told the chairman that I was afraid I would have to go on then or not at all, so he put me on, I sang a few songs, and then he gave me a check for five dollars. I looked at it in dismay, because it was of absolutely no use to me, since I didn't know where I could cash it, "Oh," says he, "the bar downstairs will take care of this for you." Down I run, and what did they give me but five silver dollars. I started running downhill and the damn things kept falling out of my jeans pocket, rolling down the sidewalk, and me trying to find then in the grass—and all the time that train whistling down at the bottom of the hill, just like it's ready to start. Finally, I never did find one of the silver dollars and ran on without it. Considering that it was 20 percent of my total capital, you can see I really wanted to catch that train.

P. S., I did.

"History of the Almanacs," 1987

From a letter to Millard Lampell, dated October
1, 1987; found in Seeger files

Dear Mill,

I was talking with Harold Leventhal[9] the other day that sooner or later somebody will try and make a novel or a play or a movie out of the story of the Almanac Singers. It is a dramatic story with humor and tragedy all wrapped in it on several different levels, personal and political and musical. A natural. I thought I'd put down my version here.

Here goes:

I returned to New York City in the fall of 1940, after having spent five or six months hitchhiking around the South and West, and most recently to New England. I believe it was the month of December, but it might have been early January, when I tackled the problem of the manuscript

---

to the book, *Hard-hitting Songs*,[10] and wondering whether I should try and find a publisher for it. At that time, somebody told me that a man named Lee Hays, who used to teach at Commonwealth College, was in New York, also trying to find a publisher for a book of union songs. And it seemed to me logical that we should get together and not duplicate each other's work, or at least not get in each other's way too much. Perhaps we could join forces. I don't know whether I called him up first or he called me; but I remember coming around to a small dark one-room apartment where Lee and Mill Lampell were staying. I believe it was on the West Side. And we hit it off right away, Lee and me, and Mill too. Lee pointed out that he could use my banjo accompaniment, and I knew that he knew a lot of great songs and was a good songleader. So we teamed up together and started singing at some little fundraising parties, I guess in January, 1941. And pretty soon Mill was joining us, although Mill made no claim to being a singer or musician. He was very quick at making up verses, which we always loved to do, adding new verses to "Crawdad," or whatever song we happened to be singing, about the latest headline of the day.

I believe it was about February when we decided really we should get a name for the group. By this time we had got a loft on the corner of 12th St. and 4th Avenue and we had Sunday afternoon songfests with a keg of beer and charging 25 cents and paying the rent. On one of those days, I took out the manuscript for *Hard-hitting Songs* and started leafing through it, trying to find ideas for a name for this trio. I came to the word, "almanac." Lee was sprawled out on another bed twelve feet away, and he says, "Wait a minute; wait a minute. You know, back in Arkansas there were really two books that a poor farmer might know about: the Bible would help him get through the next world, but the Almanac would help him through this world. And we have an Almanac too of sorts, although not everybody knows how to read it. And why don't we call ourselves the Almanac Singers." Mill and I must have agreed pretty quickly. I don't remember there being much argument.

And so we were the Almanac Singers, I think probably from late February on. And we were getting publicity in the *Daily Worker* because we had the sassiest songs about the drive of Franklin Roosevelt and others to have the U.S.A. join the war over in Europe on the side of England. Roosevelt had said, "[W]e must be neutral, but we do not have to be neutral in our sympathies." And pretty soon all sorts of help was going over to England. Well, we were making up verses according to the Communist Party line of that time, which was that this was another

---

successful group of the late 1940s and early 1950s, in 1949. The group disbanded under blacklist pressure in 1952 but regained popularity with their Carnegie Hall concert in December of 1955, an event for which Leventhal was the primary proponent and producer.

10. A joint project between Seeger, Alan Lomax, and Woody Guthrie, *Hard-Hitting Songs for Hard Hit People* is a selection of Depression-era protest and topical songs, mainly selected by Lomax, arranged and with musical notation by Seeger and Guthrie. Although the project was begun in 1940, the volume wasn't published until 1967.

imperialist war like World War I, and Hitler was bad, but Churchill wasn't that much better. He simply wanted to perpetuate the capitalist system. And we were saying, as pacifists had said for so many decades, it was another rich man's war and a poor man's fight.

Early in February, I believe it was, Lee and I had visited Helen Simon, and sprawled out on the floor of her apartment, we made up the song "Plow Under" and a peace version of "Billy Boy" and a peace version of "Lisa Jane," and these songs were getting around; and in April we recorded them. Several Hollywood actors (Lionel Stander, for one) and some people in the radio business like Joe Thompson and a script writer at the radio, Peter Lyon, arranged for a party at Pete's house near Washington Square, and in one short evening we raised $300, which in those days was worth like $3,000 now. It was a lot of money. And Keynote Records, a small independent label (there were not many independent labels in those days) agreed to put out a record. We were going to call it, *Songs For John Doe*. We recorded it all in two or three hours, and my banjo was the only accompaniment except for Josh White's guitar. Keynote handled the recording session and the distribution, which was mainly through left-wing circles. The Communist Party had bookstores in dozens of cities, and these records went to those bookstores immediately.

I am told that Alan Lomax took a copy of the record to Archibald MacLeish,[11] who was a little bit shocked but could take it all in stride but figured he should play it for the Chief himself, and he took it to Roosevelt. That's what I'm told. And Roosevelt said, "Can we stop this in some way?" And MacLeish said, "Well, not unless you want to break the First Amendment of the U.S. Constitution." And so Roosevelt, I suppose, shrugged and said, "Well, not many people will hear it. It won't get played on the air." But the songs did get around. Within a few weeks, the Almanacs' record was known from coast to coast in this narrow circle of left-wingers, and peaceniks of one sort or another. So right away Eric Bernay, the head of Keynote Records, asked us if we'd like to make another album, since that was selling well in its small way. And we decided to put out an album of union songs.

We went to the same little studio, as I remember, on Central Park South. This time I know we had Sam Gary and Carol White, and Bess Hawes[12] was there. We must have had six or eight or ten people in the studio, because we wanted to sing, "Union Train." As Lee Hays led off, "What is this I see yonder coming coming coming?" we needed a large group of people to sing like a congregation.

We weren't completely satisfied with the songs which we picked out to sing, and they asked me if I had any suggestions. And I thought of the great

---

11. MacLeish (1892–1982), a Modernist poet, was the Librarian of Congress under Franklin Roosevelt.
12. Bess Lomax (1921–2009), daughter of John and sister of Alan, was a frequent member of the Almanac Singers and lived in the Almanac House in the early 1940s. Lomax married Butch Hawes in 1942.

chorus Woody had put together about a year before when he and I were in Oklahoma City, "Oh, You Can't Scare Me, I'm A-Stickin' to the Union."

"But it only has two verses that were any good. I can't remember the other ones," says I. Mill Lampell said, "Give me 20 minutes," and we went into another room and came back with the third verse which we recorded.

Well, with Josh White's guitar and our enthusiasm, the record was off the press, and the album, three 10″ records, called "Talkin' Union," was again on sale in left-wing bookshops all across the country, and by the month of June, in this small way we were known from coast to coast. Mill, with the help of some left-wing union friends, set up a tour for the Almanac Singers which would go out to the West Coast through, as I remember, Pittsburgh, Cleveland, Detroit, Chicago, Milwaukee, Denver, Salt Lake (but I don't think we sang there) to San Francisco and then down to Los Angeles.

Just about a week before we left, Woody Guthrie knocks on the door. He'd been in the state of Oregon with his family, writing songs about the Grand Coulee Dam but had hitchhiked east, and his family had gone back to Pampa, Texas—Mary and three tiny kids. But Woody walks in the door, actually as I remember it, about one or two days after Hitler invaded the Soviet Union, and one of the first words out of his mouth with a wry grin was, "Well, I guess we're not going to be singing any more of them peace songs." He was right, of course. The day after the invasion, the *Daily Worker*, which had been preaching peace hard for the previous year, suddenly had its headline, "All Aid to the Soviet Union." And guess what: Winston Churchill comes out with a headline, "All Aid to Our Gallant Soviet Allies."

I scratched my head in wonder. Is this the Churchill who in 1920 said, "We must strangle the Bolshevik infant in its cradle"? People said, "Yes, Pete. Winston Churchill has changed his mind. He is no longer trying to persuade Hitler to go attack the Soviet Union and then back out of the war. He knows that Hitler is the main enemy, and we've got to work together to get rid of him." So we stopped singing our peace songs, although they were good songs.

Before we went West, we asked Woody if he'd like to come with us. He said, "Well, I just hitchhiked across the country to join you. I guess I'm willing to head west again if you are." Henrietta Yurchenco[13] knew a man with another small recording company who wanted to record some songs of the American pioneers and songs of American sailors. In two or three days we recorded for General Records, *Sodbuster Ballads* and *Deep Sea Shanties*. Pete Hawes joined us for these sessions. He always considered himself one of the Almanac Singers, although he lived way up in New Hampshire and only sang with us

---

13. Yurchenco (1916–2007) was an ethnomusicologist and early radio broadcaster of folk music on WNYC.

once or twice. But we weren't particular about who was in the Almanacs. Anybody who wanted to join us on a booking could come along and sing on the chorus as an Almanac Singer for the night. There must be dozens of people still living who were Almanac Singers for a night, somewhere.

We were paid $125 for each record, and with this money Mill Lampell bought a big 1932 7-passenger Buick. It was a gas hog and an oil hog, but a couple of days later four of us (Mill, me, Woody and Lee) started west on our grand tour to California of the Almanac Singers in early July or late June of 1941.

I don't know for sure how Mill did it. I think he contacted some Communist Party union leaders and got in touch with other union leaders in other cities. We had no great fame except in this narrow group of left-wingers, but we sang for a few hundred here and a few hundred there across the country. We stayed in people's homes or the cheapest hotels. I remember in Pittsburgh they sent me out to look for a hotel, and I got a cheap one, all right. There were enormous cockroaches in every room. In Detroit we sang for the automobile workers, and we took the tourist trip through the River Rouge plant and wore our C.I.O. buttons. And the workers on the beltline were waving to us and smiling because Ford had just been organized into the C.I.O. a few months before. It was a great victory.

...We didn't stay long in any one city—a few days at most. In San Francisco, our big thrill was singing for the Longshoremen's Union. There was Harry Bridges and some other union leaders up front. Some of the Longshoremen in the crowd, maybe 500 or more, turned around and I think I heard one mutter, "What the heck is a bunch of hillbilly singers coming in for? We've got work to do here today." But Harry introduced us, and when we finished singing, "The Ballad of Harry Bridges," we got a standing ovation. The applause was deafening. We sang several more songs, and when we walked down the aisle, they slapped Woody on the back so hard they nearly knocked him over.

We borrowed a very good fiddle from a liberal lawyer named Phillip Sawyer, and Woody did some fiddling. When we got to Los Angeles, I found we still had the fiddle with us, and Phil Sawyer sent another lawyer around with a legal piece of paper to reclaim the fiddle. A few years later, I met Phil Sawyer and I said, "Oh, Woody meant to return the fiddle to you," and he said, sternly, "No, he was going to take it and wasn't going to bring it back."

In San Francisco, Lee Hays said he really thought he'd better go back East and help get things set up for the fall. His health had not been too good, and he was pushing his limit on this tour, and he suggested that the three of us go to Los Angeles and then drive back and join him in New York. So Woody, Mill and I went down to Los Angeles where once again left-wingers and the C.I.O. arranged for one booking after another. I remember marching in the Labor Day Parade in early September, and they all loved to join in on, "Oh, You Can't Scare Me, I'm Sticking to the Union."

About this time Mill Lampell decided he would go back East. I don't know whether he was lonesome for his girlfriend back there or decided he really wasn't that much needed, but after a short discussion Woody and I decided we'd carry out the original plan to try and go to Portland and Seattle before heading east.

Woody and I stayed with Ivar Haglund[14] and his wife while we were in Seattle. There was a young redheaded woman and her boyfriend who joined us on a number of concerts. They were the chorus for the Almanac Singers. They were in the Almanac Singers for a week. We sang not only in Seattle but in half a dozen towns nearby. And Seattle, of course, was where we ran into the word, "hootenanny," because the Washington Commonwealth Federation used that term for their monthly fundraising parties. Terry Pettus[15] told us that they'd voted, that the word "hootenanny" had won out by a nose over the term "wingding."

In late September Woody and I headed back East, stopping off at Butte, Montana to sing a few songs for the mineworkers. We cut quickly back to New York, through Detroit into Windsor, and through Canada to Toronto, and then across the Niagara Falls Bridge and down into New York. A few days later, in early October, we rejoined Lee Hays and Mill Lampell and Pete Hawes who had rented for $100 a month, as I remember, an old building on 10th Street, about 100 feet west of Greenwich Avenue. It had three stories and a basement, but we didn't have any furniture for it. It was kind of hilarious to see this male gang trying to fend for ourselves. We had a roof over our heads, but it was the most sparsely furnished place you ever saw—a bed and a chair and a table, and things like that. But we had a hootenanny in the basement every Saturday.

Lee left the Almanacs in early November, I believe. His health was so bad, half the time he wasn't singing with us, and we thought he was malingering. My guess is he was dissatisfied with our unorganized way of working, or my unorganized way of working—my slipshod way of letting just anybody who wanted to join sing with the Almanacs. And he was increasingly dissatisfied, and he'd tell stories to one person, tell different stories to another person. I've forgotten whether Bess Hawes had joined us yet or whether Sis Cunningham had joined us yet or not, but I remember the other Almanacs said, "Pete, you've got to tell Lee that it would really be better for him as

---

14. Haglund (1905–1985) was a prominent Seattle-area folk musician and collector of folk music of the northwestern United States.
15. Pettus (1904–1984) was a newspaper reporter in Seattle, Washington. In 1936, Pettus organized a strike that earned union recognition at the Seattle Post-Intelligencer, the first Hearst-owned paper to unionize. He later became the editor of *People's World*, a newspaper associated with the Communist Party USA.

well as us if he'd leave the Almanacs. He is not adding anything to the group these days."

Looking back on it, I suspect that it was the old case of a genius who was not satisfied with the way things were going but didn't know exactly what to do about it, and he was causing trouble. I thought he was just cantankerous. And so I told Lee that we feel that you really ought to leave the Almanacs. And he went back to staying with a friend.

...I can't quite figure when we wrote the song, "Reuben James." The *Reuben James* was sunk in October, but I remember going over the song in the month of December or even January with Woody. It may be that Woody started writing it in October, but we weren't satisfied with it because it didn't have a chorus, and maybe it wasn't until January that I and the other Almanacs said, "Woody, won't you please write a chorus we can all join in on?" And that's exactly what he did. He rarely made up new tunes, but just as he wrote a musical chorus for the song, "So Long," using a melody from a verse from an earlier song, he did exactly the same thing with "Reuben James." The music for the verse was a Carter family song, "Wildwood Flower," but the music for the chorus was all Woody. And it was a great chorus—is a great chorus—and that song is going to be sung for a long long time. But I distinctly remember that chorus being made up after we moved from the East 10th Street location because it was a little expensive, over to three rooms above the Dome, which was a public dance hall on the second floor on the east side of Sixth Ave. between Ninth and Tenth Street. We were one floor above it, with our three rooms (or rather, 2½ rooms) and there was a loft right next door which we could rent every Sunday afternoon to have a hootenanny.

Sis and Gordon[16] had joined the Almanac Singers either in October or November, I can't remember which. I think it was October. In the new apartment, Sis and Gordon had a very small room. Bess and I had two single cots in one huge room, and then in a little kitchen/dining room area, we had a table and a telephone. And we started to earn some money, and Jean Karsovina's friend who did some housekeeping for her came in two or three days a week to do some housekeeping for us, mainly cooking meals. As I remember, we thought ourselves pretty well off. We made $50 or $60 a week, which was like earning $500 or $600 a week now, and we had enough for me to send a few dollars a week to my mother who lived in Florida. She was getting on in years. And Woody sent a little money out to Mary and the kids in Texas. I guess Mary was getting ready to file for divorce.

Although the Almanac Singers were bigger and looser than ever, somehow we were doing well. As a matter of fact, in January [1942] we got a chance to sing on network radio. Norman Corwin, who was the

---

16. Agnes "Sis" Cunningham (1909–2004) was a sometimes member of the Almanac Singers. She and Gordon Friesen (1909–1996) married in 1941. They were later the founding editors of *Broadside* magazine, one of the preeminent folk music magazines during the folk revival of the 1950s and '60s.

hotshot of CBS in those days, put out a big program carried coast to coast called *This Is War*. And the Almanac Singers sang, "Round and Round Hitler's Grave" on it. A day or two later, a big New York newspaper, the *World Telegram*, headlined, "Commie Folksingers Try to Infiltrate Radio." I think the investigative reporter was Frederick Woltman. At any rate, that was the last network radio job the Almanac Singers got.

However, about this time, we put out another Keynote album called *Dear Mr. President*. Eric Bernay said, "Now is our chance to make it up with Franklin Roosevelt, who is really not such a bad guy." It did not become a big hit, needless to say; but again, through left-wing circles, it sold several thousand copies, and at least one of the songs, "Reuben James," will go down in history. Of course, little by little, we were now singing, to the dismay probably of some of our erstwhile pacifist friends, entirely toward getting the U.S.A. to beat Hitler on the battlefield as quickly as possible. As good Communists, we urged all unions to adhere to the no-strike pledge for the duration of the conflict. We supported the freeze on wages, but we also pushed hard for enforcement of the control of prices. And leading C.I.O. union members were down in Washington, given important jobs.

Even though we didn't get jobs on the radio offered to us, somebody in the William Morris Agency got interested in us and tried to get us some jobs. They were the ones that took us up to the Rainbow Room.[17] This scene Woody put in his book as just being about himself; but it was actually Woody and me and Mill and Arthur and Sis, and I think Bess Hawes. We sang some of our "Win the War" songs there, and the manager sitting at a table, looking rather deadpan, says, "Yes, I think I could use you. Of course we'll want to put all the men in overalls, and we can put the girls in sun bonnets."

We didn't think much of that suggestion and started improvising verses to one of our standby songs for such improvisation, Leadbelly's "New York City":

> The Rainbow Room is mighty high.
> You can see John D. a-flying by
> In New York City, In New York City.
> In New York City, you've really got to know your line.
> In the Rainbow Room, the soup's on the boil.
> They are stirring the salad with Standard Oil
> In New York City, In New York City.
> In New York City, you've really got to know your line.

We walked out of there feeling pretty cocky, pretty sure they would not want to hire us and pretty sure that we did not want to work there.

---

17. Opened in 1934, the Rainbow Room was an upscale restaurant and nightclub catering to New York's elites. Situated on the 65th floor of the GE Building in Rockefeller Center, it hosted many famous singers and performers who provided private entertainment for its guests.

Our friends at William Morris tried once again to interest some "big-time people," and had a little reception at a hotel. I've forgotten whether Woody urinated on the balcony or not, but I know he swiped some of the silverware; and a couple of weeks later when our friend from William Morris was visiting us, he ruefully saw this silverware on our table as we served him dinner. And he mentioned that he'd had to pay the hotel for the stolen silverware.

. . . I have to admit with a laugh that I've completely left out the story of my own sex life. I guess that's typical of me. I never was much of a ladies' man, ever, and knew occasional girls who had their eye on me but stayed clear of them because I didn't want to get in deeply. This was true of two or three of the girls in Margot Mayo's American Square Dance group, which I had started dancing with in '38 and had danced with occasionally in '39 or '40, whenever I happened to be in New York, and now in the fall of '41 I went up there almost every week, held hands but stayed strictly clear of entanglements until around December, it might have been, when one of the dancers I'd never thought of romantically, I guess, asked me to take her home, or she volunteered to do some work at the Almanac House. We had to alphabetize addresses or were setting up a file of songs, and Toshi Ohta came up to help. The next thing, I was walking her home. The next thing we were necking and next thing, in June, I was taking her down to Washington, D.C., to visit my father and stepmother and saying that I hope we can marry as soon as we can, and admittedly there was a war going on and I'd probably be drafted. But we were engaged.

. . . [The Almanacs were] an extraordinary group. Alan Lomax came to New York when Lee and I first got together and started singing together, and he said, "What you are doing is one of the most important things that could possibly be done in the field of American music. You are introducing folk songs from the countryside to a new city audience, and you are learning how to do it." It had one or two geniuses in Lee Hays and Woody. And it might be that the humor between Lee and Woody and Gordon Friesen could be one of the main things in this story; because, as Joe Klein[18] brought out, Gordon would kid them both. He says, "You guys singing about hard work, how much hard work have you actually done? I was raised on a farm, and I can tell you about hard work." But the more I think of it, probably the leitmotif of [the group was] Bess Hawes, with her silvery laughter and her beautiful smile, and Sis Cunningham, with her rock-hard class consciousness. We were all very different people. And yet, out of this group came some extraordinary songs and some extraordinary music. People who heard us back in those days never forgot us. And, with the strength of the Communist Party behind us, we were not scared of nothin'.

---

18. Author of the fine biography *Woody Guthrie: A Life* (Delta, 1999).

It was exciting; we just made a go of it financially. Bess Hawes kept a job working, I believe, in the Music Division of the New York Public Library and put her small salary in to the pot. We had just enough to pay for our food and our rent and replace an article of clothing occasionally if it was not too expensive and to get some laundry done. We didn't buy a lot of cigarettes and beer. We never made enough money to deserve a regular manager. The William Morris Agency gave up on us after a couple of months. Our radical reputation was too much for them to handle as well as Woody's unconventional ways in hotels. I had tried to be the manager way back in early '41. Mill had arranged the trip west. I tried to be manager again in the fall of '41. Coming back from a trip to New Hampshire, Pete Hawes said, in a rather offhand way, "Really, the Almanacs need a manager." I was lying down in the back seat of the station wagon which Pete had, and I'd been knocking myself out trying to do the best job I possibly could and felt that nobody was appreciating it; so I lifted my foot, and it came down wham in the middle of a mandolin, and there was dead silence for a while because I didn't usually get mad.

People will probably ask exactly what kind of control did the Communist Party have over our work. It is surprising how loose things were. I'd been a member of the young Communist league at Harvard and briefly a member of a Communist youth group called Youth Arts, or something like that, in 1938 and '39 in New York. But I never joined the Communist Party until the Almanacs got back from our trip across the country. We had weekly sessions with a nice young man who tried to guide us in learning a little bit more about dialectical materialism, but none of us were really that enthusiastic about becoming great Marxist scholars. We trusted the Communists to know generally the right thing that we should be pushing for, whether it was peace or war. We read the *Daily Worker* regularly. It was one of the best newspapers in the world. It had a great sports section. It had writers like Mike Gold writing for it. Mike Gold was one of our early supporters in early 1941, writing columns about us and saying, "These guys are absolutely wonderful. They not only have great satire but they have also a sense of romance, something which the people have always demanded in their culture."[19]

Our songs were full of humor, whether they were by Mill Lampell or Lee Hays or me contributing, I was never one of the best songwriters in the group. My main claim to fame was the last two stanzas of "Talkin' Union." Then occasionally I would add verses of other songs. I also wrote a good deal of the song, "Deliver the Goods," a Grade B effort.

Lee Hays knew the gospel songs and the hymn tradition. Woody knew the ballad and the blues tradition. I would learn anything and try it out. And likewise Mill Lampell. Bess had a vast experience listening to her family's collecting and singing and sometimes would come forth

19. For more on the Communist Party, see chapter 5.

with surprising contributions. Sis Cunningham had a strong Oklahoma background not too different from Woody.

Arthur Stern's main contribution besides a big booming voice and a sharp sense of humor generally, and also a strong sense of dialectical materialism, was to make up some sharp verses from time to time. Gordon Friesen never sang with us, but he was an important part of the Almanacs—a wonderful sense of humor, an extraordinary cartoonist. Mill Lampell's big contribution, besides being the organizer of the Great Tour West in the summer of '41, was in writing new verses quicker than anybody else, even Woody Guthrie. Sometimes one person would get an idea for a song and somebody else would add to it, and when the song was finished, we knew that there was no one person who could take responsibility for it.

My own contribution, curiously enough, might not have been so much musical as just trying to hold things together, because we were all such different people and I was always trying to find some common ground, whether it was music or food or politics or whatever to keep us all working together and to welcome anybody who wanted to work with us. There were only a few times people came along, and we suggested they *not* work with us. Joe Klein said that I was the best musician in the group, but in the first place, there is no such thing as best in the field of art. I was perhaps skilled in reading music and writing it down and in playing the banjo, but certainly Lee Hays knew a lot more about music in some ways than I did. And likewise Bess Hawes knew a lot more than I did certainly about singing.

The Sunday afternoon hootenannies became a regular institution in that short year in New York City. Not only (before we called them hootenannies) in the spring of 1941 but in the fall and winter and spring and summer of 1942, the reputation of them spread as a wonderful inexpensive way for people to spend an afternoon. We'd have an average of 100 people, sometimes more, sometimes less. We'd charge them 35 cents, as I remember, the equivalent of three or four dollars now. Many wonderful people came to sing there—Burl Ives, Leadbelly, Josh White. We established the hootenanny so well that three years later, in 1945, when the Peoples Songs organization started up again with Lee Hays and me and others, it was the most natural thing in the world to call a monthly fundraising songfest a hootenanny, and later on in the 1950s, of course, "hootenannies" became a generic term.

Overall, there's something that should be kept in mind, that this was Greenwich Village, New York City. It is no accident that some extraordinary art forms arise in cities where people meet each other. Jazz developed in New Orleans and not in some small town in Louisiana. Detroit developed Motown. It took Nashville to develop the "country" field. In the case of the Almanacs, it was me coming down from New England, Lee coming up from Arkansas, Mill from New Jersey, Woody from Oklahoma, Arthur Stern down from the Bronx or wherever. Butch Hawes[20] came down from New England. Butch got into music a little later than I did, but we were both New Englanders who fell in love with Southern music and many other kinds. There in Greenwich Village we all met and we bounced back ideas against each other. It was exciting—the new combinations we worked out. My guess is, though, little would have happened if it hadn't been for the Communist Party.

And this better be the last few paragraphs. After all, throughout history, there have been groups of musicians that got together and usually they were from one tradition. Groups of Gypsies got together to play Gypsy music. Groups of jazz people got together to play jazz. But occasionally in cities, people meet each other from different places and work out a new form—somewhat new. Somewhat old and somewhat new. The Beatles got together in Liverpool. In the case of the Almanacs, we were anticommercial. We were antiestablishment. We looked upon the music establishment as corrupt. We looked upon the economy as corrupt. We looked upon the government as being corrupt most of the time, although when a job had to be done, like beating Hitler, when the government was willing to fight Hitler, there we worked right along with it as much as we possibly could. So the Almanacs never were commercial; but they'll go down in history. There were bands selling millions of records, singing groups that were famous that will never get novels written about them or plays or operas; but I think the Almanacs will some year, because we were a strange combination of people and we put out some good songs, and lived through exciting times. We participated in these exciting times. The Communist Party helped us do this. We called ourselves Communists. Probably none of us agree even now exactly on the definition of Communism. But I don't think any of us are ashamed of what we did way back in the days of 1941 and '42.

All the best,
Pete

"Diary of a Soldier, Part 1," 1943[21]

Found in Seeger files

(Keesler Field, Mississippi, March, '43: During this lull, while I am sitting here waiting for shipment, I thought I would take advantage of my free time to write the story of my time in the army. Partly to clarify

---

20. Butch Hawes (1919–1971),was an artist and occasional member of the Almanacs. He married Bess Lomax in 1942.
21. "Diary of a Solder" is a single document, begun in March of 1943, picked up again in April of 1944, added to through 1944 and 1945, and finished in 1947. We have divided the finished document into two parts, the first largely written in 1943, the second largely written in 1944, and excerpted it here.

my own impressions and conclusions, and partly because it might be of faint interest to read over sometime in the years to come (I can imagine my children: Papa, what did *you* do in the Great War? Well, if I have no wounds, no medals, I must have something to show at least that I had a little something to do with it (how little!)). And I can produce for their young eyes this small proof. Perhaps in the months to come I'll be too busy to write much for this journal. I hope so. Perhaps the months will lengthen into years of such drab routine until the armistice (which we all assume will be some sort of conclusion, at least). Perhaps there will be a few exciting events to light it up. We'll see.)

It was 3½ years ago during the summer that England declared war on Germany. I and four others were running a harum-scarum little puppet show through New York State. We were in a small town above Utica when we heard the news. We looked at each other and said, "This is it." It had been coming for long. It had come. And then we wondered how soon we would be drawn in.

In October, 1940, I was bumming through the south, and suddenly in a small mountain town above Scottsboro, Alabama, I realized tomorrow is the day we all register for the draft. I felt a sudden shadow over me—I was no longer a free agent, to roam the world at pleasure. I've become used to reporting to my draft board since then, but at the time, it was a queer and new sensation.

On December 7th, 1941, we were having a whale of a good time singing songs at a hootenanny, held in our house, the Almanac House, in New York City. Arthur [Stern] announced over the speaker what he had just heard from a new arrival: The Japanese have attacked Pearl Harbor. Some at the party thought it was just a joke; others, like myself, didn't even know where, or what, Pearl Harbor was, and paid little attention. Maybe it was some Chinese port. Only in the evening I realized what had happened: We were at war at last. We knew ... sooner or later. Now it had come.

In July, 1942, I was almost glad when I heard from my draft board to report to them on the 17th. I was sorry to have to leave Toshi, but I knew that I would have to sooner or later, and Almanac affairs had not been progressing as fast as they used to. Organizational problems continually held us back. Personnel problems. We were going OK, but not good enough, and I was secretly relieved to be able to dive into completely different work. I chose to be inducted in Alabama (though I might have been in NY, had I requested so) because I rather looked forward to hitchhiking down there, and having one last fling. Seeing the country, and a few old friends on the way.

The plump little secretary in the Scottsboro draft board said, "Why Mister Seeger! How do you do! We've written letters to you all over the United States!" And so they had, for wherever I had gone, I'd conscientiously told them where I was.

The first few days of joining the army were filled with anticipation, in spite of much long waiting—in fact, that's mostly what we did. My banjo was very popular, and in fact once the boys took up a collection for me, some 5 bucks. I was broke as hell. I looked around me at the people in Scottsboro, and later on, the draftees from there whom I was with, and wondered: These are pretty average American people. Good, hospitable. It is funny to think that at one time they were willing participants in an attempt at mass murder.[22] If I could puzzle out the solution to this one paradox, I would be able to do great things, I guess, for it would be the key to so many great problems.

You feel pretty much like a sheep, as you are herded and shuttled from room to room, into line and out of line. Finally, after two days of this, the accepted ones are lined up. A major reads off the oath which we repeat. Then, "You're in the army now," he says, and soon we march off to the train for another camp.

Camp McPherson, Georgia: For a week here, we and hundreds of other inductees from Alabama and Georgia are given tests, shots, and given clothing and equipment, and lessons in how to make a G.I. bed. The army is still new, interesting, exciting. I notice most have a good deal of anticipation, but only a few volunteer for such dangerous work as paratroopers. For most of us have been for the last week impressed inside us deep that we are entering an army. That a certain percentage of us will not come out alive. That we may never see our home and family and girls again. That we may come back wounded or crippled, or blind. We are being cautious, therefore. I remember what a man told me back in New York: "Pete, in the army, just keep your mouth closed, your pants buttoned, and don't volunteer."

Every time you get on a troop train, the main thought in your mind is: I wonder where we are going? Farther from home or nearer to home? What kind of place are we going to? Dark and early one morning we left MacPherson on the train. Again a long and dreary ride. But we watched for landmarks and names of towns as we passed. Two days later: Miami! And we're in the Army Air Force. Technical training command. That means ground work. It was just what I had asked for.

After two weeks of lectures on first aid, military courtesy, the articles of war, and after having been given blisters and stiff muscles on the drill field, and sore arms from shots—a sudden call came for me. Within two hours I shipped. Then the usual farewells: "Well, see you in Tokyo," and "Don't let Hitler get you." Then to the trains.

The trip seemed interminably long. We stopped here and waited there—and finally finally finally one morning we woke up as we crawled

22. Seeger is referencing the case of the Scottsboro boys, nine black teenagers accused of raping two white girls in Scottsboro, Alabama in 1931. Alabama Governor Benjamin Miller was forced to employ the National Guard to deter a growing lynch mob outside the jail where the defendants were held. While concrete evidence against the boys was scant, the case was tried three times, with five of the nine boys ultimately being sentenced.

into Keesler Field.[23] We could see hangars—parts of planes—it looked like the real thing to me. But I was a little too optimistic.

Shortly after arriving at Keesler I came down with a slight case of bronchial pneumonia, which is very common with newcomers because of the damp climate. When I got out of the hospital after about 12 boring days, I had to study with another squadron. Thus it was that all my friends graduated and were shipped out before I did.

...The first month and a half after I graduated I did "P&P" work—collecting garbage, laying sod, and similar work. Then I was given the easy job of runner in the orderly room, every other night. The easiest damn job in the whole army.

When I was going to school I complained of my lack of time, and was disgusted with how much time I wasted, and how little I learned in comparison with how much I wanted to learn, and I complained of the incompetence of many of the teachers (as every soldier here does)—nevertheless I was intensely glad to go to school [in the Army], and interested in learning about this subject which was so completely new to me. I was thrilled to learn to start a plane, and already had visions of myself flying through the clouds. I got good marks throughout the course and at graduation was selected with 15 others to be interviewed for the possibility of going and studying to be engineering officers. But then came a tough break: I went to the hospital again, and could not take the examination, and when I got out, all the applicants had been selected, and the quota from my class had been filled. In other words, I had missed the bus.

I did not feel too badly about it, and still looked forward to being shipped any day. But weeks went past. One day I was unexpectedly called over to the classification office and interviewed informally "just to determine my status." But when the nice young corporal who examined asked me if I had ever belonged to any committees, and then inquired rather closely about my girlfriend, I realized this was Military Intelligence questioning me, probably because they had seen the return address on some of Toshi's letters. I was very frank with them, spontaneously volunteering all I thought they would want. I thought I had satisfied them.

But more weeks still went by. Finally it was months since the last other boy in my class had graduated and shipped. I realized I was being held here purposely. I hoped it was because of Toshi, but was afraid that it was because of my work as an Almanac Singer. Today I looked to see if my mail was being opened (innocently, it had not occurred to me before that it might be) and sure enough, it is. Every envelope.

Now, I wonder what will happen.... It is almost the beginning of summer here. I take sunbaths and play tennis, and swim, and generally lead the life of Riley. But I am not satisfied. I want to feel I am doing something in this war. I want to contribute to this fight. I fill in all my

---

23. In Biloxi, Mississippi.

spare time with study (mathematics, evolution, radio, psychology) and certainly these studies will help arm me for future work, no matter what it is. Yet maybe I will live out the duration contributing only this fraction of my potential to the war effort.

"We Never Wanted It to Stop," 1966

From Sing Out! magazine, no. 16.4, September 1966

The year was 1943, and I was a draftee, studying aircraft mechanics in Keesler Field, Mississippi. One warm evening I was sitting with a banjo on the steps of the barracks, picking a few tunes to myself, when a small cluster gathered. One man steps forward and asks, "Could you bring that thing over to my barracks for a spell? I got a mandolin, and there's a buddy of mine plays a good fiddle."

Over at his quarters we found also a couple guitar players, and we sat on the beds and started playing up a storm. Just about that time the sergeant hollers that it's time for the lights to go out. "Hell, we're just getting warmed up." So we adjourned to the latrine, at the end of the building, and started going again.

The latrine was about 12 by 18 feet in size, as I remember. A dozen or more soldiers followed us into it. The echoing walls made us sound so great, we didn't want it to ever stop. From neighboring barracks they heard us and drifted in to join the party. The latrine soon had twenty, then thirty, and finally almost forty people in it, standing in the shower stalls, seated on sinks and toilet seats.

The four or five stringed instruments were going it hot and strong, and then we hit some songs that everyone wanted to sing. Some New York fellow had a good bass, and a couple southerners knew how to hit that high harmony. The fiddle screeched and soared. The mandolin twanged; the guitars whomped all around those bass strings.

After half an hour a non-com[24] came back and said we were supposed to quiet down, but as I remember, we didn't pay him any mind. Half an hour later, after several unsuccessful attempts to halt us, a lieutenant squeezes into the room.

"OK men, break it up. You sound pretty good, but it's eleven thirty. Everybody back to their own outfits."

And that was that. I never met the mandolin player again. I can't remember exactly what tunes we played outside "Wabash Cannonball" and "Steel Guitar Rag." It wasn't a very lengthy music session, as sessions go. But if anyone ever asks me where was it I made some of the best music I ever made in my life, I'm liable to reply: "In a latrine."

---

24. A non-commissioned officer, probably a sergeant or corporal, advanced from the lower ranks as opposed to originally appointed (commissioned) to a higher officer's rank such as captain or lieutenant.

"Diary of a Soldier, Part 2," 1944

Found in Seeger files

Shortly after April 30th I was given a job as a maintenance mechanic in the hydraulics branch. Not a very exciting job, but at least it was a job, and my friends on the field congratulated me. One very good thing, however: I heard I could get a furlough, at long last, maybe in June. I was bitterly disappointed, however, when I was told I would have to wait awhile. Toshi and I had just about made up our minds, in fact we had made them up, to get married on my furlough, and now I had to write her that it would all have to be postponed. One month more went by; some friends of mine were shipped away from camp. The weather got hotter and hotter, and I worked hard and it was appreciated, I think, though I was pretty much of a novice at it all. Then my furlough suddenly did come through. On a week's notice Toshi and her family had a wedding all planned, she wired me the money, and I was off. 15 days ... my first furlough in a year to the day that I left NY to join the army in Alabama.

Well, it was funny. Toshi and I wanted so to see each other we were both scared in each other's presence. We had to get acquainted all over again. But the wedding went off very well. We had a swell party afterwards in the garden. It was a regular international conference, with people of all different races and nations there, and we were all singing.

... Camp Sibert, Alabama, was another false alarm. We expected to stay there only a couple weeks and instead we stayed there 4 months, as long a time as we were in West Virginia. In Sibert we drilled, went on weekly marches, had incessant lectures and moving pictures (some of which we had seen three and four times before) and calisthenics for one hour every single morning. We were all thoroughly sick of Alabama.

However, it was from Alabama I did some of the most important work since coming into the army. When on furlough I helped make some more union records with Alan Lomax, Tom Glazer,[25] and others. Later, on a three-day pass I took a part playing the banjo for Earl Robinson's Lincoln cantata.[26] (Toshi, incidentally, was now in NY again, having given up her Washington job, for we knew now definitely that she was pregnant—and were very happy about it.) Two weeks after this three-day pass I got special permission to go to NY again (it was taken off my next furlough) to sing and play in a BBC broadcast being arranged by Alan and Elizabeth Lomax. Also at this time I helped record the Lincoln piece for Decca. And, most important, Bess Lomax, Butch [Hawes], and Tom Glazer, and I made what I think is one of the best

---

25. Tom Glazer (1914–2003) was a folk singer and writer, known in later years primarily for his children's songs.
26. Robinson's composition "Lonesome Train" is a long-form cantata detailing the life of President Abraham Lincoln.

progressive albums yet: 6 hitherto unrecorded Spanish and English songs made up and sung by the international brigade boys in Spain of '37-'38.[27] This was in April of 1944.

In June news came that finally we were to leave Sibert for overseas. Rumors galore ran through the company like packs of rats. I got my last furlough, about nine days, and spent them so happily with Toshi.

It was July before we left. As the train wended its way northwestward we gradually became certain that we were going to Seattle. Sure enough, Seattle, it was. But here too we were fools: we stayed there over a month ... doing practically nothing. Waiting for a boat that had room for us and our bulky equipment. Meanwhile I visited friends in town whom I hadn't seen since Woody Guthrie and I spent two weeks there back in the summer of '41.

At last the boat. To think that when I first entered the army I thought that I might be overseas in three or four months! It was over two years since I'd been inducted, when the boat steamed out the straits of Juan De Fuca.

For over a week we glided through placid seas, so blue and clear it was unbelievable. At night the waters were luminous, during the day we saw whales, porpoises, and later on sailfishes, Portuguese Men-O-War, and bosun birds. It was all new and strange, and interesting. The boat was crowded, but bearable. I was seasick the first day, but thereafter all was OK. Every day our company put on shows, on the deck, for the rest of the troops. I helped out a couple times. They seemed to like my singing with a banjo OK.

Early one morning we could see a lighthouse flashing through the dark. In another half hour we could dimly make out the outlines of a stern and rocky coast—Hawaii. Then we rounded the corner and saw a vast city with curving beaches and busy wharves, shimmering in the morning sun.

It is over 6 weeks now that we have been on Oahu. For the first four weeks we gave nightly shows to soldiers camped all over the island. I put on the straw hat and carried a jug and played the perennially dissolute Mountaineer in a skit with Hulett and Fletcher, a skit which turned out to be one of the hits of the show. It was very satisfying to hear the whistles and hollers of the audience for a change.

...It was one month ago, I finally received word that Toshi had given birth to a baby boy. I gave a whoop that resounded the length of the barracks, and later that night gave in to tradition and passed around cigars. I pasted the telegram and letter informing me of the fact on the inside of my locker, and still have it there, as a matter of

---

27. The International Brigades were military units comprised of progressively-minded, usually Communist or socialist, volunteers from other countries who aided Spanish Republicans in fighting against Francoist Nationalists in the Spanish Civil War. The album was *Songs of the Abraham Lincoln Battallion*, released by Folkways.

And I wanted to bring a typewriter!

fact, and don't intend to take it down 'til I get a photograph of the son and heir. Toshi and I have still to definitely decide on a name, though it is registered as Peter Ohta Seeger, for the record. Well, this makes me mighty happy and proud. It's a far cry from 1942, all right.

...While we are here [in Hawaii] doing very little, I am doing much reading, and singing about three times a week up at a Red Cross canteen for wounded men, and also I find time to explore the coral reefs with some home-made water goggles I contrived myself from scraps of wood, tape, and glass, glue, and plastic wood.

Next is the island of Saipan, in the Marianas, and 1,500 miles by Tokyo, which our Superfortresses bomb every couple days. After about 2 months on Oahu we took a 23-day trip on the calm blue sea. It was a

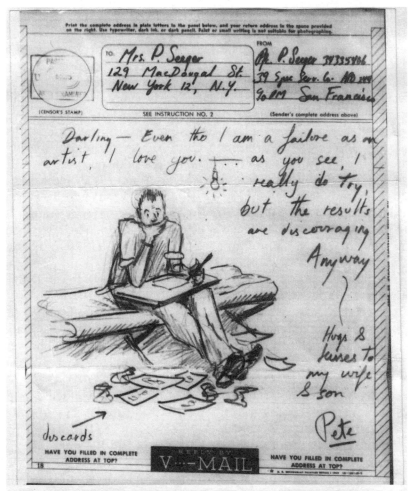

Darling.. even though I am a failure as
an artist, Ii love you... as you see I
really do try, but the results are discour-
aging. Anyway...

pity I had to leave when I did. I was just getting to know people there, and really enjoying myself. But they say there's a war on out here, and I guess they figured the 39th Special Service Company wouldn't fuck it up too much, so here we come.

"Darlingest Toshi," 1945

Letter to Toshi Seeger, dated January 15, 1945; found in Seeger files

Darlingest Toshi and my son—Pitou, later maybe to be named something else, but no matter—my son! I love you and miss you so much.

I'm writing this on such a slant because of the novelty and believe me it is easier to write! I think I shall try the next page upside down. Darling. I have just been out to see a swell movie: I recommend it to you: *Rhapsody in Blue* ... all about George Gershwin. God, how I envy that man's creativeness and productivity. Sometimes for short seconds I think I have it but then lack the talent to carry it through. "Maybe later" ... but I remember a cartoon Grandmother Edson used to have pinned up on her wall:

The first frame shows a boy running towards a beautiful goddess labeled "Tomorrow" who beckons with a graceful finger. The next three frames show him still running, and "Tomorrow" still beckons, but is a little further away. Until, in the last frame, as an old man, he suddenly stumbles into a pit, while Tomorrow stands pensively by. A rather pessimistic tale. A funny thing to realize that so many tomorrows are past and present now. The war we feared and predicted, we are in the midst of, and you and Pitou are here as I have so often dreamed of. I remember the long lonely nights in Mississippi when I wondered if I would ever see you again and wondered if we would ever actually get married and have children. How far off it seemed then.

Concerning creativeness again, I am often ashamed, as I told you, in this tent, because others around me are creative and productive while I sit and read and study and read and study ... always absorbing and never contributing. It is the eternal rut of the scholar who thinks that he can substitute learning for thinking. Of course you need both but I should have had a better sense of proportion about how much of both. All the ingredients going into the recipe of life and every individual has to determine, I guess, which is the best for him. The average will be similar but no two alike. But not even you and I. After all I can't have a baby. I can only help to start one.

I used to think that there was nothing in the world I couldn't do if I really wanted to. I have since learned some limitations ... an over-light and nervous physique and other things. Principally, I have learned that "If I wanted to" is an awful big "if." I still think that I could be an actor or an artist or a musician. Or an engineer or a scientist or a writer. But it won't spring from any intuition and unschooled genius. It would take hard study and perseverance and concentration. Therefore all at once would be impossible. Yet I could. Does this sound conceited? I don't mean it to be. There is nothing I really have excelled in, except variety. Yet, this means that I still have faith in my ability to create (besides babies) in spite of all the failures in the past.

And there have been so many of them (failures ... not babies) you don't know. Every song I started to write and gave up was a failure. I started to paint because I failed to get a job as a journalist. I started singing and playing more because I was a failure as a painter. I went into the army as willingly as I did because I was having more and more failure musically. I thought for a week or two I had failed with you, remember? A dozen times in the past year and a half I have seriously thought of transferring to the infantry and losing myself in the war because I have failed so far to do what I think I should and could do in Special Service. I have always decided against it and probably always will because of several reasons: the first and most common of course, is fear of getting my head shot off. Special Service is safe. I'm not the only one who thinks of this. I'm not proud of it but it's true; I'm not volunteering for death ... yet. The second reason and in the last analysis quite as important, if not more so, is that to transfer out would be admitting a failure which I am unwilling to admit. I still think that I have it in me to accomplish something worthwhile here. But you know, you shouldn't send me those stories of soldiers on the Russian front. They make me feel like a slacker. And it takes men who put their cause before their life to win a war.

In music, though, these are several quite definite things I want to do, which, if I could, would be a real contribution to American music. I say "I" though it really should be "we" because it is an Almanac job. Mill, Alan, Earl [Robinson], Bess, Butch, Pa, Woody and Leadbelly all figure in. Some of them like Earl and Pa seem way ahead of me but I have gone farther in certain directions than they have. So in a small way, I am a specialist too. Partly the 5-string banjo. But more in other ways because I have sung lots of songs with many different people. I want to learn all the folk songs that Alan knows, all the production technique that Mill and Bess have and the musicianship that Earl has and the honest songs of Leadbelly and Woody. Is this too much to hope for? I have a long life or should have. After the war I want to organize a very large chorus of untrained voices to see what I can do in that respect.

O, dearest, here I have talked about myself for eight whole pages. Do you shudder at being saddled for a lifetime with a man so self-centered? Believe me, I get this way only part of the time. But I am trying to think out loud and you are the only person in all the world I'd write like this to. Dearest, music is not the most important thing in the world and will not bring immortality, I know. Honesty and love and happiness are more important. But though I don't drink or smoke, I have got one helluva dissipation and that is music and I can get quite drunk on it, too and lost in it—and I hope you are a patient wife.

"I Have Some Sad News," 1945

Letter to Margot Mayo, dated April 2, 1945; found in Seeger files

Dear Margot—

Thanks for your letter and sorry for being so long in answering. At last we are fairly busy here, putting on shows and helping others put 'em on. I have some sad news, our little baby died a few weeks ago. It was a great shock to Toshi—he'd always been so healthy—but she's taken it very bravely. It seems that he'd been born with a malformed digestive system and there is nothing anyone could do about it. Have you been to I.S.E. school[28] yet?

Love, Pete

"Report from the Marinas, No. 9," 1945[29]

Dated August 12, 1945; found in Seeger files

Notes of an innocent bystander—No. 9

Sooooo—the war is over. Or least the radio says it is a matter of days, or maybe hours. We gave them an ultimatum; they were coy: said they would accept unconditional surrender terms if the emperor could retain complete control. So we reword it and fling it back. When will they got tired of playing and make up their minds?

Well, the war is over—and now the fighting will begin. That is, we will all start fighting to get home. Businesses will start fighting each other to see who can grab the first millions spent for civilian goods. The NAM[30] will fight labor (all the harder). Etc., etc.

The night before last, when the news first came ever the radio that Japan had offered to surrender, there was whooping and shouting. It was about 11:30 PM—one boy burst into the barracks, turned on the lights and shouted the news. We rolled over rubbing our eyes, and thought, Chrrrist, Peileke's drunk again. But then we heard the midnight report on the radio, and for some there was very little sleep that night. A neighboring outfit promptly rounded up some beer and had a party, with much singing. I confess I was so sleepy, though, that after that midnight newscast I rolled over and slept soundly from then on.

Next day came the reports of indecision back in the States. Reports of sidewalk interviews which said 60 percent in favor of holding out for complete unconditional surrender, 30 percent for taking the offer, and 10 percent in favor of leaving it up to the experts.

You should have heard the resentment of some guys. I was surprised and, as it went on, disgusted. "Those lousy c … g civilians making a lot of money, want to keep on fighting the G … D … war. Every single one of that 60 percent ought to be stuck out on one of these islands for two years!"

I nearly got into a couple fights about it. To me it seemed silly to debate the point. A few more atomic bombs, if necessary, would bring

---

28. The meaning of "I.S.E." is uncertain, but Mayo was an active participant in the Women's Auxiliary Army Corps, and this was likely part of her training.
29. The "Reports from the Marinas" were shorter pieces that Seeger wrote throughout the course of his military service. They seem to be designed as expressions of single moments or events that Seeger found particularly poignant, as opposed to his diary, which was used more as an ongoing chronicle of his time in the army.
30. The National Association of Manufacturers, an industrial trade advocacy group that opposed the formation of unions in industrialized labor.

the Japanese government to its senses. Furthermore, on the other hand, what's wrong with leaving the Emperor there if we take away the two main groups whose support gave him his power: the militarists and the big trusts?

I only regret that one has to show any deference to any emperors anywhere. I foresaw that the Allies would do just as they did: reword it to say that the Emperor could stay but we'd tell him what to do.

From the looks of things, it's my own personal opinion I won't get home any too soon, in spite of this quick surrender. A large force will be needed to occupy Japan, and garrison troops like me who haven't borne the brunt of combat so far, would naturally be picked for such a job.

So, as the gagman said, I'll see you in the spring if I can get through the mattress.

Pete passed by censor (I hope)

P.S. I forgot to mention Wendell (an actor in my office) trying on his civilian suit yesterday, to our amusement. (He had it here for a show.) Nor did I mention the comment of another: "Think of the poor officers who will have to give up their private empires out here." Tsk.

"A Shoestring Operation," 1961

From *Reprints from The People's Songs Bulletin 1946–1949,* Oak Archives, 1961

In 1945 Americans came home from the war. We dived enthusiastically into long-deferred projects. A number of us who loved to sing folk songs and union songs thought it the most natural thing in the world to start an organization which could keep us all in touch with one another, which could promote new and old songs and singers, and in general bring closer the broad revival of interest in folk music and topical songs which we felt sure would sooner or later take place. We called our organization People's Songs to distinguish it from the scholarly folklore societies, and started a bulletin. I wanted it to be a weekly; others persuaded me to be more conservative and make it a monthly.

It was strictly a shoestring operation. The first issue was mimeographed. When we had to start paying a salary to at least one person ($25 a week) we felt we were being wildly extravagant. Monthly hootenannies in New York paid the office rent.

We had the utmost contempt for normal commercial musical endeavors. We were convinced that the revival of interest in folk music would come through the trade unions. After all, it was New Deal money which had sparked the great Library of Congress folk song archives in the '30s. Union educational departments had already put out many fine songbooks. There was the singing tradition of the old IWW to build on. We envisioned a singing labor movement spearheading a nationwide folksong revival, just as it was the Scottish progressives who sparked a folksong revival at the time of Robert Burns,[31] and the Czech progressives who sparked another at the time of Dvorshak.[32]

How our theories went astray! Most union leaders could not see any connections between music and pork chops. As the cold war deepened in '47 and '48 the split in the labor movement deepened. "Which Side Are You On" was known in Greenwich Village but not in a single miner's union local.

But here is the interesting thing: the revival of interest in folk music and topical songs did come about, and the existence of People's Songs helped to do it. How? Because the young people in summer camps and schools grew up and went to college. Because the very banishment of singers such as myself from labor union work forced us to make a living in commercial ways, such as nightclubs, or in concerts for schools and colleges. Because, basically, these were good songs, as any fool could plainly see. And our theory about singing them in an informal and enthusiastic way was correct.

The organization People's Songs closed its doors for lack of funds in early 1949. We couldn't raise the (for us) huge sum of $3,000 to pay printers and landlords. But the singers and songs carried on. A few years later, the magazine *Sing Out,* started up on similar lines, and with the devoted work of a few volunteers, slowly grew. Looking over the pages of the little mimeographed bulletin of 1946 I am at times appalled by its amateurishness, and at other times filled with a flush of pride for bravery and honesty. Maybe fools walk in where angels fear to tread, but here's to the young and foolish, and may the world have more of them.

---

31. Burns (1759–1796) was a progressive Scottish poet and collector of folk songs.
32. Dvorshak (1841–1904) was a Czech composer who incorporated folk songs into his symphonic music.

3

Mentors and Influences

"Too Many People Listen to Me—And Not to the People I Learned From," 1958

From *Caravan* magazine, October 1958

When an audience applauds me for some little banjo piece like "Arkansas Traveler," I get a funny feeling inside me. I feel like telling them: "You should hear Hobart Smith[1] of Virginia play that; he makes great music out of it." Or when someone writes that they like the way I play "Coal Creek March" I write them and suggest they listen to a man who really knows how to play it: Pete Steele,[2] of Hamilton, Ohio. He recorded it for the Library of Congress twenty years ago, and I can't imagine it ever being done better by the greatest musicians on earth.

Frankly, it's embarrassing to think of the number of people listening to me, when they should be listening to the kind of people I learned from. Write to the Folklore Section, Library of Congress, Washington, D.C. They'll send you a list of the recordings they have available. Or get hold of the Folkways Records *Anthology of American Folk Music* with eighty-four sides dubbed from the early country music recordings of Victory, Columbia, Brunswick, et al. And I'm looking forward to the day when some company reissues a whole 12″ LP full of nothing but the singing and banjo picking of the late Uncle Dave Macon.[3]

---

1. Smith (1897–1965) was a Virginian banjo virtuoso who was recorded many times by both Alan Lomax and Moses Asch, beginning in the early 1940s and continuing until his death in the mid-1960s.
2. Steele (1891–1985) was a Kentucky-born banjo player, most famous for his rendition of "Coal Creek March," recorded for the Library of Congress in 1938.
3. Macon (1870–1952) was a banjo player and Vaudeville performer who became one of the first stars of the Grand Ole Opry.

Perhaps the role of performers such as myself should best be thought of as that of an intermediary. We can introduce music to audiences to whom the straight stuff would seem too raw, crude, or unintelligible. We also have the advantage of being able to present a broader picture of folk music than any true folk musician could. A true folk musician may be a genius at his or her own kind of music—but that one kind is liable to be all he knows.

However, having been introduced to folk music, the listener should go on and hear it done by people who have been raised on it since they were knee high, who have it in their bones, whose music blends in with their lives, the way music always ought to.

… Of course, when it comes to making music yourself, I don't think it's possible or desirable to imitate slavishly and mechanically, any more than it is desirable to have anyone slavishly imitate me. We are all in the process of building up new traditions out of many old ones, and as folks change, folk music will. But we will do a better job of building up new traditions when we take time to learn the best of the old. How else can we pass it on?

"Charles Seeger: A Man of Music," 1979

From *Sing Out!* magazine, no. 27.3, May/June 1979

On his desk when he died of a heart attack in February, musicologist Charles Seeger had letters going to half a dozen countries, and a folder on which he had noted, "Take to Yale to discuss next week." Although he was 92, he was living life as fully as anyone could, doing what he loved best, discussing and theorizing with other musicologists and folklorists.

His seven children, eighteen grandchildren, and hundreds of devoted colleagues on several continents are sad that he did not keep on for another ten or twenty years, as he gave indications of doing, but know that his long, active physical and intellectual life sets a good example for them. For most of the past twenty years he lived alone, cooking for himself and keeping his kitchen, like his desk, neat as a pin.

He came from a long line of New Englanders, ranging from abolitionists to sea captains, except for a German great-grandfather, Dr. Carl Ludvig Seeger ("Zay-gair") who eagerly emigrated from the Neckar River Valley to join the country of Thomas Jefferson in 1787. Charles Seeger was born a century later in Mexico City, where his father was in business. When he entered Harvard in 1904 he was protected against Harvard snobbery by already having a strong inoculation of what he later called "Seeger snobbery." And when he was appointed to head the music department of the University of California at Berkeley, at age 25, he self-confidently revamped things, including teaching the nation's first course in musicology.

He also got in hot water politically. To broaden his own education he monitored courses by anthropologist Alfred Kroeber (who worked with the American Indian, Ishi).[4] A socialist colleague took him to visit the migratory labor conditions in the huge California valleys. Deeply shocked, Seeger came back and was giving a speech about what he had seen when a burly voice from the audience said, "Sit down, you lily livered bastard. You've just found out about these things. We've known them all our lives."

Seeger searched out the speaker afterwards and said, "You're absolutely right. I am just learning." The man was a Wobbly,[5] and became a good friend. Soon Seeger was publicly joining others in denouncing World War I as an imperialist war, and when one October evening he read the headlines about Lenin's followers storming the winter palace he whooped with delight. "Of course Seeger whoops," said Robert Minor, the San Francisco socialist cartoonist, who was present. "He's an artist."

So the following year he took a sabbatical, realizing that it was probably a permanent separation. (Fifty years later he got an honorary degree at Berkeley.) Back east, he meticulously built one of America's first automobile trailers, and with his wife Constance, a concert violinist, set out for a tour "to bring good music to the people." With a portable pump organ to serve as accompaniment, and a big iron pot to boil laundry over an open fire, a baby still in diapers and two small boys, they set out for Florida.

They only got as far as Pinehurst, North Carolina, before the impossible muddy roads of 1920 brought the tour to a dead stop. Camped out in the woods of the MacKenzie family, local farmers, they played some Bach and Handel one evening at the farmer's house. Afterwards the MacKenzie family reciprocated, unlimbered banjoes and fiddles, and Seeger realized that "the people" already had some pretty good music. Next spring the Model T Ford sadly hauled the trailer back to New York State and the two musicians got jobs teaching at Damrosch's Institute For Musical Art, later Julliard Institute.

During the 1920s Seeger encouraged his student Henry Cowell to tour the Soviet Union and bring back recordings of Asiatic people's music which enthusiastic Soviet ethnologists were documenting. And in 1928, Cecil Sharp and Maud Karpeles[6] were collecting Appalachian

---

4. Kroeber (1876–1960) was the first professor appointed to the anthropology department at University of California, Berkeley. He worked extensively in the study and preservation of Native American cultures and was appointed head of the University's Museum of Anthropology in 1909. Shortly thereafter, he became acquainted with, and studied, Ishi (c. 1860–1916) a Yahi Indian, believed to be the last American Indian in the San Francisco Bay Area to have lived the majority of his life outside European-American civilization.

5. "Wobbly" is an informal term for a member of the Industrial Workers of the World, a radical anarcho-syndicalist union most prominent between 1905 and 1924.

6. Sharp (1859–1924) was an English folksong collector, credited with sparking and encouraging the folk music revival in England in the early 20th century. Sharp often

ballads. Seeger shrewdly picked out some of the best to show to his youngest boy, who at age 7 was learning the ukulele and would repeat any sort of song that caught his fancy.

In 1931, his first marriage having broken up, Seeger married the talented composer Ruth Crawford,[7] and started raising a new family. In those Depression days it seemed to many that the capitalist economic system was on the verge of permanent collapse. Seeger joined with other radical musicians to start the Composers Collective of the Pierre DeGeyter Club in lower Manhattan. Bertolt Brecht[8] and Hans Eisler[9] were having great success in Germany with a starkly modern style of proletarian marching song, and attempts were made to transplant it in the USA. But outside narrow circles it didn't catch on.

By 1935, most political radicals felt that only a broad coalition could defeat worldwide fascism, and Seeger took a job as assistant director of the WPA music project[10] in Washington. Soon he was working with young Alan Lomax, trying to plan how a revival of interest in folk music could avoid the mistakes which had bogged down the European folk music revival.

In Europe, folklorists had selected what they felt were the "best" melodies, arranged them for pianoforte, orchestra, and chorus, and told young people, in effect, "Now don't change a note." Nothing was left for improvisation. Lomax and Seeger felt that it would be better to let young people learn by ear, listening and seeing authentic original performers, so as to preserve the spirit of improvisation. As we know now, their theories worked. A colleague complained, "Charlie, your son will ruin his voice unless he gets vocal training."

"If I catch him taking voice lessons, I'll stop it immediately," Seeger replied.

In 1952 the Cold War was closing in on former radicals of all sorts. The FBI asked Seeger to tell them all about his past affiliations. He said, "I'm willing to undress, figuratively speaking, myself. But I will not

---

worked with Karpeles (1885–1976), a social worker and dancer whose dance troop supplemented Sharp's lectures on English folk traditions by demonstrating folk dances. Sharp and Karpeles traveled together to Appalachia, where they compared American folk songs to their presumed English antecedents.

7. Charles Seeger's second wife and Pete Seeger's stepmother. Crawford (1901–1953), who studied under Charles Seeger before they married, was perhaps the most prominent woman composer of the American avant-garde of that time. For more on the Seeger family lineage, see chapter 1.

8. Brecht (1898–1956) was a hugely influential figure in 20th century theater. His lifelong commitment to radical politics was reflected in many of his theatrical works, which he used as vehicles to express leftist ideas.

9. Eisler (1898–1962) was an Austrian experimental composer and Communist activist. He frequently collaborated with Bertolt Brecht, writing music for many of Brecht's plays. With the Nazis ascendant in central Europe, Eisler moved to the United States, where he found initial success. However, he was quickly blacklisted at the onset of the Cold War and moved back to Europe, settling in East Germany.

10. As part of New Deal–era legislation, the Works Progress Administration (WPA) Federal Music Project employed musicians and composers who were out of work during the Great Depression.

tell you anything about anyone else." This was not enough for the FBI. Seeger resigned from his job as music coordinator for the Pan-American Union.[11] A year later his wife died tragically just as her own career as a composer was getting underway again after raising four children. Seeger was soon in California, working with the Institute for Ethnomusicology at UCLA. In his 70s he was still going strong, increasingly deaf but able to hear with a powerful hearing aid. His circle of colleagues and students continued to expand worldwide. He worked with his oldest son, a scientist, to develop a machine called a Melograph. Into one end of it a melody could be played. Out the other end came a sheet of graph paper with the exact melody recorded as a wiggling line, showing exact pitch, all slurs and wavers. For the first time musicians could see clearly what they were arguing about.

Seeger increasingly centered his interest on the relationship of speech communication to music communication. "If the human race fails to survive, a large part of the blame should go to an overdependence on one form of communication—words." (I believe I am quoting him correctly.) In his eighties, his colleagues insisted that he must prepare a volume of his musicological theories, and in his ninetieth year *Studies in Musicology* was finally published by the University of California Press. He was in constant demand to attend conferences and seminars, and every few months was flying to some corner of the world. He had lived long enough to see many ideas which he had helped start off gain general acceptance. His good health was no accident, but came from a combination of yoga exercises, careful diet, and daily afternoon walks, often of several miles. A major biography of him tentatively titled *Seeger, Music and Society*[12] is in preparation.

All of us who knew him know how lucky we are. His enthusiasm was infectious, his self-discipline inspiring. I can see him now, in these new times, pursing his lips, gazing into space briefly, wrinkling his forehead reflectively. Then swinging his long spare frame around in his chair to his typewriter, he straightens his back, gets to work putting words in their proper order.

"Woody Guthrie, Songwriter," 1963

From *Mainstream* magazine, no. 16.8, August 1963

Woodrow Wilson Guthrie, one of the great folk song ballad-makers of this century, was born in Okemah, Oklahoma. Childhood in an oil

11. Currently, the Organization of American States, the organization is comprised of countries from North, Central, and South America brought together in an ostensibly collaborative union.
12. While no biography of Seeger by this name exists, a major biography was published in 1992 by the University of Pittsburgh Press, entitled *Charles Seeger: A Life in American Music,* authored by Ann M. Pescatello.

boom town. In 1935, he drifted to California, along with thousands of other "Okies" forced by dust storms and Depression woes to leave their homes. Made a living singing in saloons, occasional fly-by-night radio programs and later on for union meetings, parties, political rallies, dance and theater groups, the Library of Congress Folksong Archives. Dozens of restless trips across the U.S.A. Three marriages and many children. And over one thousand songs.

Woody has described his musical education pretty well. The lonesome old ballads sung by his mother, the honky-tonk blues, and the wild hollers that he heard from his father and other men in town. And it is worth emphasizing that his style of guitar picking was picked straight off the recordings of the Carter Family, who were popular around 1931 when Woody was eighteen years old. He also learnt some of his favorite songs directly off their records. Another favorite of his, of course, was Jimmie Rodgers, "the yodeling brakeman." Woody also used to accompany his uncle Jeff, who was a fiddler, and they played on the radio occasionally. And so you see, he fits right in with the usual "country music" category of a small town in Oklahoma in the '20s and '30s. So much so that I know some people in New York, when they first heard him, would say, "Why, he's just a hillbilly singer, isn't he?"

After he had gone to California and was singing for $1 a day on a Los Angeles radio station, he attracted the attention of a man named Ed Robbin, a news commentator for a radical newspaper, the *People's World*, over the same radio station. This man got interested in Woody and Woody's ideas, and Woody got interested in him and his ideas. The year was 1938.

Woody was introduced to Will Geer, the actor, who was doing benefits to raise money for the migratory labor camps. Woody came along and dived into the struggle. He became a close friend of Will and his family. Through Geer, Woody started to make a living singing at fund-raising parties around Los Angeles.

Will sent me a copy of Woody's mimeographed songbook, *On a Slow Train through California*, and told me I sure ought to meet Woody when he came to New York. I met him in March of 1940, at a midnight song session on the stage of a Broadway theater. It was again a benefit for the California migratory workers. *The Grapes of Wrath* had been published a year before, and there were many in New York who felt that we wanted to learn more. Will Geer was MC of the show. Burl Ives was on it and also Leadbelly and Josh White. And there was Woody. A little, short fellow with a western hat and boots, in blue jeans and needing a shave, spinning out stories and singing songs that he had made up himself. His manner was laconic, offhand, as though he didn't much care if the audience was listening or not.

I just naturally wanted to learn more about him. I became a friend of his, and he became a big piece of my education. I was working for

Alan Lomax down in the Library of Congress in Washington, D.C. Woody came down several times, usually on some kind of booking or other. We hit it off pretty well together. Around May 1940, he came down driving a car which he hadn't finished paying for, and asked me if I'd like to come with him to Oklahoma.

I quit my job—such as it was—and we "hitchhiked on credit," as he said, down through Virginia and Tennessee, on to Oklahoma, and then to Pampa, Texas, where Woody's wife and children were staying with her parents. I don't think we stayed in Pampa more than a week or two, and then went back to Oklahoma City where the finance company came and took his car, as I remember it. We went back east with Bob Wood,[13] and were learning things all the way.

…Anything worth discussing was worth a song to Woody: news off the front page, sights and sounds of the countryside he traveled through, thoughts brought to mind by reading anything from Rabelais[14] to Will Rogers.[15]

I remember the night he wrote the song "Tom Joad." He said, "Pete, do you know where I can get a typewriter?"

I said, "I'm staying with someone who has one."

"Well, I got to write a ballad," he said. "I don't usually write ballads to order, but Victor[16] wants me to do a whole album of Dust Bowl songs, and they say they want one about Tom Joad in *The Grapes of Wrath*." I asked him if he had read the book and he said, "No, but I saw the movie. Good movie." He went along to the place where I was staying—six flights walking up—on East Fourth Street. The friend I was staying with let him use the typewriter.

Woody had a half-gallon jug of wine with him, sat down and started typing away. He would stand up every few seconds and test out a verse on his guitar, and sit down and start typing some more. About one o'clock my friend and I got so sleepy we couldn't stay awake. In the morning we found Woody curled up on the floor under the table. The half gallon of wine was almost empty and the completed ballad was sitting near the typewriter.

Later, at Almanac House, I saw him compose other songs over a period of months. He'd have an idea and fool around with it a little bit, wouldn't be satisfied; then maybe he'd come back to it in a month or two and fool around with it some more.

---

13. Wood was a union organizer and head of the Oklahoma chapter of the Communist Party.
14. Francois Rabelais (1494–1553) was a French Renaissance author whose writing was noted for its irreverent and satirical tone.
15. Rogers (1879–1935) began his career as an Oklahoman vaudeville performer and comedian. A skilled and multi-talented performer, he quickly rose to fame in the then-fledgling American film industry. Known for his sharp wit and populist bent, Rogers wrote a widely syndicated newspaper column that extolled the virtues of common American life, especially on the Western frontier.
16. RCA Victor, the record label.

When World War II came along, I went into the Army, and he went into the Merchant Marines. He's written about his experiences there better than anybody else could tell them. He got torpedoed, visited half a dozen countries, or at least saw their ports, and kept writing verses every day, unconcerned by who thought he was what kind of a character by the way he dressed or acted.

After he got out, he had a new family and had to take care of them; I also had a family I was starting, so we saw each other only at occasional hootenannies.

In 1952, at a party in California, I heard him sing for the last time. He'd come out west hoping to start a new life, not realizing that his occasional dizzy spells were soon going to get worse and send him to the hospital forever. He sang one or two of his old songs. Then somehow he and I got started making up verses to "Acres of Clams." Woody improvised an unforgettable couple.

The first describes how he was sitting at home one day and the doorbell rings, and there's a man who says he's from the FBI, and would like to ask a few questions. Woody's following verse:

> He asked, will you carry a gun for your country?
> I answered the Effbee-aye "Yay!
> I will point a gun for my country,
> But I won't guarantee you which way!
> I won't guarantee you which way-y-y-y!
> I won't guarantee you which way!
> I will point a gun for my country
> But I won't guarantee you which way!"

Arlo Guthrie tells that when his father went into the hospital he was asked what religion he was, so it could be entered on the correct form.

"All," replied Woody firmly.

"Mr. Guthrie, we must know which religion to list you as."

"All."

"I'm sorry, Mr. Guthrie; it must be one or another."

"All or none," replied Woody.

While he was in the hospital with Huntington's disease, the wasting illness that finally killed him, young people with their guitars and banjos were already singing Woody's songs and making them famous. And of his thousands of verses, I think a large number will outlive this century.

Alan Lomax, perhaps America's foremost folklorist, calls Woody "our best contemporary ballad composer." Others say: "a rusty-voiced Homer," and "the greatest folk poet we've had."

Why are the songs great? Look through his songbooks, only a small sampling of his huge output.

Yes, the words show a fine sense of poetry, of reaching out for exactly the right word at exactly the right place. He used some fine time-tested tunes. The songs are honest; they say things that need to be said.

But above all else, Woody's songs show the genius of simplicity. Any damn fool can get complicated, but it takes genius to attain simplicity. Some of his greatest songs are so deceptively simple that your eye will pass right over them and you will comment to yourself, "Well, I guess this was one of his lesser efforts." Years later you will find the song has grown on you and become part of your life.

Woody took his tunes mostly from different kinds of American folk songs and ballads. He had a deep respect for the ballad form. He knew enough about other song forms to choose many others, but he felt that the old four-line stanza, which told a story and slowly unfolded a moral, was as good as any he could use. Woody said, "I'm not saying some of your tunes from other countries aren't good. But I wasn't raised to them, and neither are the people I'm trying to sing to. So I'm going to use the kind of tunes we understand."

Woody was a great poet; as a prose writer too, I think him a genius. He wasn't pretending to be anybody else—he was just himself. He learnt from everybody, and from everything. He learnt from the King James Bible; he learnt from the left-wing newspapers and publications; he had a devouring curiosity. I'll never forget the week he discovered Rabelais, and read through a two-inch-thick volume in a couple of days. During the following weeks I could see him experimenting with some of the techniques of style that Rabelais used, such as paragraphs full of images, adjective after adjective getting more fantastic.

In early 1940, Woody had gotten a job paying $200 a week—a lot of money then—to sing one or two songs a week for the Model Tobacco network radio program. One of the things the Model Tobacco people wanted him to do was quit writing columns for his favorite newspaper, *The Sunday Worker*, weekend edition of the *Communist Daily Worker*. Woody euphemistically called it "The Sabbath Employee." Those columns of his are classics. He got the idea from the columns Will Rogers used to do for the *New York Times*. Just a few sentences with a few sharp comments on the news of the day. For example, when he went to Washington in the spring of 1940, Woody wrote: "I'm down here looking at the Potomac River; they say that George Washington threw a silver dollar across it once. It looks a little bit too far for me to do that trick, but maybe he could. After all, a dollar went further in those days."

If Woody had been willing to play along with the Model Tobacco Company and sing the songs they wanted him to sing, and quit doing these columns and his left-wing bookings, he could have stayed with them and had a successful commercial career. But he quit after a month or so.

The Model Tobacco Company tried and failed to force Woody into a respectable mold. There were other attempts. John Greenway's

American Folk Songs of Protest, published in McCarthy-ridden 1953, contains the following:

> Once more in New York, Guthrie became associated with the Almanac Singers, and through them with People's Songs, an organization in which his individuality was quickly submerged. Before any harm was done to his style, however ... he gradually dissociated himself from the group.

The best person to answer this is Woody himself. In 1951—just after he signed a contract with a major recording company—Woody wrote to *Sing Out* (founded by People's Artists, the successor to People's Songs):

> Dear Editor: When some super-reactionary friend of mine looked through several issues of *Sing Out* and failed to find any songs of my own making he wrote me and said: "Thank God you're not having anything to do with that bunch."
>
> I've read just about every word of every issue of *Sing Out* and I just want to say right now before any more of you write in to thank me that I could not agree any more or any plainer nor any stronger with *Sing Out* if I had wrote every single word of it, and every song myself by my own hand.
>
> I know everybody on this *Sing Out* staff just as good as I know any of the members of my own family, or any of my sisters and my brothers. I believe in peace and *Sing Out* believes in peace; I do my best to fight against war and *Sing Out* fights just as hard to stop wars as I do; I make ballad songs about the news of every day and show you how Jim Crow and race hate hurts and stings and kills off a good part of my country every minute that flies by; and *Sing Out* sings out with songs to teach, to show, to prove to you these same terrible things; *Sing Out* sings out, too: to tell you about every little inch we gain in our fight against all of this reaction of hate.
>
> One little issue of *Sing Out* is worth more to this humanly race than any thousand tons of other dreamy, dopey junk dished out from the trees of our forest along every Broadway in this world. I don't know of a magazine big or little that comes within a thousand million miles of *Sing Out* when it comes to doing good around this world.
>
> More of my songs, my latest peace pieces and my later and older ballads too, will be printed in the pages of *Sing Out*s to come. I don't want your Tommy Glazzeye Mackarthurish[17] cold bloody handshake nor your word of thanks nor your anything else. Whichever side Mac ain't on, I'm on, whichever side MacCarran[18] ain't on, I am; whichever side Taft-Hartley's[19] not on, I'm on double watch.

17. Tom Glazer had just written a song glorifying General MacArthur.
18. Pat McCarran (1876–1954), a U.S. senator who authored the McCarran Internal Security Act, which became a central part of congressional efforts to prosecute suspected Communists during the Cold War. Notably, the act provided the legal justification for the revocation of Paul Robeson's passport.
19. The Taft-Hartley Act, enacted in 1947, aimed to monitor and curb the activities of labor unions, specifically unions' abilities to strike effectively.

Let this be the end of those remarks that I will use my record contract to fall in love with my bellybutton and forget all of the Peekskills that I've been through with Pete Seeger, Lee Hays, and Earl Robinson, and lots of others. If I do fall into ten per cent ownership of this Record Co. in the morning soon, that will not change one little word of this letter as to which side of things I am and am not on.

Your Buddy,
Woody Guthrie.

Woody always claimed that he could not theorize, that he couldn't keep up with us and our book-learning. He'd bow out of an argument rather than get tangled up in four-syllable words. He had outspoken contempt for mere cleverness. A joke was fine, a pun, a gag—he put plenty of humor into his songs. But humor was not enough by itself. There had to be some solid meat there. So in some of his most humorous songs, like "Talking Dustbowl," there's an undertone of bitter reality.

I remember in 1948, when he was listening to some friends trying to write clever political parodies. Suddenly he asked, "Why are you guys scared to be serious?"

Woody was not averse to having his songs sung on the hit parade, but to my knowledge he never wrote a song with the hit parade in mind. He considered most commercial music men as slick people who foisted their own idea of music upon the country. He thought of them the way an Oklahoma farmer thought of Wall Street bankers. So Woody put out of his head the idea of making a lot of money from his songs. He'd write and sing them himself, and mimeograph copies for friends from time to time, and trust that if he put together a song which hit the spot, people would take it up as their own.

Since he frankly agreed that he couldn't tell which of his songs would be good and which would be soon forgotten, he adopted a kind of "scatteration" technique—that is, he'd write a lot of songs, on the theory that at least some of them would be good. For example, as a "research consultant" for the Bonneville Power Authority he wrote several dozen songs. Nearly all of them have some special charm. But it was one, "Roll On, Columbia," which seems destined to last for generations.

Woody scattered his genius so that it will never be all collected: rhymes, letters, notes to himself. In 1960, for instance, I came across a notebook from 1940, when he and I were singing for our supper in the Pacific Northwest. On one page there were some financial memos from me. On the next page was Woody's own memo to himself:

The worst thing that can happen to you is to cut yourself loose from people. And the best thing is to sort of vaccinate yourself right into the big streams and blood of the people.

To feel like you know the best and the worst of folks that you see everywhere and never to feel weak or lost, or even lonesome anywhere.

> There is just one thing that can cut you to drifting from the people, and that's any brand or style of greed.
>
> There is just one way to save yourself, and that's to get together and work and fight for everybody.

I learned so many different things from Woody that I can hardly count them. His ability to identify with the ordinary man and woman, speak their own language without using the fancy words, and never be afraid—no matter where you were: just diving into some situation, trying it out. When he and I used to go around singing together, we hit all kinds of places: CIO unions, churches, saloons, meetings, parties.

I learned from him how just plain orneriness has a kind of wonderful honesty to it that is unbeatable: he was going to cuss, he was going to speak bad language, he was going to shock people, but he was going to stay the way he was. He wasn't going to let New York make him slick and sleek and contented. He was going to stay a rebel to the end.

Well, that's Woody for you. He didn't always pay his bills, and he made life hard for his family and friends sometimes, always traveling, itching heels, ants in his pants. I guess I first learned what an undependable husband Woody must have been when we visited his family in Pampa in 1940. His first wife, Mary, gave up on him when he called it quits on his job with the Bonneville Power Administration. She went back to Texas.

Is that the price of genius? Is it worth paying? Maybe it's easy for me to ask that. It wouldn't be as easy for poor Mary, who was trying to build a home and a family.

But Lord, Lord, he turned out song after song after song!

I have traveled around the country and around the world singing his songs and, although Woody was in a hospital for years before his death last year, I always felt he was very much with me, very much alive. Woody is right beside me, strumming along. I know his songs will go on traveling around the world and will be translated into many languages during the coming century, and will be sung by many people who never heard his name.

What better kind of immortality could a man want?

"We Are All Your Children," 1956

Letter to Woody Guthrie, found in Seeger files

Dear Woody,

You know the reason you don't get more letters from me? I feel you're here all the time. Singing your songs, and whanging away on mandolins and guitars like I first heard you do.

Same way everywhere I go. All the camps I've been to this summer, where the kids holler out in that nice open way kids do, not covering up or trying to make their voices sound pretty, "THIS LAND IS YOURRR LAND, THIS ..."

In a way, we are all your children, Woody. You may have thought you only had eight kids, but you ended up having several hundred thousand, and there's several million or billion not even born yet. Now you always knew you were prolific, but I wonder if you knew just how much.

Up at Moe Asch's I heard a whole batch of children's songs you wrote—songs I never heard before. They made me feel like backing off and taking off my hat and bowing. What I mean is, they were so good. They put all the rest of the kids' songs being written today to shame.

The country as a whole, as you may hear, is doing better. There are a lot of people all over who are sick and tired of the blacklist, and we are breaking more holes in the paper curtain every day.

Down in Washington they are stuttering and fumbling and trying to claim that Russia is still out to destroy America, but thousands of visitors coming back from there say that after the jolt of hearing that some bad injustices were done during Stalin's hard driving (and he did some mighty valuable things, too)[20] they are simply cruising along in higher gear than ever.

Now the talk through this country is, "We got to hurry, them Russians are getting more doctors, engineers, and schools than we are"—and even old Jim Crow is taking more and more of a back seat because the rest of the world won't stand for it. The holdouts for the KKK in Alabama are desperate and crazy with fear, because they see it won't be long before their kids will be going to school together, black and white, arm in arm.

You may have heard, I've been cited for contempt of Congress, because I refused to answer questions before that committee last summer. It may mean a costly court battle, and even a year or so in jail. But it may not. Times are changing. And Toshi and I aren't scared. Our neighbors up here in Dutchess Junction are just as swell to us as ever, and we feel confident that whatever happens, Danny and Mika and Tinya won't be hurt. In fact, I think they'll learn a lot.

I want to take them across the country next summer if I can. Show them the dustbowl and the wheatbowl, the fruitbowl and the desert. I'd like 'em to see skid road in Seattle, and some of the little mining towns down south. Do you remember Brooklyn Speedy, the paregoric addict? Do you remember the big Redwood trees, and the red-haired

---

20. Here, Seeger has handwritten "Sic!" in the margin. In his accompanying cover letter, written in December of 1997 to Nora Guthrie, Woody's daughter and the manager of the Woody Guthrie Foundation, Seeger explains this note: "Dear Nora, I thought you might want [this letter] for your files. I put 'sic' in the right column because in '56 I still didn't realize what a cruel misleader Stalin was."

gal in Seattle who sang with us? I met her again last year. Stouter, and she has three children, but that same warm smile. Calamity Jane[21] no longer lives in Duluth. Her husband died, and her kids are married now. She lives in San Francisco. Win Stracke[22] is "Uncle Win" to a couple thousand kids on Chicago TV—he sings your songs to them every week. Studs[23] is still on the air there, too. In Canada we get played on the air even more. The CBC has us both on from coast to coast on their folksong hours, every couple weeks. Everywhere I go people ask after you and send you their love and best wishes.

And me and my kids do too.

Pete

P.S. Me and Mill plan to get the script for that testimonial show you saw us give in May all printed up, so other people can put it on across the country. I'll keep you up on developments.

"The Bound for Glory Concert," 1957

From Seeger's regular "Johnny Appleseed, Jr." column
in *Sing Out!* magazine, no. 7.3, Fall 1957

One of the most unusual evenings of folk music that I ever participated in was the program of songs of Woody Guthrie called *Bound For Glory* put on in New York over a year ago. When we first proposed such an evening, some friends said, "Won't all the songs sound alike?"

Well, there was plenty of variety, especially considering the variety of voices which sang Woody's songs. They ranged from Ed McCurdy's rich baritone to the Kossoy Sisters' sweet harmonizing, solos, duets, Earl Robinson's children's chorus, and audience participation.

What the evening DID have, which was so unusual, was homogeneity. You know how the average hootenanny has a rather scattered imagery, to say the least? Your mind is led off in this direction and then that. There's variety all right, often too much.

But here, in an evening of Woody's songs, we saw the face of America as it was seen by one man, so no matter how widely we circled, we kept returning to a center. Furthermore, none of the singers on the stage

---

21. Irene Paull (1908–1981), known pseudonymously as Calamity Jane, was a political activist from Minnesota.
22. Stracke (1908–1991) was a Chicago-area musician and actor, well known for his membership in the Chicago Repertory Theater, where he worked with Studs Terkel to create topically progressive theater. As Seeger mentions, Stracke was also a presence on Chicago television for many years.
23. Studs Terkel (1912–2008) was best known as an historian who chronicled the lives of ordinary Americans through different periods in American history, making extensive recordings of individuals' oral histories. Terkel was also a longstanding and influential presence on Chicago radio, hosting an interview show, *The Studs Terkel Program,* for over forty years.

did any talking themselves. Millard Lampell had done a deft job of selecting certain paragraphs of Woody's to introduce each number. These were read from the side of the stage by bass-voiced Lee Hays. Therefore Woody's prose flowed into Woody's poetry and then back into Woody's prose without a break, and without the contradiction that so often occurs when a song is introduced with one vocabulary and sung in another.

Altogether, it made a fascinating evening, and I look forward to the program being put on many times throughout the land. It tells a good story, and would be fun for those who put it on as well as those in the audience. One ingredient the New York premiere of this script had which no other could duplicate was an ending which almost proved too melodramatic. It couldn't have been planned. The show was over, the performers were taking their bows, when the spotlight shifted to the balcony, where sat Woody himself. He'd been let out of the hospital for the occasion. Earl Robinson whispered in my ear: "Sing the last chorus over again." The whole crowd of over 1,000, mostly teenagers who had never seen Woody before stood up and sang his song to him, as though to tell him they would carry on his music across the land. Tears were in the eyes of many old-timers as they listened to the strong, young voices sing:

> This land is your land
> This land is my land
> From California to the New York Island
> From the Redwood forests
> To the Gulf Stream waters
> This land was made for you and me[24]

"I Knew Leadbelly," 1955

From *Sing* Magazine, no. 4.3, August/September, 1957

I was seventeen, in New York City, when I first met Huddie Ledbetter. He was not tall—perhaps five feet seven or eight—but compactly built, and he moved with the soft grace of an athlete. He was grey-haired—in his late fifties, I'd say. Always neatly dressed. There I was, trying my best to shed my Harvard upbringing, scorning to waste money on clothes other than blue jeans. But Leadbelly always had a clean white shirt and starched collar, well-pressed suit and shined shoes. He didn't need to affect that he was a workingman. His powerful ringing voice, and his muscular hands moving like a dancer over the strings of his huge twelve-stringed guitar, his honesty and pride, showed he was a workingman.

---

24. c. The Richmond Organization, 1963.

He was wonderful with children. He'd get them singing with him, clapping their hands and swaying their bodies. It was hard to believe the stories we read of his violent youth. I have always figured that here was a clear example of what naturally brings otherwise gentle people into violence. Those little southern honky-tonks were and still are known for fights and killings. And the southern prison farms to which Negroes are sent are murderous places.

That Leadbelly survived prison at all is remarkable. Perhaps the guards liked to keep him to entertain them with his guitar. I guess he learned what so many Negro entertainers have had to learn to do upon occasion—"make a fool of yourself and take the white folks' money." But he stayed alive and got out of prison.

Up north he met a new kind of white people, the enthusiastic young people in the progressive movement in New York City. He never wanted to live in the south again. He and his wife Martha had a little flat on the lower east side. Woody Guthrie and I visited him often there, and made music together with him, till the neighbors complained of the noise. I was proud that he accepted me. Perhaps he wondered at my earnestness, trying to learn folk music.

What a tragedy he died! It was just six months before his song "Goodnight Irene" was selling two million copies, and making Hit Parade history. If he could have lived ten more years he would have seen all his dreams as a musician come true—young people by the millions learning and singing his songs. But in the nineteen thirties and forties, the hit parade was dominated by the big bands, and all entertainment, to be successful, had to be geared to Hollywood standards. So Leadbelly sang for left-wing causes, Greenwich Village parties, and occasional college concerts. We loved him, but I wish we hadn't been his only audience.

Too bad he was never in movies. He was an expert at country-style buck-and-wing clog dancing. In one number he would imitate the gait of all the women of Shreveport, high and low. And another dance accompanied the story of a duck hunter. His guitar became the gun. Pow!

He'd sometimes get on a rhyming kick. For a couple hours on end every sentence that came out of his mouth was rhymed. Sitting in the car, on our way to bookings, he'd go on fanciful flights of poetry and imagination.

O Huddie! How we miss you. Sometimes audiences couldn't understand your Louisiana accent. Sometimes young people thought your style of music was old fashioned. But you were always honestly yourself, never trying to pretend you were someone else, never trying to be a chameleon for the fashions of the day.

He was not the cleverest guitar player; he didn't try and play the fanciest chords, the trickiest progressions, or the fastest number of notes. Rather, the notes he played were powerful and meaningful.

Perhaps this modern age is not liable to produce again such a combi-nation of genuine folk artist and virtuoso. Because nowadays when the artist becomes a virtuoso, there is normally a much greater tendency to cease being folk. But when Leadbelly rearranged a folk melody he had come across—he often did, for he had a wonderful ear for melody and rhythm—he did it in line with his own great folk traditions.

Looking back, I think that the most important thing I learned from him was the straightforward approach, the direct honesty. He bequeathed to us also, it is true, a coupla hundred of the best songs any of us will ever know. I wish people would stop trying to imitate his accent, though, and rather learn from his subtle simplicity, and his powerful pride.

Well, one year, in 1949, he started having to use a cane to go on stage. His voice, always soft and husky when speaking, still rang out high on the melodies, but his hands grew stiffer and less certain on the guitar. Then one day he was gone, and we were left with regrets that we had not treasured him more.

"Remembering Lee," 2004

Foreword to *Sing Out, Warning!, Sing Out, Love: The Writings of Lee Hays*. University of Massachusetts Press, 2004

It's been twenty-two years since Lee Hays died, but I think of him con-stantly. Either when singing some songs he wrote the words to, like "If I Had a Hammer," or relaying some joke he told me, like the old woman who had only two teeth left: "Thank God they're hitters," she said.

Or the planter rocking on his porch, saying, "Come breath; go breath. Damned if I draw yuh." When a brisk young man drives up, walks up to him, says, "I'm from the county farm bureau. I've come to show you how you can be a better farmer than you are." Pause. "I already know how to be a better farmer than I am."

Lee had such a highly developed critical faculty he threw away some of his stories and songs. A hilarious Rabelaisian novel about a young fellow named "Little Diddy Wot" was lost in typescript, and he refused to rewrite it.

He influenced a whole generation of singers and songwriters, and at least one important TV reporter. Young Charles Kuralt[25] had come to New York City from North Carolina to try and break into television. Lee was living next door, blacklisted, trying to write, and watching the then little black-and-white screen. "Think what a wonderful tool this could be for the human race," said Lee, "if it were used right."

---

25. Kuralt (1934–1997) was a journalist and correspondent for *The CBS Evening News with Walter Cronkite*. He was best known for hosting a recurring segment of the Evening News entitled On the Road, wherein Kuralt and his crew would travel the back roads of the United States and conduct interviews with the people he encountered.

I used to think Lee was just cantankerous. Now I think he was some kind of genius. May he influence many generations to come. A gardener like my wife, he mailed her this poem, a year before he died.

> If I should die before I wake
> All my bone and sinew take.
> Put me in the compost pile
> To decompose me for a while.
> Worms, water, sun will have their way
> Returning me to common clay.
> All that I am will feed the trees
> And little fishies in the seas.
> When radishes and corn you munch
> You may be having me for lunch.
> And then excrete me with a grin
> Chortling, there goes Lee again.
> (After a pause) 'Twill be my happiest destiny
> To die and live eternally.

"Welcome Back, Alan," 1959

From *Sing Out!* Magazine, no. 8.3, Winter 1959

Alan Lomax, considered by many America's foremost folklorist, has returned to the United States after nine years in England. He left the U.S.A. as an "*enfant terrible*" and he returns as a legend. It is most probably not an easy experience. Thomas Wolfe wrote a book, *You Can't Go Home Again*. Why? Because homes can change too, just as much as an individual can and when you return home, home can be unrecognizable.

I welcome back Alan Lomax, not just because he is an old friend, but also because, in my opinion, he is more responsible than any other single individual for the whole revival of interest in American folk music. Until he came along, most folklorists, good antiquarians and scholars though they were, had only succeeded in transferring dead bones from one graveyard to another, so to speak. That is, they dug folksongs out of the hills and buried them in libraries.

In the late 1930s Alan was put in charge of the Archive of American Folksongs in the Library of Congress. He listened to tens of thousands of variants and version of folksongs. With a keen sense for a good melody and good poetry, he began selecting and combining the very best of the best. He got Burl Ives and Josh White to become professional performers of folk music and taught them some of the best songs they know. He got me started. He persuaded recording companies and radio networks to take a hesitant first step towards an idiom which most of urban America then scorned.

Well, of course the folksong revival did grow, and flourishes now like any happy weed, quite out of control of any person or party, right or left, purist or hybridist, romanticist or scientist. Alan Lomax probably looks about him a little aghast. We wish him well in his many projects and hope that we will be hearing from him. We think we will. He is not averse to speaking his mind.

"Remembering Paul Robeson," 1998

From *Paul Robeson: Great Forerunner.*
International Publishers Co., 1998

It was in the late 1930s: 20,000 crowded Madison Square Garden to protest the growing world menace of fascism. I was one more teenager in the upper tiers. There had been many speeches that evening, mostly by white people, some lecturing, some shouting and declaiming at ever-higher pitch. Then this tall, broad-shouldered black man stepped up to the microphone.

"Good evening, friends." The voice was so low, so deep and resonant, it seemed to represent the whole vast mass of rank-and-file humanity. The entire auditorium responded with one big warm and loving exhalation. This man represented us, all of us.

In subsequent years, hearing Robeson speak and sing at rallies, in concerts, I never failed to be amazed at the combination in one person of great strength, great tenderness and great intellectuality. In an individual any one of these qualities might be highly developed, but here were all three, kept in beautiful balance in one man.

He was the hero of my youth. Several million other young whites must have also felt so. When I was in the U.S. Army in World War II, my wife wrote me a long description of the huge birthday party given him in New York City. After the encomiums, the ceremony, he sang, and some would have wanted him to sing all night, but others knew he had a hard schedule, playing six nights a week in Othello, and their admonition was picked up by thousands, "Save your voice, Paul!"

After the war I met him in person. I waited in line after a concert, knocked on his dressing-room door, and asked if he would be one of the sponsors of our fledgling organization, People's Songs. "Why, of course," he said with that broad smile. With all the other things on his mind he took time to help us, to advise us.

During the Henry Wallace campaign of 1948[26] I heard him speak many times, and saw how that combination of physical strength

---

26. Wallace (1888–1965) served as Vice President under Franklin Roosevelt from 1941 to 1945. In 1948, he ran for President as the nominee of the Progressive Party. The Wallace campaign platform was highly controversial, advocating for friendly relations with the U.S.S.R., equal rights for black Americans, and universal health insurance.

with delicate tenderness was driven by extraordinary courage and honesty.

In Peekskill, September, 1949,[27] ultra-rightists tried to kill him. I was a relatively unknown performer at the time, but was honored to be asked to sing a few songs on the first half of the program. After the great concert was over, the audience of thousands got into cars to drive home. The police (secretly in league with the KKK) stood at the gate, ordering all cars to turn right. Along that road were stationed men with waist-high piles of stones which they heaved at every car. Ten thousand car windows must have been smashed that day. When my wife and I got home we rinsed the broken glass out of the heads of our babies. Inside the car we found two rocks which had actually come through the glass. I later cemented them into our fireplace.

The rulers of America never dared put Robeson in jail—I'm sure because they feared international repercussions. But in the early fifties, every single concert hall was closed to him. Every "respectable" person and organization were running for cover. As Martin Luther King later said, "the ultimate tragedy is not the brutality of the bad people, but the silence of the good people." In 1954 the Oberlin College chapter of the NAACP told me, "We wanted Robeson to come and sing for us last year, but we were told by the National Office that they would revoke our charter if we did so."

If, if, if! If we had only fought harder for him. If Americans had seen through the Cold War lies quicker. If his health had only held out for another twenty years. No use. We only know that one of this country's greatest Cold War crimes was the stopping of his voice, so it could not be heard by hundreds of millions.

Well, for me, Paul Robeson will live forever. His strength made us stronger; his artistry inspired us to be better artists. The day will come when the hard-working people of the world will put an end to class exploitation, an end to racism, and militarism, and poverty. Another step on Jacob's Ladder was brought closer and sooner by this tender giant of the twentieth century, Paul Robeson.

"An Extraordinary Person," 2012

Dictated to Sam Rosenthal, January 2012

It was early 1939. The great novelist, Sholem Asch, said to his son, Moses, "Moe, you've bought a recording machine. Will it fit in the trunk of my car?"

Wallace was endorsed by the U.S. Communist Party and supported by many high-profile left-wing folksingers, including Seeger, on his campaign stops.

27. For more on this event, highly significant to Seeger, see chapter 5.

And Moe said, "Yes, I'm pretty sure, why?"

"We have to drive down to Princeton," said his father, "and record a short message, maybe one or two minutes, from Dr. [Albert] Einstein, which can be played on the radio here in New York, and I hope, elsewhere, urging American Jews not to waste one minute getting their relatives out of Germany now, right away."

So they put the recording machine in the trunk, they drove to Princeton, and they recorded a message. Over supper, Dr. Einstein says, "Well, young Mr. Asch, are you a writer like your father?"

"No," says Moe. "I make a living installing public address systems in hotels. But I've made enough money to buy this recording machine, and I'm fascinated with what it can do. There's a great Negro folksinger I've met in New York. He's named Leadbelly. But nobody's recording him because they say he's not commercial.[28]

"I think his records should be available. This is American culture! Leadbelly has recorded for the Library of Congress, but you have to drive to Washington to hear the records."

Einstein said, "You're absolutely right. Americans don't appreciate their own culture. It will be a Polish Jew like you who will do the job."

Moe did record Leadbelly. He only sold 100 copies the first year, and Asch Records went bankrupt. He started another company with one of his distributors, called Stinson Records—that went bankrupt. He started another company called Disc—that went bankrupt.

But, in 1949, LP records and tape recorders became available, and now the whole situation was different. Within the next 40 years, Moe Asch recorded over 2,000 titles on Folkways Records.

He worked out a most ingenious way of marketing them. He didn't spend one penny on advertisements. But, he would rent a table at a convention like the American Anthropological Society, or the Music Educators National Conference, and he'd spread out his records on the table. Teachers and professors would wander by and say, "My, I didn't know records like this were available."

And before they got any further, Moe would have their name and address, and every single year they'd get a new catalog from him with many more new records.

His financial arrangements were interesting too. He'd get a phone call: "Mr. Asch, I'm Professor So-And-So and I've just returned from a trip to northern Afghanistan, recording religious songs. My students want to listen to the tapes, but I can't risk them making a mistake and everything being lost or erased. Would you be interested in putting out a record?"

---

28. "Maybe I should explain. In 1939, it was still another ten years before tape recorders and long playing records became common. In 1939, records were [made of] shellac. It was very expensive to mail them and they were only sold in music stores." —P. S.

Moe would say, "Give me your telephone number and how do I spell your name? I'll call you back."

Now, Moe kept a retainer with Harold Courlander,[29] an anthropologist. And now he'd call him: "Harold, who is this professor?"

"Oh, Moe, he's very well known, you can trust that whatever he sends you will be authentic."

So now Moe calls back the professor. "Professor, I would like very much to put out your record, but here's what you must do: you must give me two pieces of tape, 20 minutes long, and leave ten seconds between different songs so people know where to put the needle down. Also give me five or ten pages of information with pictures perhaps, maybe translations of the songs. I will give you $100, and that will be all the money you'll ever get from me, but I can promise you that as long as I'm alive, and I hope after I die, your record will never go out of print."

Well, the professor's delighted. Now there's a new title, *Religious Songs of Northern Afghanistan*, in Moe's catalog.

Moe was an extraordinary person, and I recorded for him for 40 years.[30] I'd be walking down the street, having just learned or made up a new song, and I'd find myself on 48th Street, and I'd say, "Moe, can I record a new song for you?"

He'd prop up a mike in front of me, and ten minutes later I was on my way down the street. And some new record came out.

I'm not sure if there is anything else I could tell you about Moe, except that after he died they turned down many offers from people who just wanted to reprint a few of his best-selling records. Finally, they found the Smithsonian, and set up a special branch that's called *Smithsonian Folkways*. My nephew, Dr. Anthony Seeger, an ethnomusicologist, was in charge of it for several years. He said, "Yes, Pete, some of those records literally don't sell more than three copies a year, but when we don't have any more we print another five copies and Xerox another five copies of the brochure that goes with it."

So Moe Asch's complete life's work is there.

---

29. Courlander (1908–1996) was an anthropologist and folklorist who specialized in issues of the African and African American experiences in the Americas, especially in Haiti.
30. "With an interim where briefly I went along with John Hammond and recorded for Columbia, but Columbia wasn't interested. Only one record sold. It was *We Shall Overcome*. And that did get around the world, thanks to Columbia Records." —P. S.

Part 2
Life as a "Folk Singer"

Section 1
A Framework

4

What Is Folk Music?

"Folk Music?" c. 1965

Found in Seeger files

In prehistoric times, our communist common ancestors knew only one kind of music. In each village, men knew the same hunting songs, the same warrior chants. Women all knew the same lullabies, the same digging songs.

Then, at various times in various places, agriculture was discovered, and now a ruling class could have talented musicians making music for them, the first fine arts music. In West Africa, it led to magnificent drum orchestras; in Indonesia, gamelan orchestras. In Europe, it led to symphony orchestras in the castles.

When cities arose, some musicians found they could pick up coins making music in the market place. The first pop music! They didn't hesitate to borrow a good melody (or any music) either from the castle, or from the villages. Pop music still does this. In villages, poor people still made music for each other.

Within the past two centuries, in many parts of the world, a few people visiting the villages started writing down the music they heard. It was ancient and anonymous, sometimes limited and repetitious, but often subtle, beautiful, and very honest.

In Europe, about 1850 the term "folk music" was invented for this kind of music. In the early 20th century in the USA, a man named John Lomax used the term when he wrote down the songs that cowboys sang around their campfires. Later, with his son Alan, he used bulky disc recording equipment to capture the songs of old sailors, coal miners, industrial workers, and of African-American prisoners swinging axes in southern prison farms. In some musical families he found women singing long ballads brought over from England, Ireland, and other places.

In 1938, I dropped out of college and started trying to learn some of this music. In a few years, I learned that there are as many different kinds of folk music in the world as there are different kinds of folks. When people call me a "folk singer," I tell them that in some ways, I'm just a new kind of pop singer. Most gospel singers and blues singers are more "folk" than I am.

However, now there are tens of thousands of singers like me, using songs to teach history to young people, to help workers organize unions, to help all people organize for peace, and to save this world from pollution. Tens of thousands of songs are being made up. Most will be forgotten, but the best will be remembered, changed, added to by "the folk process."

And if the world survives these dangerous times, the folk process will go on, and music and poetry can help us teach love and common sense to foolish people who think that money and power are the important things in life.

And maybe ancient truths will confront modern myths, such as the belief that an infinite increase in empirical information is a good thing. And maybe we'll all learn to laugh at our mistakes, and learn to live with our various different opinions.

"A Definition of Folk Music," 1960

From Seeger's regular "Johnny Appleseed, Jr." column
in Sing Out! magazine, no. 10.1, April/May 1960

The newcomer was dragged to a folk song concert by an over-enthusiastic friend. Previously the newcomer might have been strictly a fan of classical music, or progressive jazz, or rock and roll. She says, "This is folk music? But it doesn't sound the same as some of those folk music records you were playing me. What *is* folk music?"

Here the confusion begins. For no two people, not even the professors, have been able to agree completely on a definition. The *Funk and Wagnalls Dictionary of Folklore* lists many which only partly overlap each other. One definition says, "A folk song must be old, carried on for generations by people who have had no contact with urban arts and influence. A folk song must show no trace of individual authorship." At the other end of the scale is the definition of the late Big Bill Broonzy,[1] the blues singer. He was asked if a certain blues he sang was a folk song: "It must be," he replied, "I never heard horses sing it."

---

1. Broonzy (1898–1958) was a singer, fiddler, and guitar player, first active in the 1920s. Originally a rural, acoustic blues performer, he was an early pioneer of the urban electrified blues scene developing in Chicago in the 1940s but returned to acoustic guitar when "discovered" as part of the folk revival in the 1950s.

How would it be to say that folk music is not so much any particular group of songs or singers but rather it is a process, an age-old process of ordinary people making their own music, reshaping old traditions to fit new situations. Some songs have more of this process; others have less. But even old ballads like "Barbara Allen" were probably influenced at some time in their long history by individuals in the popular or fine arts music professions. And even the pop song on the radio has been influenced in some way by folk music.

Yes, folk music is a process. And the history of any folk song will show continual change, contradictions, action and interaction of opposing influences. Now, this might be called, in the term of my mother-in-law (a wonderful woman), diabolical materialism. But we have support here from scientists; such as the late Alfred North Whitehead, mathematician and philosopher. He said, *"The process is the actuality."* In other words, if you want to understand any phenomena, study it in motion. If you could suddenly solidify all the water in a brook, and measure it, would that be the brook? An engineer wishing to throw a bridge across it must study it in motion, its origins and destinations, fluctuations, and test its qualities at many places and times. He must study the stream as a process. A pail of its water dipped up would not be the brook.

Likewise, a song is ever moving and changing. A folk song in a book is like a picture of a bird in midflight, printed in a bird book. The bird was moving before the picture was taken, and continued flying afterwards. It is valuable for a scientific record to know when and where the picture was taken, but no one is so foolish as to think that the picture *is* the bird. Thus also, the folk song in the book was changing for many generations before it was collected, and will keep on changing for many generations more, we trust. It is valuable for a scientific record to know when and where it was collected, but the still-picture of the song is not the song itself.

If you think of folk music as a process, you know that words and melodies may not be so important as the way they are sung or listened to. For the process includes not only the song but the singer and the listeners, and their situation. In this sense, perhaps a mountaineer singing a pop song to some neighbors in his cabin might have more of folk music in it than a concert artist singing to a Town Hall audience an ancient British ballad he learned out of a book.

After defining folk music (as a process, rather than any set repertoire of songs) to a class at the Idyllwild Music School in California last summer, I was still asked by a student, "Just how do you define *a* folk song, then?" I tried to dodge the issue.

"It's like two geographers arguing the exact boundaries of the Rocky Mountains. One says they run all the way from Mexico to Canada and beyond. The other says no, they are just a few big peaks in Colorado.

Perhaps it is necessary for the geographers to be able to draw a line on their maps some place, but for you and me, does the exact name matter that much? We climb a mountain for the view. Likewise, we can sing a song because it is a good song, not because of its classification."

"Not me," says the student. "I am a classroom teacher. My music supervisor says I can teach folk songs to the students, but not pop songs. I have to know."

Ah ha! Here is the source of the trouble, is it not? A phony value judgment. "Folk songs are good. Pop songs are bad." Is this not similar to all the trouble the fascist racists have in defining the difference between colored and white races? "White is good; colored is bad." Now maybe it is important for an anthropologist to analyze physical and cultural differences of peoples. But for you and me, the important thing is to accept a man or woman on their individual worth. Only by ignoring phony value judgments based on such trivial aspects as skin coloring and eye-slanting can we see our way to a peaceful world.

So can't we agree that there are good and bad folk songs: Good and bad pop songs?

"Yes," says the student, "but I still have to be able to define a folk song. My supervisor insists."

All right, let's define our process, and see if we can put it to work. It's an age-old process, of learning and singing mostly by ear, of formally untrained musicians, singing for fun, not for pay, to friends and neighbors, and from time to time changing or creating verses or melodies as events move them to.

"That lets me out," says the student. "I'm a trained music teacher, teaching songs from a book for pay. And my supervisor would chop my head off if he found me changing any of the songs."

Hm.

Hmmmmmm.

I do believe the only solution is to confound the enemy. If he asks, "Is it a folk song?" tell him, "Frankly, no. None of the songs you have ever taught in the schools are strictly folk songs." Back up your claim with copious reference to the experts. You can do it. Be so damn particular in your definition of folk music that even the supervisor will beat a retreat. Show him that a lot of what he has been calling folk music is not really authentic folk music. When he finally throws up his hands and says, "Well, it may not be folk music but it's good music to teach the children," then you've got him licked. For if he can say it, you can too.

Sometimes a method of arguing like this is the only way. It's like when a Unitarian friend of mine, a minister, was asked by a fundamentalist, "Do you believe, or not, that Jesus Christ was the son of God?"

"Of course he was," says my friend, looking the other straight in the eye, "and so are we all."

"Extroduction," 1965

From *Bits and Pieces,* Ludlow, 1965

One of the best lessons I learned from folk music is that there is nothing wrong in borrowing from older songs in order to help create newer songs. So let me freely acknowledge that in all my songs I have tried to put together, I have consciously or unconsciously borrowed. (A year after finding a tune for "Bells of Rhymney," I realized it was another variant of "Twinkle Twinkle Little Star.")

I urge you continue this folk process by realizing that you will probably have to change these songs in some way, more or less, if you want to sing any one of them and make it your own. You may have to change the key, raising it or lowering it to fit the range of your own voice. You may want to change the chords to suit the style of your own accompaniment.

... You may want to change the melody or words slightly—or even more than slightly. You may want to add a verse. Except for printing or recording it, you are not liable to get much kick from me. I might like your changes, I might probably not. In any case, I have faith in the folk process, which will over the years sift the good from the bad. Think how many thousands of different ways the song "Barbara Allen" has been sung (and printed) over the last three hundred years. Today we have a handful of beautiful versions handed down to us, shining like gems. If you don't feel like changing the song at all, don't be ashamed of that, either. Some of the first banjo tunes I learned, thirty years ago, I still play almost the same way I heard. I so admired them then, I thought they were the greatest American music I ever listened to, and never since found any special way I wanted to improve them, except to play them better.

And remember the aim of civilized man: to bring order and harmony—to simplify life. Any fool can get complicated. We are born in simplicity but die of complications. You may decide that you prefer to sing some of these songs with no accompaniment at all (as I do). In any case, the decision is up to you, and you are the next link in the chain.

"On Sing Out's Subtitle," 1990

From Seeger's regular "Appleseeds" column in *Sing Out!* magazine, no. 35.2, Summer 1990

Readers should know that at last October's meeting of the *Sing Out* Board of Directors, I once again proposed that we change our subtitle, "The Folk Song Magazine." I even got a majority vote. But I had to admit that there was not time for a full discussion, so the matter was tabled until this fall. If you'd prefer doddering Pete to cease and desist, now's the time to write.

It's worth pointing out that we got along without *any* subtitle from 1950 to 1960. Why do I object to it? First, the word "The" is misleading. "A" would be better—there are hundreds of different kinds of folk music in the U.S.A. (and, in the world, thousands). No one [magazine] can begin to keep up with them all. There are even other magazines which cover English-language folk-type songs just as fully in their own way. Mainly I guess I'm unhappy that the pop definition seems to have taken over.

Last year I decided that one of the stupid things I've done in my life was to allow people to call me a "folk singer." It was 50 years ago, when I was young and innocent, and I thought these other people knew more than I did; but I still had not woken up to my mistake 30 years later, when I titled a book *The Incompleat Folksinger*.[2]

The word "folk" should have been kept a scholarly term, like "dichotomy" or "parameter." The moment any word gets to be politically or commercially valuable, you can assume that it will be misused and in the end perhaps worthless. Historians feel this way about a word like "civilized," anthropologists likewise about the word "culture." Way back, 150 years ago, when the phrase "Folk Music" was first invented, the people who invented it should have been smarter. If they had kept this word to be used only by limited circles, everybody else could sensibly call their favorite music by some old word, whether it was ballads, love songs, cowboy songs, peasant songs or dirty songs. Many styles get associated with a geographic area so that we have such things as mountain songs or western songs or island songs. Nowadays if anybody asks me what kind of singer I am, I say I'm a river singer.

On the other hand: "Folklore is not an attempt to escape into the Age of Homespun; it is an attempt to enrich today with the humanism of yesterday."[3]

"Why Folk Music?" 1967

From *The American Folk Scene,* Laurel, 1967

Why should the guitar be the favorite instrument of many a college campus? Why are there books and LPs of "folk songs" on every shelf? Why should these songs catch on in many a school and summer camp,

2. *The Incompleat Folksinger,* published in 1972 by Simon and Schuster, and edited by Jo Metcalf Schwartz, is the closest Seeger has come to producing an autobiography. The book is a first-person account of Seeger's life, supplemented by song lyrics and sheet music.
3. "From the late Norman Strider, director of Camp Woodland in the Catskills, who puts on a festival every year using local fiddlers and ballad singers, as well as songs from the campers, NYC kids." —P. S.

not to speak of coffee houses, and Washington Square Park on a summer Sunday?

I think there are four main reasons.

One: Since World War II there has been evidence on many sides that Americans were curious to rediscover their roots, to learn about their own country's heritage. I'm thinking of the numerous historical recreations dotted around the United States, of the magazines like *American Heritage,* the movies and novels of American life.

Two: There's been a general increase in a great variety of do-it-yourself activities during these same years. Skiers, bowlers, boaters, Sunday painters, ceramicists, weavers, furniture builders, gardeners, camera bugs, hot-rodders—all these and many more wanted to be more than passive spectators. And the millions of guitar pickers are one more sign not all Americans are satisfied to simply sit and watch TV.

Three: We were handed on a silver platter a lot of the world's best songs, by the folklorists who dug the gold out of the hills and presented it to us. Our country is rich in many different traditions, with variety to suit almost any taste, from the old classic ballads, to rough work songs and raucous fun songs.

Four: It takes a certain sophistication to sing an old hillbilly song without being worried that someone will call you an old hillbilly. Or to sing an old spiritual without wondering if someone will call you an Uncle Tom. Maybe we had to wait a few years till we were far enough away from our past, to be able to pick and choose the good from the bad.

The revival of interest in folk music, which has mushroomed in the sixties, actually has its roots over half a century ago. Scholars like John Lomax of Texas and England's Cecil Sharp spent years going from one section of the country to another. Their efforts were usually scoffed at, especially in the very regions richest in music. Lomax went to a cattleman's convention trying to trace some of the old cowboy ballads. A rancher stood up and said, "There's a man named Lomax here who wants to know if anyone knows some of the old cowboy songs. Why everybody knows those damn fool songs, and only a bigger damn fool would try to collect them. I vote we adjourn to the bar." And they did. But thanks to the persistence of Lomax we know songs like "Whoopee-ty-yi-yo, Get Along Little Doggies," and "Streets of Laredo," not to mention "Home on the Range."

But another Texan, J. Frank Dobie, once observed many collectors simply "dug up dead bones from one graveyard and buried them in another." The songs, having been dug up in the hills, were now buried in libraries. A determined effort was therefore made by a few people to interest city audiences in the music. Carl Sandburg[4] would end his

---

4. Sandburg (1878–1967) was a writer and poet known for his poems of American life, especially the Midwest, and for his lauded biography of Abraham Lincoln, *Abraham Lincoln: The War Years* (Boston: Mariner, 2002).

poetry recitations with some songs. Alan Lomax (son of John) persuaded an actor named Burl Ives that he could make a living as a professional singer of folk songs. Alan showed Leadbelly, Josh White, and Woody Guthrie that there were audiences up north for their southern songs. And he got me started.

Maybe, in trying to answer why hundreds of thousands of young city-bred Americans today should be wanting to sing folk songs, I could best simply tell my own story.

In 1935 I was sixteen years old, playing a tenor banjo in the school jazz band. I was uninterested in studying the classical music which my parents taught at Juilliard. That summer I visited a square-dance festival in Asheville, North Carolina, and fell in love with the old-fashioned five-string banjo, rippling out a rhythm to one fascinating song after another. I liked the rhythms. I liked the melodies, time tested by generations of singers. Above all I liked the words. Compared to the trivialities of most popular songs, the words of these songs had all the meat of human life in them. They sang of heroes, outlaws, murderers, fools. They weren't afraid of being tragic instead of just sentimental. They weren't afraid of being scandalous instead of giggly or cute. Above all, they seemed frank, straightforward, honest. By comparison, it seemed to me that too many art songs were concerned with being elegant and too many pop songs were concerned with being clever.

So in 1935 I tried learning some of this music. In 1965 I'm still learning. I've found out that some of the simplest music is some of the most difficult to do. I've also found, of course, that America has in it as many different kinds of folk music as there are folks. We have not only the strains from Ireland and Scotland, France and Germany, but Africa and Mexico, and a hundred other countries. We have regional varieties from the north woods to the western plains, with hundreds of different hybrid idioms in different places.

Maybe this last deserves more than passing mention, because I've come to feel that America's restless habit of creating new hybrids is typical of our whole culture. We know that the English language is a hybrid of Germanic and Latin roots. Similarly, a great number of typical American folk songs use western European melodies, with a rhythmic style or vocal style that owes more to Africa, or perhaps to Mexico.

... This process is still going on. There are many definitions of folk music, but the one which makes most sense to me is the one that says it is not simply a group of old songs. Rather, it is a process, which has been going on for thousands of years, in which ordinary people continually re-create the old music, changing it a little here and there as their lives change.

Now that our lives are changing so rapidly, obviously there will be lots of new songs. We'll find songs about subjects like events of the day, problems of war and peace and the bomb. There will be as many different opinions as there are singers and songwriters. One little mimeographed magazine in New York started three years ago to try and print the topical songs coming out of college campuses, and has been swamped by thousands of contributions.[5] Soon after the prizefighter, Davey Moore, was killed in the ring, twenty-one-year-old Bob Dylan had a ballad out, "The Ballad of Davey Moore."

Is it all folk music? Obviously not, according to some old definitions ("Songs sung by a peasant class, age-old and anonymous"). But definitions change. What was called a "play" in the sixteenth century is hardly what is called a "play" today. I try not to get in the argument over defining folk music. I like to climb mountains too, but I don't get in a big argument over the name of the mountain range. The important thing is for America to rediscover how strong and honest a song can be. The best songs of these decades will be remembered and passed on to future generations. The rest can be forgotten.

Meanwhile, Americans who love to sing can learn two things from this music: we can learn about ourselves, and we can learn about each other.

Learn about ourselves? Learn where we came from, the trials and tribulations of those who came before us, and the good times and bad. Learn about each other? How many white people have rediscovered their own humanity through the singing of American Negro songs? How many town dwellers have learned a bit about a rougher outdoor life from songs created by men with calloused hands? Old can learn about young; men about women.

And, as I said before, we have such a variety of idioms and traditions in our country that you can take your pick. You can take the fun songs, or the slow, sad ones, the angry ones or the satirical ones. Some are good for solo singing, some are best for a chorus to join in on. Some call for a lot of instrumental fireworks, some are best sung unaccompanied.

The best thing about it is that the individual can choose his own, and the music is best when it's live.

"There's Gold in Them Thar Hills," c. 1966

Found in Seeger files

In [the early 1940s] the popular music business was dominated by the big swing bands. The typical pop song was full of "June, moon, croon and spoon." Woody Guthrie and I used to go around singing for the CIO labor unions on the theory that only the organized working people would promote the kind of music we liked. After World

---

5. A reference to *Broadside* magazine, actually begun in 1962 by Sis Cunnigham and Gordon Friesen, a key journal of politically oriented folk music during the folk revival.

War II we started a little magazine called *People's Songs—Songs of Labor and the American People.* We had a limited success in a few big cities and some of our hootenannies attracted audiences of over 1,000. The word "hootenanny," Woody and I discovered in Seattle, meaning an informal party. In New York City we gave it more of a folk song flavor. It was not a concert; it was not a community sing; it was not an amateur contest. It was a little of each all rolled together. A democratic-minded song session where racism would have no place and where songs about peace and freedom would be scattered between the old ballads, blues, spirituals and humorous songs.

But the Cold War kept us in a box. The American union leaders wanted to become respectable and would not listen to us. In 1949 four of us formed a quartet called the Weavers which surprised ourselves as well as everybody else by suddenly getting a record called "Goodnight Irene" selling 2,000,000 copies.

The Weavers were blacklisted off the national television networks and split up temporarily in 1953. I started singing for students in colleges and universities, the one section of the population which refused to knuckle under to McCarthyism. Within five years there were dozens of successful performers putting on college concerts of what was called folk music. The sale of guitars went up to over half a million a year. My little banjo instruction manual which sold 100 copies between 1948 and 1951, sold 20,000 copies in 1963. The circulation of *Sing Out!* magazine, the successor to *People's Songs*, zoomed up to 25,000 copies per issue. This is not a big circulation in a country of 190,000,000, but now the commercial publishers finally decided, "There's gold in them thar hills," and decided that here was another temporary fad which they could make money on.

In 1963 came a national television show calling itself *Hootenanny*. But their version of a hootenanny only slightly resembled the kind of hootenannies that Woody Guthrie and Leadbelly used to sing on. It is true the singers usually accompanied themselves on guitars but gone was the strong sense of social consciousness. The TV producer carefully avoided hiring many performers "because they did not have a broad enough appeal." I was not the only one blacklisted from the program, but because I was not on it, a number of other performers, such as Joan Baez, refused to have anything to do with it. *Hootenanny* went off the air a year later, mourned by no one. And by 1965 the word went around Tin Pan Alley, "Folk music is dead." As far as Tin Pan Alley is concerned, it was never very much alive. I wonder if any reader remembers 1944, when Freddy Martin's Orchestra had a swing version of Tchaikovsky's Piano Concerto? It was a popular hit. For a while other orchestras tried to make similar moneymaking swing arrangements of the classics. A year later the fad was over. Would one then say, "classical music is dead"?

On the contrary, the Newport Folk Festival in 1966 had some of the largest audiences, 18,000 a night. There were more varied local folk festivals held throughout the country. Some of them concentrated on one kind of music. Some on another. Half a million guitars are still sold every year. The circulation of the various folk music magazines is holding up. Numerous small recording companies keep on with their labor of love, which is issuing recordings of little-known singers and musicians who usually accompany themselves with a guitar. One of the interesting developments is to see city people experimenting with autoharps, dulcimers, harmonicas and various forms of whistles and recorders. Some singers concentrate on singing old songs. A great many of the younger ones concentrate on singing newer ones. They are called "protest" songs because they are not simply love songs nor religious songs nor humorous songs. Although they may be all of these at the same time.

I feel somewhat like old Grandpa. Alan Lomax is busy with his anthropological investigations these days. Woody is in a hospital and hopelessly paralyzed. Leadbelly is dead. But I still exercise my tonsils around the country and enjoy listening to a lot of other musicians, most of them young enough to be my children. I count myself to be a lucky musician indeed. First, I make a living at my music and this is rare. After all, automation hit the music industry 40 years ago. I also make a living at the kind of music I like. Many well trained musicians have to do hack work in some hotel orchestra. And in spite of the fact that I am still blacklisted from the major network television shows, I have consistently had audiences to learn and to grow with. So what should I protest about then? If I am an honest artist I must face the fact that my country, rich as it is, still has slums in city after city. These slums are full of demoralized people who feel themselves, as we say, "behind the eight ball." There the rate of unemployment is ten times higher than in the rest of the country. I have to face the fact that my country, the same country of Benjamin Franklin, Thomas Jefferson, Abraham Lincoln, and Frederick Douglass, is dropping napalm bombs on innocent women and children on the pretext that we are "fighting communism." I have to face the fact that the rivers of my country have been turned into open sewers and the air which many city people breathe is poisonously polluted. I still like to sing old songs. I like love songs and lullabies. But I will continue to mix them up and continue to explore the story of the human race trying to learn to live on this earth.

. . . "So where does folk music go from here?" I am also often asked. Believe me, I am no seer. I am no trained folklorist or musicologist. My guess is that the homemade music of the American people will go in many different directions at the same time. Some will stick with traditional music if they happen to come from a family with strong traditions, or if they are psychologically happier sticking close to one tradition. I think many more will continue to experiment with combining several traditions. This has been the principal feature of most American music: it combines African rhythms and syncopation with European melodies and harmonies. Others will experiment with new musical instruments, especially the electronic variety which can make such a vast volume of sound that they are suited for playing at noisy parties. And the habit of folk song writers to comment on issues of the day is now being picked up by the young rock-and-roll singers in such an exciting way that many of their songs are not being played on the radio. The networks have even come out frankly and said that they are going to "screen" the lyrics of the new popular recordings before they are played on the air. Ostensibly, this is done "to make sure that references to sex or narcotics are not in the lyrics." But one can be sure that it will be also used to keep off the air such songs as "Society's Child."[6] And even more outspoken songs.

Personally, I try to avoid arguments about what is a folk song and what isn't. As a singer I am looking for good songs, no matter where they come from. I will leave the classification of them up to the experts. Strictly speaking, I would say that I am probably not a folk singer, since I am a professional and perform on a stage. I have always deeply admired, though, the straightforward manner of traditional musicians. I have tried to learn from them and will continue to try. My guess is that future music historians will report that in the mid-twentieth century a wave of interest in bygone traditional styles of music revitalized the field of popular music and possibly fine arts music as well. Thanks to the LP record and the tape recording machine, we are now able to exchange music throughout the entire globe. We can learn from each other as never before. It seems to be that in every region of the world the same basic problems exist, and not only in the field of music:

1) How to continue to learn good things from far off places no matter where they come from.

2) How to continue to maintain the best of one's own traditions so that one does not lose one's own personality in the rush of absorbing new things. No one must lose his birthright for a mess of potage.

I hope that these comments of mine will be accepted merely as points to be argued about. I am flattered that people in a land which has produced Verdi and Toscanini and so many thousands of great singers, here asked me for my opinions.

---

6. "Society's Child," written and performed by Janis Ian in 1965, describes a teenager's interracial dating relationship and the adult forces that seek to end it. Although it was a Top 10 hit in some cities, many radio stations refused to air it.

"Progressive and Fascists Both Sing Folk Songs," c. 1942

Found in Seeger files

The last eight years have seen a tremendous upsurge in the popular consciousness of America's great heritage of folk music. The people knew about folk songs all along, of course, but the housewife humming an old lullaby, or the stevedore rolling out a work chant, or the country boy playing fiddle never called it "folk music." Nevertheless, what started thirty or forty years ago as a small trickle of professors going out to collect songs and ballads, write them down and publish them in expensive volumes, small editions, has grown now to an avalanche of "Americana" phonograph albums, radio programs, popular collections of cowboy songs, sailor songs, ballads.

Look through this newspaper any week and see the names of Huddie Ledbetter, Joshua White, Tony Kraber, Burl Ives, Andrew Rowan Summers, Aunt Molly Jackson, Richard Dyer-Bennett, Woody Guthrie, the Almanac Singers.

Five years ago who had ever heard of these musicians? Yet today all of them are busy singing night and day here in New York alone, and we will hear many more like them and better, too. The mass critical judgment which caused this upsurge is basically sound, of course, and out of it all, we will see created within the next few years music never before equaled in America. The best of the *Ballad For Americans*[7] came from what Earl Robinson learned listening to folk musicians. The best songs of this war will come from it.

Yet we should keep in mind that there are several different attitudes of people listening to the songs. Does the professor recording a ballad like it for the same reason as does the old mountain woman who sings it to him? Does the Café Society[8] patron like the Golden Gate Quartet for the same reason that the Arkansas sharecropper does?

Hitler, too, likes folk music. German propaganda is full of buxom Bavarian maidens singing old Tyrolean carols, and Benito [Mussolini]'s fascist youth hiking organization publishes many gay traditional Italian melodies in its songbook.

Where does the difference lie between the democrat's and the fascist's love of folk music? The answer, to me, seems to lie in the fact that

---

7. *Ballad for Americans* is a historical cantata written by Earl Robinson and John La Touche. Originally created for a Works Progress Administration theater project in 1939, it quickly gained national popularity, recorded by many well-known singers of the day, including Bing Crosby and Paul Robeson, and sung at the 1940 Republican National Convention.

8. The Café Society was a nightclub opened in Greenwich Village in 1938. The club's owner, Barney Josephson, conceived of Café Society as a place where all customers were treated equally, regardless of race, and where bourgeois pretension was shunned, as evidenced by its ironic name. The club was a showcase especially for African American performers.

the fascists like to think of a great, simple, and credulous "folk" with their superstitions and their myths, and their naïve culture, whereas the progressive feels proud that the people, of which he is a part, have produced art of such great truth, and lasting reality. Furthermore, the fascist emphasizes the quaint and picturesque, the static (and therefore dying) side, while the progressive responds most keenly to the expanding, militant side, the old song which rings with present day significance, and the contemporary ballad.

Take picturesqueness, for example: the farmer's wife who sang me an old ballad her father taught her does not think herself picturesque, any more than you or I do. She thought it was a beautiful song, too, and it helped remind her of the old man, who was dead some twenty years. And I think that Elie Siegmeister's[9] American Ballad Singers recording of "Springfield Valley," where his singer tries to imitate the accents of the Kentucky ballad singer, is the most reactionary piece of music Siegmeister was ever responsible for. That record is a farce, really. I guess he didn't know any better. It would insult the farmer's wife I spoke of.

"The Folklore of Prejudice," 1962

Early draft of a piece that eventually saw publication in *The Incompleat Folksinger,* Simon and Schuster, 1972

At a lecture at Columbia University, during the question period, a slip of paper was handed me, asking, "Is there such a thing as a bad folk song?"

Surprised that anyone should have asked, I answered, "Of course." Many are uninteresting musically and poetically to all but a few who wrote them. Further, if one considers that in folk music we can find reflections of every facet of the life of working people, one can find songs expressing weakness as well as strength, unthinking injustice as well as generosity. The folklorist interested in compiling a complete record may try to collect them all, good and bad, better or worse, but the musician and poet (in the form of editor and singer) will use a far narrower selection, and any individual with a normally contemporary bundle of opinions will have sharp tastes in selecting songs to sing with his or her friends.

I did say that *I* felt there was a tendency for folk music to be more honest than popular music (because there was less money in it?), and that furthermore, over the centuries, the folk process seems to weed out the bad and preserve the good.

In America, many prejudices have long been preserved in folk song. Because they are "folk," are we automatically interested in perpetuating

---

9. Siegmeister (1909–1991) was a composer and music theorist whose primary interest was the development of a specifically American orchestral music. In addition to musical works, he also wrote a number of books on music theory and appreciation.

them? I am referring to such common sayings as "Jews are avaricious," "Negroes (Indians, French-Canadians) are dishonest and lazy," "Irish are dirty," "Scottish are stingy," and so on, *ad nauseum*. That this is more than simple unfairness can be seen by the way it fits into the overall picture of the chauvinist, which in a thousand billboards, magazines, and other cultural media, urges every one of us to distort the well-known melting pot theory into "You must melt into an Anglo-Saxon" (because unless you do you can't possibly be a Real American). Emma Dusenberry, the great blind folk singer of Arkansas, recognized this when she stopped singing the old ballad "The Jew's Daughter." "That song was made up a long time ago," she said, "and it just ain't true now." She knew it wasn't because she had met Jewish youth at neighboring Commonwealth College. Not all ballad singers are so lucky.

Akin to this problem is the one brought out by the great number of songs echoing a past where the man of the household reigned supreme, and if his wife objected, she was just a nag or a shrew. In these days, when I sing at a college, looking at hundreds of eager, ambitious young women getting degrees (which I never got), how could I possibly sing "The Farmer's Curst Wife" without at least coupling it with "Old Grumbly," the ballad about the man who foolishly claimed he could do more work in a day than his wife could in three? But male supremacy dies a hard death, and many put up with it simply because they are so used to it.

Does not the folklorist who publishes a popular folk song collection owe it to the hundreds of thousands of American Indians who are struggling against great odds to regain a sense of national dignity, to amend the way the words "Injun" and "squaw" are used in some pioneer songs? Remember, millions of American schoolchildren may be learning these songs, and parroting the slander.

How can a well-known singer of folk songs stand up in New York's Town Hall (as I witnessed a few years ago) and sing the verses of "I Am a Rebel Soldier"?

> *I hate to see a ni__r*
> *Dressed up in Yankee Blue.*

And this with young American Negroes sitting in the audience! Some of them risked their lives to save this country from fascism in World War II—fighting in segregated units because of the prevalence of the above quoted opinion. "'Tain't no jokey song" as Fibber Mc-Gee[10] would say.

---

10. Fibber McGee, played by Jim Jordan, was the fictional protagonist of *Fibber McGee and Molly,* a radio comedy series that ran on NBC from 1939 to 1959.

I think the sad truth is that the folklore of prejudice runs deep, and infects the scholarly as well as the illiterate. The first task is to recognize its existence. Then what?

The singer, the student, the editor of anthologies obviously has a more selective job. Well, the librarian may be anxious to preserve all, the bad as well as the good, for future record. But, many of us are involved in this tremendous nationwide phenomenon called the Folk Song Revival.[11] We are actually creating something new, not just a static repetition of the old. Do we not want to create our new folk traditions out of the *best* of the old? If my friend has had his skin rubbed the wrong way so often that the flesh is raw, so that he now winces at my slightest touch, it is not for me to say, "Oh, you're too sensitive."

"Not a Leading Troubadour, Only a Notorious One," 1968

Letter to Bert Snow,[12] dated April 1968; found in Seeger files.

Dear Bert,

I'll attempt to answer your questions off the top of my head as best I can.

"After 33 years as one of its leading troubadours, where do you see folk music going in the future?"

I don't think of myself as "a leading troubadour," only as a notorious one. There are so many more talented than I, and usually unknown, let's stop here. Rephrase it: "After 30 years as a troubadour, where do you think this thing called folk music is going?"

OK?

Answer: Back to the nooks and crannies of the country, perhaps, where it always lingered. Songs will be sung and instruments will be played by people in their own homes for their own amusement. That is, if they have the gumption to switch off the TV, put down the book, lift the needle from the hi-fi occasionally. And I have enough faith in America to think that there will always be a minority of people who will do this.

Pop music, which for centuries has borrowed from folk music as well as art music, will continue to do so. In the past we've seen banjoes, blues, and various Latin American idioms influence pop music. Right now we're getting a faint whiff of Indian music. One of these years there will be an enthusiasm for Indonesian gamelan orchestras. You wait and see.

---

11. "400,000 guitars were sold last year." —P. S.
12. Snow was the Director of Public Relations at KCET Television in Los Angeles at the time his original letter to Seeger was written.

"Is this reflected in the *Rainbow Quest* series?"[13]

Only slightly. The series reflects one man's curiosity about different kinds of people and their music, either old or new. That's why only a few of the performers are well-known.

"Do you feel more comfortable working as a soloist or with a group of people?"

I love the solid sound of singing with a group of other people, but singing by oneself gives more flexibility in trying to make contact with strange audiences. The *Rainbow Quest* gives me a chance to swap songs with many different kinds of performers. And remember, the same songs can mean different things to different people. This is fun to explore.

"What was your personal reaction to the furor caused over the performance of 'The Big Muddy' on the *Smothers Brothers*?"[14]

I expected a little furor. TV should have some furors. It would be good for the country. You can't have education without controversy and modern man needs education. H. G. Wells once said that we are all in a race between education and disaster.

"Are there any songs of this type included in *Rainbow Quest*?"

Unfortunately, not many. These shows were taped two years ago. It was my first TV series. Since the series has been well-received in seven cities where it is shown, I hope it will be continued. Then the new shows will have a better balance of old and new songs.

"Do you consider folk singing more suitable as a vehicle for pure entertainment or a 'message' to express a point of view?"

This question reflects what I consider a common misconception. All art carries some message, just as everything in this world, even a blank wall, has significance. The message of the average entertainer is, "Eat, drink and be merry because you don't know what is going to happen tomorrow and you can't do anything about it anyway." The message of a concert virtuoso is, "Look what extraordinary things a human can do if he practices." The message of a sing-along song leader might be, "Look what fun you can have even if you don't practice." In olden times the messages of songs to placate the gods were much more common than they are now. A hymn is a controversial song. Sing one in the wrong church; you'll find out. A lover sings about unrequited love. He's protesting unrequition. The message of this show?

---

13. *Rainbow Quest* was Seeger's short-lived television show, running from 1965–1966. *Rainbow Quest* featured live performances from contemporary musicians selected by Seeger as well as archival footage of other performers or world musics. Thirty-nine shows in total were produced, airing on WNJU-TV, and later on New York public television station WNDT.

14. For more on the Smothers Brothers controversy, see chapter 5.

God gave Noah the rainbow sign
No more water, but the fire next time.
Pharoah's army got drownded;
O, Mary, don't you weep.

Hope the above is not too longwinded for you.

Sincerely,
Pete

"A Too-Narrow Definition," 1989

From Seeger's regular "Appleseeds" column in
Sing Out! magazine, no. 33.2, Spring 1989

I think that *Broadside* and *Sing Out!* and other "folk" magazines make a mistake not to print the best new rap songs. If they are listened to and imitated by new rap singers, they are important parts of this swiftly flowing stream we call the folk process.

I'm thinking of such lines as, "Junkies in the alleys with baseball bats," and "pushers drive big cars, spending twenties and tens, and you just want to grow up to be just like them."[15]

"But we're folk music magazines," some of their editors will tell me. "If somebody wants to put out a rap magazine, let them do it."

This is a too-narrow definition of folk music. It is like the Christians calling Native Americans unreligious because their rites and words were different.

---

15. These lyrics are excerpts from "The Message," the leading single from the album of the same name, released by Grandmaster Flash and the Furious Five in 1982 (c. Sugar Hill Records, 2004).

Section 2
Social Movements in the United States

5

The Labor Movement, the Communist Party, and the Blacklist

"Union Songs Must Be Fun," c. 1946

Found in Seeger files

Union songs must be fun to sing. Too often they are sung as a painful duty. How many union folks know the verses of "Solidarity Forever"—Ralph Chaplin's[1] labor hymn? But nearly all know the pleasure of rolling out on the chorus, which contains poetry of a high order.

Too often union folks will perpetrate bad verses. Yes, they mention the boss. Yes, they mention the strike, the picket line, local slogans, all the odds and addendum of local parlance. But of the local spirit, the gaiety, the fun, the horseplay, the romance, the anger—how much of these human qualities?

"Song of the West Virginia Miners" mentioned no specific coal company; or if it did, these verses have been forgot and instead we have a powerful union song.

Unions are organized for the purposes of bettering the living and working conditions of the workers. They are economic organizations, their struggle is economic. Union folks, having won union gains, enjoy a new life, geared to the economic interests of their unions. Their culture, therefore, becomes related to their union life. There may be as much social understanding in the singing of "Clementine" as in the singing of "Solidarity"—depending on the economic unity of those who sing.

---

1. Chaplin (1887–1961) was a member of the Industrial Workers of the World who became the editor of the IWW magazine *Solidarity*. Chaplin wrote many poems inspired by the labor rights struggle of the early 20th century, including "Solidarity Forever," the famous union anthem set to the music of "John Brown's Body."

Life goes on about the same. But now bosses are for poking fun at because they are ridiculous, and union women are for dancing with and falling in love with and marrying, and picket lines are for battle.

Singing is a form of battle; it is not battle. There is a time when the fist is labor's only weapon.

"Whatever Happened to Singing in the Unions?" 1965

From *Sing Out!* magazine, no. 15.2, May 1965

In the first place, except for a few unions, there never was as much singing as some people now suppose. From listening to the *Talking Union*[2] record and reading a couple of novels about the labor struggles of the '30s, one might jump to the conclusion that the United States was full of class-conscious harmonizing in those days. 'Tain't true.

The singingest union America ever had was the old Wobblies. Their official name was the Industrial Workers of the World, started in Chicago in June of 1905 by Big Bill Haywood,[3] of the Western Federation of Miners, and others who were dissatisfied with the lack of progress of the little old craft unions under Sam Gompers' A. F. of L.[4]

The IWW quickly grew to 150,000 before World War I, were put down then by the government because of their opposition to the war, made an upsurge after the war, and then in the 1920s dwindled to a fraction of their old strength.

They were a defiantly radical group, mostly anarchists-syndicalists[5] of a sort, and they argued bitterly with socialists as to the value of trying to elect working class congressmen. Their idea was to ultimately sign up all the workers in One Big Union, improve their conditions, and eventually call a general strike to decide who was going to run the world—the workers or the bosses.

---

2. *Talking Union and Other Songs* was an album of union songs collected from various parts of the United States, released by the Almanac Singers on Keynote Records in 1941, and again by Smithsonian Folkways in 1955.

3. Haywood (1869–1928) was one of the founding members and leaders of the Industrial Workers of the World. As a highly visible and combative proponent of workers' rights and unionization, he was a frequent target of politicians and law enforcement who were opposed to the labor movement. Haywood was tried for murder in 1907 and acquitted, but was arrested again in 1917, accused of conspiring against the United States, and, in 1921, sentenced to twenty years in prison. He fled to the Soviet Union while out on bail after his conviction and never returned to the United States.

4. Gompers (1850–1924) was the founder of the American Federation of Labor (AFL) one of the first major federations of labor unions in the United States. Gompers and the AFL promoted job security, high wages, and humane work conditions, but in harmony with the preexisting economic framework, as opposed to more radical labor unions like the IWW, which advocated creating an alternative to wage-based labor and the capitalist system.

5. Anarcho-syndicalists call for the replacement of capitalism and the state with federations of workers' self-managed enterprises and direct democracy.

With every new union card, they also handed out a little red song-book. The cover carried a motto: "To Fan the Flames of Discontent." Inside were the words to about fifty songs, usually parodies of well-known melodies: pop songs of the day, hymns, or older tunes commonly sung. Their best-known songwriters were Joe Hill[6] and Ralph Chaplin, both of whom rose from the ranks to become full-time organizers for the IWW. The latter's song, "Solidarity Forever," is still officially sung at many a labor-union convention, but I'll bet Joe Hill's "Casey Jones" becomes a more permanent part of American folklore.

The songs were roared out by Wobblies at meetings, on picket lines, in jails (where IWW men were often put by the dozens and hundreds), on freight trains through South Dakota (black with harvest hands for the wheat fields), or wherever Wobblies happened to meet. If the Salvation Army was preaching against them from one street corner, they might set up a soapbox on the opposite corner. When the Salvation Army band started up "In the Sweet Bye and Bye," Wobblies would use it to accompany their own singing of Joe Hill's parody, "Pie in the Sky."

Prior to the IWW, labor songs were not unknown, but they were by no means common (the eight-hour-day movement of the 1880s had some). By researching old union records and newspapers, one could probably compile a list of thousands of songs made up during this or that strike. But when the strike was over, usually the songs were forgot-ten, as might be the songs of some war after the armistice is signed.

The music of these songs often reflected the folk background of the workers involved. Thus, the anthracite miners of Pennsylvania might have Irish or Slavic tunes for their strike songs. In the Southern states, one could find old English ballad melodies or hymn tunes, with new words made up by the country people who came down to work in the textile mills.

During the 1920s and '30s, some of the Northern city unions, such as the International Ladies Garment Workers, also printed songbooks. They had many immigrant members who had an Old World love of singing; often, they joined choruses which rehearsed to perform at rallies and May Day parades. In 1935, the CIO[7] was formed, again to try to

---

6. Hill (1879–1915) was a Swedish-born labor activist who joined the IWW around 1910. He was a prolific writer of poetry and music and wrote many songs extolling and encouraging participation in the labor movement. In 1914, Hill was accused and convicted of robbery and murder in Utah. The trial was widely publicized and many prominent public figures of the day called for clemency for Hill. Despite a lack of evi-dence and no demonstrated motive or connection between Hill and the victim, he was found guilty and executed by firing squad on November 19, 1915.
7. The Congress of Industrial Organizations (CIO), originally organized by John L. Lewis in 1936 as a committee within the AFL, became its major rival as a national labor federation following a split in 1938 until 1955, when the two merged into the still extant AFL-CIO. The CIO's decision to leave the AFL reflected the former's support for industrial unionism, the belief that workers should be organized into large, industry-wide unions, as opposed to smaller, skill-specific craft unions. The CIO argued that under industrial unionism, the union's bargaining power would be greatly increased, while simultaneously ensuring greater equality for all individuals in the workplace.

do the job not being done by the conservative old craft unions. There was a wave of organizing drives throughout the country that produced a flood of parodies to pop melodies. The Flint sit-down strikers who took over the General Motors plant there in 1935 sang:

> When we walked out on you,
> We set you back on your heels,
> Goody goody!
> So you lost some money and now
> You know how it feels
> Goody goody![8]

And they had many more songs like it.

But again, when the strikes were over, the songs were usually forgotten. In 1940, 1 learned the song "Which Side Are You On?" from a folklorist who had been researching in eastern Kentucky in 1932. Later, I met Mrs. Reece,[9] who wrote the song. At that time, it was unknown except in the memories of her family and the miners of Harlan County who heard her daughters sing it at the 1932 union meetings.

In the 1930s, as in the 1960s, it was the Negro people of the South, with their fine traditions of church singing, who provided some of the best songs picked up throughout the country. "We Shall Not Be Moved" is supposed to have come out of one of the organizing drives of the Southern Tenant Farmers Union in the early '30s. It was originally "Jesus Is My Captain, I Shall Not Be Moved." But, significantly, the new words were not antireligious, as were the Wobbly parodies. They simply emphasized a militancy that was always present in the older spirituals.

"It's That Union Train A-Coming" was once "The Old Ship of Zion." "Roll the Union On" recalls "Roll the Chariot Along," and also came out of the 1935 sharecropper struggles. This and a number of other songs were put together by union people studying at Commonwealth College, Arkansas, a union school of the '30s. A teacher at Highlander Folk School in Tennessee, Zilphia Horton, first heard the song, "We Shall Overcome" (originally "I Will Overcome"), on a tobacco workers picket line in 1936.[10]

The 1941 *Talking Union* recording represented an attempt to carry on this tradition and spread it through the North and West. But then the war came, and union drives were shelved until Hitler was beaten. In 1946, a number of the former Almanac Singers and others joined

---

8. This was a (radical) reworking of a popular 1936 Benny Goodman Orchestra hit, "Goody Goody," by Matty Nalneck and Johnny Mercer. The original lyrics were "So you met somebody who set you back on your heels, goody goody/You met someone and now you know how it feels, goody, goody."

9. Florence Reece (1900–1986) was an activist and folk singer who wrote many political songs including "Which Side Are You On?" written during a strike by the United Mine Workers of America.

10. For more about the Highlander Folk School, Zilphia Horton, and "We Shall Overcome," see chapter 6.

to form the People's Songs organization, with the idea of reviving folk and labor songs through the unions of the nation. But now the Cold War came along and American labor unions kicked out most of the militants and radicals, the very ones who had always been the enthusiastic singers and songwriters. Even unions with left-wing leadership felt they had to concentrate on pork chops to the exclusion of songbooks and choruses. A West Coast longshoreman told me that at the 1952 ILWU[11] Seattle convention, a group of newly organized Hawaiian workers marched enthusiastically into the convention hall singing union songs. "Why! all our mainland delegates turned around in surprise. They hadn't seen anything like that in a long time!"

Today, a few unions still publish songbooks, and a few even have choruses. But an average of only three percent of American union members attend union meetings, except during crises, and the songbooks are by and large unused. "Union Maid" is far better known on college campuses than it is in the average union hall.

If this little article is disillusioning, let me add one thing: History shows that there is a hidden heritage of militancy which comes and goes, but never completely dies. It undergoes transformations and permutations from century to century, but the lessons learned by one generation, even though through defeat, are passed on to the next. Right now, many of the song traditions of the 1930s are seeing new life as never before—in the freedom songs of the South and in the topical songs of many a campus.

And this is what happened to singing in the unions.

"Organize the Unorganized," c. 1991

Early draft of a column for *Solidarity* magazine; found in Seeger files

The editor of this good union journal has given me the honor of letting me shoot my mouth off on this page. I'm an old singer of union songs, and I read *Solidarity* from time to time. Here's a couple things on my mind worth discussing these days.

Let's learn from some of our past mistakes. When free labor was undercut by coolies brought from China,[12] west coast labor pushed for an Oriental Exclusion Act[13] and finally got it in 1922. When the

---

11. The International Longshore and Warehouse Union.
12. The term "coolie" was used in the late 19th and early 20th century for laborers brought from Asia to the United States, particularly Chinese immigrants who worked building the Transcontinental Railroad. The term is usually associated with negative and sometimes xenophobic opinions concerning the use of Asian immigrant labor in the United States.
13. The act, also known as the Immigration Act of 1924, limited the annual number of immigrants admitted to the United States from any given country to two percent of the number of people from that country already living in the United States. It aimed specifically to curb immigration from Eastern and Southern Europe as well as East Asia.

Oriental Exclusion Act was overruled by a new immigration act, labor sensibly went along with it and most unions today are a rainbow of different ethnic backgrounds, like most of the country. Hooray. The Oriental Exclusion Act was a bad idea.

We can learn from some of our right decisions. When free labor was undercut by slave labor, most unions joined the bloody struggle to end the system of chattel slavery. And in the 1930s American labor had its biggest period of growth, when, led by John L. Lewis, it pushed for signing up African-Americans by the hundreds of thousands.

"Organize the unorganized" was John L.'s slogan and I believe it should be ours now, when labor is pushed to the wall by imports. "Buy American" is going to be of limited use. Too many Americans want the high quality products now available from both agriculture and industry overseas. In the long run, our only hope is to push harder for a world where *every* worker has decent wages. Impossible? A utopian idea? No, it's the only practical thing. Organize the unorganized in Taiwan, in Brazil, Mexico, everywhere.

"My Political Bio," 2005

Letter to Pat Fry, dated November 2005; found in Seeger files

Dear Pat,

I've been a member of the Committee of Correspondence[14] for a long time now, but when people ask me is that a communist organization I say, "Not exactly, although a lot of us were long ago members of the Communist party." I also am a member of a nice little local chapter of the Veterans of Foreign Wars, and once when handing out poppies outside the doors of a local Catholic church, a man angrily asked me, "Seeger, are you still a Communist?" I started to answer, "It depends on what you mean by that word," but he angrily stomped off. Now I try to put on paper as best I can my political bio.

I became a communist at age 7. An older brother who became a radar astronomer was at that time reading the *Amazing Stories* magazine about rocket ships. I thought they were stupid. Another older brother was reading stories about knights in armor (by Henty)[15]—I thought they were stupid. I started reading the books of Ernest Thompson Seton,[16]

---

14. The Committee of Correspondence for Democracy and Socialism was founded in the wake of the dissolution of the Soviet Union, in 1991, by dissidents within the Communist Party USA. Since that time it has grown to include a variety of radicals advocating democratic socialism.

15. George Alfred Henty (1832–1902) was a novelist, known for his adult and children's fiction, usually situated in an actual historical period, and revolving around the adventures of a virtuous and heroic protagonist.

16. Seton (1860–1946) was an outdoorsman, writer, and artist, best known for his stories of nature and particularly of his adventures with wild animals.

JH

The Big Joe Blues

PEERY
HOTEL
Historic Elegance

Sept. 2 1990

I got thinking last month about what songs Woody Guthrie
would have made up say, in 1956 after Kruschev's
speech about Stalin — or in 1968 after Soviet tanks rolled
into Prague. My guess there might have been a cowboy
blues along this line it ain't a good thing to lie
Joe Joe Joe he didn't you know it's not good to lie? (3x)

I'm not singing about little Joe
My nephew, still going to school
No, I'm not singing about you, Little Joe
Even though, you like to break the rules
Joe Joe Joe don't you know it's not good to lie? (3x)
Joe Joe He didn't   I'm not singing about middle-aged Joe
the Senator who died a while ago
He wanted to be a new dictator
Joe Joe Joe he...etc   But he was only small potaters
I'm singing about old Joe, cruel Joe
He ruled with an iron hand

PS —
1990

He put an end to the dreams
Of so many in every land
He had a chance to make
A brand new start for the human race
Instead he set it back
Right back in the same nasty place
(I Got The Big Joe Blues —
(Keep your mouth shut or you will die fast.
Do this job — no questions asked   ) Now, a joke in Moscow
is an epitaph
Now : "They pretend to pay us — and we pretend to work"

the nature writer. Over the next five years I read every one of his books.
He was my guru. He held up American Indians as a role model: brave,
truthful. The middle-aged Indian in "Rolf In The Woods" tells the
13-year-old white boy, "You can read your books, but I can teach you
the book of nature." I made myself a tepee, lived in it, tracked animals.

And Indians shared within each tribe. If there was food, everyone
ate. If there was hunger, everyone was hungry, even the learned chief
and his wife and children. When I was twenty I learned that anthropologists call this "tribal communism."

Age 13 I started reading Thoreau's *Walden*,[17] then the autobiography of Lincoln Steffens,[18] and Mike Gold's *Jews Without Money*.[19]

I was not into joining things though until age 18, in college, a friend persuaded me to join the American Student Union.[20] Those were the days of Italy invading Ethiopia, Japan in Manchuria, and Hitler helping Franco take over Spain. Litvinov, the Soviet representative to the League of Nations urged the world to "quarantine any aggressor." This made perfect sense to me. I got so interested in politics I didn't keep up with my studies, lost my scholarship, dropped out of college, and in NYC joined a "Youth Workshop" part of the YCL (Young Communist League). I met Woody Guthrie and we sang together for unions and for Communist groups too. After WWII, I was a card-carrying member for about 4 years. Woody tried to join but was turned down. We both used to laugh at the long words and special definitions they tried to give out. "Revisionism?" said Woody. "I revise myself every morning."

And of course after Khrushchev's speech in '56 detailing Stalin's anti-Semitism[21] and other brutalities, millions of us asked ourselves "What is Communism?"

"The Peekskill 'Riot,'" 1972

From *The Incompleat Folksinger,* Simon and Schuster, 1972

In September 1949 the baritone Paul Robeson was asked to give an outdoor concert near Peekskill, about forty miles north of New York City. Although he was an internationally famous star, he had been under attack because of his outspoken opinions. In Paris he had said that American Negroes would refuse to fight against the USSR, as it was the one nation which had outlawed race discrimination. In Peekskill there had been talk of opposition to his concert.

---

17. Henry David Thoreau (1817–1862) was an author and prominent American transcendentalist, whose works focused on modern individuals' attempts to overcome and "transcend" culture and society. *Walden* is a first-person account of Thoreau's time spent living on the outskirts of mainstream society in the woodlands on the edge of Concord, Massachusetts.
18. Steffens (1866–1936) was a New York–based journalist who wrote widely on government corruption and scandals. He was an early supporter of the newly formed Soviet Union.
19. Gold (1894–1967) was a Jewish author and Marxist whose writing largely concerned the problems faced by the proletarian immigrant classes and advocated for Communist revolution as a solution to these problems.
20. The American Student Union was a national amalgamation of Communist and Socialist college student groups.
21. This speech, officially named *On the Personality Cult and Its Consequences*, was given by Nikita Khrushchev, then the leader of the Soviet Union, on February 25, 1956, during the Twentieth Party Congress. In his speech, Khrushchev detailed many then-unknown abuses of power perpetrated by Joseph Stalin during his tenure as Premier of the Soviet Union. Although critical of Stalin, the speech also emphasized Khrushchev's belief in Leninism and his continued commitment to the Soviet Union and communism.

Pianist Leonid Hambro and I had been asked to do a few numbers in the first half of the concert. But when I and my mother drove up that evening, the roads near the concert area were impossibly jammed with cars and we could not get near. I hailed a state trooper, "I'm one of the performers on tonight—can you help me get through?"

He gave me a peculiar look, but only said, "The concert has been called off. It's impossible for anyone to get through." After vainly trying to get ahead, I managed to make a U-turn on the narrow road and drove home. Next day we learned that an American Legion[22] mob had got to the site early, had overturned stage and equipment, had beaten up some of the young people preparing things, including a pregnant woman.

Robeson and those arranging the concert said that this is America and the concert would be put on the next week. They would not be intimidated. Next Saturday afternoon, a lovely sunny day, several thousand cars were parked in the large field, and a huge audience listened to a great concert. Bodyguards stood close by Robeson, as there had been threats on his life. A crowd of 300 ignorant people stood near the entrance to the field shouting epithets: "Go back to Russia! Kikes! Nigger-lovers!" But they were not allowed on the field. A thousand staunch union members from Local 65, New York, stood shoulder to shoulder around the entire field, to make sure no one broke in to cause a disturbance.

When the concert was over, we all congratulated ourselves that things had gone smoothly. But the cars seemed to leave very slowly. When our car—a station wagon, carrying my wife, two babies, their grandfather, and two friends—pulled out of the gate, the policeman would not let us turn left or go straight ahead. He directed all traffic down one narrow road, several miles to a parkway. The crowd of 300 was still shouting insults, but we breathed easier and turned right and picked up speed.

Suddenly we saw a lot of broken glass on the road. "Uh oh. Watch out," said I. Sure enough, up ahead were young men with piles of fist-sized stones heaving them at every car that passed. "Crash, klunk!"—we got it. Only a hundred feet away was a policeman. "Officer, aren't you going to do something about this?"

"Move on! Keep moving!" he shouted angrily. Our car was holding up traffic and the cars in back of us were getting it worse.

I started up again, but in the next two miles ten or fifteen rocks hit us. Every window in the car was broken. Being tall, I sat as straight and high as possible; the glass flew around below my eye level. Everyone else ducked low. Fortunately no one was more than slightly cut. Only three stones actually came through the plate glass. (I cemented them into a fireplace for mementos.)

---

22. The American Legion is an organization of United States military veterans, founded in 1919. From its inception, and particularly during the Red Scares in the first half of the twentieth century, the American Legion displayed marked opposition to socialism and all entities and individuals with perceived affiliations, such as the Communist Party USA.

We were told later that down near New York, gangs of men threw more rocks at any cars passing with smashed windows. And a bus full of Negroes who had not even been to Peekskill but had been visiting Roosevelt's home at Hyde Park, was stoned as it drove through Westchester County on the way back to the city.

Many of my friends assumed that American fascists were ready to take over the country. Signs were put in car windows throughout Peekskill: "Wake Up America, Peekskill Did!"

But here's the interesting thing. After about three weeks these signs disappeared. I rather suspect that in many homes there were arguments. "You mean you threw rocks at women and children? Well, I don't like Commies any more than you do, but still you don't throw rocks at women and children."

Years later I met a young man who had become a popular guitar picker in coffee houses. When he knew me well, he said, "You know, that riot was all arranged by the Ku Klux Klan and the police. I was living in Peekskill; my father was a police official. They had walkie-talkies all through the woods. They had that place surrounded like a battlefield."[23]

"In Defense of the Weavers," 1951

Letter to Leonard Schneider, then executive vice-president of
Decca Records, dated October 22, 1951; found in Seeger files

Dear Leonard,

For nearly two years we have been proud to record for Decca. And now we understand that there have been certain rumors and allegations about The Weavers.

We feel that you might like to hear the facts directly from us. We would like to tell you that we have never in our lives knowingly participated in nor contributed to any action or cause disloyal to this country; that we are not engaged as individuals or as a group in any activity of any kind, whether professional, artistic, organizational, or personal which is unrelated to our main business of singing.

To put it another way, we're singers who make recordings of the best American folk songs we know, who appear in theaters, clubs and television. We collect and arrange songs, and we write new ones. And this is all we do.

---

23. "I did not realize then that, in effect, this was like an inoculation against fascism. The pictures were in the newspapers, and on radio and television you could hear the people shouting, 'Go back to Russia! Kikes! Nigger-lovers!' People saw it all around the country, and it was an ugly thing, like a lynching. J. Edgar Hoover had been pressing Truman to round up so-called subversives and put them in internment camps, just like the Japanese in World War II. But J. Edgar Hoover was never able to get Congress and Truman to let him fill up those concentration camps because the whole country saw what fascism looked like."— P. S.

Through our association with you and our friends at Decca, we believe you know that we have always sung the best songs we know. We think that not one line or chord of any song we have recorded for Decca can be construed as harmful to our country—indeed, we believe that our songs have helped Americans in these troubled days to know themselves and understand the great traditions of our country.

We have been fortunate in being able to work with Decca. Folksongs were a risky experiment only a year or two ago, and the results have proven that the experiment was worthwhile. Surely the more than 4 million persons who have bought our recordings have found nothing objectionable in them. We are proud that so many of our fellow citizens have liked our songs.

We often wonder whether the persons who have questioned us have ever honestly listened to our songs. We would like to invite them all to listen, and to sing with us. If they did we think they would have more faith in this country.

Sincerely yours,
The Weavers

P. S. As the fellow says, "We deny the allegations and defy the allegators!"

"On Propaganda Songs," 1955

Letter to Art Goldberg of the Queens College Folksong Club, dated March 22, 1955; found in Seeger files

Dear Art Goldberg,

Many thanks for your letter. I am glad of this opportunity to reply to the charges that have been made against me. Thought I do not know exactly what they are nor who made them, I have a general idea.

First, you should know that it was a man named Harvey Matusow[24] who in 1951 testified before various committees that I was a traitor to my country. Of course his charges were ridiculous. After some consultation I decided to ignore them. For what can one say? You can argue 'til you are blue in the face that you are a loyal American, but it doesn't mean a thing before such committees. Lattimore and Oppenheimer found this out.[25]

---

24. Matusow (1926–2002) was a former member of the Communist Party USA who turned informant for the FBI and agreed to provide HUAC with information on people with ties to the Communist Party in return for avoiding being blacklisted himself.

25. Owen Lattimore (1900–1989) and J. Robert Oppenheimer (1904–1967) were two accomplished and revered academics who were investigated by HUAC in the late 1940s and early 1950s. Lattimore, a well-known scholar specializing in Asian cultures, and Oppenheimer, a physicist best known for his integral role in the design and production of the atomic bomb, were publicly tarnished by the Committee for their Communist affiliations. Both men's careers suffered significantly after the HUAC hearings, and neither fully regained the status he had held prior to the hearings.

I have decided, instead, simply to continue singing the songs I have always sung. They show clearly what I do believe in. Let us see if there is anything traitorous or disloyal in these songs.

Do they believe "Goodnight Irene" is designed to lull honest citizens to sleep while the forces of darkness take over? Does "John Henry" indicate a suspicious favoritism towards hard working people?

"No," perhaps they will say, "it's these propaganda songs you keep singing."

Well! This *is* a hard one for me to answer. In my own opinion any song worth its salt has a point to make, and if one disagrees with that point, it is called "propaganda." (My children know what a propaganda song is. When I try to sing them a lullaby they howl me down, and demand something livelier, so they can stay up later.) Yes, the history of our country is a history of causes struggled for, and some of our most famous songs, like "John Brown's Body," were propaganda.

So which of my songs do they disagree with? Perhaps it is the ballad by a Negro sharecropper, "Hallelujah, I'm A-Traveling", which contains the lines:

> I hate Jim Crow,[26] and Jim Crow hates me
> And that's why I'm fighting for my liberty.

Now, it has been said that Communists are against Jim Crow. To avoid being called a traitor, must I avoid singing a beautiful song I believe in? No. I will sing it because I love my country and want to help make her still better.

The same thing might be said of the song, "The Strangest Dream."

> Last night I had the strangest dream
> I never dreamed before
> I dreamed the world had all agreed
> To put and end to war.[27]

Because Communists are said to talk of peace, must everyone in our nation stand mute before the threat of holocaust, because to speak would brand them?

Now, frankly, because you have asked me, I will say I am a radical—in a conservative sort of way. I come from a long line of radicals, some of whom felt so strongly that they exiled themselves from their homes and left for strange shores on a little ship called the Mayflower. And some of my great-grandparents were followers of William Lloyd Gar-

---

26. Jim Crow laws were legal statutes in effect from the end of the Civil War until the passage of civil rights legislation in 1964 and 1965. They usually operated at state and local levels, and generally served to maintain segregation under the theoretical guise that blacks and whites could live apart while still enjoying the same rights.
27. By Ed McCurdy, c. The Richmond Organization and Almanac Music, 1955.

rison, who was nearly lynched in the streets of Boston 120 years ago, for his abolitionist opinions.

I wouldn't bore you with all this, except that you asked for it! I'm a singer, not a politician. I had looked forward to the possibility of returning to Queens—you all were a wonderful singing audience. I hope we will have that experience many times, of swapping songs with each other. Ballads, square dances, blues, lullabies, and hymns—put together they tell a wonderful story of our people, who built a new land out of the wilderness. Do we want to forget it?

Best wishes,
Peter Seeger

"Legal Defense Fund," 1956

Dated June 3, 1956; found in Seeger files

To all of you who have so generously contributed to my legal defense fund:

Deep thanks to you all. I feel humble and proud at the same time, that you should have faith in me and our songs—and in our country too—that we shall see these bumpy times through. Thanks to you and many more, we'll see a day when peoples and arts and sciences can flourish and exchange together freely. This all sounds mighty flowery and perhaps pretentious, but I do believe it.

See you all,
Pete

"The Acadian Folk Festival," 1956

Draft of a letter to the editor of the *Teche News* of St. Martinville, Louisiana, dated October 25, 1956; found in Seeger files

To the good citizens of St. Martinville,
Though my home is many miles from here, I was proud to have been invited to participate in your Acadian Folk Festival. However, to avoid embarrassment to your congressman, Mr. Willis,[28] I am not appearing. Fact is he demanded I not appear and to fight it might have spoiled the day.

How is this? Let me explain.

---

28. Edwin Willis (1904–1972) served in the House of Representatives from 1949 to 1969. He was the chairman of HUAC from 1963 to 1969 and strongly opposed Communism and movements which he perceived to be influenced by Communism, including the civil rights movement.

It was a hard decision for me. Tuesday afternoon I went with one of you, the gracious Mrs. Carmen Montagut, to pray, in your church, for guidance—(though, it is true, I am not a Catholic by background. My children go to a Quaker Sunday School).

You see, last August, I was one of several people questioned by Mr. Willis and his House Committee. I declined to discuss what I considered were my private American opinions and feelings on matters whether religious, philosophical or political.

Why did Mr. Willis want to question me? You see, in 20 years of singing folksongs, I have sung for every imaginable type of American. I have sung for the Rockefellers, and in hobo jungles, too. I have sung in churches—and in saloons and honky-tonks. I have sung for Americans of every creed and persuasion. For Republicans and Democrats, yes, and for vegetarians and prohibitionists—and communists. What songs have I sung them? Nothing that I would not be proud to sing at your Acadian Festival. Folk songs.

Is it not ironic that at a time we commemorate the 200th anniversary of the sad expulsion of the Acadian farmers from their homes, not because they had done anything wrong, but because their opinions were suspect, that now some people would like to continue the same idea?

Actually, I think that American Catholics can be proud that it was the Catholic leaders of the young colony of Maryland who wrote into law the first guarantees of Religious Freedom in the colonies, almost three centuries ago. That's much better than what some of my New England forebears were doing then—burning "witches" at Salem! (Not all of mine, of course. My grandmother, may she rest in peace, told me that another forebear was Elder Brewster of the Mayflower—as you know, Longfellow,[29] the author of *Evangeline*, also traced his lineage to him.)

Perhaps this is beside the point. Some will ask, what are my opinions anyway? Now, I have never had anything to hide, and, though I am not the kind of guy to go spouting off about such things, will tell you.

As I stated under oath to Mr. Willis: "I love my country very deeply. I have never in my life done anything of a conspiratorial nature, nor said anything conducive to conspiracy." And in favor of my family I share the use and ownership of 17 acres in the beautiful Hudson Valley. I will say that I look forward to a time when there is not such a disparity between rich and poor. As it says in *Evangeline*, "The poorest lived in abundance," that is, when all mankind can, with justice, share the fruit of their own labor on God's great green earth. Did not the gentle Jesus foresee this?

---

29. Henry Wadsworth Longfellow (1807–1882) was a poet, specializing in morally didactic epic poetry concerning legendary subjects. *Evangeline*, published in 1847, tells the story of an Acadian girl named Evangeline who is deported from British-colonized Canada to the United States whilst searching for her lost lover.

All this, however, should not matter; whether one agreed with me or not. For should not your great Acadian Folk Festival be above such differences of opinion? You have fine and noble traditions here in southern Louisiana—traditions which should not be forgotten. The beautiful French language (my mother's grandfather came from old France)—the lovely Acadian songs, the fiddle and the accordion. Love of these should knit us all together in common humanity.

I live in a small community, Dutchess Junction, outside the town of Beacon, N.Y., sixty miles north of the big city. We have wonderful PTA square dances in our one-room schoolhouse. I should like to invite any of you, traveling up there, to stop in at one.

And perhaps one of these years I will be back to sing with you all again. We've already sung together, you know, on such songs I have recorded as "Goodnight Irene," "On Top of Old Smoky," "So Long, It's Been Good to Know You."

Would Mr. Willis say it would be better for America had I never recorded them?

Au revoir—but not goodbye!

Sincerely,
Peter Seeger

"Letter to My Grandchildren," 1956

Sealed letter, bearing the address: *Not to be opened 'til after death of both C. L. Seeger II and Peter Seeger. Or around the year 2000 A.D.,* dated November 30, 1956; found in Seeger files

A letter to my grandchildren,[30] across the years.

Dear ???—Dear descendants:

I write this in the 38th year of my life, to try and give a few unvarnished facts, in case some of you ever get curious as to who or what this character, namely me, is or was.

First, you have to understand that this mid-twentieth century has been torn by fears, doubts, confusions, and arguments about such things as peace, prosperity, civil rights in every country, and so on. Central in all these matters has been a much-discussed word: communism.

Some say communism means tyranny over mind and body. They say that under communism one has no political democracy, and that people can be railroaded to jail for simply disagreeing with those in power.

Communists in America always denied this. They said that on the contrary right here in the good old US people, namely they, were often railroaded to jail just because they disagreed with those in power.

---

30. Seeger had no grandchildren in 1956; his own children were not even teenagers.

However, in this year of 1956 it now appears by admission of Russians themselves, that all was, and possibly is, not as sweet as American communists hoped or believed.

But when I think of communism, I not only think of this. I think of the communists I have known. Bravery, steadfastness, and, yes, continual intellectual searching and thinking. Every communist leader I have known has lived his life in the frank knowledge that it was unlikely that he or she would live their lives through without suffering jail sentences and possibly cruel death because of their beliefs. I never knew people so intent upon a long-range goal to make this a better world to live in. They were not content to say, "tsk tsk" about such a thing as Jim Crow. They organized a committee or something and agitated and propagandized for its abolition. They gave of their time and money to a fantastic degree. Their entire lives were dedicated not to personal success, but to changing a selfish and evil world into one where all mankind could truly be comrades.

I once heard a communist leader saying in a speech: "One principle thing distinguishes communists. They hate capitalism." Note that he did not say, "They hate capitalists." They hated the system which encouraged men to be greedy, rather than hating the greedy men themselves. This to me has always seemed an important point. Anthropologists now know that you could take any hundred babies and raise them in any one of a dozen different societies, and they would turn out completely (well, maybe not completely!) differently. We all today know now a most polite and cordial man gets behind the wheel of a car and in crowded traffic acts like a selfish boor, cutting in front of cars, and doing his best to get ahead of the next car. He feels that in the traffic there is no alternative. He must crowd out others or be crowded out himself.

Similarly, undoubtedly many a man of good intentions finds himself leading a big business, and starts to behave as bad as anyone else. He pays his workers as little as he can get away with paying them. He manufactures goods no better than they need to be to sell. He cheats and lies to his friends and neighbors, because he feels that he couldn't stay in business if he did not.

Communists always believed that if the history of mankind were scientifically studied, that future changes could be predicted, and that furthermore these changes could be considerably improved upon by even a small number of people if they used intelligent leverage. It now appears that they didn't always study quite carefully enough, and their leverage was not always used correctly.

I joined the Young Communist League in the fall of 1937, when I was eighteen years old, and a student at Harvard College. Prior to that time I had read a few radical publications such as the *New Masses*, and had marched in a few New York May Day parades with my father, who was an intellectual radical. (He had been a pacifist and a socialist during the First World War.) A few years later I graduated to the Communist Party and have been, according to my own definition, a Communist ever since. Not that I went to meetings often. Because so much of my life has been spent traveling, or in the army, many years passed when I attended no Communist meeting at all, and even dues paying was irregular, to say the least. By that definition I have been a very poor Communist! I'd say that probably in the last twenty years I have attended probably fifty or seventy-five communist meetings all in all. Oy!

I said "according to my own definition." What is my definition? Well, if you ask, am I in favor of slave labor camps, of stifling of opinion, of violent revolution, etc. I say "NO!" You bet I am not. On the other hand, if you ask, am I in favor of a cooperative ownership and planning production and consumption, and do I believe that only under such socialism will eventually wars cease, and arts and science truly flourish, then I say: "You bet!"

This question of "violent revolution" has been a big bone of contention and perhaps it would be best to examine it a little more in detail. Now there are only a few people in the world so in love with fighting that they truly welcome the murderous art of war. Most people would say that violence should only be used "when there is no alternative." At the far opposite end of the scale there are few people in this world who so disapprove violence that they would not use force to restrain a maniac from chopping their children up with an axe. I have been told that in India there are religious sects (Jain monks) who will not slap a mosquito because they will not destroy life. (I wonder if they have thought about the poor microbes.) Here in the U.S. there are pacifists who will go to jail rather than enlist in any army, no matter in how just a cause. Communists, generally speaking, are not pacifists. While they may abhor violence more or less, they point out that the ruling class has always used violence to keep itself in power, and that the people should be prepared for the possibility that working people may have to oppose force with force in order to effect the popular will. Communists used to say "probability" instead of "possibility," but now, with the example of Gandhi in India, and other successes of the advocates of nonviolence (including the communist-led peace movements), and with the threat of global catastrophe should another World War be unleashed, most American communists work toward the end that socialism come through parliamentary processes.

So I think I'll stick with communism, in spite of its mistakes and excesses. I still feel that the basic Marxist analysis of history is correct. And I'll stick with Russia and China, too, in spite of their mistakes. After all, American democracy has made undemocratic errors, too: Washington's troops forced the deportation of thousands of citizens just because they were Tories during the revolution. Later these troops suppressed the Shays Rebellion. In 1812 American troops sacked and burned Toronto needlessly. And of course, slavery and Jim Crow have been a great blot on our life. Yet, taken all in all, I think American life and thought, and culture, have been and will be a wonderful influence in the history of the world. And I believe that Russia and China will also be. If I deplore Hungary, I also deplore America's past actions in the Philippines, or Nicaragua, or, more recently, Guatemala. But I'll stick with America because I love her, and with the communist states because I admire their achievements, too.

Being a communist has helped me, I believe, to be a better singer and folklorist, and a more selfless citizen. I can't say so openly, unfortunately, at this period. Thus this letter must not be opened for many years. Otherwise I would be hard put to earn a living for the family, and more important, it would put great hardships on my wife and children, in causing them to be ostracized from their neighbors and friends.

But I'll continue to be a communist. Contrary to common belief at this time about such matters, I have never been forced to accept any opinion I did not believe in, nor vote for someone I disapproved of. I have had full chance for discussion of possible paths and tactics. If occasionally we communists all planned our actions to be pointed a certain way, it is no more than any political party does. Or a union that votes to hold out for a certain contract. You stick together 'til it is won. I feel that far from holding any tyranny over my mind, communism has urged me on, to continually learn, to continually better myself in every way, to always give more for the common good of the working people of America and the world.

Perhaps all this sounds a little corny to you, has the ring of ancient history. Well, know that at this time, it is almost a life and death matter for many of us. We do not know what the future will bring, but we will be loyal to what we feel is a sensible appraisal of the facts of past and probable future. At this time I am cited for contempt of Congress and may go to jail. We will see what the future brings.

Your loving grandfather,
Peter Seeger

"The Bar of Judgment," 1957

From Seeger's review of *Sea Songs* (Ballantine, 1956) by
Burl Ives in *Sing Out!* magazine, no. 6.4, Winter 1957

This is one of the very best collections you can find of sailors' chanteys and ballads. And thanks be from all impecunious guitar pickers to Ballantine Books and the inventors of the high-speed rotary printing press, it only costs 35 cents. It has in it some of the well-known ones, such as "Blow the Man Down" and "Whiskey, Johnny," but it also includes a raft of little-known and highly singable songs, many entirely new to this reviewer, who thought he knew 'em all. Some duds slipped in too, but every man to his taste.

This book gives brief introductions to each song—penetrating pictures showing how the songs grew out of the lives of the sailors. Also to its credit, the book omits the racial dialects which have marred so many previous collections of folk songs. Altogether, it is a far better volume than its predecessor, the *Burl Ives Songbook,* which tended to get bogged down in the 19th century and then stopped safely before risking an opinion on the 20th. So let us give thanks to Burl Ives.

Such accolade may seem surprising, particularly when it comes from this reviewer. But let me ask the reader to keep the following in mind. Burl Ives went to Washington, D. C. a few years ago, to the House Un-American Committee and fingered, like any common stool-pigeon, some of his radical associates of the early 1940s. He did this not because he wanted to but because he felt it was the only was to preserve his lucrative contracts; and that makes his action all the more despicable.

Those who consider it so, however, should be careful not to set up a blacklist of their own. A good book is useful no matter who wrote it. Many of us ride in Volkswagens, though they were originally designed by Hitler's technicians. John Copley, one of America's greatest painters, turned Tory in 1776, and I have read that Degas[31] was anti-Semitic. Burl Ives, whom I have known for almost twenty years, has always seemed to me like Falstaff,[32] the character from Shakespeare. Falstaff was gross, gargantuan, talented and clever; he was also not quite intelligent enough to be honorable. Many will never forgive Burl. But when he comes up before the bar of judgment, let us be generous enough to allow him to present his positive contributions, which have been many, before his sins are weighed on the other balance.

"Rather, a Strong Link," 1956

Letter to Woody Guthrie; found in the Woody Guthrie
Foundation Archives, dated November 27, 1956

Dear Woody,

I just got back from about three months of one night stands. All across Canada, down the West Coast, and then through Detroit, Chicago, and so on, back home. Sang an awful lot of your songs, and met

---

31. Edgar Degas (1834–1917) was a French Impressionist painter and sculptor.
32. Sir John Falstaff appears in Shakespeare's *Henry IV,* parts I and II. Falstaff tempts the titular Henry, then a young prince, not yet king, into mischievous or immoral acts and is ultimately forsaken by the ascendant prince.

a lot of your friends. A miner in British Columbia, an Auto worker in Detroit, a preacher down in Kansas City, they all asked after you.

My being cited for contempt didn't matter to most of the people I sang for. Occasionally there was an argument or discussion—but that's good. America hasn't seen enough good arguments in the past few years.

Alan Lomax writes from England that he may be able to come back to the U.S.A. next spring. I sure hope so. He's been gone too long. It'll take a while to recognize all the things that have happened since he has been gone.

Do you have a guitar now? Harold Leventhal told me he would take care of it.

And what are the visiting days now? I'm going to be around here for a couple months now, and would like to get down to see you, and swap some songs, and some ideas, and see what all you've been writing. Sounds mighty interesting.

No, don't worry about Toshi and me and jail. I feel mighty optimistic about the future. Anyway, we're all just links in a chain, and the important thing is not to be a long link, but rather a strong link. There's lots of kids around the country who will pick up what we can teach them, and add a lot more to it. Like the old song said, I only wish I could live a thousand years to see how it turns out. Well, bless you too for thinking of us, and I'll see you soon.

Your friend and student,
Pete

"A Hassle with the Government," 1957

Dated March 30, 1957; found in Seeger files

Because newspaper reports have been incomplete, inaccurate and sometimes downright malicious, set forth here is the story of my hassle with the government, which has now led to my being indicted for contempt of Congress.

1) In August, 1955, Representatives Walter (D. Pa.), Scherer (R. Ohio), and Willis (D. La.)—the "House Committee On Un-American Activities"—questioned me for over an hour in New York, trying to establish a connection with the left-wing movement in the United States.

My reply, if I can remember my exact words, was: "I have never done anything, supported any cause, nor sung any song either conspiratorial or conducive to conspiracy, and I resent the implication, in being called before this committee, that because some of my opinions may be different than yours, that I am any less of an American. You have a right to your opinions, and I have a right to mine."

Rereading the statement, it sounds awfully self-righteous, but I'll stick by it. Some will say it was foolishly pigheaded, but I said that they were asking the kind of questions that no American should be asked.

2) So at the tail end of that session of Congress, in the summer of '56, I was formally cited by the House, for contempt of Congress, along with Arthur Miller, the playwright, Dr. Otto Nathan (Einstein's friend and the executor of his will), and half a dozen others, all of whom had quoted the First Amendment as the basis for their refusal to answer similar questions. (P. S. My wife felt quite complimented, in a way—to be in the same class with Marilyn Monroe[33]).

The difference between quoting the Fifth Amendment or the First is roughly this: The Fifth means "you have no right to ask me this question"—and the Supreme Court has supported this position. The First means "you have no right to ask anyone this question." So far the Supreme Court has avoided making a direct ruling on the First. Some witnesses have thereby served from three months to a year in jail. Some have had their cases dismissed by lower courts. Though I quoted no Amendment, the First Amendment ("freedom of speech, press, assembly") covers me.

3) This Friday, March 29, I was arraigned at Foley Square courthouse in New York, by the Federal Department of Justice, and charged with contempt of Congress. I pleaded not guilty. (I have very honestly the highest regard for Congress—it is the legislative arm of our democracy, and the instrument through which to channel our hopes for the future.)

Fortunately I was able to raise bail of $1,000 and am free for the moment to continue to travel and sing. There will be a hearing June 10, and a trial probably within the next three to eight months, and possibly (some think probably) appeals which can last a couple years or more. This is what really costs dough. I've discovered that the average workingman is really at a disadvantage here. Before we are through, Toshi and I will have to raise between three and ten thousand dollars, whether I stay out of jail or not.

We have a really wonderful lawyer—Paul Ross—he used to be Mayor LaGuardia's[34] right hand man, a mature, sensible, and humane man. He's promised to stick by us even though there is no chance of us being able to pay him a normal fee.

4) Well, that's how the situation stands. I still feel that I committed no wrong, and that my children will not feel ashamed of me in future years. I think that it is significant that the committee did not

---

33. Monroe (1926–1962), a leading movie star of the era, was married to Arthur Miller from 1956 to 1961.
34. Fiorello LaGuardia (1882–1947) was a hugely popular and powerful three-term mayor of New York (1934–1945). He was a liberal Republican, and a supporter of President Roosevelt's New Deal policies.

even question my statement (see second paragraph, above). If they felt I really had been a part of some conspiracy, they should have cited me for perjury, not contempt.

If only we could transport ourselves, in the mind's eye, to look down like the Gods upon the scene, it might even appear funny, if it were not also tragic that in our country with so many fine traditions of freedom, it is still possible to be penalized for opinions.

"March 1, '58," 1958

Found in Seeger files

I spent my youth with "the Twelve Disciples."
And it was a long love affair
How can I describe those early days?
If you've never been in love you wouldn't know
The tension of discussions, where history was being lived and made
The May Day parades, the rallies at the Garden

Now—well, let's just say that we are mostly separated
I'll not say she's dead—though you could hardly call
Those shreds of mind and body—torn alike
By friend and enemy, plain for all to see—
The creature I once loved
And loved till even I could see she'd changed

And should a miracle occur and she revive
I would again—
Though here am I, a balding forty
And could I ever be so ardent?
(Some will say "So blind,"—they lie!)

My love, here's to you, and to the memory of our days together
I'll try to carry on and do as you'd have wished
Nothing that we ever did was false or phony
Never was our affair dirtied by love of money or fame
And though I thought to live and die with you alone
Now I face a widower's world

And know this: we sired many children who'll live
Long after our romance is far forgotten
The books we wrote, the melodies composed
Lines written on the page of history
The world is richer for our love
A good thing that has happened
Cannot be made to unhappen
O my love, my love, O my love.

"Statement to the Court," 1961[35]

From *Sing Out!* magazine, no. 11.3, Summer 1961

Thank you, your honor. After hearing myself talked about, pro and con, for three days, I am grateful for the chance to say a few unrestricted words.

First, I should like to thank my lawyer for his masterly presentation of my defense. He has worked over many long weeks and months, knowing that it is beyond my power to pay him adequately for his work. I believe that he, and great legal minds like Justice Hugo Black[36] and Dr. Alexander Meiklejohn,[37] have explained far better than I can why they believe the First Amendment gives American citizens the right to refuse to speak upon occasion.

Secondly, I should like to state before the court, much as I did before Congressman Walter's committee, my conviction that I have never in my life said, or supported, or sung anything in any way subversive of my country. Congressman Walter stated that he was investigating a conspiracy. I stated under oath that I had never done anything conspiratorial. If he doubted my word, why didn't he even question it? Why didn't he have me indicted for perjury? Because, I believe, even he knew that I was speaking the truth.

Some of my ancestors were religious dissenters who came to America over 300 years ago. Others were abolitionists in New England of the 1840s and '50s. I believe that in choosing my present course I do no dishonor to them, or to those who may come after me.

I am 42 years old, and count myself a very lucky man. I have a wife and three healthy children, and we live in a house we built with our own hands, on the banks of the beautiful Hudson River. For twenty years I have been singing folksongs of America and other lands to people everywhere. I am proud that I never refused to sing to any group of people because I might disagree with some of the ideas of some of the people listening to me. I have sung for rich and poor, for Americans of every possible political and religious opinion and persuasion, of every race, color, and creed.

The House committee wished to pillory me because it didn't like some few of the many thousands of places I have sung for. Now it so

---

35. *Sing Out!* magazine reproduced Seeger's statement to the court after his conviction for contempt of Congress in a jury trial, six years after his initial testimony before the HUAC.
36. Black (1886–1971) was a Supreme Court Justice from 1937 to 1971. Known for his support for liberal causes and civil liberties, Black strictly interpreted the First Amendment, arguing that the federal government had no right whatsoever to abridge free speech, even in extreme cases.
37. Meiklejohn (1872–1964) was a university professor and administrator who wrote widely on the First Amendment, arguing that free speech and democracy were inextricably linked.

happens that the specific song whose title was mentioned in this trial, "Wasn't That a Time" is one of my favorites. The song is apropos to this case. I wonder if I might have permission to sing it here before I close?

[At this point the judge refused to hear Seeger sing.]

Well perhaps you will hear it some other time. A good song can only do good, and I am proud of the songs I have sung. I hope to be able to continue singing these songs for all who want to listen, Republicans, Democrats and independents. Do I have the right to sing these songs? Do I have the right to sing them anywhere?

"The Ironies of Blacklisting," 1961

Draft of a letter to the editor of *New Yorker Magazine,* dated August 14, 1961[38]

Dear Sir,

I wonder if the time is not ripe for you to have an article on the subject of blacklisting—the general ironies of it, and the 1961–USA specific of it. This thought occurred to me as I read the last two sentences of the excellent article on Stephen Crane[39] by A. J. Liebling,[40] and the note about the work of John Hubley,[41] in the same issue. Your reporter must have known that Hubley had to leave UPA during one of the congressional red hunts a few years ago, and perhaps one reason that he has time to work on a UN film is that he is not so tied down by Hollywood jobs as he otherwise might have been.

The emotions behind the practice of blacklisting certainly are ancient: people do not like to buy the product or labor of someone whose activities or opinions they despise. My grandmother would not keep a book by Owen Johnson in the house ("That man has had *five* wives!") and a Jewish Community Center director told me he had wanted to buy a Volkswagen for a staff car, but too many members would have felt uncomfortable riding in this product of Nazi engineering.

The origin of the term "blacklisting," I don't know. I first read of it being used in labor union struggles of the late 19th century, such as

---

38. This letter was likely never mailed to the *New Yorker* magazine.
39. Crane (1871–1900) was a fiction writer and journalist, most famous for his novel *The Red Badge of Courage.*
40. Liebling (1904–1963) was a journalist best known for his pieces that appeared in the *New Yorker* magazine. Considered one of the greatest press critics of the 20th century, Liebling wrote on a wide variety of subjects, and was an active war correspondent during World War II.
41. Hubley (1914–1977) was an animator who worked for Disney and invented the cartoon character Mr. Magoo. In 1952, he was forced to leave United Productions of America (UPA), a prominent animation studio, because of his refusal to name members of the Communist Party when called before HUAC.

those of the Molly Maguires[42] in the Pennsylvania mining areas. It seems to have been common practice for employers to circulate amongst each other a list of known "agitators" to insure that they would not get a job in any similar mine or factory after they had been discharged from one. But the practice must be far older; it is similar to quarantining an infection.

Today the term is used mainly in our part of the world to describe the difficulties in gaining employment for persons suspected of having Communist sympathies. It is most common in the radio-TV-movie field. But even here there is probably not one list, but many lists, of varying effectiveness. Those having only mild trouble with them are called "grey-listed."

The situation is full of illogical surprises, contradictions, paradoxes, and considerable humor. The work of European authors and artists such as Sean O'Casey,[43] Picasso, Brecht, or even G. B. Shaw, is not banned here, though if they were American citizens their sympathies or affiliations would have had them up before the HUAC long ago. Jules Dassin[44] was blacklisted from Hollywood, but "Never on a Sunday" becomes a hit in U.S. movie theaters. The Broadway and off-B'Way theater is full of actors blacklisted from Hollywood or radio. Often it seems as though the right hand doesn't know what the left hand is doing: The New Yorker magazine occasionally gives my own folk songs records favorable reviews, but its advertising department told Folkways Records in 1960 that it would not accept advertisement for my records.

Most performers do not go out of their way to tell of their blacklist problem, if they have one. It doesn't help their careers any, for one thing. Also, they may be accused of trying to make martyrs of themselves. However, I'm convinced that the overall situation is one that ought to be better known by the American people and have never tried to avoid questions on the subject. These come fairly frequently nowadays since I am under conviction for contempt of Congress. If you do decide to assign some writer to look into the matter, I'd be glad to supply what data I know about firsthand. I am one of those who, with hindsight, is rather grateful for having been kept out of the normal type of commercial work for many years.

Sincerely,
Peter Seeger

---

42. The Molly Maguires were members of a secret society comprised of Irish-American miners who were also labor union activists. The members were arrested, and some were executed, on hearsay allegations and aggressive prosecution, mostly carried out by individuals who stood to gain financially from the dissolution of the society.
43. O'Casey (1880–1964) was an Irish playwright and socialist whose works focused on the lives of the Irish working class.
44. Dassin (1911–2008) was a filmmaker, mostly in the crime and noir genres, who was blacklisted and subsequently moved to France, where he continued his career.

"A Perennial Committee," 1961

Letter to Bess Hawes, dated September 9, 1961; found in Seeger files

Dear Bess,

Finally I get around to answering your letter of July 22nd. I know how busy you are and how difficult it was for you to take the time to write your letter and this makes me all the more sorry for my long delay in answering it. But the last couple of months have been completely hectic. First of all, I worked on getting out a revised edition of my banjo book; instead of the job requiring two weeks (as I had with typical over-optimism hoped), it took all of two months. And then during August I had to take a couple of trips away from home. Now, as a result of all this, I find myself in September trying to catch up on a two months' accumulation of mail.

Toshi and I have been kind of walking a narrow line every time someone asks us about my case, because on the one hand we have the desire to be perfectly and normally frank with anybody who asks the question, especially with those who ask it with completely friendly intent; then on the other hand, we have stern injunctions from my lawyer for me not to go shooting off my mouth about legal matters. He says that can only lead to trouble and he can't do an adequate job of defending me if I'm trying to give my opinion on legal matters which I don't really know anything about. We had to get his permission before even the booklet Harold Leventhal printed could go to press. And each time I suggested bringing up more information that could be included in such a booklet, why it would get cut down on the grounds that it just confused the issue.

This also comes up in regard to people who are trying to raise funds for our legal defense, especially those in other countries. My lawyer says that while there is no need for me to stop them from doing it, he said that if I want to go to England to sing I must definitely not participate in any function that would be trying to raise money for my legal defense.

I think perhaps the best thing is for people to actually read the hearing of 1955 and let them make up their own minds about it, without me trying to go into elaborate explanation of why I answered some questions—such as my name and address—but refused to answer other questions such as who did I know, and where and when did I ever sing. In these hearings I stated that I didn't want to cast any aspersions on people who had used the Fifth Amendment; I simply did not feel that I wanted to use it myself. As my lawyer has explained it to me, using the Fifth Amendment is in effect saying "you have no right to ask me this question," but using the First means in effect "you have no right to ask *any* Americans *such* questions." Since I felt I was in a strong enough position to make a broader attack upon the committee, I chose, in effect, the second course.

Unfortunately, it is very difficult to get copies of the original hearings since they are out of print now. Harold Leventhal is having a few photostats made of the copy which I have, but I'm not sure whether my lawyer would let us print them up in quantity for wide distribution.

In an interview a couple of weeks ago with a professor from Southern California who is making a detailed study of my case and others like it, I was asked, "do you think that Congress does not have any right to have investigating committees of any sort?" Naturally, I had to agree that Congress does have a right to investigate things, and some of its investigations have been extremely important and have brought out things which the normal investigative bodies do not bring out, such as the Teapot Dome scandal,[45] and the La Follette findings on the labor spy racket.[46] However, when Congress investigates something it is quite a different thing from having a perennial junket to expose perfectly legal activities. Supposing there were a few Congressmen who thought that all oil companies were run by a bunch of crooks, and they kept up every single year since Teapot Dome for the next twenty five years a running investigation where they could call the executives of any oil company on the stand and by asking them pointed questions with no chance for rebuttal, make it appear that they were engaged in shady business practices. Supposing even that following the La Follette investigation there was a perennial investigation into the use of any detective agency. Now it is perfectly legal to run detective agencies, but a perennial committee could make it look as though any detective agency was literally a labor spy racket.

In effect, this is what the un-American Activities Committee has been doing for 25 years now. Under the pretense of investigating conspiracy, they have actually been in the perennial business of exposing heresy—that is, exposing to the public view all the names they can possibly get of anyone who ever had anything to do with any so-called radical organization, however legal this organization might have been. This, to my mind, is a complete distortion of the correct practices and the legal practices of Congress. And my best defense, frankly, is a hard-hitting offense to try and put this committee out of business. It's hurting all of us—it's hurting America and the world. In other words, it's not enough to simply try and claim "Pete is innocent." I'm no more innocent than any other normal sinful human being. However, this committee is harming America, and the sooner we get rid of it, the better.

---

45. The Teapot Dome scandal erupted during the administration of Warren G. Harding when it was revealed that his Interior Secretary, Albert Fall, had leased oil reserves at Teapot Dome, Wyoming, to oil companies friendly to Fall, without competition, in return for bribes.

46. The La Follette Committee was a Congressional Committee that investigated and uncovered evidence of widespread espionage within labor unions. The spies were hired by opponents of organized labor who sought to undermine the effectiveness and integrity of the unions.

To understand why it is harming America is difficult and can't be done in two or three words. The newspaper headlines of literally decades have to be rebutted. Perhaps the best way they can be rebutted is to tell a detailed and specific story about one person. If this one person has to be me, why then I guess I'm perfectly willing to have it told. This is why I usually preface any statement about this trial with quoting what I told the committee and what I told the judge—namely, "I have never done anything conspiratorial in any way." This is a very broad statement to make. The committee claims to be investigating conspiracy. They had witnesses who claimed that I was a member of organizations and had supported organizations which they claimed were conspiratorial. Either the committee should indict these witnesses for perjury or should indict me for perjury, or else the committee itself is lying, and the question is not one of conspiracy but heresy.

The fact that neither Congressman Walter or Judge Murphy questioned this statement, to me, exposes the fact that they know they are not really investigating conspiracy. They have got to be put on the spot and forced to admit this basic fraud. In America one does not have the right to conspire to overthrow the government by force and violence without getting thrown in jail for it. But America has been proud that you have a perfect legal right to believe in heresy of whatever form you want as long as this does not include any overt act which would be illegal. These guys have simply got to be pinned down and made to prove what overt acts that are illegal have been committed. Congressman Walter has a perfectly good right to proclaim his belief that certain ideas are harmful to America, but he has absolutely no right to go unchallenged with his claim that these beliefs are illegal and conspiratorial and un-American. America has plenty of room for heresies. It would not be such a good country without them.

Well, Bess, I hope you can make some sense out of all this rambling. I've made a carbon of this letter to send to my lawyer along with your letter in the hopes that we can get something out that will be of supplementary use to the small brochures which Harold has already sent out—about forty thousand of them, I believe.

Love to all the family, and see you perhaps in March.
Pete

"As Communist as My Songs Are," 1963

Letter to Harold Leventhal, dated
October 11, 1963; found in Seeger files

Dear Harold,

Here in far off Tokyo I have read in the pages of *Variety* that ABC-TV will be willing to hire me for *Hootenanny*[47] only if I will "explain in

---

47. For more on the *Hootenanny* TV show, see chapters 4 and 15.

full my past and present relationships with the Communist Party," etc., because it is their policy not to hire people who are associated with the Communist movement.

On the face of it, this is a reasonable request. The only thing is, I consider myself a musician, not a politician. They are trying to make me a politician, not a musician. Sure I have opinions, and I've voted on 'em in just about every election. I think it's the right and I guess the duty of any citizen of a democracy to do so. But I also believe that the U.S. Constitution proclaims that a man has the right to keep his political opinions to himself if he wants, and not be harassed on account of them, be he royalist or anarchist. And because I was acquitted by the courts last year, I believe that the best legal opinion of the U.S.A. agrees basically with this approach.

Actually, everyone knows there are lots of questions you can't settle with a yes or no answer. After all, why did Jesus Christ refuse to give a yes or no answer when Pilate asked him "Are You King Of The Jews?" The reason was, that either a yes or a no answer would have been misleading or untrue. Jesus did not consider himself any temporal ruler, but in the deepest spiritual sense the King of all Mankind.

And who is a Communist in America? According to the Birchers,[48] Eisenhower is. According to anthropologists, the American Indians were.

I'm afraid any one who wants to find out my opinions can do so easily enough by simply listening to the songs I have sung. Darn near a thousand different ones, during the last twenty-five years or more. I am about as much a communist as my songs are. I'm about as anti-communist as my songs are. I'm as American as my songs are. I'm as international as my songs are. I am as right as my songs are. And as wrong.

Yours for more and better songs—and singers.
Peter Seeger

"Is the Blacklist Over?" 1967

Letter to unknown recipient, dated
September 5, 1967; found in Seeger files

Dear Dave,

Thanks for your letter!

I certainly do not think the blacklist is over, just because I got a job on network TV. The next step is to get Phil Ochs[49] and Tom Paxton[50]

---

48. "Birchers" refers to members of the John Birch Society, a conservative political advocacy group, well-known for its opposition to Communism in any form.
49. Ochs (1940–1976) was a folk singer and political activist. He was part of the Greenwich Village folk music scene of the early '60s, and wrote primarily topical songs, addressing current social and political issues. Although Ochs never achieved the level of fame of some of his contemporaries, he was a prolific songwriter who was greatly admired within the folk scene.
50. Paxton (b. 1937) is a folk musician and political activist, who has performed with

and a lot of others on—singing their best controversial songs. And there will be a lot of steps after that.

In my view, blacklisting of artists for their personal political views is only one minor aspect of a worldwide problem which the human race has been facing for many centuries and probably will for many more: the repression of ideas unpopular with the Establishment.

When printing was the only mass media, the Catholic Church had a list of banned writings. America was first started as a nation by ex-Europeans who objected to this kind of thought control. But by the mid-twentieth century America had a new mass media, radio and then TV, and America's new powers-that-be have effectively kept out of it opinions that challenged its security. Blacklisting didn't start with Mc-Carthy. Back in the 1930s the story *Grapes of Wrath* had to reach the public through print. The airwaves were closed to that kind of message.

Today the American people face domestic and international crises partly because the information they should have got through their airwaves has been denied them. I accepted the Smothers Brothers invitation because they agreed to let me sing "Waist Deep in the Big Muddy" —my best new song—along with a couple of my best old songs. At the moment I write you, CBS is still threatening to cut the song from the show. In any case the blacklist problem is now brought out into the open where the networks cannot deny its existence, and where the American people must face up to it also.

I am no expert in tactics and strategy. I think all of us who love music, and love America and the world, must figure on how we are going to take the next steps. Unless we prefer to get off in a corner by ourselves and congratulate each other on our exclusiveness.

Keep publishing,
As ever,
Pete

Seeger on numerous occasions. Paxton first began contributing his songs to social movements during the civil rights era, and has continued a successful songwriting career since.

6

The Civil Rights Movement

"I'll Tell About Your Heroism," 1963

Letter to Chico Neblett, Bob Moses, and Sam Block,[1]
dated May 31, 1963; found in Seeger files

Dear Chico, Bob and Sam:

I just read that all three of you are in jail because they didn't like the way you walked down the public highway. All I can say is that I and a good many thousand others are going to tell your heroic story everywhere we possibly can. We'll sing it, we'll speak it until the whole country knows about it. You guys are working for the freedom of our whole country and every single American, no matter what the color of his skin, owes you a deep debt of gratitude, admiration and eternal thanks.

I and my family are leaving this August on a trip around the world. I'm putting on concerts in Australia, Japan, India, Africa and about twelve other countries before coming home next June. I'll be singing in schools and universities, concert halls, villages, radio and TV.

I hope to show them that we have a lot of good old music in this country besides what they probably usually have heard. I'll pick the banjo and guitar and sing "John Henry" and "Michael, Row the Boat Ashore," but most especially I promise you I'll sing songs that tell of the great freedom fight you are putting up—songs like "Woke Up This Morning," "If You

---

1. Neblett, Moses, and Block were all members of the Student Nonviolent Coordinating Committee (SNCC) in Mississippi. Neblett was a founding member of the SNCC Freedom Singers, a touring group of musicians who sang songs of the civil rights movement around the United States, raising awareness of the movement and funds for SNCC. Block and Moses both played leadership roles in SNCC, and, in 1964, Moses became codirector of the Council of Federated Organizations (COFO), an amalgamated association of many prominent civil rights activist groups.

Miss Me at the Back of the Bus," and of course "We Shall Overcome." Above all, I'll tell about your heroism and your love for freedom.

As ever, your friend,
Pete Seeger

"The 'We Shall Overcome' Story," 2009

From *Where Have All the Flowers Gone,* Revised Edition. W. W. Norton & Company, 2009

Some fine songs were first published by our 16-page *People's Songs.* In 1948 we printed a song, "We Will Overcome."

Where did the song come from? In 1909, the *United Mine Workers' Journal* printed a letter from a biracial local in Alabama that told how the state's "tyrant governor" shut down an organizing drive. "That was one of the saddest times that the miner ever experienced in the state of Alabama," the letter said. "The Empire local met everyday, 351 strong—open air exercises, with prayer—and that good old song was sung at every meeting, 'We Will Overcome Some Day.'"

It seems most likely that the song we know now started in the late 19th century when some union member put union verses to an old spiritual. The latter is still sung.

In January 1946, some 300 workers—black women, mostly—were on strike at the American Tobacco factory in Charleston, South Carolina. Some recall one of the strikers, Lucille Simmons, leading the song on the picket line very, very slowly, "long meter" style, so that the harmony could develop, with high and low voices. "We ... will ... o ... ver ... co ... me."

That year some of the strikers visited a small labor school in Tennessee, the Highlander Folk School. Zilphia Horton, the music director (her husband Myles started the school), had a good alto voice. "We Will Overcome" became her favorite song. In 1947 in New York she taught it to me, and the next year I printed it in our little newsletter *People's Songs* (circulation 2,000).

Sometime during the '50s "We Will Overcome" became "We Shall Overcome." No one is certain who changed "will" to "shall." It could have been me, but it might have been Septima Clarke, the director of education at Highlander. She always preferred "shall," since it opens up the voice and sings better.

Zilphia died in 1956. In August '57 Myles wrote me: "We're having a 25th anniversary of our school in August. Would you come down and help lead some singing?"

About 75 people were in the main room at Highlander, an old farmhouse. Present were two young black preachers who had just led a successful bus boycott in Montgomery, Alabama, the Reverend Martin

Luther King and the Reverend Ralph Abernathy. Anne Braden drove King up to Kentucky the next day, and she remembers him in the back seat saying, "'We Shall Overcome'—that song really sticks with you, doesn't it?"

But the person who really got the civil rights movement singing it was Guy Carawan. His parents were from North Carolina, but he was raised in California, where he and his friend Frank Hamilton heard the song from Zilphia when she was in Los Angeles on a fundraising tour. Frank had been learning gospel music at a local black church where they used $\frac{12}{8}$ time for some slow songs—that is, each of the four beats was divided into three short beats. This is an important rhythmic change.

Guy started working at Highlander full-time as music director in 1959. In 1960 he organized a weekend workshop, "Singing in the Movement," for 70 young people from all over the South. The hit song of the weekend was "We Shall Overcome."

Six weeks later Guy was in Raleigh, North Carolina, for the founding convention of the Student Nonviolent Coordinating Committee or SNCC (pronounced "snick"). Somebody hollered, "Guy! Teach us 'We Shall Overcome'." They started the tradition of everyone crossing arms in front of them and grasping the hands of the persons at right and left, swaying slowly from side to side, shoulders touching, while singing.

A month later the song was all across the South. In '63 I recorded it at a Carnegie Hall concert. Within a few years it was known worldwide. In 1994, in a small village near Calcutta, India, a man and his daughter sang it to me in Bengali.

My manager and publisher, Harold Leventhal said, "Pete, if you don't copyright this song, some Hollywood character will. He'll put new lyrics to it like, 'Baby, let's you and me overcome tonight'." So Guy, Frank and I allowed our names to be used, but we set up the "We Shall Overcome Fund," chaired by Dr. Bernice Johnson Reagon.[2] All royalties from any recording of the song go to this nonprofit fund, which distributes the funds "for black music in the South."

And here we are still making up new verses to it. After the 9/11 attacks people reached out to each other's hands and sang it.

Incidentally, not everyone has been enthusiastic about the song. Lillian Hellman[3] once scornfully remarked to me, "Overcome *someday*? *Someday*?" But Bernice Reagon, when I told her this, replied, "If we said 'next week,' what would we sing the week after next?"

Toshi and I were on the Selma to Montgomery march in '65, and by then some had found a new way to add to the song. Right after it was

2. Reagon (b. 1942) is a singer, professor and activist, and founder of the all-female, all–African American a cappella group, Sweet Honey in the Rock. In addition to her career as an activist musician, she has worked on many documentaries and radio series chronicling the history of African American life and protest music.
3. Hellman (1905–1984) was a playwright and author, who was blacklisted in the 1950s due to her many associations with left-wing activists and artists.

sung, someone would shout "What do we want?" and everyone within earshot would shout "FREEDOM!"—"When do we want it?"— "NOW!" It was a good answer to Lillian Hellman's criticism.

"Dispatch from Meridian," 1964

Letter to Seeger's mother and father, dated
August 5, 1964; found in Seeger files[4]

Dear mother and father,

I thought that for the moment I would take up the idea I tried to follow overseas, of sending carbons to you, to let you know how our travels were going. Just now, for a few days I am down here seeing if I can help in some small way these very wonderful people here to bring more democracy to their state. The family is all in New York. Toshi wanted to come, but didn't want to worry Takashi,[5] who was worried about us both coming.

Everything has been going smoothly. The only discordant note was a man in the Jackson airport, who overhead me talking with a *Life* reporter on the plane. In the airport he accosted me with blood in his eye. "Are you coming down here to sing for the ni__ers?"

"I've been asked down here by some friends to sing," says I, trying to be at my most gracious. "I hope that anyone who wants to hear me can come, either Negro or white."

"Well you just better watch your step. If we hadn't been on the plane when I heard you talking, I would have just knocked the s ... t out of you." I tried to mollify him, but he wasn't interested in listening.

The friends who picked me up, Bob Cohen and his wife, are two young Yankees who are spending the summer here. They have organized what they call the Music Caravans, and have written hundreds of musicians such as myself, asking us to spend a few days, or a week or more here. They gives us food and transportation while we are here, but nothing more, and the time is spent in giving a number of short programs for what is known as "Freedom Workshops."

There are dozens of these workshops through the state—perhaps over a hundred. The NAACP, CORE, SNCC, and SCLC have pooled their forces in what is known as COFO (Council of Federated Organizations).[6] They run classes in voter registration requirements, and now

---

4. This letter was subsequently reprinted (although in a different form) in *Sing Out!* magazine, no. 14.5, November 1964.
5. Takashi Ohta, Toshi Ohta Seeger's father.
6. In his postscript, Seeger writes: "NAACP stands for the National Association for the Advancement of Colored People, the 55-year-old, conservative group. CORE stands for Congress of Racial Equality, an 18-year-old, Yankee-led group. SNCC is the Student Non-Violent Coordinating Committee, started by southern Negro college students. SCLC is the Southern Christian Leadership Conference, led by Martin Luther King."

classes are held in history and geography, mathematics, languages, and other subjects. The students are mainly young. Older people are often scared of losing their jobs, or being evicted from their homes, but they get the materials through their children.

The teachers are mainly college students, both white and Negro, mainly from the north or west, who are volunteering their summer vacation time. About 800 are in the state, I'm told. But not all are young. I met a woman of 55 whom Woody and I stayed with 25 years ago when we were singing for the lumberjacks in Minnesota. Her husband then was a labor lawyer. Now she is a widow, and a California schoolteacher.

Most of the schools-classes-workshops (whatever you want to call them) are held in churches. Since a number of the churches have been bombed (a stick of dynamite thrown from a moving car at night) when they can't get a church, they buy or rent some other building. My first concert was held in the backyard of such a building. It, too, had been slightly damaged by a bomb three weeks before, but none of the young people seemed scared. I think, like soldiers in the trenches, they had survived initial nervousness, and learned to live with danger. There are certain routine safety measures always taken, such as always checking in and checking out, especially when any trip is taken.

My program was essentially not too different from what I always give. A few old songs, hinting at the history of our country. A few songs from other countries, hinting at the different types of people in this big world—but also good songs, which will give us a feeling of friendship to them. A few stories or songs for kids, such as "Abiyoyo," the allegory on the power of music. But my audience was happiest when near the end I concentrated on what they call "our" songs, the spirituals and gospel songs with freedom verses, which have swept through the south in the last few years.

And when I started one of these songs did they sing! It was inspiring to me to hear them.

My audience was mostly young—from ten years to 25 years. All Negro, except for a handful of white college students. And the town sheriff stood silently in the back during the whole performance. Just two local white people dared to come. I was told they worked at a local radio station, and were students at a nearby college. They'll take some rough questioning when they get home. I spoke on the telephone with three members of a rather prominent local white family. "We wanted to come, but you understand it's just impossible." He was a businessman who had already lost his office because of inviting some of the college students to dinner.

I also spoke to his wife on the phone. "We just wish you all the best. There's some true Christian people there." And the daughter added a word, "I've heard all your records at school. Would you send me an autograph?" The father said, "If there's communists behind this thing, they sure must be lower echelon communists. They're the most disorganized bunch I ever saw in all my life," and I heard a chuckle on the earphone.

And what am I accomplishing some will ask? Well, I know I'm just one more grain of sand in this world, but I'd rather throw my weight, however small, on the side of what I think is right, than selfishly look after my own fortunes and have to live with a bad conscience. The voters registration campaign is inching forward slowly, and there's no doubt that within a few years Mississippi is going to be a much freer and happier place in general.

No doubt there's some hurting going on now. There was during the American Revolution, too. And G. B. Shaw once said: "I can no more show a play without causing pain than a dentist can do his job without causing some pain. The morals of the country are in a bad way and of course it hurts to touch them."

The right to vote is the crucial thing. Better schools, jobs, and housing will flow from this. And if we believe this is one country, America, then we must be concerned with a part of it which has for so long lagged behind the rest of the country. How long will it take? It will be easier to predict this after the coming elections. If Goldwater[7] is elected, God knows what will happen. If the Negroes who do vote are able to continue without losing their jobs or homes, tens of thousands will follow their example next year.

And perhaps this is one of the more peaceful revolutions of history. Last night I had to announce to my audience that the bodies of the three young civil rights workers had just been found. But no one was shouting for revenge. Rather, one felt simply an intense determination to continue this work of love. Afterwards people came up to me to get the words of a new song I've been singing:

> O healing river
> Send down your water
> Send down your water
> Upon this land
> O healing river
> Send down your water
> And wash the blood
> From off the sand[8]

Much love,
Peter

---

7. Barry Goldwater (1909–1998) was an Arizona Senator who ran against Lyndon Johnson as the Republican Party's nominee for United States President in 1964. Goldwater's politics tended toward conservative libertarianism, leading him to oppose the Civil Rights Act of 1964, which effectively outlawed all forms of racial discrimination, on the grounds that it infringed on states' rights. Goldwater was also a staunch anti-Communist, and highlighted this aspect of his political outlook as a core tenet in his 1964 campaign. Johnson handily defeated Goldwater, who only carried six states, for a total of 52 electoral votes.
8. c. Appleseed Recordings, 2009.

"You Can't Write Down Freedom Songs," 1965

From *Sing Out!* magazine, no. 15.3, July 1965

As three hundred foot-weary but light-souled people stopped for a rest, sitting in the grass along Alabama's Route 80,[9] I tried to write down the melodies of some of the dozens of new songs I had heard. A woman watched me and laughed, "Don't you know you can't write down freedom songs?"—which I know has been said by everyone who ever tried to capture Negro folk music with European music notation. Furthermore, when I asked, "Can you give me the words to 'Oh, Wallace'?" they kept answering, "Man, there are no words, you just make them up."

I finally learned to ask for *some* words, and soon wrote down seven or eight verses and a triumphant chorus. If the song is going well, it can last for five or ten minutes or more, depending on the skill of the soloists in remembering or ad-libbing verses. If it only lasts for three or four verses, that means the spirit isn't moving the singers.

The songleader can repeat and ad-lib verses at will. When I say "songleader," of course I am not speaking about any official person. In the march, anyone who felt like singing could start off a song, and it could continue as long as anyone within earshot wanted to keep it going. My wife and I were fortunate to have a group of teenage girls walking right behind us. They started song after song. Some were the well-known freedom songs and spirituals which have spread throughout the South during the last five years: "Ain't Gonna Let Segregation Turn Me 'Round," "Hold On," "Which Side Are You On," "Woke Up This Morning," and, of course, "We Shall Overcome." Sometimes, they'd start a song learned in high school, such as "America the Beautiful" or the "Theme from 'Exodus'."

Altogether, any folklorist would have found the day a fascinating experience in living folk music. I've read arguments about how folk songs of the past must have been created. For me, there's no argument anymore. I've seen it. One talented person gets an idea, usually borrowing from traditional sources, and starts it off. If it is good enough, others seize upon his creation, add to it, and change it. I am positive that this is how "Blow the Man Down" and "Old Chisholm Trail" were created.

Over a two-day period, I sometimes heard several clearly different versions of the same song. As my father once told me, a transcription of a folk song is like a photograph of a bird in flight. I'm hoping that Guy Carawan, Len Chandler, and other musicians who were on the march, will get more of them written down: "Jump Back, Wallace, Jump Back," "Can't You Hear Them Freedom Bells Tolling," and others. The young people of Selma were inspired to some great songwriting.

---

9. This refers to the third of the Selma-to-Montgomery marches, often seen collectively as a watershed event in the civil rights movement.

"Baccalaureate Address," 1965

First draft of a baccalaureate address, dated
June 6, 1965; found in Seeger files

"Whoever says he loves God but loves not his neighbor is lying. For if he loves not his neighbor who he does see, how can he love not God who he cannot see?"

I'm not sure I agree with the logic of the above quote, but it pertains to what I'm going to try and say during the next few minutes. Walking along Alabama Highway 80 last March 25th, with several hundred very joyous and happy people, my wife and I heard several teenage girls start up an old spiritual which, with a few changes, has become a popular new song in the Freedom Movement:

> I love everybody I love everybody
> I love everybody in my heart
> I love everybody, I love everybody
> I love everybody in my heart

And subsequent verses said,

> You can't make me doubt it, etc.

They may throw in names of friends, or leaders—and believe it or not, we heard them sing

> I love Governor Wallace[10] in my heart...

I'd like to commend this spirit to you, because I believe that in the period of history we are entering, it is going to be very difficult to love a large portion of the human race living here in the USA. What do I think we are headed into? Unless our military interventions in other countries are soon stopped, we are heading into another McCarthy period, or worse, when to speak out for sanity in international relations will cause a person to lose his job, home, or worse.

...Nevertheless, the purpose of my talk today is to try and persuade you that if we love our country, this means loving the people in it, and not deserting them, or running off to more comfortable places in the globe, even though we might be able to do so.

...You and I are not only the children of pioneers and hardworking peasants. Some of our forebears were crusaders of the Middle

---

10. George Wallace (1919–1998) was governor of Alabama, serving four nonconsecutive terms, ranging from 1963 to 1967 to his final term from 1983–1987. Wallace fought aggressively to preserve segregation in Alabama, defying even the passage of federal desegregation laws.

Ages, who conquered Jerusalem, killed every Moslem, man woman and child, and herded all the Jews into their synagogue and burned the building to the ground. We are the children of pilgrims who fell on their knees and then fell on the Indians. We are the children of the witch burners of Salem, and children of the witches. Children of the lynchers and the lynched. Children of Whitman, Thoreau, Jefferson. Children of Lincoln—and children of those who were glad to see him killed.

...If you have faith in the Human Race, you have to have faith in our country. I am myself quite confident that the great grandchildren of Governor Wallace will be going to school with the great-grandchildren of Martin Luther King—living and working together quite normally, arguing about brand new problems we haven't even thought of yet. Just as you and I sit here in this church, though I am quite sure that a few centuries ago some of our great-great-grandparents were at each other's throats. Read about the religious wars of Europe, and you'll know what I mean.

I believe the best thing you can do is make up your mind that you will be living in an unpleasant world for much of your lives. This is not pessimism; it is maturity—the beginning of wisdom. And once you make up your mind to this, you will realize that it involves total awareness and total involvement. The best thing you can do for your country is treat with contempt the fellows who are offering simple solutions.[11]

I myself hope you love this country enough to stick with it through any changes which may occur to her. Lincoln told of meeting a covered wagon going west. The driver asks Lincoln, "I'm looking for a place to settle. What kind of people live around here?" Lincoln asks him what kind of people lived where you were; "O they were a mean lot, selfish and gossipy." "Well, you'll find 'em about the same way around here," says Lincoln, and the man moved on. Another wagon comes down the road, and again the driver asks Lincoln, "I'm looking for a place to settle—what kind of people live around here?" Lincoln again asks him what kind of people lived where he was before. The driver says, "O they were a real nice lot, but there was no land at all for us around there, so I had to move, but otherwise I woulda stayed." Lincoln says, "You'll find about the same kind of people here," and urges the man to settle near Springfield.

If we are in for a struggle, to keep our country from falling into bad ways don't think it need be a joyless struggle. Far from it. As Jesus urged his disciples, "Be of Good Cheer."

---

11. "Harry Golden once wrote some high school students more or less to this effect."—P. S. Golden (1902–1981) was a Jewish-American writer and satirist, who wrote articles opposing (and satirizing) racial segregation.

"A Stone in My Banjo Case," 1972

From *The Incompleat Folksinger,* Simon and Schuster, 1972

These days I carry an egg-sized stone in my banjo case. Here's why. In April 1968, I got a phone call from a white-haired poet friend, John Beecher.[12] He has a job as a consultant of some sort at Duke University in North Carolina, one of the richest and most respectable colleges in the nation.

"Pete, you've got to come down here. I've never seen anything like it on any southern campus. After King's assassination about two hundred white students decided they must do something, not just talk. They went to the million-dollar home of the president, demanded he resign from his white-only country club, that he bargain collectively with the Negro employees' union, and several other things.

"He refused to talk further with them. They refused to leave. After two days he went to the hospital with a breakdown. They moved their vigil to the quadrangle. Their numbers grew to five hundred, to a thousand, to fifteen hundred. I've been reading poems to them. Will you come down and sing for them?"

I hurriedly consulted the family schedule. "How about this Wednesday?" "Fine," said John. A couple days later I found myself facing some two thousand pure and honest young people seated on the grass in the center of their campus. There was an improvised PA system; a bare electric light bulb hung from a small tree.

I sang a few songs. John Beecher read some of his powerful free-verse poems from his book *To Live and Die in Dixie.* A well-dressed older man, president of the union of Negro maintenance employees, gave a short speech.

"I wish I could speak to you like Dr. King. But I'm not an educated man. I've been a janitor here for seventeen years. Dr. King had a dream. I can't give a long talk about it as he did. But I have a vision. I have a vision that I'd like to be able to pick up after black boys here, as well as white boys."

I whispered to one of the students, "Why hasn't there been more publicity about this nationally?" He replied, "Oh, the local papers have been full of it, but the wire services have hardly mentioned it. When we called up the TV networks they said they didn't have any cameramen to spare, 'but let us know if there is any violence—we'll send someone down.'"

I felt a deep rage boil in me, as though all the experiences with TV censorship and misrule had suddenly come to a head. When my turn

---

12. Beecher (1904–1980) was a poet and activist who documented Southern American life extensively in poetry and prose. His works addressed the Great Depression, the labor rights movement, and racism in the South before the civil rights era.

came to sing again, I found myself speechifying—probably a dangerous thing for any singer.

"You read today about crime in the streets! I say there's crime in the New York offices of CBS and NBC! Crime! I'd like to make a pledge to you here tonight. I'll have to explain. I've never carried a gun since I got out of the Army twenty-two years ago. I've never thrown a stone at any person, and I don't intend to. I've had stones thrown at me, and it's no fun."

I told them briefly about the Peekskill concert of 1949, then went on. "So I don't intend to throw stones at a person. But I'll make this pledge to you. Before I leave Duke I'm going to take a stone with me, and put it in my banjo case, and if I ever meet a TV man up there who says he won't cover a story like this because there's no violence, something is going to get hurt."

Afterward a student came up and gave me a small stone.

It hasn't been used yet. In the deepest sense, I'd love to say that I hope I never have to use it. I've remembered from childhood the old Chinese maxim, "He who starts to use his fists has demonstrated the failure of his argument." But what are you going to do when some people don't pay any attention to your words? I rather suspect I shall have to make that little rock sound sometime, or confess my cowardice. You have to put up or shut up.

"Black Panther Chant," 1970

From Seeger's regular "Johnny Appleseed, Jr." column, in
Sing Out! magazine, no. 20.1, September/October 1970

Once again I heard it proved: the best protest songs are made up by people in the thick of a struggle. The chant printed here was sung, shouted, and clapped by several hundred young black people and some whites gathered on the lawn opposite the New Haven courthouse where Lonnie McLucas[13] was being tried. At the moment the jury was deadlocked. Every day hundreds appeared to bear witness to their concern, and one day I came along also. I sang a couple songs, and so did a couple other whites. Some young blacks recited poems, with that mixture of satire and intense seriousness that marks the world's greatest songs. There was some speechifying. Then a young, slim, very dark young man with a fierce look, slightly hoarse voice, and the flicker of a grin of victory across his jaw started this chant. Soon everybody was involved. They ignored armed police across the street.

---

13. McLucas was on trial (and eventually convicted) for the murder of another member of the Black Panther Party, Alex Rackley, who was suspected of being a police informant. Rackley's murder touched off a series of trials of Party members, known as the New Haven Black Panther trials. McLucas's trial, the first of these, was marked by large protests around the courthouse where the trials were held.

It was the greatest song of the day. The leader stood relaxed but powerful, with his hands at his side. He was a workingman, not a professional performer. He turned occasionally to face different sections of the crowd standing around him. He kept a steady tempo, although the chant went on for ten or fifteen minutes. At the end, the pitch was perhaps a tone or more higher, and the intensity increased. It ended, as it began, without flourishes.

I print it [in *Sing Out!*] in the hope that some black readers may want to try making up their own version. Obviously it is not for white people to sing. I don't even agree with many of the lines. As I said that day, I was there because I am against a thing called genocide, and I think right now the Black Panthers are in the forefront of the fight against genocide. If America was a free country, they would have their own hour every week on TV, like any other minority group in the country. I'll fight for their right to be heard, even when I disagree with them.

Unfortunately, I never got the name and address of the song leader. I had to leave with the young radio reporter to get a copy of his tape recording so I could transcribe this. When I returned the song leader was gone. I'm told his name was Hemmy. I've put the copyright notice in the name of the BPP in case some jerk ever tries to make a profit on his song.

I can't tell you exactly how the chant starts, because our tape started with a section which was repeated many times, like a refrain. In a certain way the leader was improvising and creating as he went along. Perhaps each day he thought of a new line or two to include. The repetitions didn't bother him. Note that the sections do not follow each other in any regular order. They vary each time. It's an African song form. He sings a line; the crowd repeats it.

> ... *'Cause there ain't enough pigs*
> *In the whole wide world*
> *To stop the Black Panther Party*
> *From serving the people*
> *We love the people*
> *Serve the people*
> *We'll die for the people*
> *We'll live for the people*
> *Power! Power!*
> *Power to the People*
> *Gonna free the twenty-one* [14]
> *Gonna pick up a gun*
> *And we ain't gonna run*

---

14. In April 1970, twenty-one members of the Black Panther Party in New York City were arrested and charged with plotting to assassinate police officers and bomb public buildings. All defendants were acquitted on all charges in 1971.

Gun totin' power
Liberatin' power
Educating power
Liberating power
Poor Black Power
Gun totin' power
Pig killin' power
It's growin' by the hour

By now you get the idea. The song could last for two minutes or twenty minutes, depending on the leader and the crowd. It is fascinating to reflect that here is a style and a tradition being carried on, using the English language instead of a West African language, in spite of a century or two separation from the old country, in spite of slavery and repression. It calls for creativity and participation. May people always keep this power.

"A Freedom Flower Garden," 1970

Draft of a letter to the editor of the *D. C. Gazette,*
dated May 5, 1970; found in Seeger files

Dear Editor,

When I was in your town a couple weeks ago an idea occurred to me which I thought I'd pass on to your readers in case anybody would like to try working on it.

All the monuments in Washington, D. C. are to white people. Big piles of white marble in European patterns. I was thinking why aren't there monuments to some of the nonwhite Americans? The blacks, the Indians, the Mexicans, etc.?

Then I thought again. One more pile of white marble would be just one more European type cultural symbol. What's needed is a new type of cultural symbol. Therefore, I suggest the following could be done.

Lay out a beautiful garden of nations. A Freedom Flower Garden along the banks of the Potomac from Georgetown down. The flowers would be natural wild flowers and healing herbs such as the Indians knew. The walks would be ordinary fieldstone selected and carefully placed by hand, rather than poured concrete or asphalt. Rustic handmade benches of logs or stones could be put along the walks at various points so people could sit and admire the view. And at these turns in the walk there could be *small* plaques with the picture of some of the great nonwhite Americans. And below that, perhaps one or two sentences in direct quotation.

One could include such people as Tecumseh, the Indian who tried to organize the Indians of the mid-west to stop the encroachment upon their land. One could have Sequoya the Cherokee who invented the first Indian written alphabet. One could have Nat Turner and Gabriel Prosser who led slave revolts. And Osceola the Seminole Chief who advised his people to seek safety in the swamps of Florida. One could include Joaquin Murieta, the Robin Hood of California in 1849. Selecting these dozen or two dozen people and the right quotations would be of course very important. If the wrong selection were made we could be in the same lousy situation that most of the school texts books are.

At the end of the little walk I would like to suggest one more little plaque with nothing but the following words on it.

"I need no graven marble pile to mark my passage through this world. Look around you. When this river flows clear, then I will know that my people are free." The statement should be unsigned. And the person reading it need only to look up to see the condition of the Potomac to know whether or not that time has come.

I feel strongly that some sort of monument as this is the only kind which nonwhite Americans should have. A big statue would be just one more thing which is co-opted by the establishment which can then say, "See we are all in this together. We of the Administration are supported by everyone."

Can it be done? Of course. All it requires is a few people to start it and get together in a committee, go down start planting some flowers and herbs, putting up a beautiful handmade wooden bench and get the Park Department to give permission for extending it little by little until perhaps it is a mile long or more.

The very fact that a garden such as this needs to be continually kept up insures that it will be a living monument, not a dead one.

With all best wishes,
Sincerely,
Pete Seeger

7

The Movement Against the War in Vietnam

"A Visit to the Benighted States," 1965

Letter to Peggy Seeger and Ewan MacColl,[1] dated
April 5, 1965; found in Seeger files

Dear Ewan and Peggy,

Harold just yesterday showed us your letter. Frankly, I don't blame
you a bit. Visiting the benighted States must seem like one of the less
important things to do in the world. In my opinion you should be
visiting Asia and Africa, if you have any spare time. Which you don't
have, of course, and your work is cut out for you right where you are.
Or rather, you have cut out your own work for yourself.

But I believe you are wrong in thinking you would have to keep your
mouth shut if you came here. Harold and Toshi and I agreed it would
be better to come, and speak out, and if necessary be told to leave by
the US government, rather than not speak out. There are hot battles
shaping up on the whole Vietnam situation. It probably will come
to a head before October, anyway. But the problem is much broader
than Vietnam, as you know. The interesting thing is that there is no
enthusiasm for the war, in the country, except for the far right, and the
generals. I bet even a lot who voted for Goldwater are not enthusiastic
about getting into a hot war. The opposition is building up—slowly,

---

1. Peggy Seeger (b. 1935) is Pete's younger half-sister and an accomplished folk singer
in her own right. MacColl (1915–1989) was already a well-known folk singer in his
native Britain, having recorded many British folksongs with the aid of folk song collectors, when their relationship began, around 1956. Together, Seeger and MacColl
became luminaries of the British folk scene, founding The Critics Group, an important
center of the British folk music revival, and producing many politically minded songs.

to be sure. Everyone is feeling their way, thinking of their job, their home, their business, etc.

Your presence here, singing out for peace, would be a real help. You know how the terrible feeling of isolation is what stops so many from standing up for their opinions. And your bringing word of things going on would be a real boost. Too bad you couldn't be at the Newport Festival.[2] The Committee wanted to invite you, but gave up the idea when I told them of your projected October tour. Alan [Lomax] and I have been talking, trying to see how Newport can help raise people's consciousness of the rest of the world, in the way it did the last two years with southern freedom songs. I am still dissatisfied with what I have been able to do in my own concerts.

Hoping you may change your mind about October,
As ever,
Pete

"America Needs Brave People," 1967

Letter to Nick Seeger,[3] Pete's nephew, dated
June 9, 1967; found in Seeger files

Dear Nicky,

I had looked forward to seeing you this month and I am sorry to hear that you won't be coming up. But I have been told that you want to join the Army or Navy and do your part to help your country.

Now, you can tear up this letter if you want and not bother answering. I am not your father nor your mother nor am I your age. But because I like you, I write you. America needs brave people in this year of 1967 and I am glad you want to help your country, but I urge that you consider best how to do it.

Seegers have fought bravely in the American Revolution and on the northern side of the American Civil War. They also fought bravely in the engagements which historians now must honestly characterize as imperialist aggressions, such as the war with Mexico in 1846 and the takeover of the Philippines in 1898. Yes! Read what Mark Twain said about the latter and why did Abraham Lincoln as a freshman congress-

---

2. The Newport Folk Festival is an annual music festival that takes place in Newport, Rhode Island. The festival was begun in 1959 by George Wein, who had already successfully established the Newport Jazz Festival. Toshi was an important organizer of the festival, and Pete sat on the first festival board. Many future stars of the 1960s folk revival received initial exposure at the Newport Folk Festival, most prominently Bob Dylan and Joan Baez.
3. Nick Seeger (b. 1950) is the son of Charles Seeger III, Pete's eldest brother. He spent much of his childhood in the Netherlands before moving back to the United States with his family in 1966.

man speak out bravely against the war with Mexico, even though it might have cost him his political career.

I am not saying that I know all the answers. I have made a lot of mistakes in the past and probably will make more mistakes in the future. But as Carl Sandburg says, there is an 11th Commandment, "Thou shalt not commit nincompoopery," and it is up to us to find out which side the nincompoops are.

Granted it is pretty hard to tell. Our Uncle Alan volunteered to help France repel the German invaders in 1914, fairly certain that he would not come through the struggle alive. His older brother Charles, your grandfather, felt that the problem of wars had to have an overall solution and that working people in all countries should refuse to support imperialist wars. This took more than a little bravery too. He knew that it would cost him a comfortable career as the head of the music department at the University of California. But he stuck by his guns and never regretted it.

In the war to beat Hitler, I joined up willingly, in spite of having for years sympathized with my father's position more than my uncle's. My older brother, John, decided to become a CO.[4] Looking back on it, I still think that force and violence was the only way to stop fascism at that time. But I know now that it took more courage for him than for me. All I did was obey orders for three and a half years.

And in my opinion the greatest people in 1967 America are those who are fighting hard to prevent America from following the course of Germany. You once asked me in Holland, "How could the German people have gone along with the Nazis?" And I answered that they were simply trying to do their duty to their country. A lot of the Germans who invaded Holland were no worse or no better than many of the American soldiers who are today invading Vietnam. And don't give me that business that we have got to fight the Communist menace. That is what Hitler said he was trying to do, and he fooled a lot of people. The question is not only what, but how, do we fight.

Well Nicky, this is a decision you have to make yourself. Not me, nor your parents, nor your girl friends nor boy friends can make the decision for you. The funny thing is, I think you can learn a hell of a lot from being in the service. You learn discipline; you learn how to get along with people from many different places and different races and walks of life. If I had my way I would see two years citizenship service for every boy and girl on the globe. Compulsory for all— rich and poor, student or nonstudent, stupid or bright, healthy or sick. I would give eight months to your country, eight months to your own city or local region, and eight months to the United Nations, to do whatever needs

---

4. A conscientious objector, who refuses military duty on the basis of one's moral and/ or religious beliefs.

to be done. Whether it is walking a beat to see that somebody doesn't break the peace or plant trees or build bridges or patrol the coasts to prevent smugglers, or doing any kind of dangerous work. The day when human beings are afraid to do dangerous things will be a sad day for mankind. You might consider what Chaka the Zulu king said when the Englishman first showed him European rifles. "I would be ashamed to use one of those thundersticks. You can kill a man from a distance. That is a cowardly thing to do. When one of my warriors kills an enemy with his short sword, I know that he has been close enough for that enemy to kill him and I know that he is a brave man."

> Yours for people brave enough to fight for the survival of the human
> race. Believe me, with love and affection,
> Your Uncle Pete

"A Peace March in Washington," 1969

Dated November 1969; found in Seeger files

The huge peace rally held in Washington, November 15th, was reported by newspapers around the world,[5] but it was not so generally reported that the afternoon was as much a musical occasion as anything else. A five or ten minute speech would be followed by five or ten minutes of music, alternating throughout the long afternoon.

The program was planned by young people who have had the opportunity during the past few years to see how music could be more than a frivolous distraction, and could serve to express the united determination of a large group of people to affect some changes in the world. Peter Yarrow, of the well-known trio, Peter, Paul and Mary, was one of the principal persons planning the choice of singers and songs.

Besides this trio, a number of other well-known performers attended. Arlo Guthrie, of "Alice's Restaurant" fame, sang two songs written by his father, Woody Guthrie.[6]

> Why do your warships sail on my ocean
> Why do your bombs drop down from my sky
> Why do you burn my towns and my cities
> I've got to know, yes I've got to know why.

And in addition to the above, [he sang] "This Land is Your Land, This Land is My Land," with some of the verses which Woody wrote

---

5. The event Seeger refers to was a protest march organized by the National Mobilization Committee to End the War in Vietnam, as part of a larger Moratorium to End the War in Vietnam, a nationwide event on November 15, 1969. The event in Washington, D.C., was attended by over 500,000 protesters.
6. Both songs c. The Richmond Organization, 1963.

but which have not until now been so widely printed in the school songbooks.

> *As I was rambling that dusty highway*
> *I saw a sign that said private property*
> *But on the other side it didn't say nothing*
> *That side was made for you and me.*[7]

Tom Paxton, another young guitar picker and songwriter, sang two quiet but intense songs. Richie Havens, a young black musician, appeared with several friends to give him instrumental support. One played a tall conga drum and Richie got the huge crowd to chant a response, "Freedom," while he sang and chanted in the African style. Leonard Bernstein, the famous director of the New York Philharmonic Orchestra, came and, of all things, sat down with a string quartet which the huge audience listened to politely, and I think were glad to see such an unusual form of music on such an occasion.

Also significant was for the first time a leading star of the country and western field, Earl Scruggs, appearing. It was extraordinary to hear America's best banjo picker send those crackling, sparkling notes across the huge audience standing at the base of the Washington Monument. He played first his traditional "Foggy Mountain Breakdown" with no words, and then his sons sang the well-known song by Bob Dylan, "I Ain't Gonna Work on Maggie's Farm No More," an antiestablishment song.

The writer of this article, together with a friend, Brother Fred Kirkpatrick, a big black singer and songwriter from Louisiana, got the whole crowd joining in on the chorus of a song which we have been singing together during the months of July and August when we were accompanying the sailboat, *Clearwater,* on an antipollution campaign along the Hudson River.[8] The problems of the world are increasingly interrelated and this song helped to unify the huge audience by giving them a short refrain to sing following every line of the song.

> *If you love your Uncle Sam*
> *Support our boys in Vietnam*
> > *(Bring them Home, Bring them Home)*
>
> *It will make our generals sad I know*
> *They want to tangle with the foe*
> > *(Bring them Home, Bring them Home)*

---

7. In 2012, Seeger remembered these lines a bit differently: "Was a great big sign there/ That tried to stop me/ And on that side it/ Said private property/ But on the other side/ It didn't say nothing/ That side was made/ For you and me."
8. For more on the Clearwater and Seeger's environmental activism, see chapter 8.

But here is their big fallacy
They don't have the right weaponry
        (Bring them Home, Bring them Home)

The world's got hunger and ignorance
You can't beat that with bombs and guns
        (Bring them Home, Bring them Home)

So if your love your Uncle Sam
Support our boys in Vietnam
        (Bring them Home, Bring them Home)

I may be right, I may be wrong
But I got a right to sing this song
        (Bring them Home, Bring them Home)

Show these generals their fallacy
They don't have the right weaponry
        (Bring them Home, Bring them Home)

The world needs housing, food and schools
And learning a few universal rules
        (Bring them Home, Bring them Home)

So if you love your Uncle Sam
Support our boys in Vietnam
BRING 'EM HOME, BRING 'EM HOME![9]

After the song was over I glanced questioningly at the chairman to see if there was time for another song. I got the nod to go ahead, so Kirkpatrick and I started a short little phrase which has been sung by a number of young people at both the October and November moratoriums. By itself it seems a very inadequate little song, with none of the militance which is going to have to come if the war makers in the Pentagon are going to be stopped. Nevertheless, this one song provided one of the most extraordinary experiences I've ever participated in. I told the audience how the day before I had walked from Arlington Cemetery to the Capitol with the name of a dead soldier on my chest. And I didn't feel like singing anything satirical or even anything loud and fast. It was too somber an occasion. [I started] humming over and over a little phrase which was on one of the records by the Beatles. I believe John Lennon composed it, but I'm not sure.[10] I told the audi-

9. c. The Bicycle Music Company.
10. John Lennon did compose the song during his famous bed-in with wife Yoko Ono to protest the Vietnam War. It was not recorded by the Beatles but as a solo single by Lennon and the Plastic Ono Band in 1969 (and appears on a number of Lennon and Lennon/Ono albums after that).

ence that if any of them knew it they might like to hum it along with me a few times. "All we are saying, is give peace a chance."[11]

Brother Kirk and I started it not knowing for sure how it would be received. It certainly was not as militant a song as some of the audience would have liked. However, after four or five repetitions, people were singing it with us, and then they were standing instead of sitting, and then they were raising their arms high, holding up the "V" sign. And then they were swaying from left to right, back and forth in a slow unison.

The well-known band leader, Mitch Miller[12] leaped on the stage to assist us in keeping everybody in good rhythm as he moved his body also from right to left. Peter, Paul and Mary joined us at the microphone. We must have sung that one little phrase over and over for eight or ten minutes. I would shout into the microphone, "Are you listening Nixon?" and "Are you listening Agnew?" And then I'd say, "Sing it for ____" and give the name of some friend or person who was with us in spirit that afternoon. The sight was tremendous, to see hundreds of thousands of people swaying slowly from right to left. The flags, the banners, the signs all swayed in unison. It was an astonishing piece of choreography.

... There will be many other analyses of the significance of this demonstration made by people who are much better qualified than myself. I'll simply point out that 90 percent of the people present were high school and college age. Their parents may have been part of Nixon's silent majority, but the young people decided to come anyway. Most of them were rather serious and hopeful of avoiding any violence and wary of joining any of the organizations. Also in Washington were organizations hopeful of persuading the larger group to more organized action. There were militant revolutionists of several brands. There were religious pacifists and nonviolent activists. There were also established liberals. And all of these three groups had strong, almost violent disagreements as to tactics in the present crisis.

But they did agree to all be present on the same field at the same time and listen to each other. Meanwhile, in the center, between them all was this huge group of young people, many of whom attended the Woodstock Aquarian Rock Festival in August. The previous night, at a smaller gathering of perhaps two thousand people at one of the local universities, I heard an argument on the stage. A young woman, dressed in blue jeans and sandals said, "We are the Woodstock generation. We believe in love and copulation, in peace and pot and we like rock music. We don't know for sure what we are accomplishing here, but we know that either we are all going to make it together or none of us will make it."

---

11. c. Sony/ATV Music Publishing LLC.
12. Miller (1911–2010) was a musician and conductor who also worked as a record producer for major record labels beginning in the late 1940s. In the early 1960s, he hosted a popular television show, *Sing Along With Mitch*.

A young black militant spoke much more harshly. "You people are gonna have to wake up. There is going to be a revolution. The shit's gonna hit the fan and you're gonna get it. Some have already got it. They don't like you. They don't like your long hair. While you're singing and talking love, they're out there killing. You'd better wake up."

A young white youth with a tremendous mop of black hair, spoke very quietly, very seriously, "I can't speak for anybody but myself. I think I know how my brother feels. If I was black, I might talk the same way, but I know that right now I want to see if we can do it peacefully."

The next year the United States of America is going to be full of arguments such as this, and there will be arguments between the older generation and the younger generation in every household of America, and music will be taking part in the arguments.

To be honest, I must state that in my opinion there were some glaring omissions on that open air stage in Washington. No member of the Black Panthers had been invited to speak. And some singers who have been giving 100 percent of their time to the peace movement were not invited to sing, simply because they were not famous stars. Brother Fred Kirkpatrick would not have been allowed on the stage had I not personally invited him up there with me. And Barbara Dane, who has been singing in the antiwar G.I. coffeehouses around the nation, was not invited. Until the U.S. peace movement looks more squarely at our problems with the star system, with racism, with male supremacy, we are begging for trouble. I would also like to see more young people, ages 10 to 14, involved in leadership as well as participating. Peace is for everybody. Everybody. Only then can the American people start digging themselves out from the morass of shame in which we are mired. Nuremberg[13] and Song My[14] are two names to be remembered.

"Obey the Best Law," c. 1969

Draft[15] of a letter to the Internal Revenue Service; found in Seeger files

Gentlemen,

I believe in law and order. I believe that when one has a bad law, one should not break it but should work actively to change it for a good

---

13. After World War II, the city of Nuremberg was chosen as the location of military tribunals which prosecuted the Nazi leadership for war crimes, known as the Nuremberg Trials.

14. This event is better known as the My Lai massacre. In 1968, a United States Army battalion massacred somewhere between 340 and 500 unarmed civilians (the exact death toll is disputed) in the village of Song My. When the incident became known to the American public a year later, it outraged many Americans and increased the momentum of the antiwar movement.

15. Seeger apparently never sent this letter; in 2010, he told us that he decided not to withhold his taxes on legal advice. See the following entry: "Action Is Needed."

law. However I believe also that if two laws disagree sharply with each other, it is the citizen's duty to obey the best law, even though the worst law seems temporarily the most expedient to observe.

For this reason I am not sending you a percentage of my income tax because this percentage will go to support an illegal intervention in the affairs of Asia.

One: The United States Constitution says that only Congress can declare war. We have now the situation where the executive branch of the government, with the support of one section of industry which profits from it, carries on an undeclared war.

Two: The activities of the United States government clearly have disobeyed the Geneva agreements of 1954, which, although the United States did not sign, we explicitly said we would observe.

Three: The activities of United States military leaders in Vietnam clearly violate international law which we helped make at the Nuremberg Trial of 1947. We are using chemical warfare in mass assault on women and children and other civilians.

Some will say, "The communists started this war. They can stop it any time they want it." This is absolutely untrue. We started it by supporting a dictator named Diem[16] who threw people in jail without trial and would not allow elections. I could go on to say that many of our activities have fundamentally violated God's Law as promulgated in the Bible. But I will close simply saying this:

I fought for my country in World War II. I did not fight against fascism then in order to have militarists in my country set up Asian nation governments in Washington. If my taxes must go to Caesar, let the records show that Caesar seized them against my will. I can be a good German no longer. Today we face a crisis of law and order in the United States. The 1954 Supreme Court decision on school integration is still only 3 percent obeyed in our southern states. Ku Klux Klan killings go unpunished. There is still discrimination in jobs and housing and all of us know there are laws against it and all of us know that these laws are not being obeyed. It is time that we, who love law and order, decide to do something about it.

Sincerely,
Peter Seeger

P. S. A check for the percentage of income tax withheld has been placed in a bank. When the Vietnam War is over, I will forward it to you.

---

16. Ngo Dinh Diem (1901–1963) was the first president of South Vietnam after the 1954 Geneva Conference, where, among other items, it was decided that France would withdraw from Indochina, leaving North and South Vietnam to each establish its own system of governance. With the backing of the United States government, which approved of his anti-Communist stance, Diem rose quickly to power in South Vietnam. He was elected president in 1955 in a dubious election in which he won over 98 percent of the vote. In 1963, Diem's government was overthrown and Diem assassinated in a generals' coup.

"Action Is Needed," 1970

Draft of speech; found in Seeger files

I love this land and the many kinds of people who live here. If I did not love America, I would not stand here today. If I hated America, I would say STAY IN VIETNAM, BURN AND KILL, till all the world is so disgusted that it unites to destroy the government and army of this country, the way the world once united to destroy the power of Adolph Hitler.

Now, the world has not done this yet to the USA. Why? Haven't we given them provocation? Haven't we spent billions to put our soldiers in bases around the world—4,000 bases! Don't we waste and pollute while the world starves? Why have they not united against the U.S.A. yet?

Partly because you and I are here today. The world still has hope. They think, "Maybe, *maybe* the American people will remember the traditions of Lincoln and of Frederick Douglass, and will change their government and put it on a peaceful path."

But here is the treacherous thing. Our Pentagon war makers also know this. They *let* us go on and talk, while they go on and bomb. For over 20 years this has gone on. The USA has spent since 1950 over 1,000 billions of our dollars on war. This is the crime of the century! Talk about crime in the streets—it's crime in the suites!

Through our government, you and I pay one dollar a day for crime and violence on the most huge scale. Planned and paid for: murder, rape, burning. Yes. All the while people have been starving and rats infest our slums, our government for two years has piously said, "We don't have money enough to take care of housing, education, health, food, pollution. We are busy fighting communism."

LIARS. What are they? LIARS. While you and I talk and pray for peace, U.S. war makers have been busy making profit and power. Liars. Criminals. Murderers.

And inasmuch as I have gone along with them and not protested out loud, I am also—I, Pete Seeger—also. Liar. Criminal. Murderer. I, who paid my taxes and did not go to jail. I would like to be a part of the solution, but am still part of the problem.

Friends, we only have a little more time. The excrement is going to hit the propeller blades. If we with words cannot stop the slaughter, then others will do it for us—and to us.

So action is needed. Young men: don't go. Wives, mothers, girl friends: don't let them go. Old folk: don't pay taxes. Everyone: speak out loud, no matter where.

We don't have another 2,000 years to act on the message of peace and goodwill. We don't have another 20 years. Or even another two years 'til 1972.

YOU AND I MUST BE HEARD. ALL OF US BE HEARD. THE PEACE-LOVING AMERICAN PEOPLE, ALL COLORS AND KINDS, MUST BE HEARD.

8

The Environmental Movement and the Ship Clearwater

"I Became an Eco-Nik," 1993

From *Where Have All the Flowers Gone,* Sing Out Publications, 1993

In the "Frightened '50s" I sang a variety of songs out of American history, going from college to college, summer camp to summer camp. I relayed songs of Woody and Leadbelly to a batch of younger folks. It was probably the most important job of music I'll ever do. I could have kicked the bucket in the early '60s—my job was mostly done. A lot of talented new songwriters came along to pick up where Woody and Leadbelly left off.

In 1962, Rachel Carson's book *Silent Spring*[1] made a turning point in my life. As a kid I'd been a nature nut. Age 15 or 16, I put all that behind me, figuring the main job to do was to help the meek inherit the earth, assuming that when they did, the foolishness of the private profit system would be put to an end. But in the early '60s I realized that the world was being turned into a poisonous garbage dump. By the time the meek inherited it, it might not be worth inheriting. I became an eco-nik; started reading books by Barry Commoner[2] and Paul Ehrlich.[3]

---

1. *Silent Spring,* by Rachel Carson (1907–1964), was published in 1962, a very early contribution to what would become the environmental movement. Carson's main claim was that pesticides were harmful and possibly lethal to plants and animals, including humans. *Silent Spring* helped raise awareness about the dangers of pesticides, especially DDT, and played a part in prompting more government oversight of pesticide use.
2. Commoner (b. 1917) is a biologist and environmentalist who has written a number of books strongly advocating for a radical restructuring of the American economy based on the principle of environmental sustainability: that all products that could potentially become pollutants should be replaced with natural, biodegradable products.
3. Erlich (b. 1932) is a biologist specializing in population growth. In his 1968 book

About this time I also fell in love with sailing. I'd started earning money and got a little plastic bathtub of a boat. Such poetry! The wind can be from the north, but depending how you slant your sails, you can go east or west. (Don't let anyone tell you, "I had to do it." The same pressures will make one person do the right thing, another a stupid thing.)

Also, 500 years ago African sailors showed European sailors that if you used triangular sails instead of square sails, you could actually use the power of a north wind to sail towards the north, first northeast, then northwest. You can zigzag into the very teeth of the gale that's trying to force you back. That's good politics, too. Martin Luther King used the forces against him to zigzag ahead.

But sailing on the Hudson, I saw lumps of toilet waste floating past me. The ironies of "private affluence and public squalor"[4] got to me.

"Prodigal Brothers and Sisters," 1975

Letter to Norman Grib, chemical engineer, dated
April 23, 1975; found in Seeger files

Dear Norman Grib,

I'm sorry for the long delay in writing you. Every environmental publication has listed ways in which Americans can save energy. Every commission, every estimate finds out that if we really want to, we can save some 15 percent to 50 percent of our energy. That is, we're wasting it. Today. This minute as I write you.

What's needed is to mobilize the people in a way the government has yet to even think of doing. We can do it by taxing the wasteful use of energy, by giving government subsidy to the ways of saving energy, such as mass transit. We can reverse the utility rates according to the lifeline system whereby working people will get low rates but those who want to have electric toothbrushes and a television set in every room are going to pay through the nose. We'll cut down on wasteful packaging and wasteful advertising. We'll institute recycling in a hundred little ways, as we did back in World War II, and we can do it again, even better.

And when some people complain or even holler bloody murder, we'll get on TV and explain exactly how the situation is. Yes, of course we've got plenty of energy right now. Just as the prodigal son (a week before he went broke) could still reach in that bucket and get more gold and silver coins in his hand. Only we're more like the prodigal brothers and

---

The Population Bomb, Erlich argues that the human population has already exceeded the natural resources available to it, and that, in order to survive, the human race must make a commitment to zero or negative population growth.
4. "Thanks, J. K. Galbraith." —P. S.

sisters and we're each saying, "Gee, the level in the barrel is getting low, I better grab all the coins faster, because if I don't, they will."

And we'll reexamine exactly what we mean by patriotism. A few years ago, there were some people ready to shoot the young men who were ready to burn a draft card or a flag, to express their outrage at governmental policy. Now we'll see who really loves this country. There's many a person waving the flag but they don't really love that flag. They just love their money.

I would take the American flag into one of these polluting factories. And I'd take a bucket of what comes out of their pipes and I'd dunk the flag in that bucket. And at first the guy would say, "Oh, how shocking." Then I would tell him, "You think it's terrible that I dunked the American flag in this stinking liquid. But you don't seem to mind that you put this stinking liquid out into America. This flag is a piece of cloth, it's a symbol. I can wash it. How are you going to wash America?"

And I would say the same thing to the people who want to bulldoze the Rocky Mountains for shale or don't mind how many beaches they cover with oil goo as long as they can get some more petroleum. And when it is possible to produce nuclear power without endangering the lives of future generations, fine let's go ahead with it. Not before then. I don't mind taking a risk myself but what kind of idea is it that we have the right to insist that our children and grandchildren for the next ten centuries also take risks?

If there's a human race three or four hundred years from now, they'll look back to these decades and shake their heads and wonder at the age of the prodigal children and wonder why it took us so long to wake up.

All best wishes,
Pete Seeger

"On Zero Population Growth," 1972

Letter to Sheldon Novick, editor of *Environment* magazine, dated May 6, 1972; found in Seeger files

Dear Sheldon,

Have just read your recent issue quoting arguments between Ehrlich and Commoner. I have learned much from both of these men, admire them both, appreciate this interchange but hope that it won't turn vindictive.

Commoner has convinced me that technology and our private profit politics and society must be radically changed quickly. But I'm still working hard for ZPG [zero population growth], because even if population growth is only 5 percent or 10 percent of the U.S. environmental crisis, it's a big world problem, and one can't expect others to work on it if we don't. The world is the concern of everyone. Lake Baikal[5] is my worry as well as the Siberians. The Pentagon is their worry as well as mine.

Furthermore, achieving ZPG will be a good education for everyone. Everyone can and must cooperate. It will be one of the world's greatest educational drives. Everyone can say, "If I'm limiting myself this way, then everyone else should do something." For the same reason I'm in favor of going back to soap. It teaches us all.

We don't need to fool ourselves that these first steps will solve the crisis of the environment, but we can all take these steps right now. ZPG is not "counterproductive." It is not "regressive." The first countries to achieve it will have won a moral victory—and incidentally I think one of these countries will be China, because the population there is disciplined, world conscious, and solidly behind their government, which is now promoting family planning as never before.

In a few decades I expect to join my ancestors underground. If the laws of multiplication hold, I know that my ancestors of several thousand years ago included millions of people in almost every part of the earth. Likewise, if I have physical descendants (or musical ones), I know that a few thousand years from now these will include people in every corner of the earth, of many colors. I want these descendants of mine to have room to walk on a lonely beach, or climb a wilderness mountain, or yodel and make a noise occasionally for the fun of it. I hope they can enjoy untrammeled nature occasionally, not live like an astronaut, tightly controlled. The less crowded this earth will be, the better for them. I'm in favor of ZPG as soon as it can be achieved by persuasion, not force.

Best wishes,
Pete Seeger

"A Hudson River Sloop," 1993

From *Where Have All the Flowers Gone,* Sing Out Publications, 1993

In '63 an artist friend, Vic Schwarz, told me they used to have sloops on the river with a boom 70 feet long.

"Oh, don't give me that," says I, unbelieving. "There never was a sloop that big, except an America's Cup racer."

"No I've got a book all about them; I'll send it to you," says Vic. Soon after he sends a dog-eared volume, *Sloops of the Hudson,* written in 1908 by two middle-aged gents, William Verplanck and Moses Collyer.

---

5. Baikal is the oldest and deepest lake in the world, located in Siberia, Russia. The lake has long been a battleground between ecologists and industrial concerns that have built manufacturing facilities on the shores of Baikal.

"Before we die we want to put down what we can remember of these sloops, because they were the most beautiful boats we ever knew, and they will never be seen again."

I read it through twice. Wrote a long "poem" about sloops. Finally after a couple years couldn't stand the temptation. Stayed up 'til 2 a.m. typing a seven-page letter to Vic. "Why don't we get a gang of people together and build a life-size replica of a Hudson River sloop? It would probably cost $100,000, but if we got enough people together we could raise it."

Then I forgot about the letter. Four months later I happen to meet Vic on a railroad station platform. "When are we going to get started on that boat?" says he.

"What boat?" says I.

"You wrote me a letter!"

"Oh, that's as foolish as saying let's build a canoe and paddle to Tahiti."

"Well, I've passed your letter up and down the commuter train; we've got a dozen people who don't think it's foolish."

"Hm. Maybe if there are enough nuts, we just might do it."

This isn't the place to go into more detail, except to say that three years later the sloop *Clearwater* was launched. It's owned by a democratic nonprofit organization of several thousand members. Since 1969, it has taken 400,000 school kids out on educational sails, 50 at a time. The Hudson is noticeably cleaner, and *Clearwater* is one of the reasons why.

My violinist mother once said, "The three Bs are Bach, Beethoven and Brahms." I retorted, "For me they are ballads, blues and breakdowns." But now I guess it's boats, banjos and biscuits. Because one of *Clearwater*'s main education devices has been riverside festivals, with lots of good food and music. Along the line, people get some ideas about getting together to clean up a beautiful river.

"To Save the Dying Hudson," 1969

From *Look* magazine, August 1969

On the surface, the whole idea seems too hopeful, too optimistic for 1969 America, for the world-doomful ecological crisis, for the cynical human race. All I can do here is tell you how the idea started, what we plan to do. Come around next year, see whether we've made some progress, or whether we're burned to the waterline, or sunk to the bottom with all hands. At least, it's probably the first time a banjo picker has been chairman of the board.

The basic idea is to take a beautiful old boat and sail it up and down a still-beautiful river, stopping at every town and city. The waterfront is public property; we'll hold a party, free for everybody, and we mean everybody. Young and old. Black and white. Rich and poor. Male and female. Square and hip. Hairy and shaven. Country and city. We can have exhibits, displays, and a PA system for songs. People who won't read pamphlets or listen to speeches may learn things through music they wouldn't learn any other way. Who knows, we may even get on radio, on TV, and get our message to millions.

What's the message? Put simply, we want people to learn to love their river again. On this basis, we've attracted help from the most diverse people, from conservative oldsters to bearded students, housewives, teenagers, and black youth in ghettos. I can only speak for myself from here on, but in all honesty, I must say I think that the messages will go a lot further than that. You see, everything in the world is tied together. You try to clean up a river, and soon you have to work on cleaning up the society. Only the most starry-eyed, head-in-the-clouds optimist could assume that the U.S.A. and the world can continue on their present course for long. I'm thinking of polluted air and oceans, of bulldozed forest land, of the population bomb, of people vs. property, of the violence-military crisis. Perhaps the sewer running past your door is as good a place to start on the clean up-job as any.

Just to learn about a river is to learn a lot about history. Scientists tell us the world is about five billion years old, and our sun has five billion years to shine. Imagine a book of 1,000 pages. The history of ten million years is written on each page: 1969 is at the bottom of the 500th page. The dinosaurs reigned supreme for about 15 pages, ending suddenly on page 494. A couple of inches from the bottom of page 500 comes the history of a hairless mammal that started walking on two feet, the better to throw sticks and stones with the two front paws. In the last half inch of the page, his ability to adapt was challenged and developed by a series of ice ages. (Question: Will there really be more pages?)

In the last ice age, 11,000 years ago, the present channel of the Hudson River was carved out. The ocean level was about 300 feet lower than it is today. What a cataract must have roared through the gap at Storm King [Mountain in New York] when the ice cap melted! In our book, skip ahead a few thousand years. The sons and daughters of Asia found their way to the shores of this river-that-flows-two-ways, now a placid arm of the ocean. By fishing and hunting, all of ten or twenty thousand Algonquians and Iroquois maintained themselves, in spite of sporadic warfare, with high moral and physical health. And their river was crystal clear.

Come along now to 350 years ago (the last 1/100 of an inch in the last line, the 500th page of our history book). The adventurous sons and daughters of Europe nosed their big sailing boats up the broad waters. The early square riggers gave way to the Dutch *sloëp*, which could tack and jibe more handily in the fickle upriver breezes. In the 19th century, the great age of sail, New York state boat builders developed the famed Hudson River sloops. They averaged 60 to 90 feet in length, with masts over a hundred feet tall. They were 20 to 30 feet broad in the beam. Washington Irving wrote, "The Dutch built their sloops on the order of their wives."

Each captain usually owned his boat and ran it as a family business, carrying farm produce to the city and returning with merchandise. In summer calms, they might drift with the tide, making barely 15 miles a day. But along comes a stiff breeze, and sloops could show their wake to the early steamboats. One captain started from the Battery and made Troy, 160 miles north, in 14½ hours. The most dangerous section was the *worragut* ("weather-hole"), the three miles from Storm King to West Point. Here the sloop *Caroline* capsized, drowning 35 of her 50 passengers. Here Benjamin Hunt was straining at a ten-foot tiller when an unexpected gust caught the sail, swung the boom over his head. The main sheet looped about his neck, sending his head spinning out into the water while his body collapsed on deck.

The water was still clear. Ice cut near Kingston tinkled in the glasses of New York restaurants. Sturgeon were common: the packing of this fish was an important industry. They called them "Albany Beef." America exported caviar to Europe in those days. We have a slogan, "Bring back the sturgeon," and some sloop-rich members are building a huge model of one, like a Chinese dragon, out of paper and cloth. When we hold waterfront celebrations this August, we plan a "sturgeon parade," with kids in costume going up one street and down the other, following the sturgeon, letting everyone know there's something going on at the dock.

The idea of building a modern replica of a typical old cargo sloop took shape in the heads of a few Valley residents three years ago. Now, we have Hudson River Sloop Restoration, Inc., a couple of thousand members from all walks of life, from all parts of the river. Most of the money raised has been in dollars and dimes at folk-song concerts and fundraising house parties. We're hiring a full-time captain, licensed by the Coast Guard, so we don't run on the rocks, but several hundred volunteers will take turns as crew members, raising the huge mainsail in the old-fashioned way—with muscle and song.

Instead of charging the public money to visit the sloop, we figure we'll let everyone on board free. Then we'll have a huge barrel with a slot in the top, and perhaps a verse to remind everyone: "No beer maker backs this boat/You and I got to keep it afloat." And instead of having the usual mass-produced food, we hope to get people to bring homemade food to share. The kids are getting ready to decorate the waterfront and give it a festive look. This means painting the litter boxes so ingeniously that people will *want* to throw trash in them. If a man throws a cigarette butt on the ground, he is liable to be tapped on the back by some youngster of eight or nine, who says, "Hey mister, you got a ticket," and shoves into his hand a card that reads: "Fellow citizens, don't be surprised./ You have just received a prize./ You are now entitled to pick up/ One live cigarette butt./ And along the way you may find out/ What this polluted river is all about."

Will it work? Come around next year, we'll tell you. Old habits die slowly. "Mankind used to swing through trees/and drop his litter where he pleased." When the *Clearwater* was launched in May, a few individuals in the crowd of 2,000 started throwing beer cans in the water. Someone jumped upon a snubbing post and hollered, "In view of the purpose for which this boat is built, let's stop throwing trash in the water." Cheers from all who stood nearby. So, five minutes later, when trash had been collected in boxes and taken into the shipbuilding shed, we heard a clatter and clunk and turned around to see the workmen disposing of that same trash in the traditional way, through a trapdoor into the bay. What can you do? You don't give up.

The exhibits that the sloop sets up on the waterfront have an important job to do. They may be historical, artistic, scientific or a combination of all three. Bulletin boards, with felt marking pens hanging every few feet, will have a big sign overhead: "Can you write a poem, draw a picture? What do you think about The Situation?" People should know that a conservative estimate says $40 billion will be needed to clean up America's polluted lakes, rivers and air. Where are we going to get $40 billion? Maybe we'll display some pie charts of the Federal, state and local budgets. Where does the money come from; where does it go? The Pentagon has spent one trillion dollars of our money in the last 20 years. That's $5,000 apiece for every man, woman and child in the U.S.A. Perhaps $200 apiece is not much to spend to bequeath our children clean rivers instead of open sewers.

The musical programs we hold on the waterfront should represent the different tastes and traditions of all the people in the town. Singers such as Don McLean, Brother Fred Kirkpatrick and me will find ourselves MC-ing a local hootenanny. We'll have to say frankly, "Folks, we at this mike are the Establishment on this waterfront. If you have any complaints, bring them here. Here's our rules; see if you agree: This mike is open to any and all, to come up and sing a song. If you hear something you don't like, don't go away mad. Come up and sing your song. We want everybody to be heard from." So during the weekend, the mikes may be used by a teenage rock band or a barbershop quartet or a jazz combo or a fiddle or a bongo drum. If someone wants to bring his piano down, he can give us a concerto. Perhaps there will be clowns or puppets for the kids, or the high school tumbling team. Who knows. All we are sure of now is that it should be a community party on the waterfront. If you who read this find yourself near the Hudson River this month or next, come on and join us—see for yourself.

...At the moment, the members of the sloop project are so enthusiastic they are quite sure that there will be several sloops on the river in a few years. There may be a Poughkeepsie sloop, a Harlem sloop. Similar projects should be possible on other bodies of water. How about a Great Lakes Schooner touring between Erie and Superior? How about some bugeyes sailing on Chesapeake Bay? A fleet of birch-bark canoes might save one small lake. There is magic in water. Once upon a time, our ancestors crawled out of it and decided to live on land. Its sight and sound awaken ancient memories! This summer, when the good sloop *Clearwater* docks along the Hudson, we expect that a number of people will feel the damp air on their faces, hear the lapping of the waves, and turn to their neighbor and say, "Gee, this river is a mess. Ought to get together and do something about it." And now you see our sneaky subversive purpose.

"A Short History of the Clearwater," 1986

Draft of a piece probably intended for the Beacon
Sloop Club *Broadside*; found in Seeger files

In 1966 a few dozen people started with a very nonpolitical idea. We wanted to build a replica of one of the beautiful sailboats that used to carry cargo on the Hudson, back in the 19th century. Some of the committee were wealthy people, some were poor, some were conservatives, some radicals, but all of them did in one way or another love the beautiful Hudson and love the idea of building a beautiful sailboat.

It took three years to raise the money before the boat was designed, built, and launched. Meanwhile, some important decisions were made. It would be a public project. We would raise money from anyone and everyone everywhere, and we postponed the decision on what would happen with the boat once it was built. We raised most of the money with concerts, but some with fundraising letters. We had some professional artists and writers on the committee. The first mailing piece was so superbly done that anybody looking at it could not fail to be impressed. The illustrations were first class. The writing and printing was first class.

In the second year of fundraising, we had our first annual meeting of some 50 "members." At the second annual meeting, held only six months before the boat was launched, the now-120 members voted that the boat should be named *Clearwater*, although some of the more conservative members wanted rather to call it *Heritage*.

When the boat was launched, then the arguments really got fierce. You know how it is. People stick together until they start to win a few victories, and then the honeymoon is over. The Board of Directors meetings were battlegrounds. After 3 or 4 years and numerous compromises on different sides, we started to learn how to run the boat as a permanent institution. We have made many mistakes but have never made the mistake of quitting. I think the beauty of the boat, as well as the beauty of the River, kept drawing people back. They'd say to themselves, "Those bunch of jerks are going to ruin that boat. I've got to stick with it and see that it is taken care of properly." One might say the creative conflict still exists within the Clearwater organization. Some wish the boat would do more to remind people of history. Some wish it would do more as an environmental group to sue polluters. Others wish it would do more with rank-and-file local projects. We cooperate with the establishment at times and at other times find ourselves criticizing or suing the establishment. For the last ten years, one of the most concrete activities of the *Clearwater* has been to take out about 10,000[6] schoolchildren every spring and fall, 50 at a time. The four-hour sail is something the kids will never forget. They help raise the sail, help steer the boat, they help net some fish, look through microscopes at the microscopic plankton in the water. Fifty students are broken up into small groups so that there is almost individual attention, rather than one person trying to speak to all 50 at a time. The programs have proved so successful that *Clearwater* had to turn down 30 school systems this year and is now seriously thinking of how to raise the money to build another boat.

In 1986 the annual budget was close to a million dollars, although the wages we pay our 27 office workers and crewmembers is pitifully small. I wince when I think of all the union songs I've sung and think also of all the low wages paid to the *Clearwater* captain and crew and the typists and other people in the office.

The organization has a dozen or so local "sloop clubs" which meet once a month and plan waterfront festivals when the *Clearwater* visits their town. In addition to several dozen small festivals, the *Clearwater* has a committee of 15 people that meet all year long planning one big festival which lasts for two days in a county park 25 miles north of New York City, attracting about 10,000 people each of the two days. It's called, "The Hudson River Revival," eleven stages going on at once, with boats and environmental exhibits and lots of good food and crafts and various activist organizations with tables and literature. We think of it as a community festival and are trying our best to reach a cross-section of the Hudson Valley population, although we still have a long way to go. As with most environmental organizations, we are stronger among middle-class whites than among minorities.

As one of the 8,000 present Clearwater members, I am an active volunteer and push hard to try and get more news in our newsletter and more different kinds of music at our festivals. At the moment we

6. "Now [in 2011] 20,000." —P. S.

have a predominance of guitar pickers. The Beacon Sloop Club, in the town where I live, is probably the most active of all the sloop clubs. Over the last 14 years, we have evolved an extraordinarily successful way of sticking together. Our monthly meeting has music and food (nothing fancy, lots of pasta) as well as talking. Families come. They bring their neighbors and fellow workers. A pot-luck dinner is spread out, and there is so much food that you can stuff yourself. After an hour or more of eating, we have a short business meeting with the agenda written down in magic marker and the number of minutes for each item clearly displayed so that if somebody starts running over, the crowd reminds the person of this fact, and if somebody actually talks in a shorter time than they were allotted, they get great cheers. After an hour, we may have covered as many as 20 different items, from the *Clearwater* report, the environmental report, the sailing committee report, the festival committee report. Most of the real discussion is done in the subcommittees. After the meeting, we may see a movie or hear a debate, a slide show, or we may just break up and sing for the entire rest of the evening. Some people will stay until midnight or after, just because they love to sing. We can usually count on three or four or more guitars or other instruments, and we'll go around the circle, and different people will lead different songs. An average of 50 or 60 people attend the meetings throughout the winter when they are held in a crowded little building that used to be a diner on the waterfront, but in summer, when we can expand onto the lawn, sometimes we'll have 80 or 100 or more. The meetings are noisy; some people throw up their hands in disgust, saying, "This gang likes to do more singing and eating than anything else."

But over a period of 14 years, the sloop club has accomplished small miracles on the Beacon waterfront. When we first had a festival, in 1969 when the *Clearwater* first came, we proposed that there be a waterfront park put in. But the City Council in effect just laughed at us, "Where's the money coming from?" However, each year more people came down to our festivals and looked around and said, "You know, this could be a beautiful place if it were fixed up." And after 10 years the Citizen's Advisory Council voted to spend the money. Today we have a million dollar Riverfront Park. The sloop club is moving beyond this, and inch by inch fixing up the waterfront so that more boats can use it. We teach sailing to the local kids as well as literally anybody who comes along. The club membership includes some rather conservative people who vote Republican. It includes some radical Christians who don't even believe in voting. We have people of various religions and no religion, devout family types, and ramblers of one sort or another.

What helps us stick together, and what has helped the Clearwater itself to stick together over the years, is having a number of very concrete jobs to do. We may disagree with each other about many things, but we want to help accomplish these jobs. And so we overlook our differences in order to work hard on them. Try and have these jobs, very physical jobs often—picking up litter, building, decorating, teaching, singing, cooking, serving. The Beacon Sloop Club has a Shadfish Festival in May, the Strawberry Festival in June, a Corn Festival in August, a Pumpkin Festival in October, and a community dance in February in the local school gym. There is a continual turnover in membership. On paper, the Beacon Sloop Club has about 200 members, but there are a dozen or two dozen who, I'll admit, do about 60 per cent of the work. But somehow every year we get some good new people at the same time as we inevitably lose a few of the good older people.

I'll add one last word. I may be fooling myself, but I think that music and poetry has been an important part in holding the organization together—by continually reminding us of the world at large and helping keep us from being sectarian and self-satisfied. Environmental groups get tunnel vision, just as scientific or business or any other kind of group. Probably no member of the Clearwater, certainly not me, is really satisfied with the organization as it is, but in spite of our dissatisfactions in one way or another, we are proud that we have been a part of the extraordinary achievement in that the Hudson has started to get itself cleaned up. We are swimming again in the middle reaches and in another five years should be able to swim near New York safely. And when we ever happen to see somewhere on the broad river the huge 100-ton *Clearwater* sailing, our hearts lift up and we think, "That's our boat," even though we may not have been able to set foot on it for several years.

"Decisions, Decisions," 1985

Letter to board members of the Hudson River Sloop Restoration committee, dated May 17, 1985; found in Seeger files[7]

Dear Long-time Friends,

I wrote the enclosed about 12 years ago, thinking that it might make an interesting article for the *Clearwater Navigator*. It was never printed, probably because the editor sensibly didn't want to hurt anybody's feelings, but I've kept it all these years because I thought it was a worthwhile description of the democratic process at work in North America in the 20th century.

Rereading it, I still hate to tear it up; so I find myself Xeroxing it and sending it to all of you to ask you to check off the following:

---

7. All names in this article have been changed to pronouns to reflect Seeger's desire that the participants remain anonymous.

- Please tear this up and see that it is never printed.
- As far as I'm concerned, you can print it. I have indicated in the margins any corrections I have felt necessary.
- I would rather not see it printed now, but I suppose 50 or 100 years from now, when we are all dead and gone, if there is a human race around, it would not harm anyone to print it then.

In any case, thank you not just for reading this, but thanks for having at some point in your life taken the trouble to help this extraordinary *Clearwater* organization grow. With all its mistakes, it is a great achievement, I think.

Sincerely,
Pete Seeger

DECISIONS, DECISIONS:

It was already midnight.

The agenda had covered such matters as chartering new sloop clubs, plans for the December 1st annual meeting, and ideas for a Hudson shore summer school.

[The] hardworking head of S. E. W. E. R. (environmental lab which does water tests for the Peoples Pipe Watch) observes that HRSR [Hudson River Sloop Restoration] does not allocate funds correctly—more money is needed for lawyers. [The lawyer, a] former assistant D. A. in charge prosecuting Hudson polluters, says that what you people don't seem to realize is that battles for the Hudson Valley environment are being lost every day for lack of lawyers to attend hearings, file briefs and push legal processes through. And a good lawyer can cost $350 a day. [He] refers to a recent case to which he contributed 30 hours of his time.

[The] ace carpenter remarks that he doesn't see why lawyers should have to be so different from other people and [one] former mate spent one solid month repairing the *Clearwater*'s rudder and no one pinned any medals on him. ([The carpenter] is happy to be retiring from the board this year. After four years of meetings and arguments, he longs to make carpentry his main contribution to HRSR.)

[The lawyer] flares up, takes it as an insult. Says, you people have a proclivity for writing letters, but it is going to take more that that to win environmental battles. [The] secretary, who deeply admires both men, tries to bring peace, but the four-letter words are flying. A lethargic meeting has suddenly become tense.

[The] treasurer, who has been a faithful and hardworking board member for most of all of HRSR's eight years, finally works out a solution. Yes, he says, Clearwater needs more legal help. No, we don't have money for normal legal fees. [He] proposes a special committee be set up to run some fundraising concerts in the vicinity of the Columbia and NYU law schools expressly to raise $7,500 for a year's salary for some young lawyer just out of law school who wants to help save the Hudson Valley environment, who is willing and can afford to work for such a nominal salary for at least a year or two. This person will try to get a group of more experienced lawyers to contribute advice and help from time to time. [The treasurer's] motion passes. Tempers cool. A few minor matters are discussed. The meeting adjourns. [The treasurer] and I smile at each other. Four years ago at an occasion like this someone would have been jumping up and saying, "You apologize for that remark or I'm resigning right now."

I ask [an attendee from] Newburgh if she has ever attended meetings quite like sloop meetings. A gentle and elegant woman, [she] laughs and says, "Oh, no; these sloop meetings are unique."

I'm attending the meeting, as I do once or twice a year, as an observer, when some project I'm involved in comes up. I commiserate with [the secretary], who admits that at one point he was close to tears. "You see," [I say], "It's like the old military analogy of the spear. A spear needs a sharp, hard point. It needs also a handle. Some people who know how crucial is the sharp point can forget the importance of patiently shaping a long handle for many to grasp. And sometimes amateurs grasping the handle can forget how important it is to have a razor sharp point."

Peter Seeger

"What Can a Sailboat Do?" 1970

Foreword to *Songs and Sketches of the First Clearwater Crew,* North River Press, 1970

What can a song do? What can a sailboat do? Some would say music exists just to soothe or distract people from their troubles. Some say sailboats are just rich men's toys. Wrong, wrong. In the summer of 1969 they helped to start cleaning up a river.

The sloop *Clearwater* has brought together people who normally don't speak to each other: wealthy yachtsmen and kids from the ghetto, shaggy students and crew cut Legionnaires, housewives and scientists, teenagers and golden-agers, church members and atheists, businessmen and anti-businessmen, farmers and housing developers and conservationists, DAR [Daughters of the American Revolution] members and new immigrants.

They all came down to the water's edge to look at one of the world's most beautiful boats, a symphony of curves, especially under sail. In every town was held a sort of community festival, with homemade food, exhibits, and homemade music. The townspeople felt the damp breeze in their faces, heard the lapping of the waves, got a close look at the murky waters and a thoughtful look at the magnificent vistas of one of the world's greatest rivers, now in the process of dying a shameful death.

"We hold these truths to be self-evident: that all men are created equal ..." And another of old Tom's[8] writings: "We have nothing to fear from error as long as reason is free to oppose it."

How do these ideas apply here? This is a songbook. The songs were sung by the first singing crew of the *Clearwater*. It is a sketchbook of one of America's top graphic artists who was for a time a member of that crew. We don't expect everyone to like all the songs. Some of them are mossy old folks songs. Some are scandalously satirical. Some are as controversial as today's headlines. But they all reflect the feeling of the singer that all life is interrelated—the joys and sorrows, the economic, social, and environmental crisis now pressing upon mankind. I think I can say for the other singers and songwriters, that we strongly believe the Hudson *can* be cleaned up, that the human race *can* survive, *if* we get together. All of us. And that means we must each be allowed a few seconds to speak our mind. None of this: "All right, let's everybody get together now, get together and shut up and listen." That's gone on too long. We're going to get together and give everybody, but everybody, a chance to be heard. Kids, too. Eleven-year-old Evan Gallagher of the town of Cold Spring, population 2,500, sent us a poem.

> America the Beautiful
> Where the rivers are garbage cans.
> Where the skies are ash trays.
> Where every man is free to love the beautiful.
> Swimming Garbage. Flying Smoke.
> We can do better than that.

"The Future of the Club," 1995

Letter to Allan Zollner of the Beacon Sloop Club, dated December 1995; found in Seeger files.

Dear Allan,

I'm so grateful that you agreed to be president of the BSC [Beacon Sloop Club]. I write this letter to let you know of my support and how I think I can best help.

I'll be leaving the sloop club one of these years, and Toshi too, one of these years. I'm really worried about the future of the club. Why?

1) Although 50 to 90 or more show up for the potlucks, only 2 or 3 show up for the work parties, and a handful of super volunteers do

---

8. Thomas Jefferson writing in, respectively, the Declaration of Independence and, paraphrased by Seeger, in his first Inaugural Address.

most of the work. Although I declined to be a member-at-large of the executive board, I will be there at 7:30 P.M. the 2nd of January, Tuesday, hoping that the new membership blank or something, can get *every* club member doing *something*.

2) We were once a club of 20 and 30 year-olds, with a gang of enthusiastic teenagers. Now we're a club of 40 and 50 year-olds and older—and we've failed several times to get young folks of various ages involved. We once had many Beaconites—now only a handful. *Several* outreach committees are needed, not just one.

Here's a couple ideas I throw out for your consideration:

At the *beginning* of the meeting, welcome people attending for the first time and someone give each not only a copy of *Broadside*, and a membership blank, but a one-pager (see enclosed) with a pic, a map and a 150-word history of the club.

Then, I think 15 or 20 *seconds* could be taken to tell folks where *Clearwater* is, and when the next transit sail will be, in case some members want to go on it.

Then can come the treasurer's report and the rest of the agenda.

Hey, how about specifically thanking exceptional volunteers right after the treasurer's report? This month it's Pat Freeman and Aaron Haven working in the cold wind, trying to finish the multrum.[9] And maybe "All the cooks who made all the good food we just ate." Or, "the clean-up crew which got the clubhouse ready." Or, "the clean-up gang which will put everything away *after* the meeting." In other words, let's not wait till the end of the meeting to thank volunteers.

Allan, I'll keep tending "The Ebenezer" (our wheelchair accessible toilet) until the multrum is finished. I and Toshi will keep bringing food for the potluck. But I am *quitting* being every month the "someone who puts things away," neatens up, outside and inside. I believe this was my mistake. People on the executive board just assumed, "oh, somebody always does it."

Oh—and until the club can afford its own PA system, I'll continue bringing my little one down—I'm buying an extra speaker this month, which can be put up near the food table, then maybe the folks there would be quieter. And I'll have an extra mike on a long cord, to be passed around.

Well, happy holidays, and long life to you and Rachel. Be firm with all us undisciplined club members. Keep a sense of humor. We got some *great* people. But we need to be told what to do sometimes.

Best,
Pete

---

9. The *clivus multrum* is a toilet, designed in Sweden in the late 1930s, that composts human waste. The toilets were not commercially available until the 1970s when Abby Rockefeller read about the toilets and created a company to facilitate their sale in the United States.

9

Reflections on a Life in Movements

"I Abhor Force and Violence," 1956

Letter to Max and Beatrice Krone,[1] dated
November 19, 1956; found in Seeger files

Dear Max and Beatrice Krone,

I am sorry for this long delay is answering your letter. I have been on a series of one-night-stands for over two weeks, and this was my first opportunity.

First let me thank you for the frankness of your letter. While I was saddened to hear what a reputation I had, I realized after reflection that it is quite understandable how disturbing some of my occasional radical associations must be. And it is quite possible that it is I who am confused.

Toshi and I had still not decided definitely if it would be practical for our family of five to cross the continent and back next summer. In order to pay for the trip we would have to work out a few stops. However, we had just about decided it *would* be possible when your letter came.

In deepest honesty and frankness Max, I believe I can swear to you that I abhor force and violence as a means of settling any dispute. Nor do I feel hate in my heart for any man—not even the youths who stoned my car in Peekskill, NY and nearly killed my babies, nor the men who threw rotten eggs at Henry Wallace when I accompanied him in the South during the campaign of 1948. I did not feel any hate in my heart even for Adolph Hitler, though I did participate in the war to defeat him.

---

1. Max (1901–1970) and Beatrice (1901–2000) Krone were the coauthors of many songbooks, which ran the gamut from traditional worship music to Spanish- and French-language folk songs.

... Though I do not feel hate, I confess to a strong sense of indignation. Do you know what I mean? Have you seen the exhibit (or book) *The Family Of Man?* After a number of photographs showing man's inhumanity to man, a line was quoted from George Sand: "Never forget this sense of indignation, which is one of the purest forms of love." If this sense of indignation has led me into bad company, I must apologize. But I agree also with Frederick Douglass, who said, "Those who would like progress to come without struggle are like those who would like to see Niagara Falls without the roar of its waters." Of course, there are many methods of struggle. I am extremely interested to hear of your interest in Gandhi. He is one of my personal heroes, and I often sing what has become known as one of his favorite songs ("Ragupati Ragava Rajah Ram").

Along this line, I wonder if you have even seen the little newsletter put out by the Montgomery Improvement Association? I'll enclose a copy. I feel they are putting up a truly heroic struggle down there, and are really putting Gandhi's principles into practice. I feel they are also right in the great American tradition of such causes as the NY State tenant farmers (1764 and 1840)[2] and the Coal Creek Rebellion (Tennessee 1894)[3] and some of the union organizing drives of the 1930s. It is possible that through court action and other pressure the 50,000 Negro people of Montgomery may temporarily lose their struggle for a more democratic transportation system. But in the meanwhile they have awakened a sense of justice throughout the nation which has helped immeasurably to push us along the slow and tortuous path towards brotherhood.

And in all honesty, I don't think you should be too hard on old Karl Marx. I have never read him, but another man I admire tremendously, G. B. Shaw, said his life was changed upon reading Marx in the British Museum around 1880. Now, one need not approve everything done by people who claim to follow Marx (I weep for violence in Hungary as well as Suez)—come to think of it neither does one approve of all the things which have been done by people claiming to follow Jesus. But I shall not pass blanket condemnation on all who claimed to have learned from Marx, such as Shaw, Sean O'Casey, J. B. S. Haldane, Picasso, et al.

This has gotten to be a much longer letter than I intended, and probably longer than you have time to read. I apologize for this, too! But now there is nothing to do but go on! Believe me, I have never

---

2. These refer to two of a number of rebellions by tenant farmers in Hudson Valley against what were essentially feudal conditions of employment, the land they worked being owned by landlords with vast landholdings.

3. The Coal Creek Rebellion was a conflict between Tennessee miners and coal mine owners, beginning in 1891 when mine owners tried to replace miners with convict labor leased to them by the state. The ensuing struggles, including armed conflict, resulted in the arrest of many of the miners, in tandem with the state's decision to cease the practice of convict labor.

written such a political letter in my life, either to friend or foe. And I wouldn't now, though you have asked me pointed questions to answer, like to continue longer on this tack. For my job is being a musician, and it is in this that I must stand or fall, I believe. It is on music we must see if we agree.

...From your letters and description of others, I feel that Idyllwild[4] must be a really fine place. If you feel, upon reading this letter, that it will be possible for me to contribute to its program, I should like to spend two weeks there next summer. I should like to go over rather carefully with you what you would wish me to do, so that my contribution would mesh with and develop the whole program, but I believe this will not be too difficult.

Oh yes. Though customarily I am against making "loyalty oath" types of statements, I am quite glad to assure your board that I have never been a member of any organization advocating force and violence. Nor ever do I expect or hope to be. Though wait a minute, come to think of it. I am a registered Democrat. I rather think that some of the southern members of this organization do believe in force and violence to maintain the status quo. If your Board will overlook this, I will be glad to.

In general, I agree completely that the primary need of our generation is to bring people together, to release their creative potentials for beauty and constructive work. I believe music can help do this. If you agree with me, I would welcome the opportunity to work with you on it.

Very sincerely,
Peter Seeger

P. S. You didn't really listen to all my records, did you? I shudder at the thought.

"The Apple of the Eye," 1994

Found in Seeger files

In Ho Chi Minh's[5] last letter to his people, he urged them to guard the unity of the Communist Party like the apple of their eye.

I really agree with Uncle Ho, except for one thing, "apple of the eye."

After a long life of observing human organizations in various parts of the world, I'm convinced that the leadership of any organization should treasure its opposition like the apple of its eye.

---

4. The Idyllwild School of Music, now Idyllwild Arts Foundation, was started by Max Krone in the early 1950s in Idyllwild, California.
5. Ho Chi Minh (1890–1969) was the leader of the independence movement that led to the creation of the Democratic Republic of Vietnam (North Vietnam) and then served as its prime minister and president through the period of its conflict with the United States.

There's an old saying, "If you want to live a long life, have a medical problem you have to watch carefully."

So whether it's a family, a corporation, a church, a university, a political party, a nation-state, a union, a nonprofit group—if you want it to live a long time, treasure the internal opposition. Don't just depend on external opposition. Write it into your charter, your constitution, your bylaws, that opposition can exist, can speak its mind from time to time.

"Statement of Belief in Socialism," 1999

Found in Seeger files

At age 8 I read some books about American Indians, and decided that was the way to live. No rich, no poor. Food was shared. I still think communism is a good idea, in spite of the many mistakes and crimes that have been made in its name.

Mistakes. Crimes. Well, consider some socialist institutions that have been around a long while: libraries, universities. Highways, bridges, ferries. Exploration projects. Why do some work well, others not?

Postal systems. Why is it that not one of them, east or west, invented Federal Express? Shouldn't every socialist institution have an R + D [research and development] department?

If a whole country "went socialist" wouldn't it still want some small private enterprise to exist? Arts, crafts. And in factories how would we prevent the gradual growth of inefficiency? The epitaph in eastern Europe was: "They pretend to pay us, we pretend to work."

If there is a world here in a hundred years I believe it will be saved by millions of relatively small organizations: political, religious, scientific, artistic, educational, or a combination of any of these. We'll disagree on so many things it will be hilarious. But we'll agree on a few points:

- Better to talk than shoot.
- Bombs always kill innocent people, likewise chemical and bacteriological warfare.
- And when words fail (they will often) we'll try to communicate with art, sports, good food, humor.

I used to say, "When all else fails, try strawberry shortcake," but a woman told me, "No, when food fails, try hot tubs."

Scientists use numbers, but are not always scientific in deciding when or how they use them. Let us work to see that the period of the Information Revolution we are now entering will show the whole world the danger we are in. Corporate misrule *can* and will be changed when enough people decide to become active in their own communities, local or worldwide.

"There Are Also Private Libraries," c. 1983

Letter to Bob Connors of Cold Spring, New York; found in Seeger files

P. S. To Bob Connors,

I believe I owe you more of an explanation than I did, why I believe it is worthwhile trying to help a group of citizens run the 27-acre park at Little Stony Point rather than insisting the taxpayers do it.

Part of it is perhaps simply the old saying, "The art of the possible." Since for decades the State has not wanted to spend the money on taking care of this park, we'll do the next best thing.

But part of it, I believe, is because I really do think that in almost every field of life, there is a place for citizens to be active *alongside* the government. The government runs libraries, but there are also private libraries. The government runs hospitals, but there are also private hospitals. The government runs schools, but there are also private schools. I admit some people I much admire disagree thoroughly with this idea. George Bernard Shaw would refuse to contribute to a charity, saying, "That is a job which governments should do." Of course he was an old Socialist. And why not go further. Lenin is supposed to have said, "Charity prolongs poverty."

But perhaps we are getting too far afield. We are talking about parks. I believe strongly that the nation needs *many many many* more parks. We need small ones as well as big ones. Most cities need more parks. I was in London once. I noticed they have parks every two or three blocks. I asked, "How come you people with your aristocrats seem to have more parks than supposedly democratic America?" Their answer was, "Well, we taxed the rich so much that they had to give up their private parks and then they became available for the people."

In the USA, quite often, generous wealthy people will give their land to a Nature Conservancy or perhaps to the government to make a park. But, as I look around the country, I find that time and again Park Departments are not being run well. The taxpayers do not like to spend the money to keep them up properly or make them available to people. Into this picture comes the nature lovers who say, "Better not have too many people use that park anyway. They'll destroy it. They'll turn it into Coney Island."

I believe that at Little Stony Point we have an opportunity to show that they are both wrong. Little Stony Point can be well used by many people. It can still remain natural, but in order to do this, we must develop a core of volunteers very much like *Clearwater*. People will come up and help pick up litter, help see that people are not getting drunk and getting in fights, see that people aren't throwing the trash barrels into the water. They will also be of assistance in case anybody needs help, and in return all they'll get is a place to pitch their tent and sleep out under the stars, and in their free time go hiking in the mountain. This is basically what we offer volunteers on the *Clearwater*. They work hard in return for having a wonderful experience. I used to feel guilty about the low wages paid to *Clearwater* crew, especially thinking of all the union songs I've sung in my life. But I decided that this is quite a different picture. Clearwater is a not-for-profit operation, and just as you don't expect volunteers helping the church to be paid regular union wages, whether they are passing the plate or lighting the candles or singing in the choir, one doesn't expect Clearwater volunteers to be paid either. In a sense we have our church out under the sky, and at Little Stony Point we have an extraordinary altar.

Bob, I think you have to face it. The State Parks Department is not doing its job, and frankly I don't feel like making a huge issue of it right now. I would rather make an issue of job training and schools and hospitals and homes for the homeless, and after we get that, then I'll push further for more State money for parks along the Hudson. In the meantime, I'd like to urge anybody I know who loves the Hudson to come down and help us at Little Stony Point. If we don't get any money from the State, we'll still go ahead and do it. And if we do it right, you can bet your life sooner or later the State is going to put on its mettle to do better elsewhere.

Best,
Pete Seeger

"Strive to Unite Them," 1967

Letter to Julius Lester;[6] found in Seeger files

Dear Julius,

I was just going to tell Irwin [Silber] that I thought SO [*Sing Out!*] should print your article, when he told me he'd decided to print it without waiting to hear anyone else's opinion. But because I have some disagreements with it, I thought I'd write anyway.

I'm about as ignorant as the next musician when it comes to problems of stractics and tategy [sic], so I quite realize that I may be wrong here. However, I'll make so bold as to shoot my mouth off. Because I admire you a helluva lot and that is a helluva good article, and also

---

6. Lester (b. 1939) is an academic, photographer, musician, and prolific author. His 1968 book, *Look Out, Whitey! Black Power's Gon' Get Your Mama!*, which grew out of the *Sing Out!* article Seeger is responding to here, is considered one of the first books to give a contextual and theoretical framework for the developing Black Power Movement. He and Seeger had previously coauthored *A Folksinger's Guide to 12-String Guitar as Played by Leadbelly.*

because I want to see if I'm able to sort my thoughts out enough to get them down on paper.

For 35 years I've felt that the old Missionary spirit was a fraud. "We will go and help those poor people improve themselves." Every people has had to free itself, and each time has had to seize power with force because no ruling class ever gave up graciously and legally. Not even in England, Home of Legality.

People seeking their freedom as a group have been defeated several ways though: One is when they wishfully thunk they could do it by turning the other cheek. More often they have lost through disunity. Why was Nat Turner[7] defeated? A betrayal from a slave in the big house. Time and time again, a well-to-do minority has betrayed the rank-and-filers.

But geographical separation brought disunity too. Have you ever read *The Disinherited* by Dale Every? It's the story of the Indian removals circa 1820–1838. Really, you should read it. A timely book, right now. The Indians were defeated not only because they were missionized and didn't fight back. (They put their faith in The Law and were betrayed by The Law.) Not only were they betrayed by their well-to-do leaders who sold out the struggle, but they were also defeated because the different tribes could not unite to defend themselves against the encroaching Europeans. Cherokee, Creek, Choctaw, Seminole. They spent more time fighting each other than fighting whites.

Wasn't it the same way in Africa? The different nations delivered each other up as slaves to the Europeans. Europeans conquered the world by utilizing local animosities.

So if the Afro-American people of the USA maintain unity during the next few years, it's going to take some major work. The Jews didn't manage to. (Some said "Let's abandon the struggle here and go build a new state in Palestine. Others said, abandon the dream of Palestine; fight for freedom in your hometown. Others said, keep quiet and save your own skin.)

And isn't it true that even after a revolution has been won, the guns got more of a workout when the victors disagreed amongst themselves? Having got used to using guns, it was natural that they keep on using them on each other.

I feel that the dark-skinned peoples of America have potentially among them a disastrous amount of disunity, and your article does not hardly hint at it: the young and the old, the male and the female, the north and the south, the rich and the poor, the diploma-witted and the mother-witted, the city and the country, and lots more.

---

7. Nat Turner led a slave revolt in Virginia in 1831, the bloodiest such event in U.S. history, with approximately 100 killed during the revolt, half whites, and several hundred slaves killed in retaliation after Turner and his followers were arrested. Turner was hanged on November 11, 1831.

Like most musicians, when I stand up and face an audience I strive to unite them. If I'm lucky, I do it a different way, with the help of words. And if 5 percent of the audience are left out of the unity the way they were when I sang "Bring Them Home" at Newport—I don't mind at all. Because the other 95 percent perhaps get a glimmering that this is the kind of unity that will not be content to let the world go its merry suicidal way.

But songs and music *can* unify. There has been, I venture to guess, rarely if ever a liberation movement that didn't use them, along with oration, and (in recent times) paper and print. Your article hardly acknowledges this a bit.

You are dissatisfied with the old songs. So am I. You seem to agree with the man who said, "We're too busy getting ready to fight to bother singing." I think some new fighting songs are needed, and will arise.

If they are great enough songs, they will help unify in a way that no other medium of communication can.

See you,
Pete

"Trying to Talk at a Crowded Cocktail Party," 1969

From Seeger's regular "Johnny Appleseed, Jr." column
in *Sing Out!* magazine, no. 19.1, April/May 1969

In a foreign country I met an expatriate couple who said: "We feel that a country which does not respect the rights of its citizens does not deserve support." Late that night, alone and grinding my teeth, I thought: If we won't stay to try and set our country straight, we don't deserve to have a country.

Of course, U.S.A. was largely settled by people who fled jails and executioners' axes. But now it's 1969. Sinner man, poor immigrant, where you gonna run to? If the hard rain threatens to fall, perhaps we who live in the lair of the monster can do something about it.

Part of what we can do is not keep our mouths shut, not just whisper. A young banjo picker writes me: "... here at Fort Bragg ... when we have bayonet practice, the sergeant yells out, 'What is the spirit of the bayonet?' We must answer, 'To kill, to kill!' Then the sergeant yells, 'And what does that make you?' 'A killer, a killer!' I said softly, 'Sick.'" He should have said it aloud.

Communicating in 1969 U.S. of N. America is like trying to talk at a crowded cocktail party. There is so much irrelevant communication going on that getting a sensible word in edgewise is difficult. But it's not impossible. Here's where singers have an advantage over other mortals.

... Part of what we must do is act—the most definitive communication. Not only peace and freedom workers have become actionists.

Conservationists have also. Near San Francisco a young man swiped a bulldozer, rammed it into a PG&E [Pacific Gas and Electric] power line near a proposed nuclear power plant. Then he turned himself in and took a five-year sentence, to publicize his protest. A troubadour friend of mine was driving through the western desert, admiring the scenery, when he came upon a huge billboard. Ten miles later, still seething, he turned his car around, came back and chopped it down. The conservation issue is heating up. Who has written a song about the oil blowout at Santa Barbara?[8] We need one. Amusingly enough, it's bringing together people who normally wouldn't speak to each other. But this is an old story to musicians. Underneath everyone's surface layers of opposition between individuals and classes, there are still further layers of agreement. One reason musicians are suspect is that it is often these layers we appeal to. And the conservation issue also reaches these layers. After all, there is only one ocean of air we all breathe, one ocean of water lapping every shore. If these become poisoned, of what use to inherit the earth? So I and my fellow musicians tromp over the globe, suspected by many, attractive to many. The Fascists say, better dead than red. The Wobblies say, "The working class and the employing class have nothing in common." I sing, "A Hard Rain is Gonna Fall."

And now we're back to where we started. Many people flee their homes regularly every year. They go where the air is cleaner and the water clearer. They are rich people. But maybe you too have wanted to go to a freer land, a less polluted place, a place where power is not so important as decency. I say the time for exiles is over. Stop hoping for a palace revolution, a compromise solution. Worried about the computerized pollution? Know this: there's damn fools everywhere. Uncle Octopus has long tentacles. No place in this world will be safe till the technocrat's lust is tamed. I say, stay here and fight for your home. Take it from an old blacklisted banjo picker, this land does belong to the hardworking people who love freedom, to you and me.

"Voting Nowadays," 2000

Found in Seeger files

I'm often asked these days, "Do you mind telling us how you intend to vote this November?" And I figured I might as well put on paper what I usually answer.

I'll tell you how I intend to vote this November, but first I want to say to you, whoever you are, I hope that you *are* going to vote. Yes, vote for the person you want to, but *vote*. It's a scandal that only half of all Americans bother to vote nowadays.

---

8. The 1969 oil spill in the Santa Barbara channel was, at the time, the largest oil spill in United States waters.

Think of the people, black, white and brown, who over the centuries struggled, fought, and yes, died, so that we could have the right to vote. At the time of the American Revolution, only if you were male, and white, and owned property, and were over twenty-one could you vote. Over the next fifty years, there were struggles in every state to extend suffrage to men who did not own property, but had to rent the house or land they lived on. It wasn't an easy struggle. Typical of the way the rich people thought was John Jay,[9] who said, "I think the people who own a country ought to govern it."

Then in the 1840s began the struggles for women to vote, and for African-Americans to vote. Way, way later it was President Nixon who lowered the voting age to eighteen, as a concession to soldiers fighting in Vietnam. (If they were old enough to die for the country, they ought to be old enough to vote.)

Yes, no matter what your political opinions, please, please, please vote. If you think that more criminals should be executed, and have more money for jails, and less for schools, vote for [George W.] Bush. If you want to see judges appointed who will perhaps overrule *Roe vs. Wade* (the Supreme Court abortion ruling), vote for Bush. If you want to see things stay more or less as they have for the past seven years, vote for [Al] Gore. If you would like to see election reform, so that you could run for office without having to raise millions upon millions of dollars, don't vote for either of them. If you are a conservative working person, who doesn't like abortion, but doesn't like NAFTA[10] either, vote for [Pat] Buchanan. If you don't like lefties, but neither do you like nuclear power, vote for the Natural Law Party, Mr. [John] Hagelin. If you like the idea of socialism, vote for Dave McReynolds. And I guess there are several more small parties on the left and on the right as well. If you agree with them, *vote*. No matter whom you want to see elected, *vote*.

I confess I am going to vote for Ralph [Nader].[11] I've known him for twenty or thirty years. And though I have a lot of friends who are horrified, they say, "You don't want Bush to get in, do you?" I'm still convinced we've *got* to get America out of our merry-go-round rut. Here's words of a song I sang in '48:

9. Jay (1745–1829) was one of the Founding Fathers, a governor of New York State, and the first Chief Justice of the United States.
10. The North American Free Trade Agreement (NAFTA), signed by the United States, Mexico, and Canada, was negotiated by both Presidents George H. W. Bush and Bill Clinton. NAFTA was portrayed by supporters as an attempt to lessen or completely eliminate trade barriers such as tariffs between the three countries, while opponents predicted it would facilitate the flight of jobs from the United States.
11. Ralph Nader (b. 1934) is an American political activist best known as the presidential nominee of the Green Party in 1996 and 2000, and for subsequent presidential runs as an independent. Nader's activism focuses chiefly on consumer rights and protections and implementing ecologically progressive legislation.

> It's the same, same merry-go-round, which one will you ride this year?
> The donkey and elephant bob up and down on the same merry-go-round
> The elephant's strong in the north; the donkey is strong in the south
> They look similar behind, but in front you will find that they've got the
>   same bit in their mouth
> It's the same, same merry-go-round, which one will you ride this year?
> The donkey and elephant bob up and down on the same merry-go-round[12]

Close friends of mine now disagree with me. They say, "Don't repeat the mistake of the Germans in 1934. Hitler got into power with 33 percent of the vote and then closed down freedom of the press."

But I think our First Amendment will stand, even if Bush gets in. And I bet Ralph will draw votes from Bush as well as Gore. Damn few Americans like to see U.S.A. so dominated by the very rich, the ones who give millions to both Republocrats and Demicans, and then some of them get most of it back because they own the TV networks.

A friend of mine was in Holland and a Dutchman said, "Oh, you Americans, you've got two political parties. That's just one more than the Soviets had. We have twenty."

Sooner or later Americans have to quit voting for evil, even if it is lesser. But we've got to vote! Yes, vote. People died so we could vote.

"The Airwaves Belong to Everyone," 1969

From the *Harvard Alumni Bulletin*, dated April 28, 1969

To meet today's worldwide communications crisis, the printed page is inadequate. For one, there is not enough pulpwood in the world. If other nations used paper as fast as the U.S.A., there would soon be no more forests. Second, the language barrier is a very real one, even within one nation.

I used to be snobbish about TV; I am no longer. Anyone who says, "Slobs can watch the boob tube; I prefer to read books," is like someone who says, "I don't care who swims in the polluted river; after all, I have a swimming pool."

Part I of the following was written originally for *Variety*, the Hollywood entertainment magazine. Part II is an attempt to be constructive.

Part I

The Roman emperors had a slick trick that worked—for a time. While their armies were out conquering the world, and while they enjoyed the pleasures of their villas, they kept the Roman populace from revolting by giving them free bread and circuses.

---

12. "Words by Ray Glaser, music by Bill Wolff." —P. S.

America has TV. Turn on the magic screen; you'll find an assort-ment of diverting comedy, fairy stories, and shoot-em-ups. Where is the real richness and variety of American life, with its hundreds of ethnic groups, with its thousands of conflicting opinions? Where is the exciting controversy that [Thomas] Jefferson looked forward to? He said, "We have nothing to fear from error so long as reason is free to oppose it."

Someone says, "Oh, but didn't you see that great program last week?" So what? If I knew a housewife who had a large family to feed, and a limited food budget, and I found she was spending 95 percent of it on soft drinks and pastry, I'd say she wasn't giving her kids a well-balanced diet. Someone else says, "But shouldn't the majority rule? The programs that are on TV are there because the majority wants them." Not true. How many does the most popular comedy show reach? Forty million? That's not a majority of 200,000,000 Americans.

If TV were really to satisfy a majority of the American people, in any week in any big city there would be room for programs of jazz and classical music, and for a dozen kinds of folk and traditional ethnic music. There would be room for the searing and biting new songs that are coming from the younger generation. There would be room on TV not just for the two major parties, but for George Wallace, for Eldridge Cleaver,[13] yes and the Birchers and socialists and communists. There would be room for the Seventh Day Adventists and the Mormons, and room for Madalyn Murray,[14] and room for the Evergreen Press. Why not? If a viewer objects, he can turn to the best censor of all, that little knob, and switch it off just as surely as he can refuse to read a book though it is advertised in a bookstore window he walks past. TV is not like outdoor advertising, inescapably mucking up America the beauti-ful for a captive audience.

Once when I complained of the limited range of TV fare, I was told, "You can always switch to your educational channel." If the few ETV stations were not starved for funds, and were not under such pressure to be non-controversially "educational," perhaps that suggestion would not be so much of an insult.

Viva controversy! One reason I fell in love with folk music was that its subject matter was as wide as the human race. I look forward to the day when on TV I can sing this old Irish ballad:

> An old man came courting me, fal-the-lal-loodle.
> And old man came courting me, hi-derry-down.

---

13. Cleaver (1935–1998) was a high-ranking member of the Black Panther Party, also well known for his essay collection *Soul On Ice,* a treatise on the condition of blacks in America, largely written while Cleaver was imprisoned in California.
14. Madalyn Murray O'Hair (1919–1995) was an atheist activist, the founder and president of American Atheists.

And old man came courting all for to marry me.
Maids, when you're young, never wed an old man.

He has no faloodle, falal-the-laloodle.
He has no faloodle, the divil a one.
He has no faloodle, he's lost his dingdoodle.
Maids, when you're young, never wed an old man.

I look forward to comparing some day on U.S. TV, as I did last summer before 3,000 delegates to the World Council of Churches, an old Salvation Army hymn to Joe Hill's parody of it. The former sings,

In the sweet bye and bye
We shall meet on that beautiful shore.

The Joe Hill parody, one of America's great songs, goes:

Longhaired preachers come out every night
Try to tell you what's wrong and what's right,
But when asked about something to eat,
They will answer with voices so sweet:
You will eat bye and bye
In that glorious land above the sky.
Work and pray, live on hay.
You'll get pie in the sky when you die.

Last year, after 17 years of being blacklisted from network TV, I finally got a chance, and included "Waist Deep In The Muddy," [with the line] *and the big fool says to push on.* It got the most explosive approval of any song I have ever sung. But when I asked a Columbia distributor why my record of it didn't sell, he said, "Pete, I took it to every disk jockey in town; they were scared to touch it." (I wasn't asked to sing this song a second time on TV, although it was a top request at all my concerts in 1968.)

Scientific information is, in effect, often blacklisted. "It's not entertaining." No wonder many scientists are desperately pessimistic about the future of the human race. They see the Information Gap growing as fast as is the gap between rich and poor. They write books like *The Silent Spring, The Population Bomb,* and *Is There Intelligent Life on Earth?* I tell them: Stop wasting your time writing books. Learn to speak vernacular. Demand the right to get on TV. It's our one chance.

(No, I'm not suggesting cluttering up the screen with long-winded scientists. Any industry that can sell deodorant, mouthwash, and gasoline with commercials that are more entertaining than the program should be able to do the same with other types of information.)

Someone says, "But who's going to pay for all this?" Ridiculous. Outside the U.S. Army, no field wastes time and money like TV. Recently I was paid $265 union minimum for guesting on a daytime talk show. It took all together two hours of my time, including rehearsal and make-up.

The greatest entertainers in the world have always been more than "mere entertainers." Look at Shakespeare, G. B. Shaw, Francois Villon,[15] Bob Dylan. The best folk songs in a thousand idioms also probe reality: "Where do we come from; where do we go?"

Today mankind faces a communications crisis. Entertainment is communication. If America explodes in the next few years, or if it goes the way of Hitler's Germany, it will be largely the fault of TV, because TV had the chance to do something about it. We have foolishly sold our air to the highest bidders. They give us a variety of cream puffs. We should demand more: the rich variety of all human life.

Part II

OK, what do we do about it? Agreed: let's be constructive. Any mule can kick a barn down. It takes a carpenter to build one up. The year is 1969; what can this do-it-yourself nation do about TV?

Some say, let the government run it. Numerous governments, capitalist as well as socialist, do just this. Some of them (Italy, for example) pay for it by taking commercials. I'm against it here, at least now. American TV might be even worse if it were run by bureaucrats appointed by the U. S. Congress, or by our state legislatures.

Others say, let the government run a public sector of the air, in friendly competition with commercial stations. Canada and Britain do it. Maybe the U.S. could build up the educational TV network 'til it really amounts to something.

Here's another idea; see what you think of it. I propose that Congress pass a law requiring all commercial TV stations to donate 20 percent of their time to what would be called "the public sector" of the air. Say, one hour in the morning, one in the afternoon, and one hour in the evening. In a city with five TV stations these hours could be staggered so that no two hours would overlap. The stations would make available studio space plus their standard personnel.

TV, if used right, may be able to save this world. The printed page has failed. Black and white, rich and poor, east and west, south and north, city and country, young and old, all have a right to use the magic screen. The air belongs to everyone. We must open it up to minorities. We can learn about each other's troubles. We can learn about each other's beauties.

---

15. Villon (c. 1431–1463) was a French poet and occasional criminal. He wrote poems celebrating the poorest class in Paris, and especially the criminal elements of this class.

"Freedom of Speech Versus Access to Information," 1986

Letter to Marvin Frankel, lawyer and human rights
activist, dated July 18, 1986; found in Seeger files

Dear Marvin Frankel,

I read with interest the abridged copy of your speech in "The Nation" and am writing now to ask if by any chance you would have an
extra copy of your complete speech. I think the problem of freedom
of speech and access to information may be the crucial contradiction
which the human race may not be able to solve. I have not solved it.
Though I have been wrestling with it all my life.

Twenty-five years ago I was able to stay out of jail because of the First
Amendment. "I have a right to my opinion, and you have a right to
your opinion," I told to Congressman Walter and the Un-American
Activities Committee. And I still really believe this, even to the point
of saying to my friends in Skokie that the American Nazis have a right
to march and so does the Ku Klux Klan.[16] I would even give them the
right to appear on television, although I'd be listening to every word to
see if I could find a way to sue them for libel. It seems to me the best
way to handle these home-grown fascists is to expose them and their
friends in very high places and use ridicule, as did Malvina Reynolds,[17]
the songwriter, when she wrote that great song, "The Klan, The Klan,
They call on every red-blood fighting man. If you're pure and white and
bigot, Get your courage from a spigot, And defend your racial purity
the very best you can."[18]

However, I know that at times I have acted the part of the censor. I
have been an editor, deciding what was to go in a magazine; as a singer,
I choose what songs not to sing. I have withheld information from children and grandchildren when they are very young or elderly relatives
who were ill. In one of our boats on the Hudson River, we have posted
a sign, "You can argue with the captain—some of the time," implying
that when there is an emergency, you shut up and do what you're told.
Likewise it seems to me that it is hard to criticize the Nicaraguans for
censoring the press in the wartime situation they face, although when

---

16. In 1978, the National Socialist Party of America, a descendent of the American
Nazi Party, planned a rally in Skokie, Illinois. Given Skokie's large Jewish population,
the local government refused to give the group permission to march. However, the
American Civil Liberties Union intervened, siding with the National Socialist Party
of America, and arguing that the march was protected by the First Amendment. The
case eventually made it to the Illinois Supreme Court, where it was decided that the
march should be allowed.
17. Reynolds (1900–1978) was a folksinger and social activist, who, unusually, did not
become well-known as a folksinger until she was into her 40s. Reynolds was known
as an incisive satirist whose songs, including her best known work, "Little Boxes,"
addressed issues of workaday middle-class life in America.
18. "The Battle of Maxton Field," c. Schroder Music Company, 1986.

I go there next January I would hope to persuade them that a good libel law is more effective in the long run—not just more pleasing to world liberalism.

The biggest problem, though, I believe comes up in the area of scientific information. My father, an old scholar, said, "Most scientists have at some time in their life made a religious decision from their gut feeling it is a good thing to be a scientist. But if the world were destroyed by sophisticated science, could we say that it was a good thing to have been a scientist?" My father had to admit that this way of thinking led to a very reactionary conclusion that perhaps the committee that told Galileo to shut up was correct.

Nevertheless, at the rate things are going, it is only a matter of time before some insane person will put an end to the human race on earth by misusing information that has become common property after some foolish scientist first discovered it. We are faced with the contradiction that we must either make certain that there is not such a thing as an insane person in the world or restrict super dangerous information, it seems to me.

I am not sure exactly, but I suspect I would not like to see a booklet giving the details of how anyone in the world can make an atom bomb by stealing a few pounds of plutonium, and have this book translated into hundreds of different languages and made available to people around the entire world. And I tend to think that one reason America has become such a violence-prone country is the huge amount of violence on TV and movies and the press. I don't know how to make up my mind amid these contradictions. I only feel that, unless the human race faces up to these problems honestly, there's not much chance of the human race to survive.

Nevertheless, much thanks for your work, and I enclose a self-addressed stamped envelope if by chance you have a spare copy of your complete talk. With many thanks.

Sincerely,
Pete Seeger

"Little Victories Give Us Courage," c. 1986

Letter to Tim Morris; found in Seeger files

Dear Tim,

Only today I get to read your letter of July 26th. The mail comes in to our house literally by the bushel, and I hardly have time to read it, much less answer it coherently. A skilled typist types my letters for me. I guess, if you didn't know, I'm a dictator these days.

First of all, let me thank you for taking the time to write such a beautiful and long letter. I'm going to save it and show it to other people. I hope you don't mind. I really do believe that it will be people like you that save this world. There are only hundreds of thousands right now, but there are going to be millions and eventually hundreds of millions. You will be women and men all over this entire world who realize that there will be no world at all unless we change the directions of our lives.

I urge you, however, to find some like-minded people you can work with, even though you may not agree with them 100 percent, and guard against getting too discouraged because winning the big battles seems so far off and so difficult. Pick some little struggles. Here, on the waterfront of my hometown, we've been teaching sailing and pulling up weeds and cooking food and singing songs.

These are very trivial things, but little victories give us the courage to keep on struggling to win some bigger victories later.

...What you learn from working with others will be more valuable than perhaps you realize now. It is not easy, of course; you have to know when to keep your mouth shut and when to open it and say the right thing. Here on the waterfront of our hometown, we've had a monthly pot luck supper the first Friday of every month for 15 years. No one wanted to come to a meeting; so we called it a pot luck supper, and after we stuffed ourselves for an hour or more, we'll have a short meeting, which mostly consists of who is going to volunteer for this or volunteer for that, and it is kind of hilarious because some people would like the meeting to be very, very brief and others are trying to say something.

But out of this creative conflict comes some good ideas, and our town now has a nice Riverfront Park and we've got a floating dock and a sailing program, and we don't agree about a lot of things, but we're in there working together and arguing at the same time. Music helps, but food is just as important—maybe more important. Our meeting place is an old diner that used to serve coffee to the ferry, but when the ferry closed down 23 years ago, it started rotting away. And the city lets us use it free of charge. We propped up the roof and put in a cement floor, because the old one was rotten clear through. We heat it with a couple of cheap wood stoves, and sometimes the singing in there gets real good. Nobody's famous; nobody's making money, but who cares?

All for now, as ever.
Best wishes,
Pete Seeger

Section 3
Beyond the United States

10

Other Struggles of the 20th Century

"The Coin Has Two Sides," 1968

From *Sing Out!* magazine, no. 18.2, March/April 1968

In order to visit Lebanon, I had to have my Israeli visa on a separate piece of paper or I would never have gotten permission for a Lebanese visa. But we got a nice letter from the cultural attaché at the Lebanese Embassy. Musicians and businessmen in the city of Beirut who were connected with the famous Baalbek Festival met me at the airport and drove me to my hotel. They couldn't have been more hospitable. Next evening, I was driven to the home of one of them for a party.

"Have you ever eaten Arab food, Mr. Seeger?"

"Why, yes, my family likes it a lot. We can buy Arabian bread on Atlantic Avenue in Brooklyn. We first got to know Arabian food three years ago when I had a concert in Jerusalem."

Pause.

"Was that Arab or Jewish Jerusalem?"

"I had a couple weeks of concerts in Israel."

Nothing more was said on the subject at the time. But a few minutes later when one of the men got out of the car for some cigarettes, the other leaned over and said, "Mr. Seeger, I myself am quite open-minded. But I think it would be best if, while you were in Lebanon, you didn't mention that you were in Israel. Feelings on that subject are very tense."

So, for a week, when people asked me what other concerts I was giving in the area, I had to say, uncomfortably, something like, "Well, I have to meet my manager in Rome next week; he will tell me what my schedule is."

Meanwhile, I met some really wonderful people, including some experts in Lebanese folk music and dance, and students at the university where I sang. Best friend of all, though, was a young doctor whom I shall call Sharif. He had studied in the United States and knew English well and acted as my guide and interpreter for the whole week. As we drove past snow-capped mountains and ski-slopes, visited Bedouin families and villages and Roman ruins, Sharif and I talked of many things: world problems, war and peace, art and literature—and we talked about Israel. Sharif was thirteen years old when his family fled in terror from the city of Acca in north Palestine.[1]

"Pete, I don't want to see a war. No sensible man does. But I tell you that unless justice is given to the refugees I think there will be a war. I don't blame the average Jewish immigrant but I think it was criminal of the Zionist leaders to pretend that they could build a Jewish state without unjustly supplanting the Arab population. Actually, for myself, there are many things about the Jewish people which I like. They are bringing skills and talents and techniques which the Near East needs. Of course I can say this to you here, but if I said it down at the refugee camp I would be shot."

Through Sharif's help I was shown around one of the refugee camps by a UN employee. It was crowded and the sewage problem wasn't being handled as well as it should be. A ration of food keeps everybody from starving, but men go out and earn a few pennies a day to supplement the diet with fresh meat and vegetables. The houses were crowded but inside they were scrupulously neat and clean, kept so by the women. The children in the streets had shoes on and their clothing, though simple, was also clean. I spoke to a bright-eyed boy of about thirteen. I found he spoke English, which he studied in school, as well as French and Arabic. The UN man says that all the children attend the UN grade school and that there is no trouble with any of them playing hooky because they feel that education is their one chance for advancement.

"What other subjects do you study?" I asked the boy.

"Geometry, algebra, geography."

"How big are your classes?"

"Forty, fifty or sixty students in a class."

"What do you want to be when you grow up?"

He flashed me a big grin. "An engineer!"

I asked the UN man how he could possibly have such an ambition. I was told that the brightest students go on to high school and one-tenth of the graduates are able to go to vocational schools in such fields as pipe-fitting, plumbing, electricians, TV repair, carpentry. And for the girls, teaching, nursing and dietitians, etc. A very small percentage are awarded UN scholarships to universities.

I later found that the UN is trying to get contributions from nations and from private individuals and organizations to build up a 38 million dollar fund for these vocational schools and I decided that I

---

1. "Sharif" probably left Acca during the large Palestinian exodus, which took place during the 1948 Arab-Israeli war.

would contribute to them, if I possibly could. They are a ray of hope in an otherwise grim situation.

Just before leaving Lebanon I was in a car with Sharif and two others. They were asking, "Now, when are you going to come back to visit us? We would like to have you give a concert here. There is much that we have still to show you about our country."

I could lie no longer. "I would love to come back. I would love to sing for you. I would like to do a benefit and have all the money for the tickets go for these vocational schools for the refugees. But it may not be possible. Next week I am singing in Israel."

I talked for about half an hour on how I, as a person of Yankee, Protestant-Christian background had slowly come to know what it meant to be a Jew. I had learnt this partly through their songs, partly through reading books of history and of course, largely through meeting American Jews who taught me things such as the saying, "If I am not for myself, who will be? If I am only for myself, what am I?"

"But why do they have to think they are the chosen people?" asked one of the others, who, incidentally, was a Christian. Approximately fifty percent of Lebanese are Christian-Arabs.

"It's that Great Old Book."

Another burst in bitterly, "If there hadn't been so much anti-Semitism in the United States, every single one of the refugees of 1946 could have been easily absorbed in the States. Why did they all have to be dumped in this one small corner of the world?"

I replied, "Can't you imagine what it is like for a man, who is perhaps the only surviving member of his family after the rest have been sent to the gas chamber? He is desperate. He feels that the Jews have failed utterly to find a decent place for themselves in any country of the world. He is desperate; he is determined to build a place where Jews will never be discriminated against again."

"But two wrongs don't make a right," Sharif bursts out. "We are not anti-Semitic here. Believe me, I am just as horrified as you at what Hitler did. Jews have always lived here in Lebanon and still do. But how can we make Israel admit the injustice that she has done? I attended a Friends Service Committee Work Camp in Europe and met a young man. We talked in English. 'Where are you from?' 'Acca' say I. 'Acca, why I'm from Acca too,' and he rattled on and I suddenly have a sinking feeling in my stomach that I can never explain to this young Israeli what it means to me that I can never go back to my home."

Sitting in the car we talked long and earnestly and soberly. Towards the end of our conversation one of the men turned to me abruptly and asked, "When you are in Israel will you tell them that you have been in Lebanon?" And I answered, "Yes."

At the airport the next day I embraced Sharif in the Arab fashion and we promised to continue writing.

The plane carried me to Rome, where I changed and took another plane right back to Tel Aviv. As I remembered them from three years before, the Israelis were bouncing over with energy and enthusiasm. But, especially for the first few days, I could not be happy. I had an unseen companion walking beside me the whole time. Sharif. He was looking in silent bewilderment at the streets of the old Arab cities where now few Arabs lived. He rubbed his eyes in astonishment to see tractors and other power equipment move across the scientifically planned and irrigated fields.

I was one of seven performers who sang in a huge football stadium for 26,000 people two nights in a row. The audience was too large to keep in rhythm properly but they sang the chorus of "Guantanamera" well and continued to sing it with me even after I cried, "Let's dedicate this to all exiles, not only exiles of two thousand years, but of twenty years, as I sang it to them last week at the University of Beirut."

Afterwards one man smilingly told me, "You are a very brave man to have said that." But he is the only one to have even mentioned the matter.

The next day I visited the editorial office of a small left-wing political magazine. The editor of the magazine was a friendly man about our age, who had been born and raised in the Bronx. When he found that we were anxious to visit a kibbutz[2] and to get to know how it worked, he immediately invited us to visit the one he lives in, some thirty-five miles from Tel Aviv. We drove out there the next day.

We found that this particular kibbutz was one of seventy run by a left-of-center political group. Many of the Kibbutzniks were former Americans. Nobody earns any money. No, not one penny. If you need cigarettes or books or any luxury, you simply discuss it with the appropriate committee and money is taken out of the fund for it, unless it is disapproved. It's like one big family. Everybody works hard but they all insist that each other take time to play as well. Whether it is in sports or cultural activities or simply taking time off by yourself to read or gather flowers, or to swim in the big new pool. In addition to running a huge farm with a variety of crops, they have a machine shop making pipe fittings which are sold in many countries of the world. Twenty years ago they were close to starvation and lived a very spartan life. Now, though no one wastes money, they can have luxuries such as awarding some of their members an occasional trip to Europe or even the United States.

Husbands and wives share small one-and-a-half-room apartments but children, from the time they are babies, live separately in dormitories. Marriages usually take place around twenty-one or twenty-two years of age, after everyone's compulsory two-year army service is over.

---

2. Kibbutzim are cooperative communities in Israel.

I found that it was customary for boys and girls to marry outside the kibbutz, or at least outside their own age group which they had been living with since birth. I kidded them, "That's because you have no illusions about each other. For romance you need a few illusions." They said, "After living with a girl all your life, she is more like a sister." At any rate they were the healthiest, happiest young people I had seen in a long time and reminded me most strongly of young people I met in a cooperative religious colony called the Society of Brothers back in the States. I think that it is just a clear example of what happens when you live a cooperative life without the intense competitive pressures which most city people live under.

In the kibbutz was one very dark face, like that of an American Negro. It seems that a Canadian woman had previously been married to a Negro and came to live at the kibbutz. But then she left. Her nine year old son wanted to stay and was adopted by one of the families. "Do you now consider him a Jew?" I asked.

"Of course."

That simple. But it is not so simple when a kibbutz girl wants to marry an Arab boy. This occasionally happens, and all hell breaks loose. In certain quarters.

I sang in the evening for the kibbutz and again the next day for the children in the school. But most interesting was a long and serious talk with the members of the kibbutz. I told them about Sharif and the other people I had met in Lebanon. They were exceedingly interested in listening to all I had to say. It seems that this is one of the few kibbutzim where Arabic is taught in the schools. But the point I was trying to make was that unless decent and democratic minded people among the Israeli Jews were willing to recognize the injustices which Arabs suffer, where could one start reconciliation and rapprochement?

For example, in 1948 an extremely militant Zionist group called the Irgun raided the small Arab village of Deir Yessin. Over 200 women, children and old men were massacred and the few survivors put in trucks and paraded through Jerusalem and then released with the warning, "Tell your neighbors to watch their step." Of course the Irgun would claim that this action was simply retaliation for previous massacres by Arabs. The Jewish high command condemned the action and tried to forget it as another "incident of war." But the Arabs haven't forgotten it, 20 years later.

The crowd listened to me soberly and seriously while I talked on about what I had learned in Lebanon. I had a feeling that if I were an Arab I would try my best to strengthen the hand of the honest and fair-minded and courageous Israeli Jews. Just as if I were an Israeli Jew, I would try my best to strengthen the hand of people like Sharif among the Arabs.

The following day I had an opportunity to see another side of Israel though, which is not so happy. I was taken on a tour by Achmed, a young Arab, and a friend of his, a Jewish businessman, who has been devoting much of his spare time to fight for the civil rights of the Israeli Arabs. The 140,000 who did not flee in 1948 have now increased to almost 300,000. The Israeli Jews are often apprehensive and do not allow them to join the army. Arabs often are restricted to what is known as "black work," that is, construction jobs and other unskilled labor. They are allowed to vote but are not allowed to form their own political parties unless approved by the government.

The big new Hilton Hotel in Tel Aviv, Achmed said, was built right on the site of the largest Moslem graveyard. Achmed had a job driving a bulldozer and protested when he found himself plowing up skulls and bones. But no attention was paid. He quit his job. In Tel-Aviv some 40,000 Arabs work but most of them take buses back to their village on weekends because it is so difficult for them to get housing back in the city. Some live in filthy shacks such as the United States Depression "Hoovervilles." The most damning indictment of all: hundreds of Arabs, perhaps more, have actually changed their name from an Arab sounding name to a Jewish sounding name, in order to avoid discrimination.

In some ways things have improved. Outright military control of the Arab population has been eased up in recent years. I don't believe that it is any longer necessary to carry passports wherever they go. However, we drove out to a small village in what is known as "the triangle," an area of Arab villages near the Jordan border. On a hillside was a picturesque cluster of square, stone buildings. Not a tree in sight. The roads were unpaved in this particular town, at least. There was no electricity. The children were carrying buckets of water on their heads because the town pump was on the blink. Children and women wore the most brilliantly colored costumes I have ever seen, outside of Africa. Men dressed more conservatively, in browns and grays and blacks. The women's dresses had long skirts in the traditional fashion but the men wore western clothes except that they would have a white cloth over their head and a black headband.

We drove on. In another village was a big new concrete water tower, put up, I was told, by the municipality. Here I had a long interview with a smiling sharp-eyed man who was considered a dangerous Arab nationalist by the Israeli government. He was a schoolteacher but is now under house arrest and is now only allowed to run a small store in his village to keep body and soul together.

"You see, there are not only refugees outside Israel, but there are Arab refugees inside Israel. Land is still being taken away from us. Whole villages have been closed down and Arabs have had to move to other villages and have had to go to the city to try to get work. I am not allowed to protest against it because my organization, Al Ad, meaning 'The Earth,' is outlawed. I am not allowed to run a newspaper, although for thirteen weeks we circumvented the law by changing the masthead and the editor every week."

I noticed the main decoration in the schoolteacher's living room. Not just a map of Israel. A globe.

I pointed out that in the United States and other industrialized countries the farm population was also being displaced. But he did not feel that this was the same situation. "If we could get loans, the way the Jews can, if we were allowed to form organizations and cooperatives, we too could use modern methods and scientific agriculture. But there are only five high schools in Israel for the Arabs. There is no quota on Arab students at the University but there are only fifteen of them there. No technical instruction is given to Arabs except for the construction industry. Why can't the government of Israel help Arabs the way they are helping Africans and people from other countries?"

I answered him:

"I find myself agreeing with much of what you say but there is one matter which I feel very critical about and I wonder how you feel about it. I agree that when an Israeli Arab baby is born he faces a life as a second-class citizen for no other reason than that he is an Arab here. But is it not also true that 50 percent of the Arab babies [i.e., females] are born almost as third-class citizens? They are condemned in advance to spending their lives in the kitchen."

He nodded in agreement. "You are right. But unfortunately, it is very difficult to do anything about this. We are not allowed to form organizations."

Thinking it over later, after we parted, I decided that this wasn't really a satisfactory answer. There are surely many things that can be done in this world even if one is not allowed to form organizations.

I asked if the Arab population in Israel was growing so fast, what was going to happen in the future.

"They are worried about that. The security chief says that there are measures that can be taken but 'It is best not to discuss it now.' This is a Nazi answer, yes?"

Before leaving Israel, I spent one very moving and even exciting evening. A group in Tel-Aviv was started by some intellectuals, both Arabs and Jews, called the Israeli Movement for Arab-Jewish Cooperation. I agreed to appear for them. On 24 hours notice telegrams were sent out to members and friends and over 1,000 people showed up at the Hilton Ballroom. All this with daily mounting headlines about threat of war with Egypt and harassments on the Syrian border. I sang for about half an hour and talked for about twenty minutes telling them about people I had met in Lebanon. Everything I said in English was translated twice. First into Hebrew and then into Arabic.

I told them they ought to learn each other's jokes, and related this one: A Jewish youth is reading the newspaper. "Mama, listen to this.

A Japanese scientist has invented a way to make fertilizer out of fish. What do you think of that?"

"I don't know," she answers seriously. "Is it good for the Jews?" Laughter from both sides.

Before I sang the song, "Walking Down Death Row," I said, "I think there's been too much talk about crime and guilt. When it comes down to it, I have been as much a criminal as anyone else in the world. My ancestors landed on the shores of North America and, with their guns and written language, pushed out the previous inhabitants in the most heartless way. And my country was built, in large part, on the sweat of millions of black slaves. The problem for me now is not to try to figure how to atone for crimes that were done years past, but simply to acknowledge that they were crimes and take steps to see that such things will never happen again. To see, for example, that first class citizenship is granted to American Indians, American Negroes, Mexican Americans and other citizens of minority descent."

I told them about the bright-eyed 13 year old in Beirut and told them that I felt the vocational schools were one of the brightest ways of hope in the whole situation. I announced that I was turning over my entire fee from my concerts in Israel to the UN Fund which is soliciting contributions from nations and organizations and individuals for these schools. There was warm applause from at least 50 percent of the audience. But one unsmiling young man said, "Why don't you give that money to some young Jew who needs training to become an engineer?" I answered, "I'd like to give the money to both." Then a vigorous man in the back row jumped up and said to the young fellow, "Why don't you give the money to the young Jew?" There were cheers and laughter.

Both Arabs and Jews got up to speak on the stand. Warm, earnest, searching talks. One very extraordinary man who was a member of Parliament spoke: "I am glad Peter Seeger has sung to us about Vietnam because a meeting like this should not exist if we do not mention the horror of Vietnam. When Jews were being killed by the Nazis, we asked why the rest of the world remained silent. Now it is up to us to ask each other how can we remain silent while crematoriums are being rained from the skies upon a helpless population."

This man was one of a number of Jews who threw themselves down on the highway in front of army trucks in order to present a protest against mistreatment of Arabs.

A collection was taken up. I started to play the *chalil* [flute], the song in Yiddish by Hirsch Glick,[3] then I broke down, started weeping in the

---

3. Glick (1922–1944) was a Jewish-Lithuanian poet and songwriter who participated in the 1942 ghetto uprising in Vilna, Lithuania, opposing Nazi occupation. A symbol of the resistance, his songs and poems were widely circulated among the underground partisans. He is presumed to have been captured and executed by Nazi forces in 1944.

middle of it at the tragedy of the whole situation. Ilka Raveh came up with his own *chalil* and played so beautifully that he helped me pull myself together. With him standing at my side I stood up and played the piece bravely—as it should be.

I have played this little Israeli *chalil* in 25 countries of the world and I always introduce it: "I learned this from an Israeli Jew, who learned to play it from Arabs. I hope they will get back together again one of these years."

The meeting ended off with several songs in several languages. "Wimoweh" from South Africa, "Guantanamera" dedicated to exiles of 2,000 years and of 19 years. And at the end, "We Shall Overcome," with Arabs and Jews standing hand in hand on stage.

I once figured out with the help of a little arithmetic that there are about as many grains of sand in the average dump truck, driving down the street, as there are people in the world. About 3,300,000,000. All the people in Israel would be less than a quarter of a pail of sand. In all the Arab world not more than ten pails of sand. In my hometown, 10,000 people, about as many grams of sand as would fit into a heaping teaspoon. And, of course, I am only one grain myself.

And I think changes in the world will come when more and more individual grains of sand realize that they can do something, perhaps not enough, but they can do something. In both Lebanon and Israel I told the story of the young Quaker who was on a Peace Vigil in Times Square, New York City. A passerby said to him, "Do you think you are going to change the world by standing here?"

"No," and he paused. "But I don't want the world to change me."

And on that hopeful note I close this sober little account. With much love to all of you who read it. I am no wise man but only a banjo-picker, who has loved to sing for many different kinds of people and who has had them join in with him.

"The Worst Elements," 1967

Letter to unknown recipient, dated September 21, 1967; found in Seeger files

Dear Azmi,

Just a short note of many thanks for your letter of August 13th. I have been away from home much of the last six weeks and next month I will be overseas on tour. But I wanted to get this off to you. I have shown your letter to many friends and you would be interested to know that some of the people who most agree with you are American Jews who, while they are proud of the good things in Jewish tradition, are also deeply ashamed of the aggressive acts of Israel.

I am very grateful that you have written me so freely and frankly. And I hope that we may always be able to. My own position is that until various nations stop acting in a hostile way towards each other, they simply encourage the worst elements of the opposing side to rise to positions of leadership. Thus, it is the hostile acts of the United States which make it possible for the dogmatists in Russia to clamp down on freedom of the press. Thus it is the statements like Khrushchev's[4] "We will bury you," which makes the average American feel like supporting [Lyndon] Johnson in Vietnam. And, I believe, statements like, "We will drive every Jew into the sea" simply make it easier for authoritarians like Dayan[5] to get into positions of leadership in Israel. And likewise it is Dayan's act which has made the Arab world more determined than ever to take action against Israel.

I would not say that this is an inflexible rule of human behavior. I believe that when people stand up for their rights, such as when working men go on strike in just cause, they gain the respect of their antagonists who will not mistreat them so easily as before. But I think it is very necessary in all these struggles to clearly emphasize repeatedly exactly who and what you are fighting. I am sure that you and most Arabs are not in favor of killing every Jewish baby in Israel but some of the published statements of some Arab leaders sound like this.

One of the wisest acts of Ho Chi Minh has been to repeatedly emphasize that he has nothing against the American people but only against their militarist leaders who have led them into such aggressive action. Of course, the main problem here in the States is that Ho Chi Minh's words are rarely printed anywhere or publicized on television. We only know about North Vietnam what the owners of our press and television want to tell us. I finally got on network television last week but the one song that I wanted to sing most, "Waist Deep in the Big Muddy and the Big Fool Wants to Push On," was firmly censored off the air.

As ever,
Pete Seeger

---

4. Nikita Khrushchev (1894–1971) was the leader of the Soviet Union from 1953 to 1964, succeeding Joseph Stalin. The Soviet Union saw modest liberalization during Khrushchev's rule, beginning with his denunciation of Stalin's oppressive practices at the Twentieth Party Congress in 1956.
5. Moshe Dayan (1915–1981) was an Israeli politician and military commander who served as defense minister during the Six Day War in 1967, in which Israel took control of territories in Egypt, Jordan, and Syria.

"Another Name for Crime," c. 1968

Letter to unknown recipients, found in Seeger files

Dear Ronny Avad, dear friends,

The statements that you have heard on the air or in a newspaper, that I will not come to sing in Israel now "because you are the aggressors," is not true. I have never made any such statement as this about any country.

I am singing mostly in the U.S. these days because I think the big job is here. I try to persuade any young person I know, black or white, Jew or gentile, English speaking or not, that the time for exiles is over, that we must all stand and face the struggle to put our own house in order, and not flee to Canada, to Mexico, to Israel, to Africa, nor any other land. The U.S.A. is consuming one half the world's goods; it has the greatest potential for doing good. But it sends military assistance to dictators in Greece, Thailand, Brazil and many other countries. It spends every year $100 *billion* for military purposes! That represents about $30 for every human being on earth. (500 million in India, and an equal number in other parts of the world, earn less than $80 a year.)

A song by a young black friend of mine says,

> When one man's got a million
> And another ain't got a dime
> Brother, then law and order
> Is another name for crime.[6]

In the U.S.A. we also pollute rivers so no one can swim in them; we pollute skies and oceans which belong to all. Our scientific agriculture has produced big crops temporarily, but one hundred years from now we may be cursing some of our shortsighted cleverness. We are gobbling up the world's irreplaceable resources, and yet the U.S.A. population is doubling every 63 years.

Enough of that.

I'm afraid I can't agree with you that social problems have nothing to do with militarism. You say, "Israeli Arabs generally enjoy better conditions than their brothers in Arab countries." It is also true that Mississippi Negroes enjoy much better standards of living than do their cousins in Africa. But Jews must know that the worst thing about being a second class citizen is *being* a second class citizen. When a Mississippi Negro has an equal chance to become Governor, and a Tel Aviv Arab has an equal chance to train for and get a job in a diamond factory, then we will both be making some progress.

---

6. "Brother That Ain't Good," by Matt Jones.

Down with all hardliners. They say politics make for strange bedfellows. What the hell's wrong with strange bedfellows? Mother Earth is one big bed. We better all learn to share it.

May we sing together again,
Pete

"Personally Responsible," 1970

Letter to President Gustavo Díaz Ordaz of Mexico,
dated January 30, 1970; found in Seeger files

Dear President Ordaz,[7]

I have just read of the armed attacks on political prisoners which occurred on New Year's Day in Lecumberri Prison.

It is bad enough anywhere in the world to hold people in prison for their opinions. It is absolutely intolerable that their lives be threatened. People around the world are going to hold you personally responsible for their safety.

Sincerely,
Peter Seeger

"Cuba Excerpts," 1971

Dated January 10, 1971; found in Seeger files

A Summary: If I am asked by anyone, here or there,
what do I think of revolutionary Cuba?

Let me choose my words carefully; I am 51 years old; I've made many mistakes. Here goes.

If anyone thinks the people of the U.S.A. cannot live in peace and friendship with the people of revolutionary Cuba, they couldn't be more wrong. They are learning a new way of living down here. They have some great successes and are making their own mistakes. Not Russia's or China's or anyone else's. They don't need anyone in Miami or Washington to help them make more mistakes. They could use trade with the U.S.A., but they are getting along pretty well without it. I would like to help them. How can I? By telling their story and their songs to other Yankees, I guess.

---

7. Gustavo Díaz Ordaz served as president of Mexico from 1964 to 1970. Known as an authoritarian ruler, he was widely condemned for overseeing the massacre of at least 40 student activists in Mexico City in 1968. Here, Seeger writes about an event that took place at the Lecumberri Prison, where many political prisoners were held.

Should I be more critical? I won't be in public, but if anyone asks me in private, I would say that they should value their African heritage more. It should be taught in school. I hope they don't define, as so much of the world does, European civilization as the only civilization. Tablecloths and neckties do not denote the civilized human so much as the inquiring mind.

At present Cuba may be headed for the same trouble that has hobbled USSR and China, by limiting criticism to certain prescribed channels. If these channels are ever blocked, the criticism is not made, the country suffers. The trouble is dammed up only to break out with more damaging pressure later on. I would open press and microphone to more continuous criticism and self-criticism.

But it is easy for me to say this. It is not so easy for Cuba who has a neighbor with a G.N.P. of one thousand billion dollars annually and an establishment that would gladly use some of it to subvert and tangle this little island until it no longer offered any ideological challenge to rich Uncle Sam. I think Uncle Sam will be all the healthier in the long run for having some ideological challenges. I will fight hard to see Uncle doesn't destroy revolutionary Cuba. If it tries to, as with Vietnam, it is liable to be the end of Uncle.

Question: (An important one) Will the conditions of Socialist life be able to develop and bring out heroes like Che?[8] I occasionally have some doubts. His picture is everywhere. Even more common than Martí.[9] But if there ever was a nonconformist, it was Che. Socialism so far has seemed to produce heroic, hard working, self-disciplined, selfless, cheerful people. It occasionally produces people ambitious for power or knowledge. It rarely produces people ambitious for money or prestige. But it almost never seems to produce the brilliant nonconformist. Had Che been born in Cuba, I wonder if he would have grown to be a great leader. Would he have been another restless athlete or intellectual?

It's important to note that many of the great revolutionary leaders of the world came from intellectual families. Ho, Lenin, Mao, Marx, Engels, Fidel, Che, Martí. Not Stalin nor present eastern European leaders certainly.

Therefore, I wonder what are socialist schools doing to develop workers *as* intellectuals. Even IBM needs creativity. To me, this is as important a question as how to get honest and selfless people in leadership anywhere. For example, in the U.S. Congress. U.S. life produces

---

8. Ernesto "Che" Guevara (1928–1967) was a revolutionary activist in Latin America during the 1950s and 1960s. Guevara was prominent in the Cuban Revolution, acting as a general in Fidel Castro's revolutionary army. He was captured and executed in Bolivia in 1967.

9. Jose Martí (1853–1895) was a Cuban poet, writer, and activist, a champion of Cuban independence from Spain. He wrote widely on the concepts of democracy and national freedom, and often traveled throughout Cuba to lecture on these ideas to convert Cubans to the cause of independence. The lyrics to "Guantanamera," a staple of Seeger's repertoire, come from one of Martí's poems.

ambitious and selfish people, whores, wheeler-dealers. It also produces drop-outs and failures and also by inverse reaction some brilliant non-conformists. In U.S. so far they are not killed off. They are not all exiled.

Socialism, as I have seen it, seems to have produced people who are somewhat parochial and provincial in their outlook on life. They will be shocked, as residents of Moscow and Peking are, by seeing Cubans and Africans dancing with pelvic motions. Or as Cubans are when they see barefooted people or a man with no shirt on.

In the car on the way to the airport, our host, who is one of the brigade leaders, said he had once been a prosecutor of the Batista criminals.[10] "It was a pleasure to execute them," he said. I felt I wanted to ask some questions, but there was no time. I know that most of these criminals were sadistic murderers and torturers, but still I have reservations. What has happened to their families? Should one shoot them too? Where draw the line? I am sure not every single soldier for Batista was shot. Where did they draw the line? Is reeducation impossible?[11] Who reeducates their families, their friends? Now are they reeducated? When Eichmann[12] was on trial in Israel, a little girl wrote to a Tel Aviv newspaper. She said, "Don't kill him. Take him instead and show him our life in Israel."

"The US Dollar Maintains the Dictatorship," 1972

Letter to Mikis Theodorakis,[13] dated July 9, 1972; found in Seeger files

Dear Mikis Theodorakis,

I am sorry I cannot write to you in the Greek language. I have just finished reading the book about you by George Giannaris. It will be on sale in October, and I would like to do as much as I can to see that it reaches a wide audience. It is a very good book.

---

10. Fulgencio Batista (1901–1973) was the last noncommunist leader of Cuba before his government was overthrown by Castro's revolutionary forces. Although he was first elected president in a democratic election, he soon consolidated power as a military dictator and suspended many civil liberties.
11. "Later, reading the book *Castro's Cuba, Cuba's Fidel* by *Life* magazine reporter Lee Lockwood, I found that Cuba had modern humanitarian reeducation camps for 15,000 people imprisoned for helping counter-revolutionaries." —P. S.
12. Adolf Eichmann (1906–1962) was a prominent member of the Nazi leadership and the man chiefly responsible for engineering the logistics of the Final Solution, the mass murder of Jews in Europe. Although he escaped Germany at the close of World War II, he was eventually captured and brought to trial in Israel, where he was hanged in 1962.
13. Theodorakis (b. 1925) is a Greek composer, especially known for his film scores. Classically trained at the prestigious Paris Conservatory, he expanded his musical vocabulary by incorporating elements of traditional Greek music into his compositions. In 1967, a right-wing junta took control of Greece in a colonels' coup and Theodorakis, a well-known leftist, was jailed. He was allowed to go into exile in Paris in 1970 and became a prominent voice against the dictatorship through its duration.

Americans as a whole must realize their responsibility, since it is the US dollar that has maintained the dictatorship in Athens. And Americans of Greek ancestry should realize that they cannot leave their cousins languishing in jails.

On my part, I'm conscience-stricken that I was not able to do more to help arrange a tour for Maria Farantouri[14] two years ago. I tried, but I did not try hard enough. The agony that you all have gone through is all there in this book.

...Whether or not you or I are fortunate to live until the time this world is free of imperialism, fascism, and militarism, I am nevertheless confident that this time will come within a few decades, because it must if the human race is to survive. I am no longer as confident as I was of *how* it will come, but I am confident that it will come all the same. And so all our struggles and our defeats will not have been in vain. Please give my deep love and thanks to all who are fighting the dictatorship, and may your exile soon be over.

Sincerely,
Pete Seeger

---

14. Farantouri (b. 1947) is a Greek singer and political activist. Together with Theodorakis, she wrote and recorded songs protesting the military junta in Greece.

Seeger sings at a community college in Washington State, in 1941 at age 22. It was during this visit to the Pacific Northwest that Seeger and Woody Guthrie first learned the phrase "hootenanny" to describe a folk music party. Photo courtesy of Mel Kirkwood.

Seeger performs at the newly opened Canteen of the United Federal Labor, 1944. The dance is notable for being racially integrated, although Washington, D.C., was still segregated at the time. Also notable is the attendance of Eleanor Roosevelt, seated at center, the First Lady of the United States. Seeger was an enlisted member of the United States Army during this time, and this picture was probably taken during one of his last furloughs before his unit shipped to the west coast, and, eventually, the South Pacific. Photo by Joseph Horne, Library of Congress.

Seeger performs at a meeting of the International Union of United Automobile and Agricultural Implement Workers of America in New York City, 1946. Photo courtesy of Marian Hille.

Seeger performs with his 12-string guitar, behind a lectern, sometime around 1950.

Seeger performs for what appears to be a group of prisoners, probably around 1951. Seeger recorded a series of prison work songs in Texas in that year. They are now preserved by the American Folklife Center at the Library of Congress.

A promotional photo for The Weavers, with Seeger seated on the floor, and, from left, Fred Hellerman, Ronnie Gilbert, and Lee Hays, taken around 1950.

The Seeger family, around 1960 at their home in Beacon, NY. The Hudson River is visible in the background. From left, Danny, Mika, Toshi, Tinya, and Pete.

A collection of Seeger family photos, taken around 1961. Although originally assembled as a Christmas card, it was repurposed to express thanks to Pete Seeger's supporters who had helped during his trial and conviction of contempt of Congress. The photos depict, clockwise from bottom left: Tinya Seeger, with Danny Seeger; the Seegers' cabin in Beacon, NY, snow-covered; Danny Seeger, foreground and an unknown boy; Penny Seeger, playing the guitar; Mika in the snow on the Seeger family property; Tinya with her maternal grandfather, Takashi Ohta; Toshi Seeger, hanging laundry; and Pete Seeger, splitting wood for the family's furnace.

Pete and Toshi Seeger in Cuba in 1971. Seeger and his family were finally granted visas to visit Cuba after repeated attempts. He wrote of the trip in his travel diary, "If anyone thinks the people of the U. S. A. cannot live in peace with the people of revolutionary Cuba, they couldn't be more wrong."

Pete and Toshi Seeger share a moment, around 1970.

Seeger proofreads a draft, likely a concert program, at home, around 1961. Photo courtesy of Joe Alper.

Seeger observes the activity on the sloop Clearwater *as it makes its way down the Hudson River, sometime in the 1970s.*

Pete performs for a group at a renaissance fair in New York City in 1971. Photo © Ed Barnas. Used with permission.

Seeger performs with two local folksingers at a Clearwater Festival, sometime during the 1970s. The Clearwater festivals were designed to raise awareness about pollution in the Hudson River and encourage residents of the Hudson River Valley to take action in combating environmental destruction in the area. This photo showcases the typical informality of the events.

The Seeger family, with Toshi at the rudder, aboard the Clearwater around 1972. While Seeger knew nothing about shipbuilding himself, he was inspired by reading books about the history of boat shipping on the Hudson River and enlisted the help of several knowledgeable associates to begin building the Hudson River Sloop Clearwater. Making its maiden voyage in 1969, Seeger, along with environmental activists and crewmembers, sailed the boat along the Hudson River to raise awareness about environmental pollution in the river.

Seeger performs with Bruce Springsteen at President Barack Obama's inauguration in January 2009. Springsteen expressed his professional and personal admiration for Seeger by recoding and touring behind an album of his own versions of Seeger's songs in 2006. Photo by Mandel Ngan.

Seeger shows off his road-worn guitar at his home in Beacon, NY, around 2009.

11

Travels Abroad

"One Notices the Difference Right Away," 1964

From Seeger's regular "Johnny Appleseed, Jr." column in
Sing Out! magazine, no. 14.1, February/March 1964

Ezekiel saw the wheel
Way up in the middle of the air.
There's a wheel in a wheel
Way in the middle of the air

As in the old song, there are worlds within worlds within worlds. On this trip which my family and I are taking around the world, we find each country to be like a new world. And within each country there are separate worlds, classes, groups. And within the worlds of music will be separate worlds, worlds that often barely recognize each other's existence. Naturally, since our visit in each country is brief, we barely get to see a small fraction of these various worlds, and there is always a danger that I will get a wrong impression of a country when all I have seen of it is a few of its many sides. I feel like one of the seven blind men who examined the elephant.

Since we plan to visit 26 countries in ten months, we can't spend too long in any one place. We won't get to know any country well. But I hope we will be able to see more strongly the contrasts between different countries. The human body is such an adaptable mechanism that even within a few days one can get acclimated. So I believe there is a certain truth in first impressions.

If one is in a room with a yellowish light bulb, one does not think of it. Light is light. If one is in a room with a bluish fluorescent bulb, one also does not think of it. Light is light. But if one walks quickly from one room to another, one notices the difference right away.

"They've Got to Learn to Sit in Chairs," 1963

Letter to Charles Seeger from Sydney, Australia, dated September 4, 1963; found in Seeger files

Dear Pa,

If I ever get another chance to cross the Pacific again I'll be sure to stop in at Samoa. We stopped over there for three days because a friend of mine is a UNESCO [United Nations Educational, Scientific and Cultural Organization] adviser to the school system, and started to fall in love with the people and the place.

Western Samoa is now nominally independent, but New Zealand is still very much Big Brother. It consists of two islands totaling 1,150 square miles, and about 100,000 people—roughly the size and population of Dutchess County [New York]. They have a Chief of State (like a constitutional monarch, elected for life, I believe) and a premier, and a legislature and courts, etc. All the conventional republican set up. But their basic organization is in hundreds of little tightly knit villages, side by side along the shores. There the heads of the family choose a *matai* or Chief, who, if he does not obviously misbehave, runs the economic affairs for life. He assigns the work, collects the cash, sees that all runs smoothly.

Missionaries (Church of England, Mormon, Catholic, mainly) got the schools started, and everyone dresses modestly now, and sings in rich tonic-dominant-subdominant harmony. In school, which almost all attend for at least a few years, Samoan is the language for the first three or four years and English from then on. Students usually sit on the floor cross-legged, though the New Zealanders feel this is one of the features of Samoan culture which must change. I visited in the brand new library of Apia (pop. 15,000). The young New Zealander in charge, a sincere young democrat, wished the library would be used more. I noted that there were chairs and tables about, but most Samoans prefer to sit on mats.

"Why don't you put some mats in the reading room?" says I.

"Oh, but they've got to learn to sit in chairs," says he, in a shocked voice.

The NZ uniform is also spotless white shorts and shirt, white socks up to the knee, and well cared for black shoes. Samoan men all wear a wrap around skirt called a lava-lava, and sport shirts. Women wear loose fitting cotton dresses like the Hawaiian moomoos. There is no great affluence to be seen on the island, but no slums to speak of, either. The big economic problems looming are the huge birthrate which is outstripping the copra [dried coconut meat]-cocoa-coffee income which has till now been sufficient.

Tinya visited in the schools and Danny took hundreds of photographs. I made tape recordings with the Nagra [brand tape recorder].

Even the 7 year olds sing with the most appealing soft rich harmony. We also spent two hours with an 82 year old man who was a songwriter, and who has written a story of his life in English, which he hopes to get published. This man, Mr. Inga Pissa, was deported by the Germans in 1909 to Saipan (Germany controlled both islands then) but escaped in 1915 to Guam. The U.S. helped him, after the war, to get back to his home. Mr. Pissa sang us several long ballads telling of his paddling hundreds of miles over the open sea in a tiny outrigger log canoe. "I used the Southern Cross as my compass," he said. We made both tape recordings and sound movies of him; now I hope they turn out.

The experience none of us will ever forget was a performance put on for us by the students at the agricultural college. About thirty of them, Samoans, and some from neighboring islands, put on an hour and a half of the most spectacular and beautiful dancing and singing. I'll never forget the "welcome song"—as a matter of fact, I wish I could learn it some day to teach campers at home:

One leader stands up in front of the group, seated in a tight semicircle on the floor about him. He suddenly crouches and rubs his hands, flat palmed, vigorously before him. They all do likewise. Then comes a thunderous unison handclap, and the song begins. In rich sonority, three or four parts, with handclapping in certain parts, and soft drumming on a rush mat by one man. The leader would put most of our choral directors to shame. He was a dancer, lithe, graceful. His dance was part of the Welcoming song. At times he made vigorous arm motions which, I was told later, cued certain kinds of hand claps. The faces of the singers remained impassive, but his was animated—a flashing smile, and sparkling eyes darting from right to left.

After their performance they sat back expectantly, and I realized that I was expected to contribute to the evening. I wondered what on earth I could do that would not be an anticlimax. So I started with Huddie [Leadbelly]'s "Fannin Street." I'm proud to say that they loved it. We sang several songs together then, and I wound up with "Tzena" and "Wimoweh" (which they latched right on to) and some banjo breakdowns. They stayed seated on the floor when the few white people got up to go, and one student whispered to me, "Could you teach us some of the things you do on the guitar and banjo?"

"How many of you play guitar?" I asked him.

"Almost every one of us."

Well this was an unexpected twist. As if it wasn't a big enough sin for Coca Cola to blanket the world, here I am doing the same thing in a different way. I stood up and made a little speech, saying how magnificent a performance they had put on, and how proud I was that they liked the music I had to offer in return. I promised to send them copies of my own instruction books and records for banjo and guitar. But then I spoke further, as passionately and as eloquently as I could:

"All the white people I know would feel envious of your tremendous abilities to dance and sing, as I have heard tonight. I hope you know also what a precious possession to have is this. Now, you are here to learn modern scientific agricultural methods. Fine. Learn them. But don't forget these wonderful parts of your life. Learn geography. Learn history, economics. Travel, as I know many of you will. Learn new things. But don't forget this which you have now. Don't ever forget it."

"I Hope They Keep Their Beautiful Music," 1963

Letter to Harold and Natalie Leventhal from Hong Kong,
dated October 7, 1963; found in Seeger files

Dear Harold and Natalie,

There is nothing of great importance in the letter to come, but I thought I would set me down at my new typewriter and get off a long rambling disconnected letter to you. Tomorrow we leave for Japan, and now is probably the best time to draw a breath and take stock, and let you know as much as possible what's gone on. I suppose in Tokyo there will be letters from you, but meanwhile here goes.

First, Indonesia, since it is so fresh in my mind.

There was no time (nor money) to go to Bali. I had been unaware myself quite how big Indonesia is: 4 big islands, 3,000 small ones, total land area about ¼ of U.S.A., stretching 3,000 miles east to west. Java, slightly smaller than Britain, has almost 2/3 of the 100,000,000 population. Djakarta is the big city—over 3 million. None of the others approached it in size, fortunately.

The low standard of living is evident everywhere, though there were few beggars, and no outright starvation that I saw—but millions of people living on wages of $6 a month. Poor farmers might see only a dollar or two a month cash—though of course they get their own food. A college professor might get *top pay*: $150 a month. Longshoremen $10 a month.

At the same time, prices in their market are not that much lower than the USA. Imported machinery is much more expensive. Homemade hardware about the same as the USA. Food slightly lower, but not a great deal lower. This means that the average person eats rice and fruit and not much else, and is very well off if he owns two shirts and one pair of shoes. Many go barefoot. But everyone has a clean shirt on in the morning.

Only one thing (beside wages) surprised us by its cheapness: gasoline is about 7 cents a gallon. I think this is one of the main fruits of the Soekarno government's deal with oil companies.[1]

It is a beautiful land. Terraced rice fields everywhere, neat little cottages, lovely mountains. We drove up the top of one volcano and climbed down into the crater, walking around on hot rocks with sulphurous steam pouring out from the cracks. Djakarta was like many big cities, though: too crowded, and the stink of open sewers assailed our noses more often than one might wish. The huge Hotel Indonesia was comfortable, but fantastically expensive—$10 per night per person, and after we got out of the swimming pool, we took a walk, and saw poor people craning their necks through the iron fence posts to try and see the white millionaires at play. After that we didn't really much swim there again.

Any American's first thought is: Good God, what continual waste of manpower. Produce hauled to town by foot at 3 mph. Stores—millions of little stores, each tended by a family of people squatting on the sidewalk or behind a tiny counter. Big logs being sawed lengthwise by *hand*. I said to myself, a hundred times last week, "If they only had some trucks, some supermarkets, some power saws!"

I did not give any formal concerts, but half a dozen short appearances. Most of the city office workers and the students understand English fairly well, though the poor people don't. It's a country of linguists. They know their "local language," and Bahasa Indonesian, the official national language (originally the language of the Malay traders between the islands, like Swahili was in East Africa). Then many know Dutch, some know Japanese, and many know English, which I think is taught in all the high schools and colleges now. Our interpreter, a nice violinist named Boestanul Arifin (translation: "Garden of Wisdom"), studied in Belgium and knows seven or eight languages.

Boestanul helped me when I performed and it worked perfectly. He would translate as I went along. After the students in each school performed for us and on camera and tape machines, I would sing for them. In addition I sang at a public high school, and for some Christian theological students, and at an orientation meeting for 500 guides and interpreters getting ready for the big GANEFO games this month. This is like the Olympics of the socialist and former colonial countries. The latter crowd liked the songs, and the chairman remarked simply that he hoped Mr. Seeger and the songs he sings represent some of the New Emerging Forces of the United States (GANEFO means Games of the New Emerging Forces).

"We Shall Overcome" was a hit song everywhere. I am sending to Sis Cunningham a tape I think you will like to hear. I've asked her to

---

1. Soekarno (1901–1970) was the first president of Indonesia from 1945 to 1967 and the chief proponent of Indonesian independence from Dutch colonial rule. As president, Soekarno nationalized many Indonesian industries, most notably the formerly Dutch-owned, highly lucrative, oil companies.

have a dub made of it, and send it to SNCC—it consists of the moving comments of an Indonesian upon hearing the songs, and then a verse of it sung by me and a group of Indonesian students, who sing it surprisingly well—they were a chorus kind of like the Old People's Chorus in NYC, which sings songs of many different countries. I left a tape recording of the song in Jokja, and the words and music on paper in Djakarta, and my guess is that they will have a translation of it perhaps, unless they prefer to sing it in English.

The weather in Indonesia is hot but not stifling. Not as bad as NYC in July, certainly. People get up very early, and then all offices and work usually stops from 2 PM to 5 PM. Frankly, I felt in better health there than for a long time. That afternoon nap is a great invention.

There is no winter or summer, since it's right near the equator. But the wet season begins usually in October and lasts till May. Then for five or six months there is no rain whatsoever, and only irrigation keeps the paddies from drying up.

…At the moment they are so broke they mostly ride bicycles. But cars are the big dream of many. I hope like hell the government keeps cars down for a while. The streets are crowded enough already. The air will be foul with smoke. I told them I don't think they need to ban the Twist as much as they need to ban motorcars.

In general, I sure as hell hope, as I did in Samoa, that Indonesia will be able to get some of the advantages of the modern world, without getting so many of its disadvantages. I hope they keep their beautiful music and dances, and houses and sarongs, and batiks, even if they do go ahead, as they must, and get a merchant marine, modern highways and transport, schools and hospitals.

Now, briefly to mention some other things:

…[Hong Kong is] a screwy city. Like NY, full of people who live here because there is money to be made. A beautiful city, when viewed from the peak. Spectacular mountains tumbling into the sea. A harbor full of huge modern liners, and hundreds of junks and sampans. A city of two main groups, Chinese and US-English. They do business with each other, but don't see each other socially. The city is clean, efficient, and few starve, so far as we can see. But the tin roofed shacks reach far up the hillsides, where people live on next to nothing. Water is scarce, and they count it by the cup up there, I'm sure. Some of the wealthy homes are fantastically opulent.

The whole city, so far as I can see, owes its existence to the need for an oasis in the Cold War. It is the Switzerland of the Orient. Up the bay in Canton,[2] Chinese goods are sold in all the shops here. But they can't be brought into America, even if the raw materials came from China.

---

2. Canton, now known as Guangzhou, is a major manufacturing city in China and host to the annual China Import and Export fair.

They say. Danny has bought himself a better camera here, and I got a typewriter. Tomorrow we'll take a little tour on the bay. The junks are to me the most fascinating thing of all. I would like to have one on the Hudson River. Each is owned by a family, who live on it, along with a little livestock. They carry goods from the big liners to the shore (there are far too few docks) and do a little coastal and traffic up river. A little? A lot.

We are all looking forward to Japan now, and to seeing Toshi's father. And I think it will be a relief to be able to stay in one country a little longer. Up 'til now we have just gotten acquainted with a place and we've had to go. So the six or seven weeks in Japan will be good. We'll also have a chance to check up on camera and film work. I think if Screen Gems is interested in doing anything they should contact us there. They can look at what we filmed so far, but I don't think they'll see how to use them.

I feel I know how they can be used. On an Educational TV program, of songs and dances of many countries, going back and forth from me, live, to films, and using of still pictures, and recordings, etc. In fact, I'm quite positive that the films we are taking—if they are in good focus etc.—are going to be quite useful. The Nagra tape recorder is a little heavier than I hoped, but it sure is a blessing. I actually look forward to spending about four months with a Moviola [film editing machine] in Beacon, putting all the films in shape, when we return. Danny and Toshi are taking lots of pictures, and they should be useful too.

. . . Well, finally I'll close. I have a batch of other letters to write. But it is a pleasure to type. I'm just too slow with a pen. Tires me out. Hope you two are in the pink of health. Take care of yourselves.

Pete

P.S. -Rereading this letter, it seems like a helluva selfish one, not mentioning what real good travelers and workers the rest of the family are. Oh, they snap at each other occasionally when they get too tired. And occasionally we find it best to split up from each other for a little bit. But by and large, they have done well. Swallowed all kinds of strange food. Sat up long hours on trains and planes, and worst of all had to sit around for hours listening to Pop sing or talk. The talking is worst.

Toshi has been a genius of organization, getting us on schedule from one place to the next, and getting visas, etc. Also, we have found that we can get along on a fantastically small amount of clothing. For the last two months we have all done with one or two pairs of shoes each, and one or two changes each of shirts, socks, etc. This wash and dry synthetic cloth is a godsend. Or at least a sciencesend.

Also the postal system is a governmentsend, much to be thanked, so that we don't need to keep around various things we pick up, but ship them home immediately. Books, pictures, gifts given us. I carry fewer pieces of papers with me than ever before, and find it a relief.

But now I *must* get those other letters written.

"My Programs Are Not Political," 1963

Letter to Shin Kugimoto of KBK, dated November
11, 1963; found in Seeger files

Dear Mr. Kugimoto,

I was disturbed yesterday to hear from Mr. Kishi and Mr. Fukui that some of the officials of KBK did not approve of my program in some way. Now, I am always listening to suggestions for how to improve. I and my family listen closely to reactions of the audience. I was glad to take suggestions made on artistic grounds, and I intend to try out occasionally more songs which are familiar to Japanese, such as "Clementine," as long as these are also songs which I feel my style is suited for.

But, it seems, the KBK officials had political disapproval of one song in particular: the Japanese song about the atom bomb. This I find completely un-understandable. It always gets more applause than any other song I sing. Some Japanese have told me that they are unable to keep back tears when they hear it. I have sung the song for five years in America, and will be singing it in 25 other nations of the world. It would be silly *not* to sing it now. I do not intend to take it off my programs here.

I was then told by Mr. Kishi that he and you personally had nothing against the song, but that KBK was a "Free World" organization, representing USA culturally in Japan. This was a great surprise to me. I am taking a musical tour, not a political tour. I thought KBK was a nonpolitical commercial concert organization.

I was told then that everything in Japan was political. Well, I suppose in a philosophical sense everything is political, even food, babies, and making love, since legislation can affect all of them. But my programs are not political, and I have always fought very hard for the right to say what I wanted, and to sing the songs that I felt to be true and beautiful, whether they are old or new. And I will always do this.

Very sincerely,
Peter Seeger

"As Full of Contrast as One Can Imagine," 1963

Letter to Charles Seeger from Japan, dated
November 23, 1963; found in Seeger files

Well Pop,

One final massive missive from Japan, before we fly to Calcutta Tuesday. And meanwhile you yourself are probably flying to Chile. I wouldn't burden you with another, except that I wanted to sum up this little series.

At the end of seven weeks I agree with Bill Malm: there is hardly a generalization that wouldn't be true of some Japanese and untrue of other Japanese.[3] This country is as full of contrast as one can imagine: symphonies, jazz, sing-along coffee shops, hillbilly, plus 57 varieties of traditional music from rough and hearty peasant songs to ultra refined aristocratic idioms.

Perhaps, as the physical anthropologists pointed out about races in general, there is far more variation within one country than there is difference between the averages of different countries. The rich and the poor, the young and the old, the worker and the shirker, the timid and the reckless, the wise and the fool. In Japan as in the U.S.A.

But are there any average differences? I'd say, of course, yes. How much? That's the debatable question. Certainly some things could be decided statistically: we know the average wage here is less than one-third the average US wage. Prices for many goods and services are almost the same as US. (Japan thus rates slightly below Britain and West Germany, but ahead of many other parts of the world—it has by far the highest income of any nation in Asia.)

Similarly, one could make a statistical study of the amount of time Japanese spend on music, and on what sort of music. This should be done by someone.

Meanwhile I'll stick my neck out with a few highly unsupported generalizations and conjectures.

I'd say that the onslaught of western culture has dented but by no means killed off the many forms of traditional music. It is true that schools only teach western music, it is true that millions of thatched roofs have TV antennas above them. But I hear a woman humming as she sweeps out her fish market in the early morning. Is it a western melody? Nope. Pure Japanese minor pentatonic, with all the wobbles. At a party, when *sake* has made everyone mellow, do they sing western songs? Not a bit of it. Ancient, ancient styles.

As in the streets of every city, men are dressed in neat business suits and white shirts. But at home they take off the shoes and sit on straw mats.

I asked Haruhiro Fukui, my interpreter, which aspects of Western Life he thought Japan would most likely accept, and which reject. He replied: the material things would be accepted easily, the spiritual not. (For example, Christianity hasn't made much of a dent in Japan, even in recent years.)

What basic philosophical concepts are there here which are different from ours? I'll hazard a guess: "One lives by the rules."

Now, of course Man everywhere lives by the rules, but I think here more than ever. When an art or science is studied, the rules are conscientiously

---

3. Malm's 1959 book, *Traditional Japanese Music and Musical Instruments,* was one of the early exhaustive studies of traditional Japanese music published in the West.

learned. Thus one can have one set of rules for life at home, another set of rules for life on the street. Learning flower arrangement, learning the *Koto* [a Japanese stringed instrument], one sees earnest obedience to the rules. Men all wear white shirts. If London or Paris or NYC changes the rules, that is, changes the style of shirt, then they will be followed here. But I will bet a good amount that the rules will not be changed first in Tokyo. Rules are rules. The rules for tying a kimono were set centuries ago and haven't been changed also. If you go off for a hike, there are certain ways you equip yourself and certain places to go.

The rules are kept in separate compartments, as one might keep languages cleanly defined from one another (one wouldn't teach French-germanrussianchinese all from the same book). Thus even restaurants tend to be segregated: one serves just sushi (a kind of rice ball). Another serves just buckwheat noodles. Don't we have such monoculinary traditions in the USA? Of course yes. But *more here.*

Well, the third and last generalization I'd make: that things are changing and changing fast. U.S. pressure and influence even without modern free-enterprise life will do it. Outdoor advertising can now be seen along the hillsides. Cheap paint and new building materials will change architecture in spite of tradition. Already roof tiles are cheaply made from cement and painted in bright colors.

An extended aside: I regret this a good deal. The drab Japanese house exteriors I think are really beautiful. The dark brown weathered wood, the mud, the thatch. And the silvery grey tile roofs of a village remind me of an oyster bed. All horizontal lines. No two exactly alike. No one very different. Then, as the inside of the oyster is glistening clean, so also is each house—and many a young man has found a pearl within.

I think my final question would be now: how many of these material things can Japan accept without changing underneath? The mask becomes the face.

It will be interesting to see.

Much love,
Pete

"I Am Too Numbed," 1963

Letter to Harold Leventhal from Calcutta, India, dated
December 1, 1963; found in Seeger files

Dear Harold,

Busy as your poor staff is, I wonder if anyone would have time to make copies of the enclosed handwritten letter to you, and the enclosed crumpled-page article. If anything at all is ever printed about this trip, they may be some of the most important ingredients.

Under separate cover come letters about Calcutta—Gopal [Sanyal] and his committee have done a wonderful job, and our only regret is lack of time to see and hear even a quarter of what we could if we were staying here longer.

Pete

P.S. Reading letters from the States about Kennedy's murder. Crises seem to bring out the best in America. Cause people to think of larger problems than their own personal ones. I hope my letters do not indicate a lack of concern on our own part, even 10,000 miles away. The events have been on all our minds, and influence all our work. I have perhaps grown too used to the thought that our humanly race has perhaps a 65 percent chance of surviving beyond the next 150 years, that I am too numbed to present horrors. Here our car drives over dogs in the street, and we see starvation-emaciated people on all sides.

P.

"God Helps Them That Helps Themselves," 1963

Letter to Harold Leventhal from New Delhi, India, dated December 6, 1963; found in Seeger files

On the plane to New Delhi: from the window, the grandest view of the Himalayas. We sailed past them about 150 miles away, for an hour. The hugest peaks I'll ever see, I guess. A stupendous sight in a cloudless sky. Bases all shrouded in haze. Upper ten thousand feet of them all snow and rock.

Tinya runs in giggling from glimpsing the forward cabin and the crew: "The captain's just reading a newspaper and not even watching where the plane is going!"

...I am amazed by the variety of physical types I see in India—far greater even than America. Really! Some faces very dark, some very light. Some short and fat, some tall and lean. In a village we saw dancers and singers whose skin was dark, but whose features had the lean angularity of the Scotch-Irish mountain folk of Kentucky, like Abraham Lincoln. I was told that there are 300 distinct languages, not including dialect variations within one language.

...I hear a recording of an Indian folk dance tune: it is almost note for note the banjo tune "Sally Ann." And the rhythm is basically the same, 'til it gets more complicated.

But in general, I agree with the Indians who say to me, "We feel that our folk music has a lot more in common with your folk music, because the basic content is so similar, even though the idioms may be somewhat different."

Toshi looks in the mirror and says, "Oh, my hair is getting gray so fast." I reply, "I bet I beat you to baldness before you get to grayness."

Gopal Sanyal takes us to his home, introduces us to his mother. She is the boss of their "joint family" (a common Indian institution where several brothers and their families live together). Each family has one small room. Gopal has also one room—but he's a bachelor. We kid him. "That's why you don't get married. You won't have so much space with a wife and children in here, too." Gopal really was wonderful to us. The most considerate man.

We visit Jamini Roy. Wonderful old man. I love his paintings. Like me and others, he is building contemporary art on the basis of an ancient folk tradition. His big comfortable house in the suburbs is full of his paintings, and he sits in the courtyard every day in the sun painting more. As when I sing a folksong, I repeat an old tune with slight variations, he repaints an old theme with slight variations.

My own reservations about his work: the figures sometimes seem squeezed too close for my taste. But of course this is the Indian tradition. His paintings are nowhere near as full of tight crowded figures as are the Hindu temples, or other folk paintings. If I was a figure on a Hindu temple, I'd have claustrophobia, I would.

But I love his colors, his form, his content. I think he is one of the world's great painters, speaking in his language, but intelligible to the world.

...In New Delhi we are staying in a fancy modern suburb, for government workers, and the new middle class, and the 12,000 westerners who also live here. Blocks of clean concrete. I still don't think much of the architecture. The builders of these houses were all in love with the ninety degree angle.

...Had another idea for a song (have had several). "My father's house has many rooms. Some painted yellow, some painted blue. Each has a door, but it is only occasionally locked. And we all share the kitchen and the midday meal."

Have seen so often in the evening a group of poor people huddled around a little fire somewhere. In the gutter or on the sidewalk. Another idea, "What are the pleasures of the poor?/ A live flame to watch and huddle near/ Warm arms to fold the near and dear/ Surprise, when the sun is not too hot or chill too cold/ Sudden exits, to keep us from growing old."

Went to an Indian movie yesterday. Two minutes of dialogues (comic, melodrama, or love) and five minutes of music. Typical Hollywood approach to life. I could swear that the makers were assiduously following the success routes of the Hollywood movies of the '30s.

Well, the car has arrived and we are scheduled to visit a village. So I'll close. I hope these ramblings are not too boring. I will have to work out a balance between isolated disconnected paragraphs such as the above, and more generalized observations. The latter I feel worthwhile, because I still feel that my major task is to try and evaluate the *general* cultural landscape, without paying undue attention to isolated but distant peaks. Thus one can say that India is generally flat, though Everest is on its border. Thus I say that her architecture ain't so hot, in spite of the Taj Mahal.

And my overall feeling is that this country needs more of the philosophy, "God helps them that helps themselves." I sat in a temple with a praying priest, noticing the sloppy job of paint on the ceiling, the dirty walls, and like an average American (regular old Calvinist) felt in my heart: "My form of prayer would be to get up off my knees and clean up this joint."

Tagore actually said as much in some of his writings, of course.[4] But this country needs reforestation, sanitation, vitamination and calorization, and then by God they'll have a booming nation.

Well, I'm probably way off base, and will keep my opinions to myself until I have a chance to see how wrong they are.

All for now, hastily.
P.

"The Cameras Are Grinding Away," 1963

Early draft of a piece that saw publication in Seeger's regular "Johnny Appleseed, Jr." column in *Sing Out!* magazine, no. 14.2, April/May 1964

On this trip we have so much equipment with us that to keep from paying too much overweight on the planes, our clothing is down to bare minimums. One pair of shoes apiece, two socks, two shirts, etc. The rest is banjoes and guitars, tape recording machine and cameras, cameras, cameras.

I have no desire to become the Burton Holmes[5] of the folk music world, but I hope somehow that some of the movies we have taken will be able to be seen somewhere. We have filmed in 16mm sound something in every country we have visited. Mostly unrehearsed, unposed, and in its natural habitat. The family has become a fairly efficient crew, with two cameramen, a sound man, a script girl, and the 8-year old to switch the battery on when the crucial time arrives.

In India a friend takes us bump in a Land Rover off across the dusty countryside, and way out in the hell and gone there is a village entirely

---

4. Rabindranath Tagore (1861–1941) was a Bengali writer and a core figure of the Bengal Renaissance, a period of Indian history marked by an explosion of scientific innovation, artistic creativity, and a philosophical and social transition into the modern era.
5. Holmes (1870–1958) was a travel writer, photographer, and filmmaker who also lectured widely on his travels through the world.

occupied by snake charmers and their families. Half the men were hundreds of miles away in distant cities, earning a few rupees a day with a basket of snakes, but half the men were home on vacation, and agreed to put on a show for us. We set up the cameras, not knowing what to expect. One man plays a kind of bagpipe in which his cheeks form the bag. By expelling the air in them he has a moment to gulp another lungful, and a continuous stream of notes flows out. Tambourines, drums, dancers join in. Pretty soon some baskets are brought up and set up on the ground in front of the camera. Whoops, up come two big hooded heads, three feet in front of me. Dark smiling faces indicate that it's quite safe, and push me back to my seat. But, it seems, these two six-footers are just the aperitif. Out of a couple other baskets come some monster, one I swear a good eleven feet long. After a bit one of the men picks it up and quickly loops it around the neck of Mika, our fifteen year old daughter.

Well, the cameras are grinding away. She smiles prettily, if a bit nervously.

"The Coward's Easy Way," 1963

Letter to Harold Leventhal from Bombay, India, dated
December 10, 1963; found in Seeger files

Dear Harold,

You must be getting pretty disgusted reading my pontification about this and that. Did you know I was such a goddamned opinionated person? I'm usually silent or polite, because it's the coward's easy way. I guess this is one reason I wanted to be a newspaper reporter. I could see and hear all, but did not need to betray my opinions too much in reporting it. At this late age in life, though, I've decided that in all honesty, in these letters, I ought to express opinions, right or wrong. At least to be generous to give myself enough rope so that I can be hung later.

…In Calcutta an economist insisted to me that India could solve her agricultural problem without resorting to mechanized farming or socialized agriculture. "Look at Russia and China; they are having to buy grain. Agriculture is an art, not a science. Indian peasants can look at a cloud and tell you how much rain it will release. A college trained bureaucrat can't do that."

All I know is that as I look out of our plane window at the vast brown landscape below, I feel pity for the millions there who have so little chance in this world. There but for the grace of god go we. If you or I had been born down there—and had the good fortune to survive the diseases which decimate every family—I guess we also would have that lean and hungry look, and faithfully tie our turbans in the way our forefathers had always done, meticulously different from the other tribes, groups, sects.

I think perhaps people hold on to their ancient family traditions, their group traditions, because these are the only secure truths they know. Lacking education and broader knowledge, lacking money and power to travel and change and learn, they hang on to the few solid things they know: "My father did this, and he survived, and so I shall do it too."

But so often the survival is on such a low plane, I wonder how they can accept it. I also sang yesterday at a *harijan* nursery school.[6] It is run by social worker type people. "We must uplift and help the poor." My personal reaction was that this is another case of band-aid on the festered ass of democracy. Not that people in charge are not doing good work. Giving their lives. Helping at least more than I am doing, who only sit back and criticize.

Well, this is all for now. Other letters on other subjects.

As ever,
Pete

"Harambay!" 1972 [1963]

From *The Incompleat Folksinger,* Simon and Schuster, 1972

Nairobi, Kenya
December 12, 1963

The plane lands at Nairobi. We see green grass, human beings who are not half starved. Kenya seems like an affluent nation compared to India. The greatest politicians have a strong sense of poetry. Premier Kenyatta's[7] slogan, emblazoned on the new national coat of arms, is pure genius. It is one Swahili word: *Harambay.* Roughly translated, *Harambay* means "all together now" or "heave ho." But this isn't all. The term originated on the docks at Mombassa, ancient Kenya port for the Arab ships of a thousand years ago. The dock workers used the term in lifting loads; it was also used for hauling on ropes.

It means that English and African must haul together, country and city, illiterate and Ph.D., and turbaned Indian. There are several hundred thousand of the latter here, originally brought sixty years ago to build railroads, and now comprising the large class of shopkeepers. Those who think it is impossible to have a multiracial democratic country are leaving, or keeping their thoughts to themselves now. Those

---

6. The term "harijan," meaning "children of God," was introduced by Mohandas Gandhi for the Indian *Dalit* caste to replace the use of the derogatory term "untouchable."
7. Jomo Kenyatta (1894–1978) was the central figure in the push for Kenya's independence from British rule, obtained in December of 1963, and its first leader as prime minister and then president.

who hope and think this can be a prosperous, booming nation know there is only one way:

"*Harammm-bay!*"

Nairobi population is about 300,000. Population of all Kenya is about 8.5 million—small for such huge acreage. About a couple of dozen major tribal groups. Biggest are the Kikuyu, a million and a half agriculturalists. The Masai, half a million, are nomadic herders. All speak different languages, but many understand Swahili, the language of the old Arab traders with many African words in it. Only in Nairobi do many understand English, but it is likely that as education becomes more universal, much of the country will know it as a second language.

Few Kenyans realize quite the variety of cultures in their own country and so it was a stroke of genius to put a lot of tribal dancing in the Independence Day Celebration. Let me describe the evening of Wednesday, December 11, 1963. At midnight Kenya ceased being a colony and became a member of the British Commonwealth.

For miles the highways were clogged with cars, buses, and trucks. Along the grass hurried thousands of eager people, some of whom had walked for days to get here. Finally our taxi parked and we walked the last mile over a muddy field to a huge football stadium. 250,000 people—no fooling—were there for the ceremony. Were there speeches? Not one! Dozens of groups of tribal dancers, no two alike, came on at one end of the field, and gradually circled in front of the stands.

Each would pause in front of the stand, and perform their dance for five or ten minutes, then move on a couple hundred feet and do it in the next section. Another group closely followed them. At one time I counted thirty different groups on the field, with twenty to eighty dancers or musicians in each group. The color, variety, rhythms, and movements were staggering.

Here is one group of women, hips swishing, and singing with a soft undulating feeling.

Here are tall Masai warriors, with twelve-foot spears glistening, and hair plastered down with red ocher. A shuffling ominous phalanx.

Here are fifty wildly painted drummers, each with a narrow drum, five feet long, hung between his legs. A thunderous precision, and then suddenly half of them jump on the shoulders of the others and continue the rhythm unbroken.

Here come a troupe of tall thin dancers, whose white plumed headdresses reach two or three feet above their heads. In their hands are huge rattles which swish and thump as they toss their plumes.

Here are twenty little men whose armor contains so much metal that they sound like the contents of twenty kitchen cupboards being shaken in syncopation. Next come more women in brilliant dyed gowns.

By 10 PM, spotlights wave, and in comes a motorcade. Third in line is a white convertible. The crowd roars, "Jomo, Jomo," and standing up in the back is the powerful figure of Kenyatta, waving his famous fly whisk, as his car slowly circles the field and ends at the canopied stand.

More cars. Then some cheers. It's the Duke of Edinburgh, here to formally relinquish control.

Twenty minutes later the scene takes a new turn. A precision-drilled group of English soldiers, the Gordon Highlanders, appears. Trumpets. Drums. A brass band of about 600 takes the center of the stage. Scenes of ancient barbaric splendor give way to modern barbaric splendor.

For an hour the Queen's African Rifles, famous crack infantry troops, do close-order drill, up and down, back and forth, to a succession of march tunes.

So far not a word has been said over the loudspeakers. The people have been treated to a breathtaking pageant of the past and present powers controlling the destinies of Kenya.

It is nearing midnight. Three religious leaders ascend the rostrum and intone short prayers in three languages. The band stands poised at attention. Kenyatta and the Queen's governor walk out on the center of the now-empty field, alone and unattended. All lights go off. The band plays "God Save the Queen." In starlight the Union Jack slowly comes down on a flagpole at the end of the field. The lights go on. The national anthem of Kenya is begun. Only the opening two notes are heard, because the roar of the crowd drowns out everything as the black-green-and-red new flag slowly goes up. Deafening cheers as Kenyatta and the governor walk back to the rostrum.

Now comes 40 minutes of the most spectacular fireworks we have ever seen. At the end, the crowd streams happily across the field to the exits.

A Scotsman near us (about 5 percent of the crowd near us are white) says with a smile, "I came dressed in my tribal costume too," and displays his kilts.

We slowly make our way across the muddy field to our car. It is the most orderly and happy crowd. No drunks. No pushing or shoving. And even when some stumbled in water and mud over a foot deep, no cursing. At the cars are crowds of people helping to push each other's vehicles out of mud holes. Along the roadway in the distance we can hear singing.

Next day we met some Americans who told us that some white Kenyans may have been at the *Uhuru* [meaning "freedom" in Swahili] celebrations, but others stayed home and barred their doors, certain that there was to be a riot. And another friend, who came up from Tanganyika to the celebration, was asked by shocked white farmers, "You going up there? Oh, I'd be scared to. All those Mau Mau!"[8]

---

8. The Mau Mau were members of the Kikuyu ethnic group who sought to obtain independence from British colonial rule through armed struggle. The Mau Mau uprising lasted from 1952 to 1960, with many thousands of casualties among Kenyan and British soldiers and civilians.

The Mau Mau, granted amnesty by Kenyatta, are now coming out of the woods. One of their leaders came to see the English flag go down at the football stadium. He walked up and identified himself to Kenyatta, and the photographers clustered about recording the scene. Kenyatta went back and asked the Duke of Edinburgh if he would like to meet him, but the Duke shook his head.

The Mau Mau general had long hair in ringlets below his shoulder.

"Samson lost his strength when his hair was cut, and we vowed not to cut our hair till Kenya was free."

"A Tremendously Exciting Country," 1964

Written on or near January 7, 1964; found in Seeger files

In the evening something very special has been arranged. The children stay home. Toshi and I dress in our only good clothes. Mrs. DuBois[9] has arranged for us to visit the President of Ghana, Dr. Kwame Nkrumah,[10] and sing a few songs for him. Since it is only a week since an attempt was made to assassinate him, security precautions are strict, and we have been asked not to discuss our visit in advance with anyone.

(Since this is a nonpolitical tour I'm trying to make, I haven't mentioned this before. To some Nkrumah is a messiah, to others he is a dictator. The way *Life* and *Time* magazines have been attacking him lately tends to make me feel personally friendly to him. Our teenagers don't think the newspapers of Ghana do him a service when they support him hysterically. But I explain that maybe they would be excited too, if they knew more intimately the issues at stake.)

Shirley DuBois picks us up in her big black limousine, a Russian Chaika which Dr. DuBois bought last year with the earnings from sales of his books in Russia. We cruise majestically through the streets, and suddenly turn a corner and there we are at the gate of Christiansborg Castle, the executive residence.

HALT!!

---

9. Shirley Du Bois (1896–1977) was an American-born activist and author, and wife of W. E. B. Du Bois (1868–1963). W. E. B. Du Bois was a prolific author, intellectual, and activist and the most influential thinker in the area of African American civil rights in the first half of the twentieth century. Du Bois's body of work and activism helped lay the theoretical and political groundwork for the civil rights movement of the 1960s.
10. Nkrumah (1909–1972) was the first leader of Ghana after it gained independence from British rule. In addition to his commitment to Ghanaian nationalism, Nkrumah was also an early proponent of Pan-Africanism, helping to found the Organization of African Unity, a predecessor to the African Union. He advocated for a socialist Ghanaian state and championed socialism in Africa in many of his writings. However, the end of Nkrumah's tenure was marked by increased suppression of civil liberties; in 1966, his government was overthrown in a military coup.

Toshi and I had never had four rifles pointed at us quite so intently, and flinched a bit. The driver explains who we are. The captain of the guards trots to a telephone. We are let through the gate.

HALT!!

At an inner gate, we must also be identified. Then these also swing open. The car parks in front of some grand steps. Shirley, Toshi and I walk upstairs, and are ushered into an elegant drawing room. In a few minutes with no fanfare, in walks the President, and his lovely Egyptian wife, and five-year-old son.

Kwame Nkrumah is 55, but looks ten or fifteen years younger. Medium height, a handsome Africa face—very gentle, actually. He asks about us and our trip, about America. What do we think of Ghana?

"Oh, it's a tremendously exciting country," says I enthusiastically.

He smiles wryly. "Yes, very exciting." I realize it's a faux pas. To be nearly assassinated for the second time in a year is plenty exciting. But Nkrumah doesn't let it bother him, goes on asking questions. Mrs. DuBois rattles on in the homiest way. How Queen Elizabeth enjoyed her trip to Ghana, and how well she danced the Highlife (the popular West African dance). Nkrumah is quite relaxed. Nothing high and mighty about him. After a half an hour he suggests we go downstairs.

There in a smaller room, perhaps 18 square feet, we join about twenty women and a few men. One older woman is President Nkrumah's mother. She is nearly blind, but shakes hands with us gravely. Others include some of the servants of the household, bodyguards, and wives. I unlimber the banjo and guitar, and sing some of the same songs I have been singing through other parts of the world.

"Old Joe Clarke," "John Henry," "Which Side Are You On?" "Skip to My Lou," a work song, a spiritual, some of the songs of the Freedom Movement in the South. Now, in this small room, with its very special audience, each song took on new meanings. "Who Killed Davey Moore?" "We Shall Overcome." One of the guards (dressed, incidentally, as all of them were, in casual sport shirt—no uniforms) translated for those who did not know English. And afterwards, as I was packing up the instrument, I could see Nkrumah explaining, in a relaxed way, about me, to the women.

...Well, I have never in my life circulated much with VIPs, so I don't have much to compare this visit with, but I came away mightily impressed that here was an honest man working at an extraordinarily difficult job: how to bring a small poverty stricken country into independence and freedom, culturally, politically, economically. The obstacles are staggering. Few Africans are yet trained to take over the many jobs of government, business and education. No cash in the bank. Money temptingly offered, with all kinds of strings attached. Which to take? Who can you trust? If, no matter which decision is made, someone is bound to be offended, who do you offend?

I had a feeling that some of Nkrumah's problems are the same that any scholar in politics would have. But more, he has been willing to bluntly take on some powerful enemies, in order to push quickly for a modernized, independent, and united Africa. The next few years will be crucial. When the next few crops of university graduates get their degrees he'll have lots more assistance.

"Some Fascinating Contrasts," 1964

Letter to Elie Edson and Anita Pollitzer, Seeger's uncle and aunt, dated February 16, 1964; found in Seeger files

Dear Elie and Anita,

Maybe it's all the good French food inside us, but I swear this family has more *joie de vivre* the past few days. Even the spats break up in laughter:

"Danny, you're saying that just to annoy me!"

"I never try to annoy people. I just tease them."

"You tease Tinya just to make her scream."

"Tinya, do I tease you just to make you scream?"

"Yes, and I love you so much I *do* it."

... We started off from Austria three days ago in a rented Volkswagen Microbus.

... In the Austrian Tyrol we could stand at one end of a big valley and see half a dozen small villages, each with a single needle-spired church surrounded by a cluster of red-tiled roofs. In the early morning, before we left, we could hear dimly all the different church bells ringing. A beautiful sound. They didn't try to play tunes, but it has a kind of clanging tuneful pattern anyway. The ringing overtones hang overhead like the mist above a big waterfall. I'm afraid this is another European tradition which Americans have tried unsuccessfully to copy. Also Japanese. In both Chicago and Fukuoka I've heard loudspeakers banging out (tastelessly) melodies that were supposed to be sung, on electrified bells. Ugh.

Austria's a devout Catholic section. On houses, in pastureland, by the roadside, are small crucifixes with carved figures, realistically painted with pale skin and dripping red blood. Danny doesn't like 'em, though I point out it's like the innumerable carved Buddhas one can find in parts of Japan. Maybe Danny agrees with the Moslems, that there should be no attempts to portray a deity.

... Destination: London, tomorrow night. In Arlberg Pass, we had to wait for two hours with a line of trucks, 'til the highway had been cleared of six feet of snow. Today we read that avalanches have closed it completely. But as we drove north the weather got warmer because of lower altitude. Now it is late March in New York. The rolling French farmland is already plowed.

Going quickly from one country into another, we see some fascinating contrasts: Architecture, food, clothing. The latter is far more standardized though, because of mass production, I guess. (Question: will mass production eventually standardize the other two?)

Compared to Austria, Switzerland seemed quite wealthy. (French villages seemed much poorer on the whole, though the countrysides were most excellently manicured.) Most of the bigger cities now seem to have municipal laws forbidding owners of buildings in the picturesque older section from altering the outsides of the buildings. So except for the automobiles, one could almost think one was stepping into a town of several centuries ago. Old Innsbruck, Old Rapperswill (Swiss) or for that matter, Paris. But in the outskirts of Zurich I pointed to a modern housing development and remarked, "Looks almost like the U.S., doesn't it?"

"Yes. Ugly, isn't it?" Mika is incorrigibly anti-mass production.

The French villages are not so neat as the Austrian or Swiss. (We didn't go through Germany so I can't compare.) The wooden trim on the stone houses was often painted light green, or some other gay color. We all immediately recognized where we had seen this tradition before: French Canada.

In Austria I was the family translator, with what I could remember of my high school German, thirty years ago. In France Danny and Mika get the job. Are shy at first, but getting better. Mika says to me, "French is really a more beautiful language than English. Compare 'A la voila' to 'That is right.'" (I agree. But the usual American "That's ri-" is not so bad. Our Indonesian interpreter, Boestanul Arifin, who knew seven languages, felt Italian was the most beautiful language in the world. "It sings." But Danny and I think Swahili beats all we have so far heard, including Japanese, Bengali, Hebrew, et al.)

Mika reads in a guidebook, "It says here that French beds are the most comfortable in the world."

"They are convinced of that," I explain. "The most beautiful city, the most beautiful language, the most beautiful girls. *La Belle France.*"

But as a tall man, I can state categorically that one of America's greatest inventions is the king-size nonsag bed and long blankets. In Japan my feet froze while the rest of me sweated under a too-thick comforter. And in Switzerland where not all men are short, we are presented with two (2) thick comforters, each no more than five feet square. I try tucking one around my feet, and another around my shoulder, and hope that a few inches will stay overlapped around my middle.

French cooking is something else. Even roadside restaurants maintain a standard that would put U.S.A. to shame. We get superlative soup, crusty bread, and mellow cheese in one. Mika remarks, "In America we'd get in a place like this, Campbell's soup, tasteless soft white bread, and Kraft processed cheese."

But though the average is high, still, French cooking has its highs and lows, and the lows could often be topped by good cooking elsewhere. For one thing, I think they could let it be simpler and let natural flavor be tasted more (as the Japanese do) without relying quite so much on sauces. The poorer cooks still use too much grease, as in the US. (A century ago, Mrs. Trollope[11] complained of American cooking as using "rivers of butter and oceans of gravy.")

I've heard my father say that most American teaching is afflicted with what he calls Europo-centrism. As though Europe was the center of the universe. In Austria I met a Fulbright professor who tells me that the English literature departments of most European universities think that American literature is juvenile. "Who has America go to compare with Goethe?" they will say.[12] They think the Swedes are silly giving occasional Nobel prizes to the Americans. "Sinclair Lewis? He was just a popular best-seller."[13]

I have a suspicion that Europe's big problem is this: that she has had such a great culture in her past, that she will be slow to realize that other parts of the world have also had great pasts—and will have greater futures—as Europe will, too.

In any case, we are drinking it all in—as much as we can while just driving through. Langres: a lovely walled town in Lorraine, with narrow winding streets, and well-maintained battlements. Impressive Paris (the 1918 Ragtime tune echoed in my head, "How ya gonna keep 'em down on the farm, after they've seen Pareeee?"). We stood awed under the tall arches of Reims and Beauvais, wondering how on earth masons were able to make those fantastic flying arches and lacy spires, has a more mystical aura than the Roman and Greek self-contained circles, squares, and triangles. Remember Frank Lloyd Wright's opinion that St. Peter's [Basilica in Vatican City] is essentially the Pantheon plunked on top of the Parthenon?

Who do you suppose invented the arch anyway? My history books said the Romans did. But I wouldn't be surprised if some Roman architect didn't observe a slave mason bridging over the top of a window with a slightly arched collection of small stones (perhaps because he lacked the big one to do the job). And the Roman architect swiped the idea and developed it in designing his next villa. With his mathematical training, he probably analyzed the basic principles involved, perhaps by dangling a heavy chain and tracing the parabolic curve.

---

11. Frances Trollope (1779–1863) was an English writer, best known for her 1832 book *Domestic Manners of the Americans,* which painted an unfavorable picture of American decorum and national identity.
12. Johann Wolfgang von Goethe (1749–1832) is considered the most influential figure in modern German literature. Goethe wrote works in many literary genres but is best known for his drama *Faust.*
13. Lewis (1885–1951) was a novelist, and the first American to be awarded the Nobel Prize in Literature. Lewis's books were often commentaries on the then-emerging modern American society, including the conflicts between capitalism and small-town American values.

After all, the Eskimos probably knew about arches for thousands of years, with their igloos. Perhaps other folk cultures did also.

Driving through the lush French countryside, I got to thinking of the thousands of wars that must have been fought for their possession. Prehistoric peoples, Romans, Gauls, barons. As we approached the banks of the Marne [River] I saw in my mind's eye the zigzag trenches, and the implacable tanks coughing and thundering across the fields where my Uncle Alan spent his last few minutes.

In Paris then I stood under the Arc de Triomphe. It's much larger than pictures would lead one to think. And the size impresses. A beautiful touch is the eternal flame over the grave of the French unknown Soldier: "Here lies a French soldier who died for his fatherland."

But then on the outside of the arch I see a statue of Napoleon being crowned by an angel, and wonder what would have been the thoughts of a citizen of Spain, Italy, or Austerlitz of that period of history. Where does the love of one's own country end and the despising of another's country begin? Defense, yes? But the best defense is a good offense, said Bony.

Well, the human race has been throwing stones at each other for two million years, and piling stones on top of each other for only a few thousand years. Now we are traveling through this world in the hope of discovering ways to help make it possible for this argumentative form of life to enjoy the planet for another couple billion years, for which scientists say it will be habitable.

Traveling really is a good thing. Between countries, between social classes, from city to country and rich to poor. I think there is a very good reason why artists and writers have nearly always liked to travel. The contrasts stimulate the senses, produce new ideas.

The human nervous system will send back reports to the brain if there is anything new to report. But if not, not. This is why the lover's hand keeps moving. If it rests on a hip for ten minutes, it is really not feeling the hip.

Well, I hope you will pardon this overlong, rambling letter. I started out by wanting to give you the family's reaction to a part of the world which I knew you loved, and ended by generalizing too much. I hope all is going well with you, and the apartment on 115th Street, Manhattan, USA. Do take care of yourselves. As I write this final paragraph we are in London. The [English] Channel was foggy and choppy, but no one got seasick. We drove our car off, and three hours later were ensconced in a London flat, with a kitchen yet! And Danny and Mika have promised to go shopping tomorrow and give us some home cooked meals for a change. Besides, we know English restaurant food is not liable to be as good as the French.

Much love,
Pete

"The Difficulty of Giving Answers," 1964

Letter to Woody Guthrie from Moscow, USSR, dated May 4, 1964; found in Woody Guthrie Foundation Archives

Dear Woody,

Toshi and I are sorry we have not been around to visit you, but we have been traveling. Took the kids out of school, went around the world. Paid for the trip by singing in 25 countries. We'll be back home in a month, and will come around to see you then.

In a sense, you came with me on the trip, because I was singing your songs everywhere. In some places like Australia, India, and England, the songs were well known—at least some of them. In most places they were brand new, but were well liked, and people asked where they could get words and music of them. So I was busy handing out addresses of Moe Asch and *Sing Out*, all around the world.

The language barrier made it hard to get some of the songs across, like "Talking Columbia," but others, like "Reuben James," "This Land Is Your Land," "Union Maid," "Hard Traveling," "So Long," they got right away, with the help of a little translation (I work on the stage with a translator standing beside me). But the favorite song of all in every country was "Why Oh Why." It got everybody laughing and made 'em think, in every place, Asia, Africa, and Europe. And I usually end up saying, "Perhaps some of you out there are students in school or college. Can you imagine tomorrow morning, just as your professor is about to open his mouth to give a lecture, the whole class rises and sings ..." and I go into one more chorus, 'Whyowhyowhyowhy whyowhyowhy,' and he says (I wave my arms like a distracted penguin), 'Becausebe-causebecausebecause,' (I wave them off as though to say "you all go to blazes"), "Goodbyegoodbyegoodbye."

This cuts down to a central problem of our whole world: the right and the duty of every man, woman and child to question themselves and others. And admit also the difficulty of giving answers. And admit the silliness of some of the questions.

Woody, every day I live I realize more my debt to you as a poet and musician. I mean I'm trying to be one, and what I half-learned from you have been the most valuable few lessons I ever learned in my life. Not only me, of course, learned, but a whole raft of young guitar pick-ers and verse-makers, a helluva lot more talented than me. I've been singing some of their songs around the world, too: Ernie Marrs, Tom Paxton, Bob Dylan, not to mention old Malvina [Reynolds]. I guess you know that her song about "Little Boxes" (mass produced houses and mass produced people) has been heard on all the US radios.

Right now we're finishing up a one month tour of this big Soviet land. We've been given a warm welcome in half a dozen big modern cities. It's a good country. It's way behind U.S.A. in some ways. Their average weekly income is more like ours in the 1920s—a good wage is $30 a week. But they are way ahead of us in other ways. Not a slum in a single city. Not as we know it, with demoralized people and dirt and danger in the streets. And most advanced medical care available for every single person, no matter who they are. Vacations for everyone. Jobs for all who want, and pensions for old folks. There's still a helluva lot of improvements needed, and they are only too painfully aware of it. They are all deeply ashamed of what happened when old heavy-handed Stalin started pushing people around, and are pretty determined it won't happen again.

But it's not easy to get into the habit of talking out, after you got in the habit of keeping your mouth closed, and people are by and large what you and I would call shy. The idea of singing along with me is a completely new idea to them, and I have slow going at first. But later they really break out. And I have learned just a few of their songs, so we can meet each other at least part way. I'm going to try and learn Russki so if I get a chance to come back here I can meet 'em more nearly half way.

I wish I could do this with every country in the world, to help tie in together a big rainbow colored band. But it's hard enough to learn one or two new languages, let alone a hundred. Did you know that in India alone they have 320 separate languages?

In Ghana I visited the grave of old Dr. DuBois, the great Negro scholar who died there aged 94 last year.

...I honestly do believe that no one of us ever dies as long as little bits of the things we did in our lives are still flitting around the old world, and the children we borne alternately cuss us and use us.

See you this summer,
As ever,
Pete

"Final Excerpt," 1964

Dated June 3, 1964; found in Seeger files

This morning I rolled over sleepily in bed and dimly tried to figure out what hotel I was in when after a few seconds I realized I was really in a bed long enough for me, and it was home.

The plane came in yesterday afternoon and there were friends to greet us. Customs was thorough. The first time in 24 countries that our bags were gone through in detail.

By London time, it was 2 AM when we got home, but Tinya stayed awake the whole time, chanting, "Ten more miles to go, we've ten more miles to go, around the curve and up the hill, we've ten more miles to go."

Everything in America seems rich and big. Cars seem like cruisers and our log cabin like a mansion.

No more long trips for quite a while. We've got a huge job ahead of us, editing the movies we took, developing pictures, and generally settling down to routine. Home seems awfully good.

"Still Wandering Son," 1972

Letter to Charles and Elsie Seeger, dated
March 7, 1972; found in Seeger files

Dear Father and Elsie,

Just a few more words from your still-wandering son and nephew. After six busy days in Paris the visas finally came through, and I write this from a Moscow Hotel. Day after tomorrow we leave to spend eight days in North Vietnam, at the invitation of the Artists Union. After that, the itinerary is up in the air. I have not even mentioned to our interpreter, a nice woman from the Ministry of Culture, that we might be visiting China. When she asked what we thought of Nixon's visit to China,[14] and I said that I thought that there was probably a thought in his mind that among other things he could drive the communist nations apart, she immediately said, "They are already as far apart as possible. You can't call China communist. I saw on our TV a movie made by Belgian cameramen. They line up children like robots, and have them all chant in unison. They are turning men into beasts!"

Well, we have one day here, and I'll try to learn more.

(March 9, aboard plane to Hanoi)

I'll try to mail this in Bombay or Calcutta. Since Tuesday evening there was no more time to write. I was interviewed and sang three or four songs for Soviet TV—they have excellent color quality—French technology. It was so improvised we had to tape it twice. The young woman announcer cheerfully crossed herself and breathed a sigh of relief when we had it right. My translator said, "Thank God the Ministry of Culture doesn't run the TV. Too much bureaucracy." The bouncy young director (who had formerly been a circus clown!) took us all out for a midnight snack with Soviet champagne and was kidded unmerci-

---

14. In 1972, United States president Richard Nixon visited China, the first sitting president to do so. Due to the tense state of Chinese-American relations, the trip came as a surprise to many citizens of both nations. During the trip, Nixon and the Chinese government worked out the details of the Shanghai Communiqué, which took steps to formalize a more amiable relationship between the two countries.

fully by Toshi and the other women for getting so excited during the taping and behaving like a dictator.

I had sung, "Oh, Had I a Golden Thread" (peace song, mine) and "The Bennington Rifles" (1776) and "Fixing To Die Rag," the jazzy sarcastic satire on the Vietnam War (by a popular rock singer, Country Joe). Then, in conversation, demonstrated some instrumental techniques on banjo and guitar, and ended with the Russian children's song, "May There Always Be Sunshine." I'm told the tape goes on Soviet network in a couple weeks.

Wednesday morning early I couldn't sleep, got up at dawn, and in near zero temperature, strolled thru Red Square and joined several dozen others standing in front of Lenin's Tomb. After half an hour the crowd numbered several hundred, and then "clomp clomp" out marched four immaculate soldiers in a stately ballet, changing of the guard. Their boots swung in a huge goosestep, and two of them replaced the guards at the entrance of the tomb. No shouted commands. The tomb, an artful pile of polished granite blocks, is not ugly. It's symbolic of Lenin's determination to make USSR a technologically advanced country. But I prefer St. Basil's Cathedral, 100 yards away. Stunning, with the morning sun behind it, also clouds of smoke and steam from a big factory. I'm told that Czar Ivan the Terrible put out the eyes of the two architects that built it so they couldn't build anything classier.

…Much love to you both,
Pete

P. S. Forgot to mention reading in Moscow airport a diatribe on "Chinese Maoists trying to split world communist movement." To read it, one would think there's to be no reconciliation ever. But now I know better about politicians. Words words words.

"Hanoi Diary," 1972

From *Eastern Horizon* magazine, no. 11.4, 1972

Friday, March 10

We arrive in Hanoi amid palm trees and rice paddies to our right and left. Is this the land of "the Enemy"? We are greeted by 30 members of the Committee for Solidarity with the People of the U.S. Huge bouquets of flowers are put in our arms, and we are kissed and hugged, with tears of emotion in our eyes and theirs.

First impressions of Hanoi: It is a city (1,000,000) on bicycles, mostly manufactured locally with imported steel. An amiable, courteous people, small in size. They show a love of color in spite of little money—it takes two or three months wages to buy a bicycle. Trees are everywhere, and so are bomb shelters. The city has not been bombed since 1968, but they think an all-out attack may yet come.[15]

We visit a little temple-pagoda 1,000 years old. It was destroyed by the retreating French, and later rebuilt. We also visit a lovely park, created by thousands of volunteers, who made a lake from a swamp, put in flowers, pavilions, goldfish tanks—wow! It shows what can be done with very little money only if you have love and perseverance.

Someone has "sculptured" bushes to look like ostriches, lions and deer on the lawn. And then we see "elephants" sculpted by growing four small pines and weaving their long branches around to form legs, torso, head, and trunk!

Another thing I have never seen: bicycles each carrying loads up to 800 pounds! The device was invented during the war against the French. A man walks pushing the bicycle with one hand on a diagonal stick behind the seat, and another steering by a horizontal stick tied to the handlebars. The load is on two platforms hung low one on each side of the bicycle.

Saturday, March 11

In the morning we visit the museum, which combines archaeology with crafts and modern painting and sculpture. It is a small museum, but one of the best we've ever seen. There we find a 4,000 (!) year-old bronze drum. It is four feet high and was used for signaling in naval battles. But it is still in perfect condition. Decorations covering it depict the life and times of that period.

In the afternoon we visit an exhibition of war crimes. Latest ingenious bombs and devices to carry on computerized electronic warfare from the air are on display, enough to give anyone nightmares.

Evening—we go to the circus. Performers are young, but of high quality. We see trained monkeys peddling tiny bicycles. This country is at war, but the people are not grim about it.

Sunday, March 12

We have a three-hour session at the home of the Artists' Union, a big old mansion once the home of some French family. We hear a great variety of Vietnamese music, from the Western-influenced modern compositions to ancient traditional music. They mix it up, alternating old and new almost as I do. Later at 8 PM we have a similar session at the radio station.

Here are some of the instruments we see:

---

15. [Editor of *Eastern Horizon*:] The bombing actually started in less than a month, on April 6 [1972].

A beautiful bird-like flute (the player tells us of performing this instrument for soldiers in sections where U.S. chemical sprays had killed all birds, and the bird calls he made on the instruments were the only ones to have been heard there in years).

Banjo-like instruments have two strings over very high frets, so the player can slur the notes. There is also an instrument like a cigar-box ukulele; a bowed instrument held between the knees of the player while seated; various wood-blocks, claves, drums, from huge to small; and harps like kotos.

All the Western instruments are there. I wouldn't be surprised if Hanoi, like Tokyo, doesn't have a first-rate symphony orchestra some day. (Hey, it *does* have a symphony, which I find out later.)

But what really gets me is an instrument completely new to me, a monochord—one stringed. The Vietnamese name for it is *dan bau* (pronounced "don bow"—as in bow and arrow—with falling pitch. The same words, if inflected differently, could mean "bullet pinches.")

Like a dulcimer, it is a horizontal box. Perhaps it was once set on the floor, or on the lap. The one we see stood on legs, and is amplified, so as to be heard by any audience bigger than five or ten.

The one steel string is tuned by a peg at the player's right. His left hand holds a thin curved rod. By forcing this *toward* the string, he can gradually lower the pitch as much as four or even seven notes. Thus the *dan bau* is similar to a broomstick-wash-tub bass. When moved to the left, the rod raises the pitch, but no more than three or four notes.

While plucking, the player's right hand momentarily dampens the string in order to sound the high harmonics, a bell-like tone. Thus if the string's basic pitch is low C, the first usable note is middle C, and the few notes below that. So most melodies will be played in the 2½ octaves above C. Without the left hand bending the curved rod, one could only play bugle calls. With the rod in action, one hears a warm sensuous melody. An old folk song saying has it: "Let the player of the *dan bau* be enraptured, by his own music. You, being a girl, should not listen to it." But the *dan bau* was never puritanically outlawed, as the fiddle was in America.

A week later we are given a two-hour lesson in the *dan bau* or *don bow*, as I shall anglicize it. No one knows exactly how old it is—perhaps several hundred years, perhaps much more.

Our instructor, Doan Auh Tuan, a young man in his twenties, is a member of the Vietnam Traditional Music Ensemble, playing on radio and TV, concert tours, as well as performances for soldiers and for children in parks. He plays often as accompaniment, or with accompaniment. He says that in the old days a good player might be invited to perform at a feudal court. But it was usually in the peasants' home or in the courtyard, where a few neighbors could gather to listen.

...Doan Auh Tuan played us a folksong from Central Vietnam, a lullaby, a modern composition by a contemporary composer, Huy Thuo. "But this is of course improvised upon by everyone who plays it," he tells us.

At his request, I give him several American tunes and he demonstrates by reading at sight and playing "Down in the Valley" and others. In the old days, he says, legend had it that the *dan bau* was given by a good fairy to a mother and daughter, both blinded by a ghost, and searching through the country for their son and husband. "In the old days, many blind traveling musicians played this instrument," he says.

...Later on Sunday, while I sleep, Toshi and Tinya go shopping.

...This country may be communist but on the streets there are many sidewalk vendors. Plentiful vegetables. No one seems underfed. Though few houses have running water, we smell no sewage as in Indonesia and India. Streets are very clean. No trash at all. No one is unfriendly, but everyone's eyes follow me because I am so tall, as conspicuous as a 7-footer would be in U.S.A. Such a friendly, courteous people.

Monday, March 13

At 7:30 we're off with cameras, tape recorder and musical instruments, to visit a village 12 miles out of Hanoi.

There we find a school of 500 kids, aged 11–14, studying math, geography, history, literature, etc. They have no glass in the windows, and only very simple fixtures, but all is clean and neat. A picture of Uncle Ho hangs on the wall. He is one truly loved guy. The kids sing us some songs; they also dance. I sing them a couple including Woody's "Put Your Finger in the Air," with grown-ups helping out. Toshi really leads it, by sitting on the railing; and when she raised her foot ("put your fingers on your toe") the kids all exclaim with delight to see that she is wearing rubber-tire sandals, like Uncle Ho.

No bell in this school; signals are given by a huge homemade drum made out of a wooden barrel, and hung from a tree in the courtyard. Near by is a war memorial; part of a U.S. jet shot down over the village. Its shiny aluminum, machined with the world's most advanced technology, contrasts with the mud and bricks and wood of the school. It also attests to its failure to put the village out of business.

I find out from our hosts that the town council is elected annually. Men and women over 18 can vote, and anyone over 21 can run for office. The village is one big cooperative. Public works are paid for out of profits. People build and own their own homes. No taxes are paid. School teachers' salaries are paid by the Central Government. But villagers built the school buildings. Workers at the lacquer workshop are paid on a piecework basis.

I said, "I must ask you, because people will ask me, if people here had to be forced the joined the cooperative. Americans are told that President Ho was a dictator."

General smiles and merriment and shaking of heads. "Our coopera-tive was voted in 1957. Some people were against it then, but nobody is now. The local members of the Communist Party are like anyone else; they can run for office if they want to, or not. A list of nominations is posted on the wall, and people discuss the candidates among themselves."

They ask what I think of their village. I say I can see they are proud of their progress, but that progress could bring new problems. For example, what about the population problem?

General nodding of heads. "We now realize this. Five years ago we had a four percent annual birthrate. Now it is down to three percent, but much needs to be done. We urge women to wear the ring (I.U.D. [Intrauterine Device]) after two or three children; but if they don't like it, it can be taken out. Of course our chairman here is not a good example—he has eight children. But no new ones in the last five years." This is followed by much laughter, and a few blushes.

After lunch we hear some songs in the local style, *Quan Ho*, for which this town is famous. Two people stand looking into each other's eyes and smiling, somewhat touching hands or arms gently, while they sing in lilting unison. The songs are three to five minutes long, about love, or otherwise sentimental. The voice tone is slightly reedy but not harsh. Here is a typical subject of the songs: A boy and girl, much in love, live on the opposite sides of a river. Every day they come to its banks and speak to each other longingly, and sip of the river, saying that with each sip, they drink of each other's love. If ever one of them cannot make it, the other should sip the water anyway. But once when the girl fails to come, the boy sips and sips and can never have enough.

Tuesday, March 14

We are taken on a 5-hour drive to one of the beauty spots of the world: Hon Gay Bay, which is filled with several thousand steep rocky islands, averaging 400–600 feet high with fishing junks sailing between them.

Wednesday, March 15

I am invited for a 3-hour session at the home of the Delegation to DRVN (North Vietnam) from the PRG (Provisional Revolutionary Government of South Vietnam). You see, the NLF [National Libera-tion Front, also known as the Vietcong] is not a bunch of guerillas in the forest, but a full-fledged government, with considerable light industry, including color printing, textile, etc. It includes communists in its leadership, but also a lot of non-communists, all united under one slogan: Drive out the Yankees and their puppets.

Their leader, a wiry, intense man a little younger than me, is a promi-nent writer, a man who knows literature of Europe and America well.

Thursday, March 16

I tape three 15-minute programs for Radio Hanoi.

My songs here are purposely about the same as I do in U.S.A., except that (as it always is overseas), because of translation difficulties, I do fewer wordy songs, and more repetition and instrumentals. I doubt I can learn any of their songs—language is too difficult.

... Musicians here of all types have proudly carried on for several years a slogan: "Let our songs drown out the sound of bombs." They are hoping I can make up a new song as the result of my visit. But I'm stymied so far for words except for a good idea—which needs much working on. I sing it once on the radio, with a warbly pentatonic Irish-type melody.

The song follows:

> **Land of a Thousand Songs**
> *We visited a land*
> *Of a thousand songs*
> *Voices blending clear-ly*
> *Each one see-ming*
> *To say as it sang*
> *We love our country dearly*
>
> *We visited a land*
> *Of a thousand colors*
> *Every garden many shades of green*
> *Still they told us, after peace will come*
> *Such colors then as you have never seen*
>
> *This land has heard the sound*
> *Of a million bombings*
> *Broken homes, broken lives*
> *Poisoned forests*
> *Crying out to all the world*
> *Speak out, speak out!*
> *To stop the bombings*
>
> *We visited a land*
> *Of a thousand songs*
> *Voices blending clearly*
> *Each one saying, if need be*
> *Each one of us would give our lives*
> *To keep our country free*

Friday, March 17

In the afternoon Toshi and I have a session with a wonderful man, Che Lan Vien. He is a poet about our age, who tells us many stories about Vietnam. He has a great sense of humor, and we swap anecdotes for three hours. "We say, translation is like cutting the wing of a bird," he says. "But what if cutting it helps the bird to fly in a different sky?"

"We say, if there is some skin, the hair will grow. If there is a branch, the tree will grow. Our small country has suffered countless invasions. One year we had 20 hurricanes. But still we remain optimistic. Hamlet said, 'To be or not to be.' But we say, 'To *be*, to *be*.'"

Our translator is really kept busy. We hear many stories about President Ho. It seems he had a great sense of humor, and was not above playing some practical jokes on people. For example:

A big reception was planned for him, at a military base. In the front row were officers, in the back row privates. Ho arrives at the back door, and announces, "About Face!" and gives his speech with the privates in the front row.

The state publishing house owed Ho $350.06 royalties for a book he has written. They sent a check for $350. Ho wrote back, "Where's the six cents? It's not so much, but I am afraid you may escalate."

Ho was really a poet. He said, "The U.S.A. has a long stick, but a man can't dance in a small house carrying a long stick." Some of Ho's prison poems have been put to music and widely sung.

Saturday, March 18

In the afternoon Toshi and I have a long interview with another writer our age, the head of the journalists' association, Luu Quy Ky.

Luu says that after the U.S. and puppets are defeated trouble is predicted in the south. And then he goes on, "There has been much corruption by the dollar. But we know that the job is to rebuild, not recriminate. Six hundred years ago, after we defeated the Mongol army of Kublai Khan, the king's minister brought a large box into the court of the king. "This box," he said, "contains names of all those who collaborated with the invader." The King ordered the box to be burned, in full view of the court. So today, the NLF proposes that there be no reprisals against the puppet mercenaries."

"Some Beautiful Acreage," 1972

Letter to Les and Nancy Rice from Peking, China,
dated March 31, 1972; found in Seeger files

Dear Les and Nancy,

On Monday we visited a large agricultural commune about 15 miles from Peking.

...We were received with extraordinary friendliness everywhere, by young and old. The Chinese here are about average reserved—not like the Vietnamese, who along with the Cubans seem absolutely the world's most unreserved people, and who smile back the instant you smile at them—but once introduced on the farm here, they eagerly give frank answers to all our questions. The commune has also a flour mill, a factory to make herbicides ("To keep down weeds in the wheat fields. Yes, we use many precautions."). Six big high schools ("Not one school here before liberation"). Six big medical centers and 59 little health centers manned by "barefoot doctors" with three months training and then continuing to study while they serve. ("Serve the people" is one of China's main slogans. It is emblazoned in stores, kitchens, factories, street corners.) The health center had an 8' × 5' shelf space for "traditional medicines," a 2' × 3' space for modern antibiotics, etc. They also used acupuncture, and showed us the needles (in a museum we saw acupuncture needles 1,000 years old). But recent research has developed many new uses for acupuncture anesthesia.

Everything spotlessly clean. My God you never saw such a clean country. Not a speck of dirt in streets, yards, homes. ("Chairman Mao has told us to observe sanitation everywhere.")

The health center also educates people in prevention of sickness ("because Chairman Mao has told us our first duty is to prevent illness and epidemics. In spring and winter we educate people in preventing colds and bronchitis, and caution them about poisoning from gas fumes from stoves. According to the teachings of Chairman Mao we strive to bring the best medical service to rural areas. This center is open day and night. We also deliver babies.")

I sang some songs for the kids, and they, unprepared, sang some songs for me. One said, "I found a steel pellet, and I took it, and turned it over to the waste products center because as Chairman Mao says, we must not waste anything in China today." Another song, "Sailing the Seas Depends upon the Helmsman."

Sang for some beautiful old people in an old folks home—people with no families; cheerful, spry. Spontaneous applause when I sang a peace song.

I wish a TV camera could have caught the face of the commune leader's strong friendly face as he talked to me. "We have 8,000 households, and every one has at least one bicycle. Some have two. Average individual income is 300-400 yen a year."

On the face of it, this is pretty low pay. One yen = 50 cents (US). Annual income then is $150 or $200. A bicycle costs $60 or $70. But as always in socialist countries you have to figure what they get free—rent, medical care, certain free clothing and food. In cities, workers get almost twice as much pay—average $30 monthly, here as well as Hanoi—but pay $6 or $7 a month for food. Incidentally, shops are well stocked, and prices cheap. Shoes $2.50 a pair, rubber-plastic sandals $1.75. In food market prices nearer U.S.—eggs 45 cents a dozen, chicken 23 cents per pound, rice 7.5 cents per pound—not expensive, but not fantastically cheap either. Government prices are evidently carefully fixed so everybody is clothed and fed, but no waste. CM (I have come to use this abbreviation in my notebooks for Chairman Mao) has told 'em not to waste, and they don't. Every neighborhood has a waste products purchasing center and a handcart man comes weekly to collect paper cans, bottles, old clothes, shoes, metals. A kid can get 1.5 cents for turning in an empty toothpaste tube. Orange peels saved to make medicine.

Back to the ranch. Rainfall in this region is only 16″ to 20″ annually so irrigation is a big thing. The government has given top priority to all sorts of waterworks—dams, reservoirs, canals, but still has lots to do. Two days ago Peking had one of its annual spring dust storms. You couldn't see three blocks. It seemed like half of Mongolia blew across the border without permission. I wonder how many million tons of Asia's topsoil blows into the Pacific annually?

The China-Cuba Friendship Commune is experimenting with many new techniques. Seeds imbedded in plastic. Plastic sheets to save young plants from cold. "Following Chairman Mao's teaching of self-reliance, we have progressed much, but we are still backward. We are not mechanized enough yet in our commune. We still use many animals instead of tractors in our fields. Every house now has electricity, and every courtyard has running water. We still have far to go."

We only had three hours to spend with the farm. Wish it could have been three days or three weeks. We just got half acquainted, and had to leave. That's our trouble everywhere. So in six days we've also seen the Great Wall, the Ming Tombs, the Sung Pottery, the Forbidden City, an opera, a ballet, an acrobatic show, a symphonic-Peking Opera (remarkably good combination!), a woolen mill, a cotton mill, nursery schools, market place department store, antique store, bookstore, the Institute of Nationalities, conferences with musicians, with Peking radio, with personnel, with the China Friendship Association, with Rewi Alley (great old New Zealander), a neighborhood factory, a do-it-yourself brickyard and taken rolls of film and tape and filled two notebooks with scribbles and writing down slogans up on every wall. I am a little groggy, but Tinya is doing great, having bought herself quilted jacket and Chinese shoes, and watercolor brushes, and bought baby presents for Mika's expected production in early August and for the baby expected in late August by Danny and Martha. If all goes well, Toshi and I will be double grandparents.

We go to Shanghai today, and next week to Canton and then home via Hong Kong and San Francisco and back to work. To sum up here, as you can see, no one can fail to be impressed with the material achievements. Fantastic is the only word for it. Compare this country with India today, where millions are starving, undernourished, disunited. And yet I believe the cultural cost has been greater than they realize.

In the long run, the cult of personality weakens a people even though in the short run it sustains them. I do not sense here the genuine affections and love felt in Cuba for Fidel and in Vietnam for Uncle Ho. No one here would think of talking back as they will to Castro, "Hey Fidel, when are you going to clean up the Cultural Department?" I doubt that children would scramble all over CM and sing and dance with CM as Vietnamese kids did with "*Bac* Ho" (*Bac* = Uncle). Ho had a famous sense of humor, and was not above playing practical jokes. He used humor as an educational tool.

CM has a sense of humor, from what I read and hear, but it is more sardonic. When Kosygin[16] visited here two years ago, CM told him there would be 10,000 years of polemics between their two countries. Kosygin protested that 10,000 years was too long. "I'll subtract 1,000 years. No more," said CM.

CM is quoted everywhere in conversations with peasants, factory workers, as well by cadres (party people) technicians, and foreign guests. It's like being in a mission where the Bible is quoted all the time. His slogans are on the walls of every public room, in streets, in workshops, in homes.

"Unite to win still greater victories" (everywhere).

"Serve the people" (in restaurants, kitchens, stores).

"Rely on our own effort" (in workshops).

"Only socialism can save China" (everywhere).

"Go all out, aim high, achieve greater, faster, better and more economical results in building socialism" (anywhere).

The main line for China today: "Make the past serve the present and the foreign serve China."

...Some of the quotes are quite sophisticated: "The correctness or incorrectness of the ideological line or political line decides everything." Or: "There are many contradictions in the development of complex things, but one is always the principal contradiction that controls the other contradictions." Or: "If you want knowledge, you must take part in the practice of changing reality." And: "The just struggles of the people of all countries support each other."

And lots, lots more. Most are actually pretty good. But why couldn't they quote someone else occasionally? And I suspect people get numbed to them all. Maybe I'm wrong. It's a little like Shakespeare said: "Methinks he doth protest too much." You need a change of pace. There's no doubt this country does more rank-and-file arguing than any country except maybe Cuba. But the older I get, the more I distrust words. The proof of the pudding is in the eating. The statues, pictures of CM

---

16. Alexei Kosygin (1904–1980) was a progressive Russian statesman who eventually rose to the position of Deputy Premier of the U.S.S.R., beginning during Nikita Khrushchev's tenure. Kosygin is best known in Soviet history for his attempts to reform the Soviet economy, advocating for a more decentralized model.

everywhere don't help particularly. And one thing I haven't had satisfactorily explained is this great campaign against "social-imperialism." Two years ago when there was a border clash over little Damansky Island, a U.S. magazine chortled, "Karl Marx died on the Ussuri River." Well, he certainly didn't die but he wasn't helped either. It seems to me that a few kilometers of "sacred soil" is nowhere near as important as the unity of the socialist peoples. If either nation had had the sense to back off, they would have been the victor.

Ah well. I wonder if while I'm here I dare to make a toast referring to CM's remark to Kosygin, and toasting, "To the year 10,972."

Well, this letter is now so long I wonder if you will ever have time to read it. The longer we stay here, the more we like the country and people. 700 millions inherited some beautiful acreage damn near ruined by 5,000 years of feudalism and then imperialism. They deserve all the love and help they can get.

Toshi has been wonderful. Leading discussions, keeping a sense of humor at all times, keeping Tinya and me healthy, and having a great time herself. She was raised on China; Tapapa [Toshi's father] felt so close to their struggle here. It's kind of a dream come true to visit it.

Hope you are both well.

Much much love to you and to all of Cuba linda!
Pete

"The Beautiful City," 1974

From Seeger's regular "Johnny Appleseed, Jr." column in
Sing Out! magazine, no. 22.6, January/February 1974

I feel like the revival preacher who led a wild youth and now goes around urging people to walk the straight and narrow. Having sung the praises of traveling, this reprobate is remorseful. I used to quote Woody Guthrie, "If I didn't travel you'd have to travel, because there's lots of traveling to do."

OK, agreed. The world needs diplomats, salesmen, circus performers, and revolutionary travelers too.

But after these travelers have done their jobs, the work begins to save each neighborhood of the world, and this is going to be done by people who dig in and don't run away from the job.

In America we have too long glorified the person that has pulled up stakes and moved on. The brave immigrant. "Pioneers, O Pioneers!" exulted Whitman. But Bob Dylan punctured this ideal a bit with his song, "Pity the Poor Immigrant."

You can still be world conscious while digging in. You can read, you can write. You can exchange songs, pictures, ideas with the rest of the globe. But use all this to help your neighborhood be proud of its own, while being friends to all. Neighborhood? It might be a small town, it might be a city, it might stretch along a river, a lake, a mountain range, or a city block. Who's going to save it? Not the compromisers, the cowards, the prostitutes, the people who call themselves conservatives just because they allow the rape and destruction to continue. Working people can save it, if they've organized. Who will organize them? You.

OK, travel first, learn. Ho Chi Minh traveled the world, then came back to the job of organizing the people of Vietnam. Ben Franklin spent twenty years in Europe and glorified the philosopher who could set foot on any part of the world and say, "This is my country." But then he came home. The Beautiful City that will be the world is going to have a lot of neighborhoods.

Poets and singers are essential to each neighborhood, to help keep up its morale, to cherish its traditions, to sort out false from true, to give a vision of the future worth fighting for.

... When I sang in Hanoi, March 1972, I ended with some Hudson Valley songs. A Vietnamese novelist, a fighter from South Vietnam told me later, "That was when I decided I could believe you. For only when Americans realize that they too have no place to run to, that they too must stay home and fight to free their own corner of the world, as we are fighting for ours, can the world live with Americans."

Come home from Canada, you exiles.

12

Musics of Other Countries

"Thus Poetry Differs from Prose," 1952

Found in Seeger files

All arts use a combination of design and imagery to convey deeper meaning than would normally be given by a casual use of the same medium.

Thus architecture differs from a haphazard pile of sticks and mud brought together for a dwelling.

Thus poetry differs from haphazard prose speech.

Thus a painting might differ from the result on film of a camera casually aimed and clicked.

Of course, all nature has a certain amount of design in her. Man simply intensifies these designs in his arts. For example, dancing.

Looked at from this broad point of view, music, as an art of the design of sounds, has developed many subtle elements of design, and no two parts of the world have seen anything like a similar or even development.

Do we think a sustained pitch, "a musical tone," is the cornerstone of musical art? Listen to the Plains Indians, or Maori chants.

Do we think an ordered series of pitches (a scale) is ordained by God? Don't refer to Pythagoras.[1] Our tempered scale is as far from him as a hundred variations throughout the world. India, Africa, and the New World, all hold to other scale standards.

Europeans like to sound several pitches at once, but prefer a single and simple rhythmic pattern. India prefers to hear one pitch alone, with a multiplicity of rhythmic patterns interweaving at the same time.

---

1. Pythagorean tuning is an early version of the interval system used in most Western music, based on strict mathematical ratios between tones, said to have been discovered by Pythagoras. This system was supplanted by "even-tempered" systems of tunings by the late Middle Ages.

South Africans like harmony, but it is based upon different pitches than those we prefer.

The subtleties of rhythm: sharp, smooth, soft, irregular, crisp or surging—and the subtleties of pitch: flat, wavering, sliding, strident; and of tone and overtone: brilliant, mellow—all these vary from place to place.

"A New Folk Instrument," 1972 [1956]

From *The Incompleat Folksinger,* Simon and Schuster, 1972

I went to Trinidad last winter to try to learn more about the steel drums I had first heard at a recital by the dancer Geoffrey Holder. By great good luck I met Kim Loy Wong, leader of one of the champion steel bands. He and his friend Renwick Walker made six "pans" for me in their backyard, and permitted me to make a film of them.

The steel drum was invented for use in the annual 48-hour spree known as Carnival. As in Brazil and in New Orleans, Carnival is celebrated just prior to Lent, usually late February or early March. It was introduced to Trinidad in the late eighteenth century by French planters fleeing revolutions on other islands of the West Indies. During the early nineteenth century the middle and upper classes of Trinidad celebrated the season with masques, balls, and pageants. The slaves carried on similar parties in their own quarters.

After emancipation in 1837, the lower classes brought their parties out into the open. The upper classes recoiled in horror. "Carnival is desecrated!" They gradually abandoned their own celebrations. By the end of the century Carnival was a bacchanal, an occasion for the unrespectable to poke fun at the respectable. Satiric songs (predecessors of modern Calypsos), fantastic costumes, and dancing shocked the ruling groups, who periodically tried to get the celebrations suppressed by the police.

...It was impossible. Carnival was too much fun. A person could put on a mask and abandon propriety anonymously. Finally, in the twentieth century the celebration became a truly national affair, with all classes participating. The most obscene satires were banned. Nowadays there are official contests for the prettiest girl, the best dancer, etc. Imagine Halloween, New Year's, July Fourth, May Day, and Labor Day all rolled into one!

...In 1937, the stick bands were forbidden by the police, who said that the rival bands were getting into fights too often and using the sticks on each other's heads. (The Duke of Iron—a Calypso singer—also told me that in that year there were riots of the unemployed in the south end of the island, and the sticks had been used on policemen's heads.) This presented a catastrophic situation. How could one celebrate Carnival with no rhythm? The young people refused to be discouraged. They raided the junkyards and that year danced in the streets with clanging of tin cans, brake drums from old cars, and other pieces of metal. These were the first steel bands; they had no melody or harmony.

Some genius then discovered that a dent in the bottom of a garbage can gave off a musical note. According to Winston "Spree" Simon, an early steel bandsman, someone threw a rock at the bottom of his garbage can. In hammering out the dent he found he could control the pitch. He purposely put several other dents in the can, and started an impromptu parade about the neighborhood, playing "Mary Had a Little Lamb," while an excited crowd gave him rhythmic accompaniment.

Within a few years the young men worked out, by trial and error, a system of using large and small dents, and learned means of controlling pitch and tone. Since there is a large oil industry on the island, oil drums replaced the garbage cans. Today the steel drum has grown to be Trinidad's national instrument. They are as proud of it as the Scots are of bagpipes.

At 5 AM on the Monday two days before the start of Lent, all the bells start ringing; bands start assembling in the streets. Each band has rehearsed and costumed itself in secret. Some may have fifty or more players, and several hundred similarly costumed friends and neighbors who will dance with them up one street and down the other.

The music that emerges is not what you might expect. It can be subtle, poignant, and haunting. It can also be exciting, with the compulsive drive of the bass booms, the seductive tinkle of the ping pongs, and the bittersweet cello note of the tenors.

Once in the 1940s the police threatened to ban steel drums too, but this time the whole island protested. There are now several hundred bands, totaling many thousand members, on the island. Last February literally the entire population, young and old, rich and poor, crowded the streets of Port of Spain to dance to the music of the steel bands.

In my opinion the instrument will spread around the world. Within the last five years it has gone to the other islands in the British West Indies. Another generation may see it in other parts of South and North America, Africa, Asia, and Europe—wherever there are vigorous and youthful amateurs wanting a rhythmic music.

"This Song Is Felt by Africans," 1972 [1960]

From *The Incompleat Folksinger,* Simon and Schuster, 1972

Choral Folk Songs of the Bantu Villages

What does the average American think of when he hears the word "Africa"? Jungles? Cannibals? Political unrest? Most of us, raised on a diet of Tarzan movies and comic books, actually know little about the traditions of that continent. Great civilizations there were destroyed by centuries of the slave trade and wars of conquest. Over two thousand years ago they were forging iron and casting brass, at a time when men in northern Europe still used stone hatchets. Eight hundred years ago a university flourished in Timbuktu, drawing scholars from many lands to its halls. Today one can find African cultural expressions which challenge the world to produce their equal for beauty, vigor, subtlety and rich variety. Music is one of these. You don't have to have a degree in anthropology to learn a lot about African music. Folkways and other recording companies have issued fine field recordings in recent years.

The music of Africa has become justly famous for its complex and exciting drumming, but the great variety of other music indigenous to the continent is not so generally known. In East Africa one can find large xylophone orchestras. In West Africa, the predecessor of the American banjo is still played. Flutes, bowed instruments, thumb pianos, trumpets, harps, all can be found, not only playing ancient traditional music but also in contemporary combinations which result from the influence of European music.

Africa also has a highly developed choral tradition. In West Africa, this usually takes the form of antiphony—one group of voices answering another. In South Africa, the Zulu and Xhosa people don't think a song is a song unless it has three or more parts in parallel harmony. The bass part is usually very important and helps the whole to achieve a rich sonority.

This tradition existed long before the coming of the Europeans; the first European explorers heard village choruses singing in harmony, with counterpoint and antiphony entirely African in character.

In 1946, Joseph Maselwa, an African student at St. Matthews College, Capetown Province, South Africa, transcribed traditional harmonizations for forty songs of several different Bantu peoples. For bringing this collection to the attention of Americans, thanks are due a gracious lady, Mrs. Frieda Matthews. Her husband, Dr. Z. K. Matthews, a teacher and a courageous leader of the African National Congress, lectured in New York at the Union Theological Seminary in 1952-53.

Mrs. Matthews had heard the recordings made by the Weavers of the popular South African song "Wimoweh," and told me, "Yes, your record of it was quite popular in Johannesburg. But, you know, you should learn some of our older folk songs, which have been in danger of dying out because of the changed conditions in Africa."

She then presented me with *African Folk Songs*, the rare and remarkable volume edited by Mr. Maselwa and Reverend H. C. N. Williams. It contained forty songs: work songs, wedding songs, lullabies, songs for initiation ceremonies, songs of the witch doctor, drinking songs, children's songs and warrior songs. All were written out in full harmony, with from two to six parts. No accompaniment was indicated.

...These village songs are not of the ancient type, neither are they the jazzy songs now popular in large cities like Johannesburg. In varying degrees they show the influence of over one hundred and fifty years of contact with European missionaries. "Here's to the Couple," for instance, shows a great deal of missionary influence; "Somagwaza" practically none.

Mr. Henry Ramaila, a student at Union Theological Seminary, translated some of the songs for me, but gave up on many. "This song is untranslatable; it is *felt* by Africans," he noted under "Somagwaza." Of another he said, "Don't try to render this song in English. It will make no sense. The idiom has no equivalent to give the exact emotion in English."

...It is interesting to note that in present-day Africa many Africans are likewise latching onto American traditions in music. Throughout many of the cities the guitar is being played in a style very similar to American country folk music such as is played by Merle Travis or blues singers such as the late Big Bill Broozny.

At the same time we hope that older strains of music are not driven out by modern sophistications, it is nevertheless fascinating to see the combinations of European and African traditions which are being put together by young African musicians.

There is so much of Africa already in American folk traditions that these songs can be learned very quickly by anyone familiar with spirituals, blues and square dances. Some are like rounds, which may be repeated almost endlessly.

We cannot duplicate exactly the way they are sung in Africa. African scales don't have the exact same pitches as our major and minor scales, and our voices are unused to traditional African inflections, slides and accents.

But we can try to be faithful to the spirit of the songs. There is no reason why African folk songs should not be added to the world's heritage of song. This Yankee song leader has gotten thousands of voices in Moscow and Tokyo to help him sing "Somagwaza," "Bayeza Kusasa (Oonomothotholo)" and "Wimoweh."

"My Ears Don't Mind This a Bit," 1972 [1963]

From *The Incompleat Folksinger,* Simon and Schuster, 1972

I wish I knew Bengali, or some other Indian language, well enough to learn a couple of their folk songs. They are charming, and would appeal immediately to most Americans. The vocal tone is not strange or strained, as in traditional Japanese and Chinese music. The harmony is simply that of the drone bass, as in a bagpipe. My ears don't mind this a bit. I prefer not being distracted by tonic-dominant progressions. The beautiful melodies are subtle and quick, and the rhythms too. Some polyphony is used, such as when a group of singers repeats a strong rhythmic phrase over and over, and the soloist holds a high flowing descant, usually on the fifth of the scale, and descending from it.

Western music has hardly made a dent here. It's no wonder. Their own music is so good. Folk songs: my God, 57 hundred varieties. Each province has got its own style. (There are three hundred languages in India.) Solo songs, group songs, work songs, love songs, religious songs. (Especially religious songs. This is a most God-conscious land.) Great rhythms, great melodies, and great sense of poetry in all the people. Here are a couple of themes from some of the songs:

"O people, don't get involved in love—that sticky stuff—Like glue, it will never let you go."

A man says: "I can tame the wild elements, but not a wild girl like you."

A woman's protest whose husband is taken off to war.

The god Shiva arguing with his wife. Humorous song.

And boatmen's songs. Hundreds of 'em. Mostly with the general theme of comparing the soul to a boat tossing on the waves.

The favorite Indian instruments are distant cousins of the banjo and guitar, the sarod and the sitar. Village folk have simple versions; trained classical virtuosos have elegant masterpieces. Usually accompanied by drums, tapped by hand. Many varieties of them. The most common seems to be the tabla: two drums used together, with a black rubber spot near the center to deepen the tone.

Flutes are popular too. Small cymbals, and bells, and jingles around the ankles. I saw also in a village a neat one-stringed instrument. The one string can be tightened with a peg. The other end goes through a hole in the center of the skin drumhead. Called an *ektara* (*ek*, "one"; *tar*, "string"). The string is kept taut simply by the pressure of the player's left hand. He holds the drum tight under his left arm, and strums with a wooden pick over the knuckles of his right hand. By varying the pressure with the left hand, great "quong quong" sounds come from it.

We saw this instrument played by a religious group known as Bauls, in a small village a hundred miles north of Calcutta. Bauls rarely own their own homes, but travel from place to place. Unlike most religious orders in India, they are no ascetics. They marry and raise children to follow their line of business. Women are more equal to men than in most of India. The Bauls have their own songs and styles, usually singing in a group of three to eight people. One soloist, and the rest joining in from time to time, and then as they get the spirit, dancing and whirling, like the Jewish Chassidim. They sing in the marketplace for tips, and serve God and keep alive that way.

One of their songs said, "O Lord, my boat is tossing on the waters of life. Please see me safely to where I am going—wherever that is."

Within the next three days I heard no less than seven other songs, both classical and folk songs, which had the same essential theme. And in conversation with different persons I found that this was India's main tradition: God rules the world. Our fate is in his hands. The best we can do is pray that he shows us how to act.

The city intellectuals tell me that this is just because India is a very poor country. When people have so little, they have to have faith in God. But I've seen other poor countries that didn't have it so intensely as here. And [Rabindranath] Tagore, the poet, was an aristocrat, and deeply religious too. His song "Jana Gana Mana" is the national anthem and translates roughly as follows: "O Thou who leads the minds of the people, unite us now from the Himalayas to the Ganges." It is a fine song—along with "The Marseillaise" [of France] the best national anthem I know.

But I'm afraid I have my doubts—at least concerning this definition of God. God helps those who help themselves.

"Skills Which Deserve to Live," 1972 [1964]

From *The Incompleat Folksinger,* Simon and Schuster, 1972

Ghana has a vigorous program of research and collecting, *and,* equally important, publicizing and distributing its own folk music. Their university has an Institute of African Studies, headed by Professor J. N. Nketia, author of several collections of folk music, and a composer. Folklore collecting is done throughout Ghana. But what is rare in universities: African dance and music is also *taught.* Some first-rate African drummers and dancers are on full salary, teaching intensively to students who are studying for degrees.

One of the teachers in the Institute said we might be able to find some fishermen singing at a spot forty miles up the coast. We zipped along a modern blacktop highway, traveled a half mile off of it down to the beach, and had hardly parked when we heard singing. A long rope stretched endlessly out into the blue Atlantic. Thirty cheerful people sang as they slowly pulled it up into the palm trees, cinched it, and walked down for a fresh grip. One man did no pulling but accompanied the singing with a sort of metal castanet held in his hand. He wore a *papier-mâché* mask! (We never discovered the reason for the mask. Carnival spirit? Ancient religion?)

In the distance were large dugout canoes taking fishermen out through the surf. We rope the camera tripod to the front seat of one of these boats, lash the tape recorder and battery pack next to it, cover them all with plastic against the surf, and push off. Crowds of children help us get it afloat, and then six paddlers get us through the surf. Danny and I and an interpreter sit crouched in the stern, helping by staying out of the way till the boat is safe beyond the breakers.

Finally we're out there, bobbing easily upon the swelling brine. We take the plastic off the camera, get ready to roll. The paddlers wait, however, till the drummer is ready.[2]

Now start the drums in the canoe. Metal castanets pick up a syncopated pattern. The singing starts. Very ragged at first. No one seems to know exactly what to do. But by now I realize this is a typical folk music method. They are not a rehearsed chorus coming in on cue. They have to sound each other out, see how they feel.

Mika comes alongside with another translator in another canoe. She is taking short bursts of film with a hand-held camera to cover mistakes that I may make with the main camera. The men in her boat start clapping in rhythm. Gradually the harmony and quality of singing become richer and stronger. The solos and choruses follow each other right on cue. Different paddlers take turns on the short solo lines. I am not an experienced cameraman, and I am praying that it all comes out well when developed. The sunlight glints on the strong dark muscles; the melody, harmony and rhythm all fit together. Since the camera is locked to the boat, the singers will stay in focus and not bob around too much, but the horizon tips back and forth as the boat is rocked on the waves.

Finally we run out of film, and come ashore. I suppose, within a generation, fishing around here, too, will all be done with machines. Fishermen will be paid more, fish will be cheaper. But for everything you gain in this world, you lose something; and if these songs are lost, I for one will regret it. The world is full of many skills which are outmoded economically, but which deserve to live because they are beautiful. I have a suspicion that Ghanaians, because they love their country and their culture, will find ways to keep some of these traditions alive.

"Is the Hybrid Accepted First?" 1956

Letter to Hugh Tracey, South African musicologist,
dated July 3, 1956; found in Seeger files

Dear Hugh Tracey,

At last I get around to writing a decent reply to yours of last February. I and my friends feel extremely grateful to you for taking the time to give such extended comment upon our experiment with folksongs from Africa.

---

2. "This is a characteristic of African work songs, it seems. They must have accompaniment. We passed a group of men cutting grass with long knives. Our driver hopped out for us to see if they knew any work songs, which are often sung by grass cutters. Oh yes, they knew many. But they couldn't sing them now, because they didn't have their music with them. Their 'music' was a calabash rattle and metal castanets. (Played by an expert, these become quite fantastic instruments.) One might as soon play tennis without a net as try and sing without one's 'music.'" —P. S.

G. Schirmer, one of the biggest music publishers in the U.S., wants to publish fifteen of the songs from the songbook, *African Folksongs*, edited by Williams and Maselwa, including the eleven which we recorded for Folkways. I tend to agree with the point made in your letter, that it is a pity that "the real thing" could not be published first—in other words, truly indigenous African folk music. However, they want to go ahead with it immediately, and I am writing an introduction to the folio, taking into account the corrections you noted for my introduction to the Folkways LP.

I wonder if perhaps it doesn't always turn out this way—that the hybrid is accepted first, and only later the straight stuff? In the field of popular music, the politer form of "swing music" in the '30s paved the way for the acceptance of rawer forms of jazz. And a symphony conductor planning a "pop" concert will soften up his audience with Tchaikovsky before bearing down on Bach. Similarly the folksong revival in America took to Burl Ives before they could understand the straightforward power of a singer like Leadbelly. Thus also, it may turn out that the acceptance of such comparatively westernized music as we recorded for Folkways will make it easier to teach more purely African songs to Americans. At any rate, I hope so.

…It is easy to find examples of the tendency you noted—of a conquered people adopting traits of the conquering people—as a subconscious way of attaining parity. The Indians of South and Central America thus absorbed much of Spain, and the Dutch, though kicked out of Indonesia, are still very much there culturally—and students in Calcutta will learn cricket. In America I can see on all sides children of immigrant parents disdaining a proud and beautiful heritage for the culture of the jukebox and the slick paper magazine.

Nevertheless, it would seem to be wrong, to me, to consider this the whole picture. Acculturation has always been, historically, a two-way street, and in a few generations from now it may produce some of the grandest forms of art that the world has ever known.

It is in this light that I question what you mean when you say that such hybrid songs as we recorded for Folkways are "no longer in the authentic living stream of music making." Is not the word "authentic," like the word "traditional," if not misused, at least misunderstood? It is like the almost futile arguments one occasionally hears here in the States, about "what is folk music?" I say futile, for the average laymen. For professionals, it is a different matter. Perhaps it is worthwhile for two professional geographers to argue whether the Rocky Mountains extend from Canada to Mexico, or consist of only a few highest peaks in Colorado. The average hiker can be better concerned with enjoying the climb, and leave nomenclature to the specialist.

Can one not compare the acculturative process to two students meeting at college, coming from different backgrounds? Supposing two girls room together, one from a cooking-and-sewing family, another from a literature-and-art-family. By graduation they would each have absorbed some of the more highly developed tastes from the other. Thus today in the island of Trinidad, one can see most of the young people, Negro, East Indian, Chinese, and white, quite infatuated with the steel bands, and their basically African rhythms. The older Moslems, for example, deplore this. But one might point out to them that practically the entire island accepts basically East Indian cuisine—rice with hot curry.

Sincerely,
Pete

"Here's the Wince," 1963

Letter to John Manifold, Australian poet and literary critic, dated October 14, 1963; found in Seeger files

Dear John,

I've been wanting to write you more at length ever since I saw you ever so briefly last month. By now I see the American cultural invasion as a major world problem. I was dimly aware of it before, but now I've experienced it.

And, I suppose, been part of it. Aye, here's the wince. I used to think it was simply a problem of the worst of mass culture being exported: Hollywood movies, TV, top twenty phonograph records, slick magazines, fashion. But much as I love the five-string banjo, I know now that I would be sorry to have it sweep the world, invading the music of every nation as a weed might a garden.

Unless, unless—people really wanted it, and were not taking to it just because it's the fashionable thing to do, or expedient in any other way. But then they would adapt it to their own culture, and make the banjo different. Not adapt their culture to it.

After all, one of the reasons the English language is a great one is that it combines Germanic and Latin-based vocabularies. Perhaps one reason American folk music is good is that it combines west European melodies with African rhythms.

I hope you'll forgive my rambling on at such length. But knowing something of how you feel about the need for building on Australian poetry and song, I wanted to see how you felt about some of our reactions so far on this trip.

In Indonesia, after 300 years of Dutch rule, they told us frankly when we arrived that Indonesia had two kinds of music: "traditional" and "western." The former includes the magnificent gamelan orchestras, and a hundred and one local varieties of folk music. The latter includes popular music influenced by Dutch, Portuguese, Spanish, and now American, French, etc., etc. Russian and Indian and others too. And European classical music taught at the conservatory. They have hundreds of delightful catchy melodies among the western type songs sung in that huge country (735,000 square miles, ¼ of the area of Australia, stretched over 3,000 miles and 3,000 islands).

I couldn't deny the beauty of them, though I told the Indonesians frankly that it was the traditional music which overwhelmingly impressed us. But they complained that the traditional music was too formalized—in a rut. I said why not get it out of the rut? They said they were trying to, but it was in awful deep. I watched a rehearsal of an experimental piece of music—a symphony plus a gamelan ensemble. It was a little like listening to someone trying to speak half French half English, all at the same time. And it took the English people 400 years to succeed in doing that. I told them I thought it was good to experiment, but not to be too hopeful of quick success.

Did you ever compare the growth of music traditions to the very development of traditions in cooking and eating? Very similar.

In America, one can trace wave after wave of influence from different countries, until today American cuisine is incomparably richer and more varied than it was in the days when Britain's meat and porridge held sway.

Also, the way one wife learns recipes and adapts them to her own family is very similar to the way a singer learns a folksong and adapts for a new audience.

Well, to get back to this trip. If I was horrified at the American cultural invasion of Australia, I was speechless in Tokyo. Billboards in English blinking on and off. Western dress everywhere except for occasional kimonos on the women (I guess women are always the upholders of tradition) and thong sandals quite often. The latter must be one of the dominant, cultural genes in Japanese life which is spreading around the world. And quite sensibly.

Another dominant cultural gene here is the sense of design—visual simplicity, color harmony, etc. Crowded as Tokyo is, the architecture of the average home is four or five cuts above the architecture of any other city in the world I've visited so far. I'm talking about the average, not the extremes of good or bad.

For 80 years, I was told, only western music has been taught in the schools. If one wanted to learn the Koto or *shakahachi* (the bamboo flue played vertically—mellow like a cello) one would have to search out a player in the countryside and take private lessons. In the popular Tokyo coffee houses I heard young people singing enthusiastically—Russian, French, American songs. All in Japanese translations. But the rare Japanese folk song was the exception that proved the rule. These coffee houses, incidentally, are quite different from the U.S. or Australian kind: brightly lit. Peanuts and soda pop on the table, and beer for those who can afford it. On the stage, the type of wistful solo singer I've heard in Greenwich Village is unheard of. In Tokyo, there is a small band: piano, bass, accordion, electric organ, or drums, all acting as accompaniment for two young people standing side by side at the mike, leading the audience in community singing—out of songbooks! I haven't seen anything quite like it since visiting some summer camps in the States.

Well, I shall. You've got enough to do without having to pore through more of these tourist impressions. I started out to write you about Australia anyway. One thought I had was that I hope more Australians will be able to visit Indonesia. They are wonderful people. Dead broke, but high morale. Another thought I had was trying to compare similarities and differences between U.S. and Australia. The way Kentucky mountain banjo picking has spread through the U.S. in the last few years is a little as if a type of music half white-Australian and half Aborigine-Australian were discovered by some folklorist up near Alice Spring, and because it was so good, spreading through the whole country. And after my son Danny (17) and I had attended a meeting of the Bush Music Club in Sydney, he commented, "It was nice but is that the only kind of folk music Australia has? It's as though we in the States were trying to build a folksong revival on just the songs of the cowboys." Has anyone every analyzed the effect of the WAP[3] in Australian culture? Or is it all the old story of uprooted Colonial people?

Well, I'll stop asking questions. Hope all is well. I liked your poem in the new *Overland.*

Sincerely,
Pete Seeger

"New Tools for Sound," 1975

Draft of liner notes to Boris Bergman's LP *The Gypsy and the Ant,* dated March 1975; found in Seeger files

I don't know the French language. It seems presumptuous for me to write these few lines. But I know Boris Bergman, and as I listen to this record, it is exciting to realize what is happening: young people around the world are seizing upon this thing called pop music and making it a tool for the survival of the world.

For many years—many centuries—pop music has more often been icing on a poisoned cake fed to working people to keep them quiet, to keep them from organizing to right the wrongs of society. Musicians and

---

3. The White Australia policy (WAP) refers to a series of acts throughout the 19th and 20th century in which the Australian government aimed to reduce the percentage of nonwhite immigrants to Australia.

poets who didn't want to play the part didn't get jobs. As folk musicians they sang for their families, neighbors, fellow workers.

In the mid-20th century, inventions such as the tape recorder and radio started breaking down barriers of paper, barriers of language and form. Things have got tangled up. The neat categories of scholars no longer mean much to us. Using the new tools for sounds, we are reaching out to each other across miles of space. Where we can't touch hands directly, we touch each other's minds and hearts, and give each other hope.

In years to come I can see us combining languages, as we now combine musical instruments. From Africa (the banjo), from Asia (the guitar), from the Americas (hybrid rhythms and harmonies), young people reach out to each other. But this reaching out will be most successful when there is a firm base to reach from. For this reason, digging into one's own local traditions and history becomes important. Being of service to the rank-and-file people in one's neighborhood, one's home region becomes important. The timid, the scared people need to be reached as well as the daring and adventurous. All of us are bruised in one way or another by the money systems of the world. Smile at our weaknesses. And if the French government wanted to help defend and perpetuate the beautiful French language, instead of spending the money to publish a new dictionary, they should give prizes to all the songwriters of France, young and old, men and women, amateur and professional.

But if the people with money don't want to help, we have to do the job anyway. Thanks to Boris Bergman and all the talented people with him who put this disc together.

"The Internationalism of Folk Song," 1987

From *Folk On Tap* magazine, no. 30, March 1987

John Paddy Browne asks if I would contribute a few words on the "internationalism of folk song." Over sixty years of singing, I've tried to sing songs that originated far from my home, starting as a child with Christmas carols, and in recent years, songs from Latin America.

I have to confess that most of the time it doesn't work that well. I'll try to sing the song briefly; but after a while I realize that I don't sing it particularly well, and I quit singing it and leave it to others who *can* sing it well.

But some songs become my all-time favorites, like the South African song "Wimoweh," the Cuban song "Guantanamera," and a few others. Melodies are easier. I can play on a recorder some favorite melodies from Asia as well as other parts of the world, knowing that I'll never be able to pronounce the words right; but the wooden whistle is sufficient to bring out the good melody.

At one time—perhaps twenty or thirty years ago—I might have sung five or ten such songs in a two-hour program. In recent years I'm liable to do only one or two; and I sing many more local songs from the Hudson Valley where I live.

I really do believe that the world will be saved by people who fight for their homes. We should try to think globally, but we have to act locally. I also find myself increasingly singing songs over and over that I know well and that I can do a better job of. But I guess this is true of a lot of performers.

Mahalia Jackson, the great Black gospel singer, once told me, "I love to hear people sing their own songs; they sing them so much better than anyone else." But the painter Rockwell Kent once said to me, "If you try and learn another person's language, you start to understand a little of their soul," and I think that's true too. Now that the world is getting so mixed up, in another few decades people in almost any part of the world may be heard trying to make music that originated almost anywhere else; but I still guess I would feel like urging them, "Sing your own songs mostly. You can sing them better than anyone else."

Section 4
Issues for Performers

13

A Philosophy of Making Music

"The Songwriter Can Be Most Free," 1968

From *Unicorn* magazine, April 1968

A song is such a short form that it has often been looked down upon. The novelist, the playwright, the composer of operas can explore a situation in more depth but the songwriter must give off whatever brief flash of insight he has within a few minutes.

Nevertheless, the song can be on as high a plane of art as any longer form. And out of this present outpouring of new songs in many corners of the world, I expect that at least a few will be of such quality that they will be sung for centuries. Even those songs which do not last for centuries may often do important work of the moment. Is a *soufflé* any the less great work of art for lasting but a few minutes?

Furthermore, whereas novelists need publishers, playwrights need theaters, symphony and opera composers need orchestras, painters need galleries and sculptors need whole warehouses, a songwriter is peculiarly fortunate. All he needs is a voice and perhaps a guitar and another human being to listen. If a song is truly good enough, it will not even have to be written down. It will be memorized and passed from one human being to another.

Thus perhaps in this day and age, the songwriter can be the most free of all creative artists. And if he is sensible enough to pursue his own ideas and conscience, whether or not his efforts achieve attention from the owners of juke boxes and radio stations, in the end he can be the happiest of creative artists.

We are just beginning to realize all the different kinds of songs that can be written. Some can be fifteen seconds long; some can be fifteen minutes long. Some can use a great deal of repetition, others use hardly any repetition. Some can be accompanied. Some are best unaccompanied. Some can be written for two or more singers. Others for solos. Some can go off on flights of allegory and others be earthy and direct.

The heritages of the world's traditions of folk song, popular song, and art song are ours to draw upon if we want. We are faced with an almost bottomless treasury of idioms. At the same time, however, this is our biggest danger. Obviously one cannot speak every language in the world equally well. Just as important as being able to seize upon a new idea, no matter where it comes from, is being able to say "No" to many musical or lyrical ideas, tempting though they may be. Don't be like the small boy in the restaurant who loaded his tray with more than his stomach could hold.

"Two Apparently Opposing Trends," 1972

From *The Incompleat Folksinger*, Simon and Schuster, 1972

Painting, as an art, would be similar to music, if one could imagine that it was impossible to make a permanent painting—all colors would fade in a few days. Thus a class of craftsmen would develop whose function in life would be to paint reproductions of great paintings of the past. Some schools of painting would believe in a close reproduction; others would encourage more improvising upon the old designs. They would place originality as their main aim.

In every art form known (writing, visual art, music) one can see two apparently opposing trends. One is a respect for tradition and the achievements of the past, and the other is an attempt to change these traditions in accordance with the needs of the artist and his times.

It would also appear that following either of these two trends too faithfully can be disastrous; either an artist can become sterile and imitative, or he can become so meaninglessly experimental that the audience is left behind.

The field of folk music is admirably suited to preserving a balance between the two. It would seem at first glance that maintaining a fine tradition is most important. But since folk music is a process that depends for its life upon the oral tradition, music is continually changed by folk performers, whether they intend it or not. Basic tradition is continually remolded to fit a new situation.

"Can Music Lead to Action?" 1970

From *When the Mode of Music Changes,* War Resisters League, 1970

Pop music ain't what it used to be, and I say hooray. In the 1930s, when I was a teenager, the dominant theme was June-moon-croon-spoon. One hit song was explicit in its ideology: "Wrap Your Troubles In Dreams (And Dream Your Troubles Away)." All this while jobless were marching on city hall, industrial workers were getting hit over the head for forming unions, and some young men were going to Spain to try and keep fascism from taking over that country.

In those days, Woody Guthrie mimeographed copies of his songs. The Top Forty wouldn't touch 'em. Even today, the music business and the radio stations try to keep things under control by plugging so-called "inoffensive" songs, and screening out "protest" songs. But they are being outflanked by youth, and by the ingenuity of songwriters.

A song, after all, is not a speech. Like any work of art, it bounces back different meaning to different people at different times, as life shines new light upon it. On paper, the words might mean one thing; sung with a lot of rhythm and harmony, they'll mean something else. Sung over and over, a favorite song becomes more like a basketball backboard against which you bounce the varied experiences of your life.

The key question now is whether music (or any art) can lead directly or indirectly to worthwhile action. Because unless we are careful, when we are surrounded with all this joyful rhythm and harmony we so enjoy the illusion of freedom that we forget the chains tangling ever tighter around our legs.

Our country is as full of communication as a crowded cocktail party. It is also full of people asking, "What can I do?"

May these songs help us decide.

"I Have Sung in Hopes of Unifying," 1972

From *The Incompleat Folksinger,* Simon and Schuster, 1972

It does not make me happy to be the occasion of rancor within any community; I have always sung in hopes of unifying people, not dividing them. But I don't mind being controversial, or being accused of singing controversial songs. The human race benefits when there is controversy and suffers when there is none.

It seems to me that any singer who values the future of his work and his children would want to feel that his work was helping to build world peace, and an early dismantling of all atom bombs, the burning of all military uniforms (or maybe weave 'em into rag rugs). Surely they must assume that this must come sooner or later. Are they willing to imagine closely the alternative?

A lullaby, a love song, a rip-roaring hoedown—these all tremble with love of life. Can we be so careless as not to try and figure out steps to insure Life's continuation?

"Who Can Live Without Hope?" 1970

From Seeger's regular "Johnny Appleseed, Jr." column
in *Sing Out!* magazine, no. 20.2, April/May 1970

Last fall I was wondering why the song "Worried Man Blues" remained
one of my favorites after thirty years of singing it. Was it the melody?
It's a nice melody, but not that outstanding. "Done Laid Around, Done
Stayed Around" and "Do Lord, Do Lord, Do Deliver Me" have sub-
stantially the same melody. They are all second cousins of the melody
"John Brown's Body."

No, I decided it was the words. That extraordinary ambiguity which
says, "I'm worried now, but I won't be worried long." This could mean
either of two things: I'll be dead or I'll be free. And the more I thought
about the verses, I realized that "I went across the river and I fell fast
asleep, when I woke up, had shackles on my feet" could stand for every
human being or group of human beings who thought they had solved
their problems and then woke up to find out they still had chains
around their legs. We cross that ocean. We get that farm. We get that
home, that job. It didn't matter, we fell fast asleep, we woke up with
chains around our feet. And who's the judge? Some 74-year-old man in
Chicago in a long black robe? Perhaps it is the young judging the old
or the black judging the white. Or the poor judging the rich.

But at the end hope is still held out. "I looked down the track as far
as I could see. A little bitty hand was waving after me."

Who can live without hope?

"We Don't Give Enough Encouragement," 1955

From Seeger's regular "Johnny Appleseed, Jr." column,
Sing Out! magazine, no. 5.3, Summer 1955

Last year, in Los Angeles, I stopped by at a little music store to visit
Ray Glaser, the songwriter whose death this spring saddened a lot of
people. Ray wrote the lyrics of such songs as "Put It On The Ground,"
"Everything Is Higher," and "The Union Way." He was feeling discouraged at the time, and when I asked him whether he was writing any
new songs, he answered, "Oh, who sings them?"

I told him that I'd heard kids and grownups singing his songs in
Canada, in the South, the East, and other points of the compass. Singing his songs though they never heard his name or knew who wrote
the songs they were singing.

The fact is, we don't give enough encouragement to songwriters.
Commercial pop song composers get used to living the life of a gambler
(the curse of all cultural workers in our country) and the royalties from
an occasional hit may compensate for the months or years of fruitless

knocking on doors. But people such as Earl Robinson, Lewis Allan, Woody Guthrie, and in the past, Joe Hill and Robert Burns, have never been able to make a full-time living from writing people's songs. And that is a scandal and a shame.

One result is that we, the people, suffer, by not having the songs we need—songs which will echo in poetic form the thoughts and experiences we've had. We need thousands of new songs these days: humor, to poke fun at some of the damn foolishness going on in the world; songs of love and faith in mankind and the future; songs to needle our consciences and stir our indignation and anger.

One thing we can do is write letters of encouragement and appreciation to songwriters; or letters of constructive criticism and suggestions. More concretely, in many towns we should be able to organize songwriters' concerts or hootenannies, to which performers could contribute their services and the proceeds sent to the songwriter for a change. We might send along a few ideas for songs we would like to have written, and be surprised by receiving a finished song in exchange.

Which leads one to suggest that more often songs should be commissioned. The Oil Workers Union once commissioned Woody Guthrie and the Almanac Singers to compose and record a song for their organizing drive. They took $100 out of their treasury and got a ballad, "Boomtown Bill," which for years was played in union hall juke boxes along the Texas coast.

"Your Song Must Paint a Picture," 1972

From *The Incompleat Folksinger,* Simon and Schuster, 1972

Every folk singer should consider himself or herself a songwriter on the side. If you love folk songs, consider how they have been changed and improved through the generations by singers who added their own home-grown genius.

For great songs to be written we must have an outpouring of topical songs. What does it matter that most will be sung once and forgotten? The youthful Joe Hills, Tagores, Burnses and Shakespeares and Guthries can only thus get their training.

Many articles and books have been written on the subject, "How to Write a Song." They tell the aspiring amateur to be simple, be clever, have a gimmick, be this and that—and I doubt have produced many new songwriters. Yet here we go again with another attempt.

A really outstanding song is rare. But it's easier than you think to write a "usable" song. Your song must paint a picture or tell a story, to make your ideas come to life. Learn to make a rhyme, learn to create images, develop them, and hold your listeners in suspense. A rhymed editorial is worse than useless. It is not art. Phooey. Stinko. Underline this: *An editorial in rhyme does not make a song.*

Since it is harder to make a complete song than a fragment of one, first practice by writing verses to tunes you know, or writing new tunes for verses you hear. Try them out on your friends. If it isn't good enough for you to repeat to your friends, it probably isn't good enough to print, so try again. After a couple dozen successful but random verses you may be able to carry through a conception and create a complete song. Don't be afraid to make it specific. A song which hits home, goes right to the point, is worth more at that instant than any other song in your repertoire, and is worth, for that instant alone, the time it took to compose it, even though perhaps a week later it will be out of date and useless.

"The Columbia Concert," 1961

Found in Seeger files

The following is a transcript from a concert Seeger gave at Teachers College, an affiliate of Columbia University, in 1961, the first of a series of six lectures. We publish the piece here to give readers a sense of Seeger's on-stage demeanor and program style. No song lyrics are included, but we indicate in brackets where the songs appeared in the program.

Really, you shouldn't have clapped. You know this banjo is just here for show. I am going to talk most of the evening. Seriously, I got a lot to talk about. I got notes there, a regular Toffenetti[1] menu it looks like. However, I notice you all have your pencils poised. Before we talk I guess we ought to sing one song. Have something to talk about. I am just going to get my fingers warmed up on an old one you have all heard many a time before. And if you know how to join in on the repeat of the last line, do so. [Sings "John Henry."]

That's an awful good song, and it's a very good one to start off a series like this, but really one should point out that it is only one example of literally thousands, tens of thousands, hundreds of thousands of American folk songs. Of course, a few generations ago no respectable musician would admit there was such a thing as American folk music. There was European folk music, and there was American doggerel. And yet the wonderful thing is that music has come here from all corners of the world. Not only every country of Europe, but every part of Africa, from Asia too—people don't think of it, but a great deal of the music of Asia is with us. Every time you are playing a cymbal it is a Turkish instrument. The guitar, before it came to Spain and Europe, was a

---

1. Toffenetti was a well-known restaurant in Times Square in Manhattan, which closed in the late 1960s.

Persian instrument. From every island and from every ocean, people came here and they all brought music with them.

And it is going to take us all these six evenings to really even half cover it. You couldn't possibly cover it in one evening if you tried to. What I am going to do is each evening concentrate on one particular angle and tonight, it's—what was it Shakespeare said, "The Play's the Thing"? Tonight it's "The Story's the Thing." Because it is something we have forgotten about. Nowadays we put a nickel in the juke box; you hear a little three minute record; there is a solid beat there; there is a melody sometimes; there is some harmony, but if you hear the words at all, the story is a little short thing compared to what a ballad used to be. I wish somehow you could imagine instead of a great big room like this, the little kitchen most of our grandparents would sit around, perhaps in the evening, for a few stories, games, jokes, songs before they all hit the hay. No matter what country the people came from, there was hardly a family in the world that didn't know something in the way of the old songs that they had known from their own grandparents.

During these six evenings, we will try and discuss a lot of different things like "What is a folk song?" A lot of people disagree as to definition. In fact there are no two people who do agree. It is kind of like a territory on a map that everybody is willing to agree exists, but no two people are willing to be able to decide on the boundary.

Again going back to Shakespeare, in *Twelfth Night* he says, "What manner of songs are these?" So he says, "They are old and the weavers sing of them at their work!"

Hadn't thought of it that way. Of course a lot of the ballads that used to be sung, they took the place of newspapers and history books and they are mostly very bloody. They are all just like a tabloid newspaper. They give you all the bloody details and then end off on a very moral note. There was one, "Lord Thomas Had a Sword at His Side." It takes about twenty verses to tell the story of a man who asks his mother whom he should marry, the beautiful girl or the rich girl. And she says, marry the rich girl, of course. So at the wedding feast, the poor girl comes in and confronts him, so he kills everybody including himself.

Ballads like that of "Little Matty Grove" who, when the lord was away fighting, his lady sees Little Matty Grove and says, come home with me. And the lord gets appraised of the situation and gallops home. Little Matty Grove raises out of bed and he says, "What's that I hear?" and she says, "It's just the hounds barking." Next thing there is the lord standing at the foot of the bed and they fight and, again, all get killed.

Curiously enough, though, the ballads which really lasted in this country were not the ones about the lords and ladies so much as about ordinary working people. I think it is kind of a tribute to America's democratic spirit. And you'd find a ballad like this sung. [Sings "There Was a Wealthy Merchant."][2]

...To me, one of the most interesting things is how these songs change. We say this or that song comes from England or Ireland or France or another part of the world, as though it started off there. Now, we don't know, because it is too far back to know exactly where it started off, but as far as this country goes, we are able to trace just one change after another. Here is a typical example of a tune which came to this country years ago and has had successive different sets of words put to it. Back in 1798, the Irish had a rebellion and they lost it. However, it wasn't forgotten. There were many ballads made up. "The Boys of Wexford," who fought the boys of the north, and one of the most famous of all was called "The Men of the West."

Well, the tune came over here with many Irish people who sought freedom. Around 1830, someone made a set of pop lyrics to it. Yes, they did in those days too. It was a corny set of lyrics, rather a corny pun, but you can't keep a good tune down, and parodies were made up on the pop song. [Sings "Hurrah for the Choice of the Nation."]

...Putting popular verses to old tunes is a very common thing which has happened all through history. If you think of folk music in the old fashioned European sense, this is the music of the peasant class, handed down from generation to generation. And then there's the popular music of the cities and then there's the fine art music of the aristocracy. You find that there is a continual interaction between them. A folk musician will swipe an idea he hears from a singer in the town. A town musician will swipe an idea he hears from a singer in the country. And the fine art composer swipes from them both, and they swipe from the fine art composer. In America, the situation has, of course, gotten so mixed up that you can no longer strictly say that there is folk music in that old sense. As a matter of fact, Duncan Emerich, who is in charge of the Archives of American Folksongs down at the Library of Congress, says that in fifteen years there will be no more folk music in America. Well, if you consider that old-fashioned definition, there is no more. On the other hand, my own feeling is that every definition changes. What was called a play in the fifteenth century is not what you call a play when you go down to Broadway now. And in the same way, what was called a folk song a hundred years ago does not necessarily mean what we call a folk song now. Rather, I think that one might look ahead to the future where there is music for singing, music for dancing, music to listen to with orchestras, music for fun, for work, for love, for every purpose under the sun and you won't think, "This is 'folk music,' this is 'popular music,' this is 'fine arts music.'" Rather, they will all be subject to the

---

2. "Also known by the title, 'There Was A Rich Merchant, In Plymouth Did Dwell.'"
—P. S.

rules of art. You will have a good folk song as well as a bad one and a bad symphony as well as a good one and so on.

...Now, as interesting as it is to trace as many songs, tunes, words which come from the old country, I think it is interesting to point out the things which we didn't get. The changes that took place in the tunes are just as important as the survivals. One of the things which we didn't seem to bring with us from the British Isles was a certain grandiloquence which infected English music after George Fredrick Handel. I don't know exactly how to describe it. Perhaps you know the Christmas song, "Oh, Green Grow the Rushes Oh."

I don't think I can exactly say why but it is the kind of song which never did come over here. Another thing which seems to have gotten drowned out in this country is the type of rhythm that many songs were sung to in Europe. I remember an Irish friend of mine saying, "You don't have to know how to sing Irish songs—they aren't supposed to have rhythm; they have cadence." And another Irish friend, who heard Beethoven's arrangement of some Irish melodies said, "Oh, he's ruined them. That's stamping music, that metronomic German music."

...I think that actually it is a job of this generation of ours to work out some of these new combinations. It is not enough just to say, "Let's keep the old pure." There are a lot of beautiful old songs and we may like them that way, but inevitably you will hear an idea from here and hear an idea from there and you will want to put them together. But it takes artistry to do that and there are many hundreds of thousands of folk artists in cities and towns in this country who do just that. Huddie Ledbetter was one of them. He was a genius at making new combinations. He took over one of these old melodies and I think some of you have heard me explain how there used to be an Irish song about a dead cow. [Hums "Poor Drimmer."]

Well, Huddie Ledbetter loved that melody. He used to hear it sung at parties around New York years ago. But he didn't quite dig that lack of rhythm. He took out his big twelve string guitar, "bum, bum," etc. Huddie Ledbetter never played an A minor chord in his whole life. He would sing in A minor, but he would play in A major 7th. So it was that years later, when the Weavers were reminiscing and thinking of some of the wonderful melodies we'd heard Huddie sing, we used to remember how he sang this song. And we still figured that the words didn't make any sense, so we made up some new words. Many of you know them, and perhaps you will sing along with me. [Sings "Kisses Sweeter Than Wine."]

Songs have not only been changed to make them more popular but they have been changed for many, many different purposes and reasons. Take the early revival churches in this country. John Wesley, the great Methodist, said it is a shame that the devil should have all the good tunes. So he took one ballad melody after another, one old square dance, one hornpipe tune after another, and he changed it around and put new words to them. There is a very wonderful old shape note[3] hymn from the south. In Alabama and Mississippi, go to these Baptist singing conventions, and they will bring out the old [shape note] hymn books with 300 songs in them, and they sing right square through them. Different people will take turns at leading. Not much subtlety in the music but an awful lot of enthusiasm. One person describes one of these early revival meetings. He said the leader beat time as though he was beating on an anvil and the devil was right there. [Sings "What Wondrous Love Is This?"]

Incidentally, all through these six lectures, I think I ought to be frank with you and let you know where my prejudices lie so that you will know how many grains of salt to take with what I say. Because, after all, there is no such thing as pure objectivity, and there are two sides to every question. Of course, in my own opinion, there are two sides to a piece of flypaper too, and it makes a great difference to the fly which side he lands on.

…I think there is such a thing as a bad folk song, because you will find all the weaknesses as well as the strengths that are in ordinary human beings. You will find defeatism, as well as bravery. You will find cynicism as well as optimism and so on. In our own country there are many songs which reek of chauvinism and unfairness to national minorities. It has happened with every wave of immigration from another part of the world.

The wonderful thing about folk music though is that as the centuries roll by, the ignoble songs and the bad songs get discarded. One by one, they get forgotten and the good songs, the songs that surely have the ring of truth in them, manage to last.

---

3. Shape notes are an alternate form of musical notation where the typical round note heads on a music staff are replaced with varying shapes, with the aim of facilitating group singing among a group of untrained singers. Shape notes have been in use since the early 19th century, mostly in songbooks of sacred music.

14

Participation

"For Hope, for Understanding," 1993

From *Where Have All the Flowers Gone,* Sing Out Publications, 1993

It all boils down to what I would most like to do as a musician. Put songs on people's lips instead of just in their ears.

While I don't wish my publishers ill—(I'm a lucky songwriter to be working with several honest and hardworking publishers)—my main hope in putting together [*Where Have All the Flowers Gone*] is that I can encourage other singers and songwriters in various places and times to write songs. To adapt and rewrite other songs. To use songs not to get rich or famous, but to help this world survive. I wish I could live long enough to see more people singing again, either solo or in groups. For recreation. For reverence. For learning and laughter. For struggle. For hope, for understanding.

I know I won't live that long, but if this world survives, I believe that modern industrialized people *will* learn to sing again.

"No Reason to Forget How to Walk," 1956

From Seeger's regular "Johnny Appleseed, Jr." column
in *Sing Out!* magazine, no. 6.2, Spring 1956

Some friends of mine have started a singing quartet now enjoying considerable success in West Coast nightclubs. They have a running intramural argument as to whether or not they should ask audiences to join in singing folksongs with them. Since I'm at a safe distance, I'm tempted to join in the fray. Here's two cents worth of opinion. It's a subject close to my heart.

The revival of audience singing is an integral part of the whole revival of interest in folksongs in America. Consider the matter historically. It is only within the comparatively recent history of the human race that such emphasis has been put upon professional solo singers. In primitive tribes all songs, except for the long narratives of the storytellers, were sung by everyone. If a song had a chorus, everybody in the audience naturally sang it.

Modern civilization developed highly professional specialists in the arts as well as sciences. But comes the time when the intelligent person will say, "Hold on! Just because we have oars is no reason to forget how to walk." Because we have books is no reason to forget how to tell a good story. Because we have cameras is no reason to forget the fun of wielding pencil and brush. And because we have the phonograph is no reason to forget how to make music.

The revival of interest in all folk music, which proceeds this year of '56 on an unprecedented scale, is simply part and parcel of a gigantic countertrend in American life. (The main trend is, of course, mass production and mass media.) The Sunday painters, the do-it-yourselfers, the taking up of sports like sailing, skin-diving, skiing, are all evidences of 160 million Americans wanting to do something more creative with their time than switch the TV set on and off. And this is perhaps one of the very best things that ever happened in our country. For just as the apex of a pyramid can be only as high as the base is broad, so we cannot have great professionals unless we have also many amateur participants. How can one have great big-league baseball teams unless there are many sandlot players?

If we really love this revival of folk music, we will do all in our power to get audiences singing with us wherever we go. It matters not that occasionally it may slow down a program. Tempos may drag, or we may have to abandon some beautiful harmony or spectacular effect.

Actually, the quality of audience singing has improved tremendously in the last fifteen years. When I first started singing folksongs it was like pulling teeth to get anyone to sing with me. I had to use all sorts of tricks to coax a tune out of a crowd that had never sung together in its entire life. Today I can ask people to sing counterpoint or counter-rhythms, softly or loudly, fast or slow. I can get them to revel in improvised harmony. And when I say "I can," I mean anybody can if they want to try.

This type of audience singing is a far cry from the raucous sound of "That Old Gang of Mine" on a Saturday night in Old Joe's Bar Room. People are singing here because the songs are more than maudlin sentiment. This type of audience singing is different, too, from the average church where the congregation limps along half a beat behind the organ.

The song leader should be having so much fun that the audience joins in without being able to help itself.

Some day, perhaps in our lifetime, we will see an American population which can sing as readily and beautifully together as many Slavic or African peoples can today. We will sing together with harmony, rhythm, and good tone, which we do not always have at present. Meanwhile, we song leaders have a long way to go in learning how to help audiences sing with us. Needed: not only songs with choruses, refrains and responses, not only rousing, spirited songs, but quiet and deeply moving songs as well. Composers! Can you compose for an audience?

Of course, a program of folk songs should not be all audience participation. Narrative songs, lullabies, often sound better sung by one person—just as they often sound better unaccompanied by any instrument. The art of programming is an art in itself; ninety-nine percent depends on the particular needs of an audience, and the way a performer feels on that particular day. But, if, between ballads and solos, we can help our neighbors in front of us realize some of their own potentialities as singers, we will be doing a service for our whole country.

Somehow, somewhere along the line, Americans must learn, as our grandparents knew, that it is fun to create for yourself. The problem: how to be a whole Human Being in a machine and monopoly age. Ultimately, rank-and-file participation in music goes hand in hand with creativity on other planes—arts, sciences, and yes, even politics.

"On Democratic Seating," 1957

From Seeger's regular "Johnny Appleseed, Jr." column
in Sing Out! magazine, no. 6.4, Winter 1957

An auditorium with semicircular seating is a more democratic auditorium than one where the seats are all in conventional straight lines. Why? Because the latter assumes that all wisdom and inspiration must come from the front, and that members of the audience have nothing to contribute to one another.

Most democratic of all were the council fires of early communal societies. Then, anyone could stand up in place and address his or her fellow citizens. When society became more autocratic, the lines of seats straightened out. The earliest churches in America were aware of this, and consciously faced pews in from the sides, even if squarely, so worshippers could see one another.

Similarly, folk music concerts and hootenannies should use democratically semicircular seating. When everyone joins in on a chorus, there is a mutual life from seeing each other.

"Folk Music Is Not Show Business," 1974

From Seeger's regular "Johnny Appleseed, Jr." column
in Sing Out! magazine, no. 23.3, July/August 1974

The stage is a great invention. It elevates a performer so he or she can be seen clearly by people in the back rows. With a microphone, one performer can be heard by thousands of people. The framework of the stage concentrates the eyesight of the viewer. The spotlight and a bright colored costume all help to lift the spectator's heart out of the drabness of everyday existence.

That's show business.

And what's wrong with it is that everyday life stays drab.

What's good about folk music is that it is not show business. It should not be show business. Folk music should be part of everyday life and should help keep it from being drab. It should be the song that accompanies the worker at his or her job. It should be the fiddle or guitar, bongo drum or harmonica that's brought out after supper dishes are cleared away and families make their own music, rather than switching on the magic screen. Folk music is the songs that parents sing to their children to put them to sleep. And the tunes that you can whistle as you walk down the street.

But the trouble with most "folk music" magazines (and I read an awful lot of them from U. S. A. and from other countries as well) is that they tell me what professional performer is singing here, and why that one is better than some other one. And somehow millions of people have gotten the idea that folk music is somebody standing on stage with a guitar in his or her hand. I'm sorry I ever had anything to do with giving such a false impression.

"I Suppose I Overdo It," 1994

From Seeger's regular "Appleseeds" column in *Sing Out!* magazine, no. 39.3, Winter 1994/95

I suppose I overdo it—asking audiences to sing along. Sometimes I hang the words on a banner ("De Colores") or ask 'em to repeat each line after me ("Lonesome Valley," "Long John," etc.). With "If I Had A Hammer," I call out all or some of the words of a short phrase just before the crowd sings it, without dropping a beat. Likewise "Go Tell Aunt Rhody" and a lot of other songs.

Fifty-five years ago, I learned the technique from Josh White. He did it with the song "On Top Of Old Smoky." With his mouth close to the mike, he fed each line to the crowd so that they could sing that old North Carolina love song from beginning to end. Ten years later, The Weavers recorded it this way with Terry Gilkyson.[1]

Lee Hays explained to me that this was no more than what many a country preacher did when the congregation was too poor to afford

---

1. Gilkyson (1916–1999) was a folk singer and sometimes actor who enjoyed success with his band, The Easy Riders, in the 1950s. He was featured as a guest vocalist on the Weavers song "On Top Of Old Smokey." Gilkyson continued his career in music writing songs for Walt Disney films.

hymnbooks, or (in the early days) could not read enough anyway. It was called "lining out the hymn."

"If You Don't Watch Out, People Will Be Voting," c. 2001

Found in Seeger files

A corporation must make as much money as it can, or it is betraying the trust of its stockholders. That's what we're told. Newspapers and TV networks are corporations.

Sports sections only write up star players. They never mention hundreds of participation sports—with the exception of yachting and skiing (there's money there!). Entertainment pages write up virtuosos, shows, but never mention the entertainment people make for each other. Political pages tell of victories and defeats of major players, but never tell of the thousand and one little successes of groups of people who win victories by sticking together in spite of individual differences. Books of brilliant writers are reviewed, "Read and learn, read and admire," even "Read and forget your troubles." Books of poetry are reviewed; practically never books of songs, even books of pop songs. Don't encourage people to do something themselves. Next thing if you don't watch out, people will be voting.

But there's signs of hope. (I grasp at straws.) Cookbooks sell so well they can't be ignored. Even though 60% of American meals are now eaten outside the home, printing recipes sells magazines and newspapers.

"For Art's Sake," 1971

From *Party Playbill,* November 9, 1971

The artist in ancient times inspired his fellow citizens, entertained them, educated them, helped them live more fully.

The artist in modern times does the same, but has an additional responsibility: he or she must encourage others also to be artists. Why? Because technology is going to destroy the human soul unless we realize that each of us must be in some way a creator as well as a spectator or consumer. Technology has made it possible for one artist (musician, painter, writer, dancer) to reach millions. What about the artists now unemployed? Don't let anyone lie to you and say, "They have no talent."

This is why I always ask audiences to sing with me wherever I go. As a musician, I am most proud that thousands have learned from me that it is fun to make your own music.

This is why I urge all painters to show others that they need not always rely on the outside expert, the mass-produced article. We should be showing people how they can be painting murals on garage walls, decorating garbage cans so that they are things of beauty.

Frankly, the young people are already doing this, and they are way ahead of us. They make their own clothes, decorate their own rooms, their cars, everything. Hooray.

They also know that art and life and politics are so closely intertwined that it is impossible to tell where one leaves off and the other begins. They suffuse each other. Hooray.

Let us work for an America where the continual artistic activity going on all around us is what we boast of, not the few outstanding works of genius. The latter are fine. Good. But they will mean little if we don't have all the rest going on at the same time.

"The Most Important Part About My Work," 2005

Letter to Jim Brown,[2] dated July 10, 2005; found in Seeger files

Dear Jim,

It must be hard on you, after working so hard for several years, to find I and my family want to see so many changes in your movie. But it's 3 AM and I've got up to type a few more lines.

Maybe you don't know why I'd like to put words of a half dozen or more songs on the screen so people can sing along if they want. I feel it's the most important part about my work as a musician. I've never sung *anywhere* without giving the listeners a chance to join in. As a kid, a teenager, as a lefty, as a man touring the USA and 45 countries, as an oldster.

Actually if I had my way, the title of the movie would be *Participation*, subtitled *The life of Pete Seeger, Family and Friends*. It's too late now, I guess, but besides shots of Arlo [Guthrie],[3] Joan Baez, Bernice Reagan, Bob Dylan, I'd like it if the movie had younger people sing—Jon Fromer, Pat [Humphries] and Sandy [Opatow], Stefan Smith, Dave Rovic, Jimmy Collier, unknown folks. There's dozens more.

---

2. Brown (b. 1950) is the director of *Pete Seeger: The Power of Song* (Shangri-La Entertainment, 2007) an Emmy Award–winning documentary that chronicles Seeger's career.
3. Guthrie (b. 1947) is a protest singer and the son of Woody Guthrie. He is best known for "Alice's Restaurant Massacre," an 18-minute monologue set to music that satirizes aspects of American life during the late 1960s. Guthrie has frequently collaborated and performed with Seeger.

15

Commercialization, Popularization, Authenticity, and the Star System

"Someone Who Can Bring in An Audience," 1967

From Seeger's regular "Johnny Appleseed, Jr." column
in *Sing Out!* Magazine, no. 17.3, June/July 1967

Someone said to me after a concert, "I'm so glad you haven't gone commercial." I had to disillusion her. I've been commercial for a long time. In fact, she probably would never have heard me sing if I hadn't been. Still, I know how she felt. But you have to work out a balance.

I'll admit that once upon a time I was highly against the idea of "building up a career." Sang anywhere and everywhere for all sorts of causes. Never expected, nor particularly wanted, to try and get jobs or publicity in the mass media.

In 1949 I was helping edit the *People's Songs Bulletin,* and Irwin Silber, in the same office, received a phone call from the American Labor Party in Brooklyn. They needed his help in locating a friend of mine, a well-known performer of folk songs. They wanted to run a concert series to raise some money for the organization.

"Well perhaps I can help you get him," says Irwin. "But in case he can't make it, how about getting Pete Seeger to do the concert for you?"

"Oh, we know Pete," came the answer. "He's sung on our soundtracks and parties, for years. But we need someone who can bring in a mass audience. We need to raise money."

When Irwin put down the phone and told me the conversation, I started doing some hard rethinking about my own work. Here I'd been knocking myself out all these years, congratulating myself on not "going commercial" and the result was that I was not as much use to the Brooklyn ALP as was my friend, a highly conscientious and hardworking artist, but one who also set out in a more conventional fashion to build a career. He could bring in a big audience for them. I couldn't.

"Finally a 'Success,'" 1972

From *The Incompleat Folksinger,* Simon and Schuster, 1972

The 1941–42 Almanac Singers had been undisciplined ("the only group that rehearses on the stage," said Woody). In November 1948, Lee Hays and I discussed the possibility of forming a more organized singing group, to see if we could get a solid sound on such songs as "The Saints Go Marching In." Originally we had thought of three men plus three women, but it simmered down to a quartet.

I had met Fred Hellerman right after World War II. He and Ronnie Gilbert had both started singing folk songs before the war, as counselors at the same summer camp. (In 1951, when "Kisses Sweeter Than Wine" was in the jukeboxes, an interviewer asked whether Ronnie and I were really married. "Yes," says I, "she is married to her husband and I am married to my wife.") So now Ronnie, with her exciting contralto, and Fred, a gifted guitarist who could sing either high or low, joined their voices with my split tenor and Lee's big gospel bass. To our delight we found we could give a big solid warmth to the songs of Leadbelly and to many songs which had seemed ineffectual with one voice. After long discussions we finally named ourselves: the Weavers.

We helped put on some of the world's best little hootenannies, but in late '49 we were ready to break up. We had never intended to be a commercial group. We were dead broke and about to go our separate ways. As a last desperate gasp we decided to do the unthinkable: get a job in a nightclub.

Six months later we had a manager, a recording contract with Decca, and a record selling almost two million copies ("Goodnight Irene" with "Tzena Tzena" on the flip side). The Weavers sang on vaudeville stages and in some high-priced saloons. "So Long," "On Top of Old Smoky," and "Wimoweh" made the top of the Hit Parade. People coming up to me in the street said, "Pete, isn't it wonderful finally to be a success?" I thought to myself, we were just as successful in 1941 when we sang "Union Maid" for 10,000 striking transport workers. But those months of early 1950 were an interesting experience. And at that time millions of teenagers first heard the words "folk song."

In midsummer of 1950 we were offered a weekly network TV show, but a couple of days later the red-baiting publication *Red Channels* came out with a blast against us. The TV contract was torn up. We kept on with personal appearances, but it got to be more and more of a drag. Our then-manager would not let me sing for the hootenannies and workers' groups. Decca, hungry for more hits, insisted on teaming us with a big band; predictably, the result was almost the opposite of how we wanted to sound.

One night Lee and I found ourselves in a Reno nightclub discussing the theory of our poet friend Walter Lowenfels that everything in the world is grist for the writer's mill.

"Grist," says I, looking about me.

"Yeah, but where do you start shoveling when it's up to your neck?" says Lee.

In '53 we took a "sabbatical." As Lee says, it turned into a Mondical and a Tuesdical. Ronnie took time to raise a baby. Lee started to concentrate on being a writer. Fred became the arranger-accompanist of several successful singers.

Moe Asch's new Folkways company made some records of me. (Moe had already lost a shirt or two in the record business but was still obstinately determined to get more folk music into the hands of more people.) I gradually found audiences at colleges and camps for my solo programs. And I sang gratis whenever I felt like it. Toshi organized my bookings and benefits; at first, the job didn't keep her very busy. I had time to work on our unfinished log cabin and watch the kids grow—and was thankful that there wasn't any rent to pay.

Then, in 1955, the Weavers got a new manager and producer, Harold Leventhal. Although that was the year the House Un-American Activities Committee turned its beady eye in my direction, the overall climate had brightened a little. We decided to hold a reunion at Carnegie Hall just before Christmas. This concert was received so well that the Weavers were in business again. With Harold's cooperation we now made freer choices about where and how we wanted to sing, and audiences responded to the informal give-and-take which we ourselves enjoyed. (Lee's vein of satire, which had been a highlight of the *People's Songs Bulletin,* spiced every performance.) Our Vanguard LPs were for the most part recorded at live concerts—the first one by Harold himself—and controlled by our own concepts.

The TV industry wasn't noticing us; but we seldom looked at them either.

By this time, though, I was singing pretty regularly on my own; all sorts of people were getting excited about homemade music. To coordinate my schedule with that of the Weavers, and still leave time to see my family, proved impossible. I asked if Eric Darling (already well known to banjo enthusiasts) couldn't become a Weaver in my place. Later, Eric was succeeded as banjo picker by Frank Hamilton, and Frank in turn by Bernie Krause of Boston. The Weavers continued to tour for another half dozen years.

Meanwhile, their example encouraged first the Kingston Trio, and then hundreds[1] of young strummers, to become professional folk music

---

1. "Thousands?" —P. S.

interpreters. Some saw fit to parody and belittle the country people whose lifework they were looting for the sake of a fast buck. At their best, though, some of the groups introduced a commercial public to music which ignored worn-out formulas and said something about people's real lives. The commercial folk boom died down before long, but many of these performers—and new ones every year—still search out treasures of tradition to introduce to a wider audience. Other alumni of the folk groups have moved into rock music and helped to widen its horizons.

"Pure Prostitution," 1958

Found in Seeger files, dated January 1958

Last week, for the first time in eight years, I got a job in the New York radio field. Replayed over many stations, it should end up making for a profitable recording session. But if another such job ever comes along, I don't think I'll take it.

It was a singing commercial. For a cigarette company. Maybe if it had been for Vega banjoes, or stone-ground whole wheat bread, I could have put my heart into it. But as it was, the job was pure prostitution. Now, prostitution may be all right for professionals—but it's a risky business for amateurs.

If you start doing solely for money something which you would normally do for love, you're liable to find that it makes it difficult, or perhaps impossible, for you do to it for love anymore.

...Well, of course, there is no such thing as absolute purity, as everyone knows, and some say you are compromised with the world if you decide to live in it. Lord knows I can't criticize anybody for making a living as best they can. But maybe everyone has to decide for themselves what they are going to do for money, and what for love. Fortunate are they who can make a living at what they love to do.

P.S. The company didn't accept our commercial anyway.

"Herded with the Sheep," 1957

From Seeger's regular "Johnny Appleseed, Jr." column
in *Sing Out!* magazine, no. 6.4, Winter 1957

I have been accused of being anti–Tin Pan Alley. I confess it. Deep within me lurks a prejudice against the institution and its Hit Parade. I hesitate to let it be known, since some of my best friends, as they say, work there. They like to think of their jobs as channeling the best popular music of the nation so that it reaches the most people. They think of Tin Pan Alley as a funnel. Some of us think it more of a bottleneck.

Most fundamentally, though, I think I am against the Hit Parade because I am against anything that would make a sheep out of a human being. The world is too big, and its people too varied, to try and make one hit parade suit us all. True, the gods of mass production may proclaim that it is much cheaper, much more efficient, to produce everyone's music at one place and at one time. But which would you rather have—cheap music or good music? (And by good you might mean anything from Calypso to blues to bop to Bach.)

Not only every country, but every region and town, every national group, every age group, every industry, even every school or summer camp should have its own hit parade, refusing to follow slavishly the dictates of Hollywood and New York.

Fortunately, at the same time that TV has concentrated the entertainment business as never before, LPs have enabled hundreds of minority idioms to receive hearings. The so-called "Hit Parade" is, today, simply the most popular songs of the 14–18 age group, and is supported by them and a few saloon-goers who help feed the jukeboxes. There have been many songs which attain Number One on the Hit Parade, yet 75 percent of the population has never heard of them.

After this, let me hasten to say that many popular songs are among my own personal all-time favorites. I don't mind being herded with the sheep a bit if they'll give me occasionally a real patch of green grass.

"Folk Songs and the Top 40," 1966

From Sing Out! magazine, no. 16.1, February/March 1966

It seems to me that popular music did not start "borrowing from folk music" with the Weavers. The Andrews Sisters sang "Bei Mir Bist Du Shein" in the 1940s. W. C. Handy wrote "St. Louis Blues" in the '20s. Minstrel show banjo tunes of the 19th century were mostly imitations of the older, more honest, plantation music. The topical broadsides of 18th century London swiped older folk melodies to carry their verses. Commercial musicians in the market places of medieval cities swiped ideas from peasant music of the countryside, as well as from the orchestra in the duke's castle. Because most of these pop musicians were concerned with making a buck, of course they turned out a lot of hackwork. They were neither worried by the "high artistic aims" of the trained composers, nor had they the simple honesty of the country musicians who only made music for the fun of it and the love of it. But pop musicians have also created some fine music: witness "Greensleeves," "Old Dan Tucker," and the works of Duke Ellington.

We should not be surprised that the process is still going on. Now the word "folk" is being taken over for whatever money it can make. What should we do, we who over the years have come to realize the variety, the artistry, the honesty of the many kinds of folk music in our land?

1. We should fight hard to see that the many "minority" forms of music are not stamped out just because any one idiom becomes suddenly popular and saturates the airwaves.
2. We should strive to see that local people are not ashamed of their national and racial traditions.
3. We should not waste time fighting pop music per se. Who knows: the electrified guitar might prove to be the most typical folk instrument of the 21st century? But we can continue to ridicule the worthless hack songs, and if we want, continue to sing the occasional good ones.
4. We should fight hard to see that any idiom, when and if it is suddenly popularized, is not debased, nor prostituted, as often happens.
5. Above all, strive to persuade the average citizens that they can like what they like, and that they can ignore the fashions of the day—which usually change for no better reason than such rapid obsolescence is profitable. We don't have to be swamped by mass manufactured culture if we don't want to. We can make our own music, new or old, loud or soft, plain or fancy, sad or silly. It may not be profitable, but it will be our own.

P. S. In ancient Arabia it was customary for poets to comment upon events of the day. If a king put a gifted poet on his payroll, and attached him to the court, it was called "cutting off the tongue of the poet."

"A Precipice Between Deadly Perils," c. 1957

Found in Seeger files

It can happen that a great and vital talent rooted in folk tradition finds—without the benefit of commercial promotion—a wide enough popular following to become interesting and useful to the communications industry. Then the deep anger and unquenchable aspiration of the common man may be echoed for a time on the Hit Parade.

But the artist who achieves this kind of success walks a precipice between deadly perils. More than a few former jazz stars have been found wielding mops or shovels, their instruments silent in a closet or a pawn shop while, perhaps, the songs copyrighted in the name of some businessman are still bringing in royalties. Others make music to the end but are pushed by the ruthless harassments of the commercial system into a lonely descending spiral of self-destruction ("self"-destruction, but imposed from outside themselves) through distorted personal relationships, dope, and the like.

The juggernaut attacks from a hundred directions; in addition to straight "legitimate" business materialism, it ramifies into the underworld and even into the machinery of the law. (Read Billie Holiday's account of how the police almost explicitly prevented her from kicking the habit, and how she was refused a cabaret license even when she was clean.[2])

Then there are those who accommodate to the system, perhaps cynically, perhaps accepting the commercial pressures as corresponding to the legitimate requirements for communication with any audience. Then the rugged affirmation fades into saccharine: the cleansing bitterness of protest turns inside out and becomes a snarl of passive hopelessness.

But it would be risky for any of us to hold himself blameless. The system can include us all; we all use the gifts offered by the frail, restless, homeless creative spirits—perhaps not for monetary profit, perhaps for honest and constructive aims. But are we never guilty of taking without giving in return, or without giving enough?

"The Star System," 1965

Letter to Irwin Silber and Moe Asch, dated
August 20, 1965; found in Seeger files

Dear Irwin and Moe,

Will you please, please see whoever pastes up advertisements for the *Folk Singers Guitar Guide Book* and get them to take out my name as one of the two authors? Check page 89 of the recent issue of *Sing Out!* and you'll see what I mean.

It should simply read "The *Folk Singers Guitar Guide* by Jerry Silverman," and, if you want to take the space, you can put the other phrase underneath, "Based on the Folkways Record by Pete Seeger."

While I am about it, I'm still turning over in my mind this whole problem of what to do about the star system which seems to inevitably come when there are professional performers and economic competition. I note the sentence in the article on the British Music Hall tradition, "They idolized their stars."

Perhaps I can take heart from this—the fact is that a hundred years later the stars are forgotten, but the good songs have lasted.

Best wishes.

Hastily,
Pete

---

2. Holiday (1915–1959) was one of the most successful vocalists of the 1930s and '40s and remains one of the best-known jazz singers today. Although prodigiously talented, Holiday's career was marred by issues with drug addiction and frequent run-ins with law enforcement officers, who followed Holiday closely, perhaps due to her status as a successful African American entertainer and her many professional relationships with Communist-affiliated songwriters and musicians.

"I've Been Too Tolerant," 1967

Letter to Irwin Silber, dated November 13, 1967; found in Seeger files

Dear Irwin,

I've been trying to bring myself to telephone you for ten days, but finally decided to write you a letter. I feel that if you are trying to kill *Sing Out!* magazine before you are no longer its editor, you're doing a good job. For 15 years I've defended you against all kinds of attacks, saying that even if I disagreed with you I appreciated your self-sacrifice in keeping the magazine going, and saying at other times, that I agreed with you, but didn't think much of the way you expressed yourself. Thirty years ago, when I was secretary of the local branch of the American Student Union, the president said to me, "Pete, you're too tolerant," and he was right then, and I suppose I've been too tolerant all along. If I have been a blind King Lear, one of the things I probably have been most blind about is your own failings.

Julius [Lester]'s article in the last issue is honest and well written. Your attempts to keep up with him are phony.

It's perfectly logical for a critic to change and develop his opinions, but you'd better beware of being too self-righteous about it, or else it will look to a lot of people like you're just hopping on a new band wagon. Let me be specific. Your opening article in the last issue can show what I mean.

You could have started the article, "Newport [Folk Festival] 1967 was irrelevant to USA 1967. Why did I ever think it would not be?" First of all, using the title "What's Happening" for a series of articles on festivals and shindigs is totally misleading of the whole idea which *Sing Out* was founded on, namely the music of working people. Maybe festivals are a small part of the total picture of what's happening, but you and *Sing Out* have continually distorted this into "What's happening with the city folknik scene." That last couple words, "Folk song scene," you also used and promoted when you knew goddamn well it is a distortion of what we are trying to do. You used it on the upper left-hand side of page one, and if it wasn't for that a nice young lady has to type up this letter for me, I'd tell you exactly what I think of people who use this phrase when they know better.

You used other sarcastic phrases, such as "stars of hollow yesterdays." Who was it that helped build up these stars, and fell right along with them? You know very well it was you as editor of *Sing Out*, who continually boosted personalities, when *Sing Out* should have been writing about working people and songs and their uses and their meanings.

Who is it thinks that "The cause of folk music won in 1967 at Newport"? Nobody but you, but you set up your straw man so that you can flourish your power of sarcasm. There are a lot of unfair little inaccuracies in your article, but I wont even bother to bring them up. Newport doesn't need me to defend it, nor, for that matter, did they need a big article in *Sing Out*. For issue after issue, after issue, I've tried to persuade you to downgrade these commercial festivals, and all you do, for issue after issue, after issue is to boost them up.

Actually, I can go a lot further than you in my criticism of Newport, I am only sorry that I have been so uncriticizing of you as editor of *Sing Out*. I am afraid that even if you leave immediately, it's too late to save the magazine.

With regrets,
Pete Seeger

"Grateful for Your Criticism," 1969

Letter to Irwin Silber, dated September 29, 1969; found in Seeger files

Dear Irwin,

When I got off the sloop, Toshi faced me with three huge piles of mail, about one foot high and I'm digging down through it and find your letter of July 24. For several reasons I am very sorry for the delay.

My definition of the word "dishonest" is not as specific as you took it to be. I feel that when someone criticizes someone else for a fault without criticizing themselves for the same fault, it is basically dishonest. Such as when Americans accuse socialist countries of not being fair to political or racial minorities. Or when policemen accuse [Black] Panthers of using violence.

It would have been more fair of me had I said, "In my opinion it was not an honest article." But I some time ago stopped trying to use that phrase, "in my opinion," because it seemed presumptuous to claim that anything I said was more than just my opinion.

You see, I feel that some of the very things you are criticizing the Newport Folk Festival for were the very things which were wrong with *Sing Out* magazine while you were editing it. I do not believe that you were forced "By the very nature of the system," to be an accomplice to the kind of business practices which you allowed *Sing Out* and *Stormking* to get into any more than someone living in a fascist country has to be forced into a practice of racism.

I have made so many mistakes myself, and am still making so many mistakes myself that I don't really have the right to criticize anyone else, except that I now realize that I don't have the right to simply clam up either, and avoid trouble by remaining silent. Believe it or not, I feel more than a little grateful to you for your sharp criticism, which has been considerably instructive to me within the past year or two, and though we may disagree strongly about tactics, if you are on the side of those who are trying to build Socialism and those who are preparing the way for the building of Socialism, we are still on the same side. I grant you there may be some disagreement between us as to who should be included in both of those categories.

Incidentally, the sloop project is no longer quite so antiseptic. We had some interesting experiences giving waterfront festivals along the Hudson. I owe you a considerable apology for not letting you print "Bring Them Home" in your songbook. It turned out to be the hit of the show all summer long. I still have reservations about the song which I tried to imply in the liner notes of my new Columbia album, but nevertheless, I think it was a distinct step forward to hear it sung by large Main Street audiences of all sizes, shapes and colors in towns like Nyack, Newburgh, Kingston and Castleton.

I guess this is all for now. It is about 4 AM. I got up early this morning to continue dictating letters to hard-working Irene Bryant, without whose assistance as typist I would really be sunk.

All for now,
Pete

"No Reputation to Speak Of," 1975

From Seeger's regular "Johnny Appleseed, Jr." column
in *Sing Out!* magazine, no. 24.2, May/June 1975

Dear friends,

I've just received your letter asking if I can come sing for your organization. It's a good cause; I know you need cash right now, but unfortunately, I can't make the date. My schedule's too full.

You ask me, do I know "some big name performer" who can help your cause. Don't you realize that we all have to fight the star system? In this technological society, we have to oppose the cult of personality. There are a lot of good performers living near you. They are young and old, black, white, makers of many different kinds of music. Many of them are concerned about the immense crisis facing the human race. You should be calling on them to help out. They should be paid, if possible—not some astronomical sum, but union minimum or at least transportation. It depends on the cause and the commitment.

…Suiting musician to audience is an art. Putting together a well-balanced program is not easy. Getting the right location, the right sound system or lighting is damn important. And don't forget excellent promotion.

…In the end, your audience will learn one of the lessons that revolutionists have always had to teach the people: that some of the greatest talents in the world have no reputation to speak of; they have just been sitting beside us all the time, and we didn't know about it.

Sincerely,
Pete Seeger

"The Feverish Search for 'Fame,'" c. 1970

Form letter, found in Seeger files

To Whom It May Concern (especially people making autograph collections):
Dear Friends,

Within the past few years I have gotten increasing requests for autographs, and I guess I'm flattered and I don't want to hurt people's feelings also; so I comply. But really I feel very deeply that the whole feverish search to get close to "fame" is not only foolish but a symptom of something very bad in modern society around the world.

Modern technology, mass production, has made some people too famous and has left billions of people feeling that they are unimportant, that they are just cogs in a big machine, that the world could get along without them. This is really false. Everybody is important in this world. Back in the days when our ancestors sat around a campfire wondering whether they should move to a new location the following day to keep from starving, it was probably true that some people were the leaders and some were the followers; but you didn't find anybody that was really unimportant. Everybody was needed. They all supported each other. There was work for everybody.

I realize that a big autograph collection is worth some money, and a lot of people figure that it's something they can do in their spare time, and if they don't use the money themselves, they could pass it on to their grandchildren. But I urge all autograph collectors to realize that the kind of fame people get in show business and politics is about the phoniest of all. To be in show business is to be in the professional publicity business. People are hired to send out releases to newspapers and to arrange for TV interviews.

If you want to have a creative and unusual autograph book, you might look through the newspaper for some people that are doing some really interesting things and combine their autograph with a newspaper story about some unusual event. There are totally unknown people who do something heroic and are briefly mentioned in the newspapers, or only known to their family.

Of course, if you want to be cynical, the way you could really get an unusual autograph collection would be to haunt the courthouses and the jails and get autographs from people who have committed crimes and are condemned to death. Do you think that's cruel and unnatural? I don't think it is any worse than the kind of publicity which comes to us people in show business.

"The Essential Purpose," 1961

Letter to Henrietta Yurchenco, dated May 25, 1961; found in Seeger files

Dear Henrietta,

For many months now I have enjoyed receiving the *American Record Guide* magazine which I assume I have you to thank for. And although I don't have time to read the whole magazine I have invariably managed to go through your column which I find consistently interesting. I have quite often clipped it and sent it to Irwin Silber telling him with envy that I wish we had anything half as good in *Sing Out!* magazine. Your recent column reviewing some of my own records along with those of Woody [Guthrie], Sonny [Terry] and others actually prompts this letter of mine.

While I think you are, in general, on the right track in criticizing modern performances of folk music, or what passes in the name of it, I'm not sure you hit the nail quite on the head. Father once said that he thought one of the outstanding traits of good indigenous folk music was a certain relaxed unforced quality, and I think you pointed in this direction. However, it always seemed to me that another very important trait of it was a certain hardness—perhaps "hardness" is not exactly the right word—but I usually thought of it that way when I first came in contact with the unflinching honesty and directness of Woody and Leadbelly, for example.

In trying to analyze what happens to my own singing as well as the singing of other city people who like to sing folk music, I feel that the most important single innovation is singing with a rather soft smooth voice somewhat like a crooner. Now it may be true that I have speeded both the songs "East Virginia" and "Cumberland Mountain Bear Chase," but do you know that both of these songs are ones I learned twenty years ago and have hardly changed a note in? You listen to the original recording of "East Virginia" sometime, which Alan made in 1938 from a man named Walter Williams with a banjo in Salyersville, KY. I haven't listened to it in several years, and it is possible that I have sped it up and it's possible that I have raised my voice more stridently. But I admired his performance so much that I have tried to sing as nearly like it as possible, and only within recent years have been singing it more according to my own standards.

"My own standards." That is not really the phrase I mean to use either. But within the past five years or so I've felt increasingly that every performer, or every singer, whether amateur or amateur making a living at it—which I am—has to be himself. When somebody asks me am I authentic I tell them of course not, I am only authentically myself which is all anybody can be in this world. At the same time I admire tremendously what my younger brother Mike is doing—making a very conscious attempt to master the idiom of certain white southern folk singers. To a certain extent I did this myself for many years. I did everything I could to destroy the Harvard accent which had been bred in me since the cradle, and I quite distressed all my relatives, except perhaps my father, by trying to shed such obvious upper-class manner-isms as I was able to.

By characterizing modern city-billy music with the term "machine-like precision," I don't think you are taking into account the fact that if you really want to hear machine-like precision you should listen to some of the records of Earl Scruggs and Don Reno, the most exciting Bluegrass musicians to be heard these days. This is not to say that theirs is bad music. As a matter of fact, it is becoming deservedly popular. I think the distinguishing characteristic of some of the commercialized folk groups, such as the Kingston Trio,[3] is not necessarily their machine-like precision—although they do occasionally have it—but rather the general softening of the approach; and next, and perhaps this is even more important, their choice of repertoire and the way they treat it.

I listened to a couple of performances of the Kingston Trio last sum-mer and was appalled to discover that they were unable to sing one single song straight, unless it was a mawkishly sentimental song. Otherwise, they always at some time had to crack a joke to let the audience know that they didn't take it seriously. This reminds me of a comment made by Woody Guthrie once to Walter Lowenfels, "Why are you guys scared to be serious?" I really think many of the college folksinging groups are a little scared to be serious, just like any teenager is scared to be serious unless he is with someone he can completely trust, because the one thing they are most scared of is to be laughed at.

Here I meander on; however, you said this much more briefly, "Cleverness, sharpness, slickness abound, but human quality—seldom!"

Perhaps instead of criticizing others I should once again turn to my own work to try and analyze how it has changed in the 20 years that I have been singing folk songs. Partly, I find that I no longer try to achieve a very hard nasal vocal tone as I once consciously imitated. I rather strike a balance between the somewhat richer vocal tone which most Negro musicians have.

Because I love the songs (and for old times' sake), I still occasion-ally sing "Cindy" or "Lolly-To-Dum," and also occasionally sing some

---

3. The Kingston Trio, which formed in California in 1957, was one of the most suc-cessful pop folk bands of the 1960s folk music revival. The Trio's albums featured many radio-friendly renditions of traditional folk songs and consistently charted in the Billboard Top 10.

of the union songs of the thirties or the Spanish Civil War songs. I also sing these songs not only because I like them but because I think that any audience can learn from them, especially the young people of today for whom the thirties lie almost as far away in the distant past as does our own Civil War. I do not bear down on these songs though, because if I am going to sing songs about the bitter realities of life, I'd rather sing some about contemporary times; it is all too easy to become romantic about the bitter realities of a past age while ignoring those of the present. Thus, in preference to singing "The Ballad of Harry Simms" (Simms died in 1931), I think right now I would rather sing "The Ballad of Fayette County" or even the classic "Talking Atom."

I say this because the essential purpose of my singing, it seems to me, is still that of any good art—namely, to help the listener to understand reality. And the path to understanding the reality of any age lies through the "here and now" and thence to the "faraway and beyond."

Keep up the good work.

As ever,
Pete

"Not Authentically Me," 1962

Letter to editor of *The London Times,* dated
January 12, 1962; found in Seeger files

Dear Sir,

I was interested to read your article on folk music which was more than a little critical of some of the things which I perhaps said and did. However, I think perhaps you also misinterpreted some of my remarks. It is not too unusual, of course, in the field of folk music to find the same word meaning quite different things to different people. "Authenticity" is one of these words.

I think I agree with you almost completely about some of the appalling commercializations of folk music which one can hear today on the jukeboxes. However, I have often been almost as repelled by some of the sterile imitations of folk music which I used to hear from effete, well-trained middle class musicians. Don't you agree that it would be possible, and has often happened, that the letter is imitated but the spirit has escaped?

When I sing in America some of the beautiful songs which I learned in Britain, I will try and keep the spirit, the strength and the truth of the songs. But it would not be authentic of me to try and sing them in an English accent. I am an American. It would not be authentically me if you want to come down to that. And for me to sing one of these songs in Britain with my American accent might sound as silly to an English audience as it would be occasionally when American audiences see English actors trying to put on Brooklyn accents.

Furthermore, it seems to me that the first duty of any artist is to produce good art. The only artists who are exempt from this first commandment are those who are in a very specialized field of creating historical reproductions. The first commandment for these, of course, is to be authentic to what they are trying to reproduce, as in a museum restoration of an 18th century drawing room. As far as those people are concerned, they can only hope that the original was good art.

Since in the field of folk songs, the authentic original is best captured on an authentic field recording, I think it would not only be futile, but completely wrong of a singer such as myself to try and produce exact imitations. Rather, it is my duty to be authentically myself and to make as good music as I possibly can, and to transmit the truths as well as I am humanly able to do to those whom I am fortunate to sing for. Do you feel that I am incorrect in this?

Sincerely,
Peter Seeger

P. S. Of course, let me add that in my own opinion good music can be interpreted in almost infinitely different ways. My definition, for example, of a good vocal tone is the resonant rasp of a real country singer which has no vibrato to speak of and often strains the upper registers. And with no such things as pear-shaped tones placed in the proper cavities.[4]

"My Own Songs?" 1964

"Parting Views," from *Overland* magazine, no. 29, April 1964

So, what were "my own songs"? I had none.

But [Ralph Waldo] Emerson said, "We have what we enjoy." I enjoyed a lot of good songs I heard, but I wanted to sing 'em.

In some cases I try and translate. I feel I have to translate, because otherwise my listeners will miss 90 percent of the song. I translated literally some foreign language songs into English, like "Oleanna" and "Zhankoye," halfway successfully. I translated musically some songs from Africa, Indonesia, Japan, singing the original words, but playing a U.S.A. style banjo accompaniment while I was singing the foreign language words. I translated some old folk songs from an archaic style of singing into a more conventional modern style, while trying to retain the basic honesty and content of the older song.

---

4. In some forms of vocal music, a tone which is sung "correctly," such that it is heard as having a rich, full tone, is called "pear-shaped."

I figured I was justified in doing this because this is what folk musicians throughout history had done, so far as I could find out. Well, at least while there was always the desire "to sing a good old song in the good old way," there were in every century young people who made the old songs come to life again by some sort of translation. After all, don't parents translate the precepts of their own parents to train their children? Don't lawyers try and translate old laws to fit new citizens? And cooks translate old recipes to fit new stomachs?

And sailors took old shore songs and made new shanties of them. Cowboys took old Irish songs and made new frontier ballads. A Yankee pop tune ("Old Zip Coon") was remade into a humdinger of a new Australian song called "The Old Bullock Dray." An Irish fiddle tune ("Irish Washerwoman") became "Starving To Death On My Government Claim" and also a slow pulsating spiritual, "Rock-a My Soul in the Bosom of Abraham."

I'll grant you there are such things as unsuccessful translations. I don't like curry sprinkled on the pizza. And I don't think Tchaikovsky sounds well on a saxophone. But the virtue of the democratic old folk process is that the unsuccessful hybrid, and its brief notoriety, are forgotten, and the successful ones are remembered and improved upon. I think one thing I would be sorry to see, though, is for the good old songs to be forgotten. And another thing I'd be sorry to see is people stop writing new ones.

"Nothing Underplayed, Everything Overplayed," 1963

From Seeger's regular "Johnny Appleseed, Jr." column
in Sing Out! magazine, no. 13.2, April/May 1963

I'll probably get in Dutch with a number of people for writing these paragraphs. I'm relaying information which, while not exactly given me in confidence, was told me by people who thought I was a mere musician, not a journalist. However, the story needs to be told now, not next year nor even next month.

It looks as though the much ballyhooed national TV show, *Hootenanny*, will be a bitter disappointment for anyone who loves folk music, or who thought the word "hootenanny" meant a healthy mixture of the old and new. The ABC network, the advertising agency (Ashley, Steiner) the sponsor (Proctor and Gamble) are all charging ahead with the idea of making a "fast-paced show, 26 minutes of screaming kids in the studio audience." All strictly professional performers will be used. Real folk musicians such as Doc Watson, Horton Barker, or Bessie Jones and the Sea Island Singers will not stand a chance of being considered. Even the Tarriers were first turned down because they are an interracial group. (All-white, or all-Negro groups are allowed.)

Perhaps it's worthwhile reviewing briefly the history of the situation. After many years in which Alan Lomax and others tried to get the airwaves interested in folk music, the networks have finally got this sponsored show. How? Because about a year ago the Greenwich Village coffee house "The Bitter End" let Ed McCurdy start Tuesday evening jam sessions for new and old talent to drop in on. The term "hootenanny," developed in the '40s by Woody Guthrie and the Almanac Singers into its present definition was common property by 1962, and the "Hoots at the Bitter End" became fabulously successful. The directors of the coffee house, two young former advertising men, sold the name and the idea for a show to ABC. Each week the show would be videotaped at a different college. One "star"—a different one each week—would sing three or four songs, and then introduce a couple or three other artists, each to do one or two songs. The students grouped closely around would join in on the choruses.

It could be a nice format. The folk song revival on its home grounds. With good performers allowed to ad lib, with meaningful songs and youthful participation, it could be a breath of fresh air on TV. But with the producers of the show knowing little about folk music besides what they learned from the pages of *Billboard* and *Variety* (listing "top sellers"), and with their usual concern that every song be "socko!"—nothing underplayed, everything overplayed—it will be a miracle if much meaningful music gets to reach the TV screens. How I hope I am wrong. I would love to be proved wrong.

When will TV producers learn that some of the greatest music in our country is made by unlettered farmers, miners, housewives, people with generations of folk traditions in their veins? The great thing about the old hootenannies was their ability to put together on one stage the old-timer and the new-timer, the city-billy and the hillbilly. The professional and the amateur. But the TV networks have not learned this lesson.

What can you do about it? Two things, it seems to me. First, the way is still wide open for a decent folk music show to be put on the networks. Fight TV with TV. Second, anyone who knows how to use pen and paper can sit down and write a letter to ABC, to the ad agency, and the sponsor, and give a considered opinion of the shows when they're aired in April. Those hucksters have no mind of their own, you know.

"Songs Are Forms of Love," 1957

> Letter to Lynn Riggs, playwright, dated
> September 1957; found in Seeger files

Dear Lynn,

Someone once said that work is love given concrete demonstration. I think even more songs are forms of love, even when bitter or silly. And there was no song ever written to which the writer ever contributed more than a miniscule fraction. The great part of the song was composed by untold thousands who handed him his language, syntax and vocabulary, his forms of harmony, traditional scales and traditional ways of using them. Two musicologists once argued whether Beethoven's symphonies were 10 percent or 20 percent Beethoven and 90 percent or 80 percent traditional—and ended up agreeing that the proportion was more near 90 to 10, than 80 to 20.

Thus it is that I have tried never to place any restriction on any song I have ever written or sung. I let people tape my singing and am proud when someone reprints a song. I would be proud of having a song I'd written reprinted in either the *Wall Street Journal* or the *Daily Worker*—or a Hearst tabloid. If it was a worthwhile song, it could do nothing but good for its readers.

I believe it is true that the American people owe a great debt, for all the wonderful songs they have learned, to you (and to Alan Lomax, and to me). A debt far greater than will ever be paid. But I think it is also true that you (and Alan Lomax and I) also owe a debt we can never repay, to the uncounted songwriters and singers who have given us the songs we have been so fortunate to be able to pass on.

The reason I dragged poor Alan L. into the argument, is that I've been having a trans-Atlantic conversation with him over this very subject. After several years of seeing literally millions of dollars being made on the Hit Parade by people who changed a word or two in songs he had laboriously collected, he is finally copyrighting them himself so that he can afford to make some more collecting field trips. I pointed out to him that he never would have gotten into such a pickle if in his original books he had only given a fairer shake to the people he collected the songs from. Now at last he is doing it, and I expect his copyrights will hold. I, too, this year, have finally been persuaded to copyright the various songs I have either written new words to, or music, or both—in order to keep them from being restricted by the Broadway pirates. But it is one thing to copyright a song in order to prevent restrictions upon it, and another thing to copyright a song in order to restrict it.

…I hope I may continue to send you good songs I run across, or that I help arrange, and that you will be free to use them as you wish.

As ever,
Pete

"The Gambling Man Rich, and the Working Man Poor," c. 1957

Letter to Alan Lomax, found in Seeger files

Dear Alan,

This is in no way a proper and sufficient response to your letter, but I wanted to get something off without too much delay.

If you will send me a list of titles of all songs to which you are attaching copyright claim, I will be very glad to notify any record company, radio or TV station, or publisher that I use these songs with, of such claim. I agree that I have been remiss in this respect in the past.

Generally, I have come around to your view (which Moe [Asch] has come around to, on his own) that the only way to protect folk music from the Lonny Donegans[5] and the Mitch Millers is to do some copyrighting on your own. I myself would still rather not be involved, unless I have actually written some verses (as in "Kisses Sweeter than Wine") or made up a new tune, even though I know that my selections of verses and my research is being used by singers reaching millions through the Hit Parade.

However, I certainly won't raise my voice in objection if you plan to do this. I agree that your research has been fundamental to the present folksong revival. I regret that you feel it necessary, but under the circumstances of our society, in which research must suit the scholars or the big business firms (as in scientific research), there seems to be no other way for you to pay for your field work and other work which does not pay for itself directly.

If you include as coauthors your original informants such as Ironhead, Mrs. Ball, George Turner, et al, you will be on firm ground, moreover. If you don't do this, I feel you will be in for more trouble than you realize.

...You see, Alan, I feel that above all you weaken your case dreadfully by being in any way bitter yourself. You demean yourself, getting bitter about the Lonny Donegans. If you are going to be bitter about anything, be bitter about this cockeyed system where the gambling man is rich and the working man is poor. Be bitter about Ironhead, and Aunt Molly, and about the Cold War.

The truth is that you, and I, and others like us have been *lucky*, far luckier than we realize. You with stepping into a Library of Congress job when you were so young. Me for meeting you. If we realize this, and realize also that we are all just links in the human chain anyway, isn't the important thing to be a strong link rather than a long link, if I think I mean what I think I'm saying?

I'll grant you, all the city-billies are doing better than the true folk sources, such as you mention: Ironhead, Georgia Turner, et al. Here's an idea. Why don't you write an article: "Why I Am Now Copyrighting Folk Songs," and include in it personal accounts of some of these fine people. Also include stories on exactly what you did, in a couple of cases, to change their songs. Or would this be endangering your copyright?

---

5. Donegan (1931–2002) was a British musician, known as the "King of Skiffle," famous for his fast-paced pop music covers of American folk songs like "Rock Island Line" (with authorship legally attributed to him). Until the rise of the Beatles, he was Britain's most commercially successful musician.

Take care of yourself, Alan. A lot of us love and admire you, even when we think you are wrong, as occasionally happens, or when we think you sound condescending, which occasionally happens, too. Take it easy, but take it.

Pete

"The 'Guantanamera' Story," 1978

Letter to an unknown recipient, dated November 29, 1978; found in Seeger files

Dear Peter,

In 1971 I was welcomed warmly to Havana by Joseito.[6] Three years earlier (maybe 4) I wrote the Cuban society of composers explaining why my name was listed as one of the authors [of "Guantanamera"], and that I did not intend to keep one penny of any royalties for the song.

Perhaps something since then has happened to make for a misunderstanding.

...Keep in mind that when a white singer sings an Afro-American song, he/she is in effect stealing. This has happened with banjoes, with jazz, calypso. I used to try and ameliorate the situation by giving a rather detailed translation and story of the composition of "Guantanamera," but it became so well-known that I had to spare my audiences all this talk.

But here is what I said: It was 1964. I was singing at a children's camp (Camp Woodland) in the Catskill Mountains of New York. The children said, "You must hear the song our counselor has taught us," and they brought out a very shy young man, Hector Angulo, who sang "Guantanamera" into a tape recorder. He told me that the 3 verses were from [Jose] Marti's last book, *Versos Sencillos* (*Simple Verses*), and the tune and chorus was an old one that everyone knows.

...As the years went by I gradually learned to pronounce and sing it better, but I never got into the Cuban style of improvising verses anew each time I sang it —nor do I "tear the melody to shreds" in the Afro-Cuban style. I sing the notes pretty much as Hector gave them to me, except I sing the 6th note of the scale on the opening syllable "Guant-" of the chorus.

Because of U.S. policy to Cuba, Harold Leventhal suggested to me that unless someone copyrighted the song, it would become "public domain" and no money would ever reach Cuba, or Hector or Joseito. So I agreed, on the understanding that all royalties would go into escrow, until they could all be sent to Cuba. My name on the copyright (along with Hector's, Joseito's and Marti's) was simply to facilitate this.

---

6. Jose Fernandez Diaz (1908–1979), sometimes known as Joseito, was a Cuban songwriter, best known for his contribution to "Guantanamera."

I did not want my name on it, but I was told that unless it were, the copyright could not be controlled, and no money—or credit—would ever get to Cuba.

I think Joseito should get major credit for the song, although the words most of us sing are by Marti. But I think Angulo deserves credit, too. It was a stroke of luck or genius that coupled Marti's patriotic stanzas with a popular barroom melody and chorus. I wish my name were not connected with it. All I did was change one note.

"A Musical Story and a Money Story," 2009

From *Where Have All the Flowers Gone,* Revised Edition, W. W. Norton & Company, 2009

Following are two intertwined stories, as true as I think I can get them, of how a South African song was changed and added to (and profited from) in the U. S. A. during the last 60 years. It's a musical story and a money story.

In 1929 a young Zulu sheepherder, Solomon Linda, made up a song consisting of a few wails and shouts, and a chanted background. It had a great bass part repeated over and over.

In 1939 Linda was in Johannesburg singing with five other young men. For a flat fee he recorded this song for the local record company, Gallo Records. It was the biggest hit of the decade, in South Africa: "Mbube," by Solomon Linda and the Evening Birds.

> M-bu-be-wo, w'm-bu-be
> W'm bu-be w'm-bu-be

In 1948 Gallo sent a dozen of their recordings to Decca Records in New York City. Decca was not interested in promoting them, but folklorist Alan Lomax, who was working at Decca then, grabbed the 78 rpm discs before they were thrown out, and gave them to me. I was in bed with a cold, got pencil and paper, transcribed the music, mispronounced the two words, and taught it to the Weavers, a quartet just organized.

> Hey yup boy! Wi-mo-weh
> Wi-mo-weh wi-mo-weh[7]

In 1950, when the Weavers, to everyone's surprise, "hit the big time," we had a hit (Number 6 on the "Hit Parade") with "Wimoweh," accompanied by Gordon Jenkins' orchestra.

---

7. c. Hallmark, 2009.

Flash forward to 1966. I was at a Newport Folk Festival committee meeting at the New York City apartment of Chairman George Wein. A telephone call came for me from a secretary at Columbia Records. "Mr. Seeger, I need to know copyright information for songs in your new records."

She listed several titles, then listed the British ballad "Barbara Allen." "That's public domain," said I.

"Oh, thank you," said she with surprise in her voice. Back at the meeting I told George of the call. He said, "Pete, I don't think you're being nice. I think you're wrong. Columbia Records didn't write 'Barbara Allen.' You gave them the money as if they did."

It was the first I knew that since about 1940 it had been standard practice in the music industry for performers, when recording an old song in the public domain, to copyright the song, because they had "adapted and arranged it." Now they received royalty payments as songwriters as well as performers.

Flash back to 1951. Howie Richmond, the Broadway publisher, had published "Goodnight Irene" and paid royalties to Leadbelly's family, and to John and Alan Lomax, who first printed it. With the Weavers' (then) manager (not Harold Leventhal) he now published all the songs the Weavers "adapted and arranged." I distinctly remember being told, "Pete, money is coming in for 'Wimoweh.' Where should we send it? Gallo says send it to them."

"Oh, don't send it to them," says I. "Solomon Linda will never get a penny of it."

"Well, get his address. We'll send it directly to him." I didn't bother to ask exactly what "it" was. Foolish me. A year later I'd located Linda and a check for about $1,000 was presented to him at a grand banquet in Johannesburg. I assumed this was the first of many such payments, and that a standard songwriter's contract had been signed with Linda. Again, foolish me. Linda received 12.5 percent, not the usual songwriter's 50 percent. Gallo got the same 12.5 percent. The Weavers' manager and the Weavers each got 5 percent, and the Weavers' manager got another 37.5 percent because he set up a new publishing company with Howie, to get most of the publisher's 50 percent.

…I'm mainly happy that Solomon Linda's children are now getting the full 50 percent songwriter's royalties. The contract has been rewritten. How come? In 2004 out came the lead article in *Rolling Stone* magazine:

> "It is one of the great musical mysteries of all time: how American music legends made millions off the work of a Zulu tribesman who died a pauper. After six decades, the truth is finally told."

I wrote the editor, "Hooray for muckraking journalists and journals that will print their muck." The author, an antiapartheid white South

African, did not get every fact straight, but basically taught me how wrong I'd been to leave finances entirely in the hands of others.

"The Committee for Public Domain Reform," 2001–2002

From Seeger's regular "Appleseeds" columns in *Sing Out!* magazine, nos. 45.3 and 46.2, Fall 2001 and Summer 2002

Twenty years ago Mike Cooney[8] put out a record of traditional American folk songs, and told the record company to send the royalties to the nonprofit fund at the Library of Congress which supports the archives of folk song. I thought of this when I read in the May 25, 2000 issue of *Rolling Stone* magazine, about the song I heard on a record from South Africa with one word on it, which sounded to me like "Wimoweh." Because of mistakes I made back then, it seems that Solomon Linda, who recorded the song in 1939, got only a half or a quarter of the money he should have got. And in 1991 the man who wrote ten words ("In the jungle ..." etc.) won a court case against the Weavers' publisher. The judge said that if those ten words are used, the man who wrote them (George Weiss) gets *all* the royalties for the song. That's what the copyright law says now: If you adapt and arrange an old song "in the public domain," you can keep all the royalties.

At first I was bad-mouthing George, and then I looked through my own songbook and found I'd done the same thing on a lot of songs. What to do? Well, you have to start somewhere. One of my publishers is rewriting the contract on the story-song "Abiyoyo." Some of the royalties will go to me for writing the story, but some will now go to a nonprofit fund of the Xhosa people in South Africa, because it was a traditional Xhosa lullaby. The two publishers I've worked with for half a century have worked out with me a statement. See what you think of it:

The Committee for Public Domain Reform

Songs have been written all over the world which have fallen into public domain. These songs continue to be used by contemporary recording artists and record companies as sources of inspiration for new songs. In these cases, the new copyrights and recording masters owe a monetary debt to the original sources.

It is our quest to recognize and honor the original sources of lyric and/or music content which have and continue to be included in contemporary music.

We propose that a share of mechanical, print, and performing royalties from such new works be sent to the "public domain commission"

---

8. Cooney (b. 1943) is a folk singer and activist who was active on the board of the Newport Folk Festival.

in the country of origin. Such commission will determine where the funds can be used.

This income will serve the cultures and countries which have helped inspire us.

Please join us in this effort.

Continuation in Summer 2002

I got a few letters from friends who read my proposal in the Fall 2001 issue of *Sing Out!* proposing that when someone "adapts and arranges" an old song which is in "the public domain" they no longer collect 100 percent of the royalties which come in for this version. They think I am proposing abolishing the idea of "public domain." Not at all. Not at all. When after a number of years copyright runs out on a song, it goes into the "public domain" and can be reprinted and/or recorded free of charge. What I and my publishers are recommending is finding some way to get money to third world countries when someone puts new words to one of their ancient melodies.

Joseph Shabalala (of Ladysmith Black Mambazo)[9] told me with a rueful smile several years ago, "I've found that when the word 'traditional' is used about a song, it means that the money stays in New York."

…It's true that a record company now could hire some singers to record some old traditional song and have each singer sign a statement that these songs are in the public domain. They could do it, but the standard thing is for the record company to have to pay eight cents for mechanical royalties to someone for every copy sold, because the song has been "adapted and arranged." It's true that half a century ago Moses Asch of Folkways Records practically never paid royalties to any publisher, and thus kept his tiny company alive, but it's not so easy now for Smithsonian Folkways, which bought the company when Moe Asch died.

So this is why I and the two publishers that I work with have started this Committee for Public Domain Reform and are hoping that some other publisher and songwriters will want to join us. Eventually we hope to reach the WIPRO office in Geneva, Switzerland. That's the World Intellectual Property Rights Organization, which tries to get world copyright laws into some kind of agreement with each other. We think that every country in the world should have a Public Domain Commission. They wouldn't have to bother with all the tens of thousands of songs written every month, but when a song somewhere starts to earn money they'd consider it.

For example, a hundred years ago an English lawyer looked through a book of *Irish Traditional Airs*, and wrote the words of "Oh Danny Boy"

---

9. Ladysmith Black Mambazo is a South African choral group founded by Joseph Shabalala in 1960. Ladysmith Black Mambazo has sung of the political struggles of black South Africans since the 1960s, as vocal opponents of apartheid and other social injustices. The group garnered international recognition after appearing on Paul Simon's 1986 album *Graceland*.

to one of them. The singer John McCormack made it world famous and the lawyer collected royalties whenever the song was printed or sung. What should have happened then was the lawyer could have received half the royalties and the other half could have gone to the Irish Public Domain Commission. They would have said, "Oh send this money up to County Derry on the north coast." That's where the song was written in 1603 by a blind harper (I think they even know his name)[10] when Castle Derry was captured by the English and its defenders slain. The harper wrote it in memory of his slain kinsmen. The royalty money could now have gone to the County Derry School system, perhaps.

...All I know is that there are thousands of truly beautiful melodies still uncollected in small poverty-stricken communities around the world. Sometime later this century they will be collected and new words put to them in some wealthy city somewhere. The poverty-stricken village will stay poverty stricken.

---

10. "Rory O'Cahan." —P. S.

16

Reflections on a Life in Music

"A Professional Amateur," 1972

From *The Incompleat Folksinger,* Simon and Schuster, 1972

This man is advertised as a singer—but he obviously hasn't much a voice.
He is a Yankee but sings southern songs.
He sings old songs, but somehow his meanings are contemporary.
He tries to talk simply, but obviously has a good education and has read widely.
He sings about poor people, though I doubt he is poor himself.
Altogether, he is a very professional amateur.
I would call him phony, except that I think he is just another modern paradox.

"Most of My Job Is Done," 1961

From Seeger's regular "Johnny Appleseed, Jr." column in *Sing Out!* magazine, no. 11.4, October/November 1961

For many years I figured I pursued a theory of cultural guerilla tactics. I could not hold a steady job on a single radio or TV station. But I could appear as guest on a thousand and one disc jockey shows, say a few words while they played a few records. I could not hold down a job at the average college or university, but I could appear to sing some songs, and then be on my way. I kept as home base this one sector of our society which refused most courageously to knuckle under to the witch hunters: the college students.

Now, I figure, most of my job is done. The young people who have learned songs from me are taking them to thousands of places where I myself could never expect to go. Though I cannot get on network

TV, many of my friends do. Though I cannot get a job in a university, those whom I have helped get interested in folk music are getting them.

But even more important are the literally hundreds of thousands of amateur guitar pickers and banjo pickers—and each has an important job. Like fireflies they light up the night.

"A Songwriter Whose Persistence Brought Many," 1963

Letter to journalist Nat Hentoff in response to an article published in *Playboy* magazine, dated May 19, 1963; found in Seeger files

Dear Nat,

...Hey—in your estimate of me, I think you're not far wrong. At the end I think it will be recognized that here was a guy limited in talent vocally, instrumentally, and as a songwriter (my main regret) but whose persistence brought many to follow some sort of interest in folk music.

...It *did* sound wonderful, in that big Victorian bathtub,[1] to hear 5,000 human beings singing "We Shall Overcome" strongly, and with feeling. I grant it's not everybody's favorite form of music, but it sure sounded better than I would have alone. Incidentally, most critics are confounded by this bit, understandably.

My principle criticism of your article was this, though: I feel you concentrated too exclusively on well-known professional performers of folk songs, in order to analyze the folk song revival. Whereas the long-run significance to the musical life of this country is in the huge numbers of people not just listening to this music, but trying to make it themselves. Half a million guitars sold every year. Individual professionals may come and go, but the music of America is never going to be the same again after this decade, I'm willing to bet. Nor, I'll say further, the poetry. Bob Dylan (and there will be more) is going to have a real effect on American poetry. Want to bet?

...I'll end up with a couple questions:

Is it any more screwy for a college student to sing a Kentucky mining song, than to memorize a Shakespeare sonnet?

Is it less phony to have a piece of African sculpture sitting on the mantelpiece than to get some tools and try to carve in wood yourself?

If you want to rebuild a healthy artistic tradition in a country, where do you start?

With thanks to you and all the tribe of word-slingers,
As ever,
Pete Seeger

---

1. This is apparently a reference to the Albert Hall, where Seeger performed in the early 1960s.

"A Record Review," 1965

From *Sing Out!* magazine, no. 15.1, March 1965

Pete Seeger will be forty-six this year. He has been singing professionally for twenty-five years, and as an amateur for many years before that. His first recording was made in 1941 (with the Almanac Singers). This review is not of any one of his discs, but makes some general comments on all of them—the forty or fifty solo LPs he has done for Folkways, and the five he has done for Columbia in the last three years.

Taken all together, they form one of the most uneven bodies of recorded music that any performer could boast of, or perhaps be ashamed of. Now, it is true that some songwriters have written thousands of songs and let posterity decide which few dozen of them were worth singing. But does a performing artist have the same right to spew out thousands of recorded performances to the commercial market, without being judged for the poor ones as well as the good ones?

Some of Seeger's earliest discs, such as *Darling Corey* (1948), have the nearest to traditional folk music on them, although a still earlier one, *Talking Union* (1941), is the most frankly propagandistic.

Scattered throughout the discs, you will occasionally hear some passable ballad singing. (Pete's sister, Peggy, is a much better ballad singer. But if you really like ballads, why not listen to the master balladeer, Horton Barker, on Folkways and Library of Congress LPs?)

As for banjo picking, Pete only occasionally does some good traditional picking. His brother Mike can play rings around him, not only on the banjo, of course, but on guitar and half a dozen other instruments which Pete does not attempt. But much of P. S.'s banjo accompaniment is mere whamming.

If community singing is your meat, you can probably learn a lot from him, since he has been at this game for a long time—according to his own account, since his mother gave him a ukulele at the age of eight. But if you prefer your folk songs less noisy, better performed, and with a smaller number of voices, best steer clear. He also has a disturbing habit of singing harmony to his own songs when the crowd is warmed up. On the stage, perhaps he can get away with it. Over a loudspeaker in one's living room, it can be just plain annoying.

If you like blues, don't even bother listening to him. He doesn't know how to sing or play blues, though he occasionally tries to.

If you like spirituals and gospel songs, he does a little better here—in fact, better than most white musicians. But still his voice tends to get tense and hard, and he rarely achieves that full, relaxed but powerful tone that most good Negro singers have naturally. No, if you like spirituals, listen to Vera Hall (Folkways) or Blind Gary Davis, or the Gospel Keys, or to the modern commercial singers such as Mahalia Jackson (her early discs, for Apollo, are some of her best).

Pete Seeger's concerts are a different matter. I will not mention them in this article except to say that while there's hardly a song he sings which couldn't be sung better by someone else, his concerts—most of them deft improvisations upon program themes he has developed through the years—are often masterpieces of programming.

This is probably why his records are rarely criticized properly. People like the guy, and hesitate to slam his discs as they should.

Sometimes the intensity of his performance can pick you up and carry you away, especially if you agree with what he is saying (not all do, of course). Jimmy Durante, the old-time comedian, is supposed to have said once, "When I face a crowd, I give 'em all I got!" and Seeger, when he walks out on a stage, often seems to follow this philosophy. Some people try to recapture the excitement by listening to his records. Others, who know what kind of music they like, will not join in on the chorus, and feel more and more repelled. You're either with it or you're not, baby.

It is probably because of his indefatigable concertizing that he has made so many records. Any recording company knows that sales follow personal appearances. Probably a number of readers of this article were first introduced to folk music through a Seeger concert at some college. They can be a lot of fun, and sometimes a deeply moving experience.

But that doesn't mean one has to like his records. Really, I don't think the guy listens to them himself. In between two pretty good songs is sandwiched a sentimental little piece of nothing. If someone recommends a Pete Seeger record to you, the standing rule should be: Don't buy it sight unseen, or sound unheard. You might like it. You might not be able to stand it. The discs range from children's songs through standard American folk repertoire to modern composed songs by people like Malvina Reynolds and Bob Dylan, and to songs from a dozen different countries. Which prompts one to say that Seeger would probably do a better job generally if he didn't spread himself so thin. Perhaps he has opened up Young America's ears to new sounds and songs, but he has also given them a bad example: "You, too, can sing in sixteen idioms."

It's not true. He can't, and you can't.

He is known to go out on a stage before a thousand people (who have paid hard-earned cash for tickets) and, sticking the words of a song with Scotch tape to the microphone, sing them for the first time in his life. You may be able to get away with it on a stage, but do you have to record it, Peter?

To sum up, if one could dub onto a tape a few songs from here and there on his many LPs, one might have quite a good one-hour tape of Pete Seeger. The trouble is, no two people would make the same selections.

Therein lies his defense.

(*"Collected, adapted and arranged with additional new material" by Toshi Seeger, Copyright © 1965 by Toshi Seeger.*)

"The Biggest Victims Are the So-Called Stars," 1965

Letter to Don West dated August 27, 1965, responding to West's article in a symposium in *Sing Out!* magazine, no. 15.4; found in Seeger files

Dear Don,

It hurt to have an old friend—and a man I have long admired—who proudly bore the title of "Poet" relaying an incorrect story.

In May of 1963 there was still some doubt about whether anything could be done to improve the *Hootenanny* television program. Some people wanted to boycott it completely. Others felt that if pressure were brought in the right way, it could be improved and in the end, do a good job.

For example, Theodore Bikel[2] threatened to raise a big fuss with the Television Actor's Union if they refused to hire an interracial singing group called The Tarriers. The producers of this show backed down and agreed to hire The Tarriers. This was a victory. The trouble is, The Tarriers had a job at a coffee house in New York City. So I agreed to take their place at the coffee house to free them, so they could be on the *Hootenanny* show. Later on that summer, it became more and more obvious that nothing could be done to improve the *Hootenanny* show and more and more people refused to be on it. However, by that time I was out of the country anyway.

The first paragraph of your letter in *Sing Out* magazine I agree with completely. The whole character and definition of the word "folk music" is being warped by the commercial image of the solo professional performer and the publicity surrounding it (him or her)—and I think that you are right that magazines such as *Sing Out* are consciously or unconsciously contributing to this bad state of affairs by continually boosting the names of performers in articles rather than talking about the music and the nameless unknown people who have created it and kept it alive.

However, I don't quite understand your use of the word "anomaly." My dictionary says this means "an irregularity." But in our present commercial system the star syndrome is the regular thing and I believe among the biggest victims of it are the so-called stars themselves. I

---

2. Bikel (b. 1924) is an actor, folk singer, and progressive activist who helped found the Newport Folk Festival.

know that I feel a victim of it personally because for ten years I have tried to persuade *Sing Out* to play down my name, but it keeps popping up in every issue. I keep sending letters to publishing companies and record companies, but the basic facts of economic life keep running against me and there goes my name up in huge letters. I consented to a normal interview with the *Christian Science Monitor* and suddenly see a headline, "A Folk Hero Is Born." What are you going to do about this kind of shit? I can tell you for sure that many times I've thought of quitting the whole music business because of it and one of these years I will. I also know that there is no easy solution to it, either for me or for anyone else. Supposing that in your community you wanted to raise a thousand dollars for some civil rights purpose and some singer, whether it was me or anybody else, agreed to come and give a concert for you. Would you be willing to publicize it in your posters as "Come and listen to an evening of singing by a good friend of ours?"

Well, I am resigning from as many things as I can and quitting my column in *Sing Out* and pulling in my horns in half a dozen ways.

Incidentally, you should know that both Toshi and I regret that whole business about the article reviewing my records which was printed in *Sing Out* last winter. I guess you didn't notice that in the following issue I explained, or tried to explain, that the article was originally written for the *Little Sandy Review* a year before. *Little Sandy* had always treated me with kid gloves, and I felt they needed a realistic hard-hitting review of me. So I wrote this review, but before it got to them, they had a better article printed. Irwin Silber happened to see a copy of it and wanted to print it. However, I didn't want it to go out—though it would be a good humorous way to break down the goddamned halo which *Sing Out* readers want to hang on me.

The big mistake was in not putting it out signed with my own name, but rather having it signed, "collected—adapted and arranged by [blank]." Well, I hope I've learned a lesson and perhaps I'll keep a sharper watch to prevent things from being printed that were not meant to be.

To my mind, we all have to be careful about slinging around words such as "phony" because what is phony and what is not phony in this world is, believe me, a very moot point. Many people including some whose opinion I usually respect a great deal, thought that *Woody Guthrie* was a phony because he was careless of his appearance and continued to use incorrect grammar, when he knew perfectly well what correct grammar was taught in school. From the viewpoint of the modest, most of mankind are phonies.

All of the best,
Pete

"Not a Usual Entertainer," 1966

Found in Seeger files, dated September 16, 1966

Dear friends,

If any of you who sit in the audience tonight hear me for the first time:

I confess that I am not an entertainer in the usual sense of the word. Oh, I like to eat, drink and be merry.

In the U. S. A. I am sometimes accused: "This man Seeger is not a musician. He's just a politician pretending to be a musician."

And an Irish girl disdained to come to my Dublin concert last year, saying, "Seeger? That clergyman?"

"It's true I'm not as good a musician as I would like to be," I would answer in protest. "But I am not a politician. I vote, as a citizen is supposed to, and form opinions. But I am a musician."

I think now this was not entirely honest. For in a larger sense, the basic purpose of all art (writing, painting, too) is to help enlarge our understanding of ourselves, and of other people. And these understandings inevitably affect our political opinions. Nothing—not love, sex, our taste in food, clothing, skin coloring, language, sports, architecture— nothing is without political significance.

But likewise, this means politics is much more than who is going to get elected next year, or how high taxes are. Tonight, you'll hear love songs and lullabies, ballads, work songs, blues, and hymns. Some will be out of the history of my own country; some will have been picked up in other places. If you can put any simple label on all this, you're a pretty slick labeler.

…I was caught up in the social ferment of the 1930s, and the struggle against fascism which, in a larger sense, is still with us today. I've made as many mistakes as anyone else, probably more, but they have all been my own mistakes. No one ever told me what to think. The long range goals seem just as clear as ever. But the arguments about the exact road to take to get there are sure confusing.

Perhaps what singers have done in the past, and what they should now, is to present a variety of stories, then let the listeners decide which are the truest ones, and what significance they carry.

I have a wonderful wife, and three fine children, two of them grown up. They've all stuck by me even though their father is traveling too much of the time. Our home is on the banks of the Hudson River, 60 miles north of the city of New York. We're involved in the campaign to clean up the pollution in this lovely body of water, which human selfishness has turned into an open sewer.

About the music: America is a more recently mongrelized nation than most and our music reflects this. Wave after wave of hybrid musical idioms have been thrown off and influenced in turn the popular music of the world: "minstrel music," jazz, blues, rock-and-roll. But even our older music is not "pure." Our old ballads came to be accompanied by instruments: the banjo (originally West African); the guitar (from Spain to Mexico to Texas and then east and north); the dulcimer (from North Germany to Pennsylvania down to Kentucky)—and so on. Negro slaves heard Irish melodies and sang them with African rhythms. And now young people in colleges are singing these old songs in still newer ways. Perhaps it is best to agree with the older folklorists and say that none of it is folk music.

Whatever you want to call it, tonight I hope you have all eaten well, and are prepared to be merry. We can get drunk on music.

"I Just Feel That I Was Fortunate," 1986

Letter to Jim and Ginger Brown,[3] dated December 20, 1986; found in Seeger files

Dear Jim & Ginger,

Toshi and I have talked over your proposal, and unfortunately think maybe this is just not the right time to do it, although we're not exactly agreed on what would be a better time.

My first thought was you could go ahead and make it but on the understanding that it wouldn't be released until after I'm dead, five, ten, twenty years from now. Whatever it is. Toshi said, make it when I'm 70 or 75 years old, not while I'm still tromping around the place.

In addition, there are some real complications. I feel funny about having the story about me and leaving out of it not just Toshi and the kids, but other people I've worked with who have taught me so much, from Alan Lomax to Woody [Guthrie] and Lee [Hays], and yes, Harold [Leventhal] and you and many others. I just feel that I was fortunate to be born with a lot of energy in the right place and time so that I was able to at least partly do a job that still needs to be done.

I say "partly" because really what I wanted to do was try and get rank-and-file people singing again, whether parents singing to children or workers singing on the job or friends harmonizing in a car as they drive down the highway. But the prevalence of loudspeakers has defeated me and a lot of others and in the end our "Revival of Folk Music" seemed

---

3. See chapter 14 re: Jim Brown; his wife, Ginger Brown, is a television and film producer. The project Seeger is declining in this letter was eventually made, entitled *The Power of Song*, and released in 2007.

more like simply starting up another minor branch of the pop music business, especially appealing to middle-class whites.

On the other hand, there is a definite value in showing people, not just in this country but any country, that a musician could lead a satisfactory and fulfilling life without hardly ever getting involved in the big-time pop music business nor without hardly ever being involved in the public school music business. And I guess I am proudest of all to see the hundreds of people in the People's Music Network carrying on the idea that you can sing a combination of old songs and new songs and make them relevant to a wide variety of people today, not just a sectarian few.

…I guess another part of the problem is that I feel more pessimistic than at any time in my life as I reexamine my own failures and mistakes and those of my country and of people in so many countries in the world where power-hungry men seem to get in charge and don't want to let go. I've tried to learn from Woody and Lee the ability to see a joke even in the grimmest situation, but I'm nowhere near as good at it as they were.

Now, of course, this is not a clear answer. All I can say is that it shows you how we're thinking, and at the moment I guess it adds up to saying, "Not right now."

I'm really sorry that you got turned down on filming the history of "We Shall Overcome."[4] That was a humdinger of an idea.

All for now.
Best,
Pete Seeger

"Jobs That Needed Doing," 1989

Letter to David Dunaway,[5] dated May 23, 1989; found in Seeger files

Dear Dave,

Thank you for your letter of April 28th. Only today, May 23rd, I really had a chance to read it through closely. I've been more swamped than ever in my life, to the point where I'm trying to figure some way I don't have to spend about 90 percent of my free time trying to answer mail and somehow never getting around to some projects that I really want to finish before I kick the bucket.

---

4. The Browns did, in fact, go on to make *We Shall Overcome* (California Newsreel, 1989), which also won an Emmy.
5. Dunaway is the author of *How Can I Keep from Singing* (Da Capo, 1990), the first published biography of Seeger.

...I didn't know that Jim & George[6] were writing you. It sounds like they are seriously trying to go ahead with a movie about me, although I've told them that as long as I'm alive, I don't want such a movie to come out.

You should know that these days when people ask me what I think of your book, I say something like, "I was once very cruel to Dave by writing in *Sing Out!* magazine, 'I thought he would seriously critique whatever successes or failures I'd had, but it seems to me the main thing you learn from the book is why I don't brush my teeth regularly.' I regret this. He spent six years working hard, and it was all a labor of love. Nevertheless, I am sorry that I gave him the go-ahead on the book."

When they ask me why, I am usually at a little bit of a loss for words and try to pass off as a joke my father's word about the lingocentric predicament. I think a good deal of it is tied up in the different definitions of the word "career." I've always been very prejudiced against the word and tried to deny that I attempted to have "a career." I rather thought that there were jobs that needed doing and jobs that I might be able to help do, but I didn't really like the word "career." Nevertheless, when I'm gone, I realize that people will talk about my checkered career, and I have to face up to the fact that I've been a bad father and a bad husband, and even today spend too much time working on my own projects and not enough time helping other people with *their* projects. I have forgotten whether you ever quoted Toshi in your book, "If only Peter would chase women instead of causes, life would be easier for me."

Right now, with my voice about 50 percent gone, I'm desperately trying to discipline myself to get a little bit of time to get a book of songs put out, which Harold has been after me to do for five or ten years, and if I get real callous about it, within a few months I may not even be reading my mail, much less answering.

Well, in any case, you take it easy but take it, and I'll try and repair some of the damage I've done in more ways than one.

As usual, hastily,
Pete

"The Most Difficult Time of My Life," 2006

Letter to Sibnath Ray, dated November 2, 2006; found in Seeger files

Dear Sibnath Ray,[7]

I owe you an apology for promising to help you in writing a short biography of me for readers in India. I have been trying for almost a

---

6. George Stoney (b. 1916) is a director, producer and social activist, particularly in the realm of entertainment media. A frequent collaborator of director Jim Brown, Stoney coproduced *We Shall Overcome* (1989) and *The Weavers: Wasn't That a Time* (1982).
7. Seeger now recalls Sibnath Ray to be an Indian professor who approached him about writing a biography of Seeger for an Indian audience but who died shortly thereafter.

week to write a short answer to you for your letter of October 22. Now today I get up early in the morning as soon as it's light and try to write a longer one.

…Now I'm facing the most difficult time of my life. From the shoulders on down I'm in better condition than most people my age (87 next May). But my eyes are not so good, my hearing, and *worst*, my short term memory also. My voice long ago started going, but I've always been good at getting a crowd to join in singing and nine days ago Arlo Guthrie and I did a fundraising concert in the Beacon High School auditorium and I was delighted at the way the *crowd* sang—several songs where all I did was to play the accompaniment and just speak a line or so, so they could remember the words. They did an especially good job on the famous 200-year-old hymn, "Amazing Grace," which I learned from Lee Hays 60 years ago. And when I sing it I usually remind audiences that the words were written by a man who had for ten years been captain of a slave ship, but in his thirties he quit and became a preacher in his home in the south of England, and he started the antislavery movement in England. "He turned his life around, and gave us hope that we can turn our country around."

So even though my voice is 95 percent gone, I'll try to keep on "singing" for a while, at least locally. I sing for kids at local schools and summer camps—that is, I get them singing.

I'm interviewed several times a week these days, either for the press or radio or TV. Friendly or unfriendly souls. If I get copies of them I give them to a filing cabinet in Harold Leventhal's office, but now that he has passed away I guess I'll have to find some place to put it.

…I hope *your* health is OK. I still think the human race as a 50/50 chance to be here a century from now, and I still stick with the song I wrote about 40 years ago, "Quite Early Morning."[8]

My politics, my "religion" these days is in one of my newer songs, "God only knows what the future will be; but God gave us brains. He meant us to use 'em."

And now I better quit.
You stay well—keep on.
Old Pete

---

8. "Some say that humankind won't long endure / But what makes them so doggone sure? / I know that you who hear my singing could make those freedom bells go ringing / And so keep on while we live until we have no more to give / And when these fingers can strum no longer, hand the old banjo to young ones stronger" (Bicycle Music Company, 1969).

17

Balancing Work and Family Life

"A Paradigm with Pots and Pans," 2009

From *Where Have All the Flowers Gone,* Revised
Edition, W. W. Norton & Company, 2009

After *People's Songs* folded in February '49, Lee Hays and I (and Fred
Hellerman and Ronnie Gilbert) tried to start a new quartet, the Weavers. But jobs were few and far between. In June '49 by a great stroke
of luck, Toshi and I were fortunate to find a few acres for sale on a
wooded mountainside overlooking the Hudson, 60 miles north of the
Big City. Only $100 an acre!

For two summers Toshi cooked over an open fire, helped me build
a log cabin. The third summer we moved in permanently. For two
winters I toured with the Weavers, then as the blacklist put us out of
business, we took a sabbatical in '52. Lee said it turned into a Mondical
and a Tuesdical. I started teaching in a small "alternative" school in
New York City one day a week, and on the weekend picked up a few
dollars singing somewhere.

The so-called "folk music scene" hardly existed at the time, but it was
building. *People's Songs* had folded in '49, but with an "Interim Newsletter" I kept a few of us in touch. *Sing Out!* magazine started up in 1950.

Moses Asch had me record one album after another for his tiny
company, Folkways. It encouraged me to explore a variety of old traditions and to experiment with songwriting as well.

Our kids were little then. I'm certainly not the first versifier inspired
by small children. Most of the songs or stories in this chapter [of *Where
Have All the Flowers Gone*] would not have been put together without
the existence of three small people now all grown up, with kids of their
own. Danny, Mika, Tinya. They taught me so much. I'm still learning
from their mother.

The *Clearwater* knows Toshi Seeger as an ace organizer. After having to organize me for 66 years, no wonder. But she's the wisest person I know: Perspicacious, Peppery. A Paradigm with Pots and Pans. Calling Toshi a good cook is like calling Louis Armstrong a good trumpet player. And we are both proud to be parents of those three.

"Away Singing Some Place," 2009

From *Where Have All the Flowers Gone,* Revised Edition, W. W. Norton & Company, 2009

All these songs don't mean I was a particularly good father. Half the time I was away singing some place. One year Toshi counted the days I was home: 90 out of that year's 365. That might have been the year after I was sentenced to jail for a year, for not cooperating with the House Committee on Un-American Activities. We accepted almost every job offered, on the assumption that most of them would be cancelled. But none of them were. The Court of Appeals acquitted me. It was a horrendously busy year. Toshi said, "Never again. Next time no appeal. Let him go to jail."

As for me, I'll never sing these songs without seeing in my mind's eye certain little children. Something good that has happened can never be made to unhappen. And never is a long time.

Now there are grandchildren.

"Practically Ready to Be Raised," 1949

Letter to Rockwell Kent,[1] dated October 1949; found in Seeger files

Dear Rockwell,

It's terrible that I have been so long in thanking you for sending down the tent. It literally was a life saver. The fall weather was getting a little cool for continuous sleeping out of doors. The only excuse I have is that there has been an enormous amount of work to be done since the Peekskill incidents—and also trying to get the house finished in time for the winter.

We have about given up trying to finish it off completely, but it is practically ready to be raised. We plan to spend as much time as possible all winter going up there and working on the house and land. The next main thing to be done is to some way get some water. Right now we are taking a five-minute walk to a wonderful clear stream and hauling buckets.

---

1. Kent (1882–1971) was a painter and writer who contributed to People's Songs.

The tent is standing in the spot that someday we will have a larger house built and has the most gorgeous view on the property, overlooking ten miles of the Hudson that is continuously changing depending on the weather or time of day. Someday I wish that you and ... would be able to stop by and see us there on your way to the city, perhaps.

Pete and Toshi

"Nothing to Feel Bitter About," c. 1957

Letter to Alan Lomax; found in Seeger files

Dear Alan,

A few exceptions I feel I should take to your letter. You say, "since you are not in personal difficulties over jobs, recording dates, etc., I would appreciate it if you did acknowledge Lomax sources." Why should you wait till now? Yes, I'm making a better living than before. For the *first* time in my life I hope next year to have time and money to do some original research in this field, something I have *never* been able to do before. I have been for twenty years almost blacklisted from commercial work, and have had to use ingenuity, and still do, in order to get jobs. I have never had the opportunity of working for a library, foundation, or radio company. My wife still raises three children in a two room log cabin, which only this year has an inside toilet. Thanks to her, we've been able to save enough to buy a movie camera and start our first research. At the moment I have an indictment for contempt of Congress with a possible year's jail sentence and $1,000 fine hanging over my head.

Frankly, were this not a confidential letter to you, I would feel ashamed of writing the last paragraph. For withal, I have absolutely nothing to feel bitter about. I feel I have been very lucky, all in all, having been born and raised with opportunities far beyond many other Americans, or other humans on this earth. I guess I wrote it mainly because of what you said in your letter.

...Oh, I guess this will be all for now. I have about 163 letters to answer, before leaving to go out west for three weeks. Poor Toshi. I'm going to have to dictate them into the tape machine, and she'll transcribe them. It has been a hectic spring, with her brother and his four children, and an average of two to five guests every day of the week dropping in on us. We don't want to be standoffish, but it has got so we look forward to winter when we get a little more peace and quiet to work. I'm turning down all booking, but *all*, for January and February, and don't plan to answer the telephone or write a letter unless it has to do with this movie project.

Take care of yourself, Alan.
Pete

"Most Wonderful and Unusual," 1967

Letter to Toshi Seeger, dated March 1, 1967; found in Seeger files

Toshi Darling,

1. You have a right to make whatever radical change to extricate yourself from the painful pressures you've been under.
2. I think that all along you have needed some work or recreation outside the family circle.
3. I know, that in spite of your occasional blow-ups, that this family has accomplished much in this world, and it could not and would not have been done without you. You are, with all your strong and weak points, one of the most wonderful and unusual people.
4. And I love you and always will.

As ever,
Peter

"Realistic Planning," c. 1971

Letter to Toshi Seeger from Spain; found in Seeger files

Darlingest,

It was so good to hear your voice on the phone. I miss you very much. In spite of all the things that have gone wrong on this trip, I still think it was valuable to have tried to make it, but really, I don't enjoy traveling like I used to. And I enjoy being at home with you more. I like singing with other people, but singing in a little Hudson Valley folk song club would suit me just as well or better.

I hope to learn from singing in both Cuba and Spain, and I think I will have to rely on tape recordings, movies, or books, to do it more and more. I've written Dan Moses[2] to ask when I can read proofs on Jo [Metcalf Schwartz]'s and my book [*The Incompleat Folksinger*], and I've asked Harold [Leventhal] how soon I can read proof on the Berkeley book (*Henscratches and Flyspecks*).

But I think I'd like to buckle down to work on some other ones meanwhile. What's needed is a lot more disciplined planning—realistic planning—on my part. Taking into account my own lowered energy. And then if I get my own work more under control, I won't be such a drain on you. I'm sure grateful to hear hints that you are clearing up

---

2. Moses was a senior editor at Simon and Schuster publishing agency.

things in the barn, but I'll feel awfully guilty if you aren't soon able to get back to pottery.

You would be proud to see Mika and Emilio working as a team here. They are two beautiful young people. The last two days they've been having long conversations with Raimon[3] and Analisa, and learning about the [Spanish] Civil War and Catalan history. It seem that almost ¼ of Spain is in the Catalan language area. Barcelona is now 3 million, the most modern city by far in the country. Seven million Catalans (out of 30 million Spaniards) read ¾ of the books and magazines—though all in Spanish. The Catalan language is allowed in only one or two magazines and two hours a month only on TV.

We drove (12 hours) from Madrid to Barcelona—wearying but interesting. Dry. Rocky. Half-empty little medieval towns. Occasional shepherds, fields. Driving over a ridge I spied a real live eagle. We stopped. He (or she) hovered right over us for 15 minutes or so, just a few hundred feet away. It was spectacular. I'll never forget it. Emilio took some pictures, I think, with his telephoto lens. It is a tragedy that eagles aren't around the Hudson any more. I bet a determined drive could bring them back, once DDT is no longer used—and when the DDT content of the oceans gradually abates. You know who could use an eagle in their backyard? The people at the blueberry farm. It would keep down the other bird population which devours the blueberries before we do. Really, we must get up there this year. It was a shame to miss it last year. Now Analisa is getting ready to serve dinner, and I'll close. I love you much much much.

Your slightly batty,
P.

"You Are Right," c. 1990

> To-do list/note to Toshi Seeger; found in Seeger files

Toshi,

You are right:
>   La Byteman
>   Carry It On
>   ~~Germany~~
>   ~~Japan~~
>   Walkabout
>   Also:
>   Sing Out

---

3. Raimon Pelegero Sanchis (b. 1940) is a Spanish Catalan-language singer and pioneer in the Nova Cançó music movement, which used music to denounce injustices in Francoist Spain.

U. S. Committee
People's Music Network
The Woody
Beacon Sloop Club
Little Stony Point

I must soberly face the facts. I want to stay home more.

P.

Part 3
Other Dimensions

18

Other Writings

"Imaginations Need Exercise," 2000

From *Pete Seeger's Storytelling Book,* Harcourt, 2000[1]

When I was a small child, my father, just home from work, would come into my bedroom and tell me stories of family adventures and fantastical foolishness. Lying there in the dark, I'd whoop with excitement. He'd say to himself, "I'm supposed to be putting this child to sleep. He's more awake than ever." But, exhausted by laughter, I'd soon fall sound asleep.

Twenty-five years later, I found myself putting my own children to bed. Back then, we lived in a small cabin with no electricity. So, like parents since the beginning of time, I started telling stories in the dark. And although I'm not the best storyteller, my children—and now grandchildren—still prefer these improvisations to reading something out of a book.

I love to draw and I love picture books. And we all know how strongly children (and adults) are attracted to television, videos, and computers—machines that present moving images right in front of their eyes. But instead of always relying on somebody else to make up the pictures, why not let the imagination take over? Let children learn what fun it is to imagine the pictures. Or give it a try yourself. See if I'm not right.

Of course, you don't have to wait until bedtime to tell stories. You may be on a long car trip or waiting at the dentist's office. Or maybe you're preparing your child for a new experience like the first day of

---

1. "I had what I still think was a good title and a good picture for the cover of this book: 'Telling Stories in the Dark.' The picture was of a silhouette of a small child and an adult seated in a dark room with the only lights coming from a window on the other side, lights of a city at night. The publisher turned it down. *Their* cover? A rocking chair." —P. S.

school. And naturally, you don't have to be a parent or grandparent. You may be a teacher faced with naptime, or a summer camp counselor with a cabin full of restless kids and a rainy day. Or maybe you're a visiting aunt, uncle or babysitter who simply wants to strike a bond.

As a young man, I didn't think of myself as a storyteller. Then, at age twenty, I met Woody Guthrie, a balladeer from Oklahoma. Soon after that, I met Lee Hays, son of an Arkansas preacher. Both Woody and Lee were great storytellers, and I listened to them with admiration.

I learned early that it's easiest to begin with something familiar. If you remember a favorite picture book, you can tell the highlights, the bare plot. You don't have to tell it word for word. Or pick something from a collection of folktales, the Bible, or even Shakespeare. Lately, I find myself telling about events and figures from American history: George Washington, for instance, or Martin Luther King, Jr., or Rosa Parks. And don't forget about your own family's history.

Sometimes you'll have thirty minutes, sometimes only two. Luckily, successful storytelling doesn't depend on a story's length. A quick personal anecdote can capture a child's attention as easily as a long tale.

Not long ago I thought every good story needed a beginning, a middle, and an end. Then my grandson Kitama came along. He loves to make up stories and all the names and situation that go with them. But he finds it hard to finish. One day I asked him, "Kitama, do you ever finish your stories?"

"No," he answered. "I just start them."

This makes Kitama a certain kind of storyteller, and for different kinds of stories, there are different kinds of tellers. That leaves room for all of us—for you, for me, for anybody. And while it's true that some storytellers might be better than others, and some may be truly great, what a sad world this would be if the only storytellers were professionals, and the only stories were the best ones.

I think you'll discover that the more stories you tell, the more confidence you'll gain. The first book I wrote was called *How to Play the Five-String Banjo.* On page 18 it said, for the "secret of clear crisp tone, see page 30." On page 30 it said, "Practice." It's the same with storytelling, though unlike musicians who can practice in private, storytellers have to practice right in front of their audience. And the more you practice, the better you'll get at what I called "growling them out." If it's a scary tale maybe you snarl and hold your fingers out like claws. If it's a funny tale you might puff up your cheeks and let out a funny noise.

Don't be afraid to embellish stories, to make up names or places, or to add new characters and subplots. You'll be surprised how fanciful you can get and still keep your listener's attention. Trees can talk to each other. Stars can talk to each other. My old friend, the poet Walter Lowenfels, wrote a book of children's stories called *Be Polite to the Grass.*

In it, every piece of furniture, every pot and pan, even pictures on the walls, take on different characters.

Try it yourself. Start with the question, "What would happen *if—?*" Then take off on any fanciful flight and follow it through to an illogical conclusion. The ingredients for stories are found everywhere: under rocks, perched on oak leaves, rusting behind old radiators. But don't overdo it. Pick just one or two ideas at a time, add seasonings, and savor them.

Now some of you might be thinking, this is easy for Pete Seeger to say. He's a professional. And true, for sixty years I've earned a living singing songs and telling stories to audiences around the world. But as Iona and Peter Opie, editors of the *Oxford Dictionary of Nursery Rhymes*, point out, "Four and twenty trained singers caroling in harmony are not so effective as one parent's voice, however out of tune."

More and more, it seems we're becoming a nation of spectators. On Sundays we watch professional athletes instead of playing ourselves; on weeknights we watch professional jesters instead of tickling ourselves; and on weekdays we tune the radio to professional music makers instead of singing ourselves. But perhaps it's wisest to view performers as intermediaries who show how enjoyable these things can be.

The world can be full of people with enough carpentry skills to make a table. Or enough sewing skills to piece a quilt. Or vocal skills to sing in a choir. Or gardening skills to grow some vegetables or flowers.

Just because we have cars and buses shouldn't mean we forget how to walk. And just because we have books and television sets shouldn't mean we forget how to tell stories. They needn't be virtuoso stories. And you don't have to look far. Tell about your family, your friends. Tell about the nation's history or a people's history. Tell a moral tale or a silly one. Tell stories even if they're only the bare plot.

My hope is that each of us, at some point in our lives, will say, "Hold on. I know that someone can do it better, but I want to try this myself. It looks like fun."

…The history of the United States is a long, varied, and complicated story made up of countless small stories that I've learned—and you've learned, too—from books, articles, anecdotes, and songs. I retell some of these stories, both onstage and at home, filling in where memory fails me, adding a scene here, a little dialogue there. My story's not exactly the way it happened, but it might have happened this way.

I particularly enjoy telling anecdotes that show why something succeeded; how people with all the strikes against them still managed to make a situation work. I tell these stories hoping that other people, especially young people, might learn by example.

Too often our knowledge of history goes no farther than a name or a date. We establish holidays, build memorials, and name public works to commemorate important figures and events. But soon we forget.

Presidents' Day comes to mean a day off from school, the Fourth of July means fireworks, and the Statue of Liberty means sightseeing.

But when kids get to be eight or ten years old, they start taking an interest in the bigger world around them and its history—how things got this way. How did Harriet Tubman lead slaves along the Underground Railroad? Why were the Wright brothers successful inventors? What became of Geronimo and his people? Discovering the true stories behind legendary figures can be exciting.

It's up to each of us to tell the stories that make history come alive again. In Fishkill, New York, they read the Declaration of Independence on the Fourth of July, and in schools and churches all across America, the "I Have a Dream" speech is read on Martin Luther King Day. That said, remember that history is not limited to tales of "great" people and important events. In fact, it's mostly made up of the stories of people who simply lived their lives. How did your uncle win the Purple Heart? What was your town like before the interstate came through? When did your mother open her first restaurant?

There are also family adventures, like my father's story, "The Trailer and the Flood." And still other adventures that I call "across-the-ocean" stories. How did your grandmother travel from Hungary to America? Where in China did your great-aunt come from? Why did your father emigrate from Ghana?

...The possibilities are endless if you let your imagination go. But be patient. Not every story you make up will be a smash hit. Improvised stories may have an unwieldy quirkiness. They'll have edges and bumps and meanderings like any homemade thing. Your audience's reaction will tell you when you've hit upon something wonderful. It's either, "Not that story again!" or "Tell it one more time!"

If you live in a big city, you can make up a story about city life. Every city has highways, railroad, and airports. Imagine an adventure using one of these avenues and add in a character or two. What if two long-lost friends met at the station? Where are they going? Where are they coming from? What if the two friends weren't people at all, but pigeons? If you live in the suburbs, you can make up a story about your particular neighborhood. What if a squirrel stole birdseed from the feeder? What if the squirrel got rich selling the seed back to birds? Or maybe you live in the country, and there's a bush that blooms pale blue blossoms every spring. What if one year it bloomed bright orange?

When I was a kid, most stories had one basic message: If you're strong, if you're brave, if you're honest, everything will turn out all right. It's a good message, but we can add other important messages. One I include quite often in that if we work together, we can accomplish things that we can't do alone. Another is that if the world is going to last, we must make better choices about how we live. And if we all do our part, a hundred years from now our grandchildren will be making up their own stories and retelling the ones we're making today.

"False Values Are Embedded Deep," 1974

From Seeger's regular "Johnny Appleseed, Jr." column
in *Sing Out!* magazine, no. 23.1, March/April 1974

What's necessary is that everyone be aware of the many meanings of songs, and their many uses for good and bad. We're learning this about all culture: language, architecture, clothing, cooking. Learn how much damage can be done by something we once thought was merely foolish. Listen, even if we disagree, to criticisms we once would have shrugged off.

False values are embedded deep. The English language—like most North European languages—uses the same words to describe a light colored skin and good aspects of life in general: fair skin, fair weather, a fair decision, fair (smooth) lines of a boat, a fair way or fair road, meaning open and free. One of the great cultural achievements of the '60s was the phrase, "Black is beautiful."

In general, don't think you can expose all false values at once. I doubt it can be done. Whack away at them little by little. And often this can be done without words. Ray Fisher[2] will sing a great old Scottish ballad, but part of the message is not just the lyrics, or the tune, but *she* as a free and independent woman, able to pick and choose what she wants to learn from the past and carry into the future.

"We Inherit an Outlook," c. 2000

Draft of an article apparently intended for the Beacon
Sloop Club *Broadside,* found in Seeger files

Folksong collectors John and Alan Lomax, like other collectors before them, used to try to locate a singing family, whether in the countryside or town, among African-Americans, European Americans or Hispanic-Americans. That is, a family that liked to make music for an evening or a weekend—rather than play cards, or wrestle, or whatever. He found the Gant family in Texas, Vera Hall's family in Alabama, the Garland clan in Kentucky—Aunt Molly Jackson and Sarah Ogen Gunning were both sisters of Jim Garland, who wrote, "I Don't Want Your Millions, Mister."

When they find singing families, collectors tend to find both ancient songs and stories and new stories and songs, reflecting present day times. But what makes a singing family? Often it's inherited. Woody Guthrie's

2. Fisher (1940–2011) was a Scottish folk singer and activist who played a large part in the British folk music revival of the 1950s and '60s.

mother sang old ballads; his father made up stories and rhymes, sang cowboy blues and hollers.

I've wondered similarly why one nation will be famous for one trait, and another famous for another trait. Often it's geography: the Inuit (Eskimos) are good at building snow houses, Hawaiians good at surfing, Himalayan sherpas good at mountain climbing. But I bet it's often inherited. I bet the first French tribes made a big thing out of cooking. I bet the first tribes invading what is now Japan were conscious of visual beauty in every article of everyday life.

So while I still agree with Marx that the way we make (or steal) our living tends to set our style of life and outlook, I also think we can inherit an outlook and a style. Maybe it's like a path zigzagging up a bluff from a beach. Why does it zigzag that particular way? Perhaps a hundred years ago a vacationing family set it there, and subsequent families used it and wore it deeper.

Well, in these mobile video days, perhaps everything will be different. Someone who loves music may leave her or his non-music-loving family and settle far away. Someone who loves jazz may settle in New Orleans; someone who loves fiddling may settle in Ireland. American painters and sculptors have gravitated to Italy.

But I still believe that this world will be saved by people who fight for their homes. I urge people everywhere who love music that they can learn from anywhere, but they ought to try to make their own singing families. Start with little kids. Keep things loose. Have fun. Accept that teens have their own priorities. Honor special holidays.

And many an organization becomes like a big family, whether it is a church, camp, school, a political organization, club or whatever. On the Hudson River, the Clearwater organization has spawned a number of smaller groups that act like families, and the singing gets better and better. In 1971 we started a "Beacon Sloop Club." At first nobody wanted to come to another meeting.

"Don't call it a meeting; call it a potluck supper," said my wife Toshi. Thirty people showed up. Had a feast, sang some songs. A few announcements were made. We agreed to have another potluck supper in exactly one month. And for twenty-nine years, regular as church, we've had monthly potluck suppers on the waterfront. No one knows what anyone else is bringing, but it's always a feast. Short meetings; most work is done in the subcommittees. The ramshackle building the city let us use has been gradually fixed up. We repay the favor by picking up waterfront litter and putting on little waterfront festivals.

As folks gradually learn the songs, the music gets better and better. Never twice the same. And the word spread. "If you like singing, visit that gang." And a hundred years from now someone will say, "How come they have such good singing there?"

And someone will answer, "I guess they inherited it."

"The Human Race Diet," 1977

Found in Seeger files

From time to time religious leaders or political prisoners go on hunger strikes or undertake fasts of some sort in order to convince others of their serious intent. In this year of 1977 we would like to propose something slightly different. We think it would have educational value.

If all the food in the world were parceled out on the U. S. dietary level it would feed only about 1/3 of the human race. Americans should try at least once a year, perhaps twice or more times a year, living for *one or two weeks* on the amount of food that would be available if all the food in the world were divided up equally.

Admittedly, it's hard to figure this out exactly. The shortage of calories would not be so extreme. There would be more than 2,000 calories available daily. Keep in mind that a 25-year-old man weighing 130 pounds would normally require about 3,200 calories per day. However, the shortage of protein and other nutrition would be hardest to take. There would be extremely small amounts of meat, milk, eggs or cheese. The exact figures on this we do not have yet, but we are trying to get them. There is also the problem of a shortage of green leafy vegetable and yellow vegetables or fruit with vitamin C.

The big shortage in the world is in protein. There are huge areas throughout Africa and Latin America, as well as Asia, where entire populations grow up with not enough protein. Growing children need protein, especially in the earlier years for the development of brain cells. However protein does exist in grains and legumes (beans to you). Furthermore, it's worth keeping in mind that one can get as much protein from one acre grown in legumes as one can get from two acres in the form of milk and cheese. Or from four or five acres if the protein is in the form of beef.

In other words, considering the world food shortage, it would be better to grow legumes rather than to raise meat.

Our suggestion is that people look into this question. There are books on the subject. There are United Nations figures. There are nutritionists that can help. The basic thing to remember is that if the world is going to find its way out of the present crisis, it is not only going to take a reordering of our scientific and technological development. It will take a sharing of the world's resources. It's an important old word: S–H–A–R–E. If we don't share, we will not get the human race together and civilization will be destroyed.

No sense being gloomy about it though. Has anybody got a good name for this diet? "The Human Race Diet?" How about "The Nobody Hungry Diet?" How about "The Seconds For Everyone Diet?"

Sincerely,
Toshi and Pete Seeger

"Like the Brief Flare of a Match," 1963

From Seeger's regular "Johnny Appleseed, Jr." column in
Sing Out! magazine, no. 13.1, February/March 1963

In traveling around the country, I get a chance to meet some of the hundreds of talented young performers coming up in the folk music field. This year, returning to one city, I found a young fellow I'd especially admired was experimenting with narcotics—the hard stuff, with needles. I felt sick at heart, almost like weeping. This guy was talented. Now his career will be like the brief flare of a match, instead of a fine hearth fire which could have warmed us all, for years.

I felt I'd like to kill the guy who got him on it, if I only knew him, and then realized that, for all I knew, the pusher was helpless himself, and behind him there was a bigger villain—and behind him reached the shadowy world of organized big money crime. What can you do? Well, maybe you can't stop the steamroller, but you can snatch someone out from in front of it.

I feel almost as violent about the milder but more common forms of narcotics—the happy dust, the ether sniffs, the tea sticks. Partly because they pave the way for the needle, part because they're all so unnecessary.

OK, OK, trim your beard, patriarch, I hear someone say. So the world is full of habits. Sure it is, but there's a damn big difference between common ones like smoking, which might cost a few hundred dollars a year, and forms which drain every cent you've got and leave you willing to steal or prostitute to get more.

Furthermore, the need for secrecy opens this field of folk music wide open to some of the most vicious kind of blackmail. Artistic, political and otherwise. So don't tell me it's none of my affair. That monkey on his back is the concern of us all.

On the two acres of land my family and I cleared on the mountainside by the Hudson, birds occasionally drop seeds of poison ivy. But my father-in-law and I rip it up, every time old three leaves makes his appearance. So, though the plant is common throughout this region, on our two acres friends can roam safely, lie on the grass, even if they're highly allergic to poison ivy.

If the smallest seedling of it makes an appearance, we just tear it out by the roots.

"Duck Down a Dozen Blind Alleys," 1965

From Seeger's regular "Johnny Appleseed, Jr." column
in *Sing Out!* magazine, no. 14.6, January 1965

The country seems to be full of ambitious young people with guitars in their hands. I get letters every week asking, "How can I get started as a folk singer?"

I used to beg off, protesting that I was no one to hand out advice. I was singing for the fun of it for twenty years before anyone paid me for singing. And then, I sang for another ten years for five- and ten-dollar bills, and, very occasionally, for a big fee like $50. Only in the last five years have I been able to turn down work, during summer vacation, for example, so I can spend more time with my family.

I guess I feel like urging people who would like to spend their lives making music not to be in too much of a hurry to make money from it. It is true that artists must eat, but if you are in too great a hurry about eating, sometimes the art isn't so good. You can make the same kind of mistakes as the girl of sixteen who is overanxious to marry. Consider, also, that if you really enjoy making music, you are liable to enjoy it for many years longer if you keep it for a hobby and do not make it your profession.

But, if you love people as well as love music, okay. 1964 is a good time to start. It's an expanding market and there are jobs. Get a friend with a tape recorder to help you make a few small audition tapes, and start mailing them around. And insist on honest criticism, rather than a polite turn-down.

Meanwhile, sing for as many different kinds of audiences as you can. Experiment widely. Duck down a dozen blind alleys and duck back out again. Sing for hospitals and veterans homes, orphanages, golden age clubs, indoors, outdoors, in small and big places, for rich and poor, drunk and sober. Summer camps are often good for a job. The pay is not astronomical, but it is sometimes adequate. The worst hazard here is that you can very easily get hoarse. But learning how to pace yourself so you don't strain your voice is one of the most important things a singer can learn. So, in this respect, a summer camp is as good a training ground as a saloon. (Saloons are good experiences, too; Woody Guthrie used to advise all kinds of young singers to try them.)

All this will force you to experiment with different kinds of songs and different kinds of idioms and approaches. How can you decide what path you want to follow if you can't poke around a bit and see what the various paths are like? After a few years, you'll have a couple of hundred songs stored in your memory, and will have the know-how to fit the right song to the right occasion. (Is it hard? It's always hard to do something well, and that goes for baking a cake or teaching a class. Any fool can do something sloppily, and some can even get away with it for a few years and make a living at it.)

The biggest mistake you could make would be to think you have to "make it" quick while you're young, while the fad is on. Quick fame can be one of the headiest of poisons, and the aftereffects are rough, to say the least.

I hope you don't take all this as an attempt to discourage you from being a musician. On the contrary, I feel like urging every talented person I know to take up the profession. The world is full of human beings who live in little boxes and don't know about each other, and you can teach them and encourage them more freely than perhaps with any other art form. Novelists need publishers, actors need theaters, composers need orchestras, and painters need galleries, but all you need are some songs in your head, a guitar in your hands, and people with ears to listen.

True, it's a rough life. Like a gambler, you'll not be sure from month to month what your future will bring. It's hell on trying to raise a family. It is so hard on the health (irregular sleep, irregular food) that a person in poor health usually can't keep up with it.

But the things you'll see! The people and places, and, most of all, the warm feeling that you've raised somebody's spirits and helped them "keep on keeping on." Go to it. Once, it was argued that the pen was mightier than the sword. Nowadays, there is at least a fighting chance that the guitar may be mightier than the Bomb.

"If I Had an Axe," 1997

From Seeger's regular "Appleseeds" column in
Sing Out! magazine, no. 41.4, Spring 1997

There's another new book, *There But Fortune*, a bio of Phil Ochs by Michael Schumacher. It's a good book, but I'm sorry it repeats the lie that I tried to axe the mike cable at Newport in '65 because I didn't like Bob Dylan going electric.[3] Not true. I didn't mind his using drums, bass and electric guitar. I *was* furious at the distorted sounds so no one could understand Bob's great words. He was singing "Maggie's Farm." I tried to get the sound people to improve it. They shouted, "No, this is the way they want it." I shouted back, "God damn, if I had an axe I'd cut the cable."

Ah, well, in a way I hope that the rest of the bio is just as inaccurate, because it makes out Phil to be a too self-centered guy, needing women, consumed with ambition for the big time. I loved him and I loved his music.

---

3. By the 1965 Newport Folk Festival, Bob Dylan was already established as one of the stars of the folk song revival. For his set at the festival, Dylan eschewed his usual acoustic guitar accompaniment and performed with a full band playing electric instruments. Commonly referred to as the "Electric Dylan" incident, the radical departure from form was received by the audience with mixed reactions, ranging from enthusiasm to outrage. Seeger's involvement has played a prominent role in the mythology of the incident, in particular the claim that he was so perturbed he attempted to cut the sound cables with an axe. See the next chapter for more on the incident.

"Haul in Rhythm upon a Rope," 1977

Found in Seeger files, dated February 1977

I don't know for sure who Clio[4] was, but I know that the ingenious men and women, the daring and hardworking people who during the last ten thousand years developed the art and craft of sailing, deserve to be remembered. They live on in us, of course, but we'll do a better job of steering for the future if we knew better from where we came.

The Bible says we all came from Adam and Eve. Professor Leakey[5] said the Human Race started off in Africa. The history of boats and ships show that good ideas have come from every corner of the world. It's well-known that the invention of the compass came to Europe from China. Less well-known is that the idea for retractable keels—daggerboards and later centerboards—also came from the Orient.

The idea of tacking against the wind came to Europe from North Africa. In the 15th century, Italian sailors with their square-sailed ships were amazed to see Arab ships literally sailing rings around them with their triangular lateen rigs. The first Italian admiral who tried such triangular sails was threatened with excommunication if he used them. "Only someone in league with the devil could sail against the wind." Obviously somewhere along the line the admiral must have persuaded authorities that the triangular sail was just a devilish good idea that ought to be swiped.

Our nautical language holds bits and pieces from every continent. "Catamaran" from Malay; "starboard" from the Viking's "steerboard" where the steering oar was held. And in tools, ropes, and materials we draw upon dozens of ancient cultures, perhaps hundreds of cultures.

Now some say that technology, having made it easier and easier for fewer and fewer people to do more and more damage, has doomed the Human Race to an early death. They may be right, but they may not be. Old-time sailors knew that some mighty heavy jobs could be done if enough people hauled in rhythm upon a rope. And we know that the strongest ropes are only made up of tiny fibers which are only strong because they are in close contact with each other. May our four billion humans get in ever closer contact with each other, knowing our common past. Then we, and history, will have a future.

---

4. Clio is the muse of history in Greek mythology.
5. This is a reference to Louis Leakey (1903–1972), who, with his wife Mary, established the theory that humans first evolved in Africa.

"Of Good Cheer," 1987

Found in Seeger files

I do feel I am more pessimistic than I used to be. I do believe that nuclear weapons are going to be put behind us. Probably some of the most conservative people in the world will eventually come to realize, and some of them already have, that it's too dangerous and too big a risk that all life on Earth may go back millions of years. I'm not quite as optimistic about toxic chemicals being put in their place. They're so handy and we all use them. I'm not even as optimistic as that about a third problem: the new information that scientists uncover every year. How do you keep some things out of the hands of insane people? What would Hitler have done had he known about recombinant DNA for example? So I'm not as optimistic as I used to be. But I do believe we have a slim chance. I do believe that the happiest people in the world that I've ever known were those who were struggling, even though against great odds, and even though they knew they would not live to see any kind of victory. They struggled, and they rejoiced. As Jesus said: they were of good cheer. As Woody Guthrie was of good cheer, as Victor Jara[6] was of good cheer.

Did you ever stop to think that what we're doing today is carrying on an extraordinary tradition that I think dates at least from the Phoenicians in the Mediterranean? Early human society was pretty ruthless. The neighboring tribe spoke a different language: it was the enemy. One tribe captured the other and destroyed everything they had. Any symbol of their culture represented the devil: their idols, music, and song. I don't mean to run down ancient tribal society. Actually, when I was age seven I read Ernest Thompson Seton's book about the American Indians, and I decided that was the way to live: no rich, no poor. If there was food, everyone ate; if there was no food, everyone went hungry. So I've called myself a communist since I was age seven.

But, nevertheless, tribal societies have tended to treat each other cruelly. The Phoenicians realized you could swipe a good idea from an enemy and use it. The Greeks, Egyptians, and other people living around the Mediterranean started learning, borrowing, and stealing from each other. The wonderful thing is, you can steal something cultural, and the person whom you stole it from keeps it.

I'm a musician. I steal every day of my life. I hear an idea on the radio and say, "gee, what a nice idea," and I start trying to imitate it on the banjo. I hear a melody and put new words to it. A good melody is

---

6. Jara (1932–1973) was a Chilean musician and activist, a critical figure in the *Nueva Canción* Latin American folk song movement of the 1960s. Shortly after the military coup of 1973, in which Socialist president Salvador Allende was deposed and replaced by the far-right commander in chief of the Army Augusto Pinochet, Jara was arrested, tortured, and killed.

like a well-constructed house; it's built so strong that generation after generation uses it, often for different purposes. It might have been a warehouse at one time, then a dwelling place at another time, and then it becomes a workshop. Likewise, some of the great old melodies have been used for hymns, love song, marching songs, and for many other purposes.

I want to pay tribute to the extraordinary musicians of Chile. I'm thinking of Violeta Parra.[7] Her songs are going to last generation after generation. People will learn Spanish just in order to learn them, because it's very difficult to translate poetry. You know, Robert Frost[8] was once asked, "Mr. Frost, what is your definition of poetry?" Frost thought a moment and said, "Poetry is what gets lost in the translation." Nevertheless, one tries to translate; we're all translators. Cooks translate old recipes for new stomachs. Some of the best Irish tunes had English words put to them.

[Jose] Marti wrote a verse which should be remembered by everybody in the world:

> I cultivate a rose
> For the friend who gives me his hand
> And for the cruel one who would
> Tear out this heart with which I live
> I do not cultivate thistles nor nettles
> I cultivate a rose.

Here's Marti's poetic way of saying something said by every other person who's thought about the world, ever since agriculture was invented and class society came along, whether it's Jeremiah, or Marx or Jesus. He says, "With the poor people of this world, I want to cast my lot."

---

7. Parra (1917–1967) was a singer and a leader of the *Nueva Canción* movement in Chile. Her most famous work is the oft-covered song "Gracias a la Vida."
8. Frost (1874–1963) was one of the best-known American poets of the 20th century, noted particularly for his depictions of rural life in New England.

19

Other Correspondence

"More Clever Ways to Crucify a Person," 1963

Letter to Bob Dylan, dated November 1963; found in Seeger files

Dear Bob,

Once a week we try to look at an American magazine so we don't get too out of touch with U. S. events. So what should we see but the article about you in the November 4 *Newsweek*.

All I could think of was, "Bastards."

These guys can sure think of more clever ways to crucify a person. I have hopes and a feeling though that you are not going to let it all bother you too much, but just keep on doing what you think best, and making up good songs.

Hastily,
Pete

"Here It Hit Home," 1963

Letter to Bob Dylan, dated December 3, 1963; found in Seeger files

To Bob Dylan
Somewhere in the US of A
Dear Bob,

When I sang "Hard Rain" for 3,000 folks in a public park here [in India] yesterday, it got an ovation—far more than any other song I sang. Most adults know a little English, and many speak it very well, since it's the nearest thing to a common language India has just now. I've sung the song everywhere on this trip (Australia, Japan) but here it hit home the most.

...I think if you ever get a chance, you ought to visit here. You'd get a tremendous reception. There would be no language barrier (as you would find in Japan, or many other countries) and you would have a very good influence on thousands of singers and songwriters here.

All this plus some of the world's greatest virtuoso music on sitar and sarod. You've never heard fancy picking unless you've heard it here.

All for now. Take it easy but take it.

As ever, with thanks for your songs,
Pete

"The Confidence to Sing a Song," 1986

Letter to Joe Boyd, record producer, dated
March 25, 1986; found in Seeger files

Dear Joe,

I just read the good interview with you in "Folk Roots." If I am ever fortunate to meet you, I hope you won't be surprised if I put my mouth about one inch from your ear and shout at the top of my lungs, "Hiya, Joe." I did not object to the loud volume of sound when Bob was singing at Newport in 1965. I was outraged at not being able to understand his words.

Some kinds of music, like steel bands, I like to stick my head right inside the speaker, I like it that loud. And, while a good deal of rock music is not my favorite kind of music, I have to admit that it manages to get the listeners' bodies moving far better than I have been ever able to get an audience singing, hard as I try. And "Maggie's Farm" is, in my opinion, one of Bob's greatest songs, right up there alongside "Dear Landlord" and "Hard Rain" and a batch of others. Incidentally, I accompanied Floyd Westerman, the Native American singer, with his own version of "Reagan's Farm."

The main problem which amplification it seems to me, is similar to the problem with instruments. They tend to discourage the ordinary average person who just likes to sing a song into thinking that they can't sing without it. And in the long run what the human race needs in the way of music is the ability and the confidence to sing a song, whether it is at the fireside, bedside, tableside, workside, sidewalk side, or anywhere side without having to think of it as a "performance." And none of the "folk revivals" in any country nor any festivals, magazines, recordings that I know of have really attacked this problem and made much headway in solving it. Skiing and swimming are participation sports for millions, but music seems still to be in hock to the experts, and most of the millions listen. The best thing about rock is that millions have been dancing.

All best wishes,
Pete Seeger

"The Frail Star on the Stage," 1965

Dated July 28, 1965, apparently revised
August 20, 1965; found in Seeger files

Memo to: Myself

It isn't pretty to see a corpse—man or beast. We usually bury them in earth or sea or nowadays, burn them in expensive incinerators. Indians and Indonesians do it more poetically, sprinkling perfumed oil upon the flesh before setting it alight. Ancient tribal customs often let animals dispose of it. In the Arctic, polar bears. In Africa, hyenas. Our plains Indians tie the body to a scaffold and let the birds pick the bones clean. But I wonder if relatives stood around to watch and listen to the process; I doubt I could.

I know that last week in Newport, I ran to hide my eyes and ears because I could not bear either the screaming of the crowd nor some of the most destructive music this side of Hell. Bob Dylan, the frail, restless, homeless kid who came to New York in '61 was now the frail, restless, homeless star on the stage.

Once a year I like to lie on the grass or sand at night and look up at the stars for a few hours. When family or friends are also there, we call it a star party, and when we see a flaming streak across the sky, we all exclaim, though the light has died before the echo of our voices. But I am glad I saw this shooting star and thanks to the invention of written language and the more recent inventions of paper, printing and LPs—I can recapture a bit of its flame and pass it on. The songs Bob wrote in 1962 and 1963 will be sung for many a year.

Why, you ask?

I suppose the painstaking analysis of poetry is one of man's more foolish endeavors. Who wants to analyze the aerodynamics of a seagull or the meteorology of a sunset? But I think scientists also love beauty, even though they have analyzed it. So I now try. Analysis:

The author of "Hard Rain" said: "I'll walk to the depths of the deepest black forest where the people are many and their hands are all empty." The author of "Mr. Tambourine Man" said: "There is no place I'm going to." The intriguing snarl of his voice now held no hope.

I sang the first of these two songs in 24 countries around the world and found new meanings for it in every place. I don't think I'll be singing the second except in memoriam to Bob.

Why? What is the reason for the change—I don't know. A girl gone perhaps. A manager come. The claws of fans. Or was he killed with kindness?

I will still keep singing "A Hard Rain Is Gonna Fall," and "Who Killed Davy Moore?" and "Fair Thee Well My Own True Love." Bernice

Reagon sings "Playboys and Playgirls;" Joan Baez still sings "With God On Our Side" and Peter, Paul and Mary sing "The Times, They Are A-Changin'" and of course, "Blowin' In The Wind," which is also sung by millions of people in other parts of the world as well.

His more recent songs—who is going to sing them? And for how long? And of course this bring up a whole question of "What's Wrong With Rock & Roll?"

I like some Rock and Roll a good deal. Chuck Berry and Muddy Waters. I confess that, like blues and like flamenco music, I can't listen to it for a long time at a stretch. I just don't feel that aggressive, personally. But I have a question. Was the sound at Newport from Bob's aggregation good Rock and Roll?

I once had a vision of a beast with hollow fangs. I first saw it when my mother-in-law, whom I loved very much, died of cancer. This beast came and fastened itself upon her back. It had a hundred hollow claws and fangs which it sunk into her neck and shoulders, into her upper arms and up and down her spine. Its two huge eyes glared at us silently, as if to say, "you'll never unfasten me till I have drunk my fill." For each fang was hollow and sucked the juices of life from her body till it was left a lifeless shell.

And who knows, but I am one of the fangs that has sucked Bob dry? It is in the hope that I can learn that I write these words, asking questions I need help to answer, using language I never intended. Hoping that perhaps I'm wrong—but if I am right, hoping that it won't happen again.

"A Certain Independent Originality," 1967

Letter to Charles Seeger, dated 1967; found in Seeger files

Dear Pop,

I passed a music store today and on the spur of the moment stopped in and ordered a copy of the new Bob Dylan record [*John Wesley Harding*] to be mailed to you. I know you don't have time to listen to all the pop records that come out, but I'd be curious to know what you think of this. I like it a lot.

Bob Dylan, in case you didn't know, was raised in a small town in Minnesota. His father was a Jewish owner of a hardware store. Bob ran away from home several times, was a college dropout, heard Woody's records, came to NYC in 1961, at age 19 I think, and showed himself a prolific and talented songwriter, pretty much in the Guthrie tradition—using old melodies with slight changes, and new words which were more than mere editorials in rhyme, even though they touched upon peace and civil rights and other contemporary subjects.

The left tried to lionize him; he reacted violently against this, saying fuck you to them all. He dressed outlandishly, screamed out new songs with electric backing; cynicism came to the foreground. It was common assumption that he was on drugs of some sort. For two years the pages of *Sing Out!* were full of violent arguments pro and con his new material.

In '66 he was almost killed in a motorcycle accident, spent long months in the hospital with a broken neck. After a year and a half comes this new LP to break the silence. The songs are shorter, lyrical, full of double and triple possible meanings—endless meanings.

In brief, the 1962 poet sang, "I'll walk to the depths of the deepest dark forest/ where the people are many and their hands are all empty."

In 1964 one said, "I'm not sleepy and there is no place I'm going to" (from "Mr. Tambourine Man" which some said was an ode to marijuana, but I think is much more than this).

In 1967, as you'll hear, he says, "There's many among us who think life is just a joke / But you and I, we've been through that."[1]

Maybe Bob Dylan will be like Picasso, surprising us every few years with a new period. I hope he lives as long. I don't think there's another songwriter around who can touch him for a certain independent originality, even though he is part of a tradition.

Much Love.

"A Thankless Task," 1969

Letter to Tom and Edral Wilson Winslow,[2] dated
October 30, 1969; found in Seeger files

Dear Tom and Edral,

Awfully good to hear from you and to hear that things went well in Connecticut.

I hope you will be able to do more bookings like this. As your name and reputation spread you will get invitations to sing at many different kinds of places for many different kinds of people. I am very glad to be able to refer people to you.

I wish I could be more helpful in the way of getting jobs for you and others that I know. Unfortunately, the average person that calls me is just as much a prisoner of the "Star system" as anybody else, and they

---

1. "A Hard Rain's Gonna Fall," "Mr. Tambourine Man," and "All Along the Watchtower," all c. Special Rider Music.
2. Tom Winslow (1940–2010) was a folk musician who was heavily involved in the Clearwater campaign, penning the song that would become its anthem, "Hey Looka Yonder (It's the *Clearwater*)." Edral Winslow (1939–2007) was active in the Clearwater organization and the author of a vegetarian cookbook.

always want to get someone with a well-known name who can help fill the hall. Toshi and I still, in effect, act as our own managers, although we now work through several different agents in different parts of the world. But for many years, the only bookings I got were those I managed to dig up myself by writing letters, making phone calls and sometimes by renting the hall and putting up the posters myself.

Being an agent is in many ways a thankless task. No wonder there are so few good agents since often the only reward is money. Yet there is a great need for creative and imaginative agents because throughout America there are many good musicians who need to be brought before the public. I must get hundreds of letters every single month from hopeful singers and songwriters and all I can do is encourage them not to give up in spite of how long it seems to take to get started.

I would suggest to you, specifically, that you make tape recordings and get photographs and make Xerox copies of any newspaper reviews which you have and send them to many different kinds of places, not only concert agents and colleges and schools and television stations, but hospitals, old age homes, orphanages, prisons, any place where there are people who you can sing to.

You are unique and individual people and the contribution you can make to the human race is something very special and I know we will be working together on programs on and off during the next few years, but please, please, please don't count on me. I cannot promise a single thing. At the moment I am sitting at my desk wishing that I could get out and work in the woods in the bright sunlight, but I am faced with a mountain of mail that has come in during the week that I was out west.

Love to all three of you.
Pete

"A Few Suggestions," 1988[3]

Letter to the New York State Commission of Correction,
dated August 1, 1988; found in Seeger files

Dear Commission,

I've just read the booklet "General Information & Rules and Regulations." Thank you for giving it to all inmates. I have only a few suggestions:

    1. On page 2, item 2C—how *does* one "clean a shower"?

---

3. This letter was written while Seeger was being held at the Albany County Jail, serving a one-day sentence ordered after being convicted of disorderly conduct earlier that year. Seeger was arrested, along with civil rights activist Al Sharpton, for blocking traffic in a demonstration on April 4, which protested the alleged rape of Tawana Brawley.

2. The entire booklet should be printed in more normal size type. Then it will be a better read.
3. How about a page of isometric exercises, with small sketches, following item 3 (page 4)? Especially for middle-aged or older inmates, this is important, mentally, as well as physically.

One other small matter: there should be more fiber in the diet. You may not want to pay for green vegetables, but you could have bran instead of Rice Krispies. And this very week, when Surgeon General Koop[4] urges Americans to cut out fat in the diet, it's unnecessary to give out so much butter.

Sincerely,
Pete Seeger

[Seeger provides his home address]—*I'm only in the Albany jail a few days (I think).*

"Without Dictating Details," 1989

Letter to the Board of Directors of *Sing Out!* magazine, dated October 15, 1989; found in Seeger files

Dear Fellow Members of the Board of Directors of *Sing Out!*:

I guess all of us must have been frustrated at the end of our three days in Madison, because there are things we would have liked to have discussed which we never got around to. This situation is going to get worse and worse unless we right now divide ourselves up into subcommittees and manage to do 90 percent of the work before we get there. So let's start now dividing ourselves up into these subcommittees.

I would not like to be on the committee looking into finances, although, as you know, I'm a fiscal conservative, even if I may be called a political radical.

I would not like to be on the committee setting policy for *Sing Out* Archives, or, as they're called, "Resources Center," because they're going to have to be handled by computer and I am a nudnik when it comes to computers, even though I think in the long run, this can be one of *Sing Out*'s most important segments for all of us singers throughout the world.

I would not like to be on the committee setting policy for publications, even though I'm fascinated with them, nor on the committee helping with the 40th anniversary celebrations nor the 50th anniversary celebration ten years from now.

I would like to be on the committee setting policy for the magazine, partly because I helped start it 45 years ago with the *People's Songs Bulletin* and have at least a couple times helped bring it back from the dead.

---

4. C. Everett Koop (b. 1916) served as the thirteenth surgeon general of the United States.

I realize that some of you may not want me on this committee because I have such strong feelings on the subject, but I think perhaps I can learn to set policy or to help set policy without actually dictating any details. This committee should never ever tell the editor what song or article must go in or what the layout must be exactly or what the illustrations on the cover should be in detail. All it should do would be to work with the editor to try and formulate proposals for policy which can be followed throughout the decades, and I hope if we all do our job right, that magazine will have a circulation up in the five figures and be known throughout the entire world by people like us.

Who would like to be on this committee? It would be convenient for me to have it in the East, but perhaps there are people in the Midwest who would want to come to Chicago for the *Sing Out* program during the month of May, and we could have a meeting out there. Or we could have a meeting in California during mid-January when I'm in Los Angeles and San Francisco. In any case, any one who feels strongly about anything in the magazine, I urge you write to this committee care of Mark,[5] so whenever the committee is put together, they'll have input from all of us, and I want to hereby apologize for my desperate act of trying to get on the agenda once again the subtitle, "The Folk Music Magazine." But as long as I have a Dictaphone in my hand and Xerox to copy these pages, I'll tell you that the reason that we have this subtitle is because in 1964, as a result of the Newport Festival, the word, "folk" was temporarily commercial, and Irwin Silber was desperately trying to raise the circulation by selling on newsstands. Up to that time, *Sing Out* had no subtitle. Consider, most magazines don't have subtitles. If it had to have a subtitle, a more accurate one would be, "A Folk Process Magazine." However, I think this is a job for the committee to discuss, whether I am on it or not.

I look forward to hearing from you. See you next October in Bethlehem [Pennsylvania].

Happy Solhanamas.[6]

Best,
Pete

"The Rule of This Class Must Be Overturned," 1987

Letter to Richard Leakey, dated June 5, 1987; found in Seeger files

Dear Friend Leakey,

I have Xeroxed many copies of your article, "I Will Not Celebrate the Constitution," as well as the article in the *Guardian* newspaper

5. Mark Moss, the then-and-current executive director and editor of *Sing Out!*
6. Among Seeger and his friends, "Solhanamas" refers to the season when (Winter) Solstice, Hanukkah, and Christmas all occur.

reporting on Justice [Thurgood] Marshall's speech in Hawaii.[7] I also Xeroxed copies of the enclosed, which I thought you might be interested in looking at.

This year, and I think for other years to come, if I'm lucky to live, I will be handing out copies of these because, while I do not feel exactly like "celebrating" the Constitution, I feel like continually studying it and trying to analyze in ever more detail its various successes and failures over 200 years as it has gradually changed and developed. Let me explain more in detail.

First of all, recognize that it was essentially a North European document. The North Europeans were, I believe, more racist than the South Europeans. The latter had fought and traded and enslaved but also mingled with Africans over several thousand years at least. When King Charles V of Spain ruled, he decreed that no single women would go to his colonies in Central and South America. He *wanted* his soldiers to intermarry with the Indians and create a stable ruling class which would be part Indian. Such a decree would have been unthinkable to the English. Among the English, one of the worst charges one could level at somebody living in one of their colonies was that they were "going native," not dressing for dinner, eating local food, etc. Nevertheless, the North Europeans had some interesting traditions. [Karl] Marx harked back to the "communist" tribes of Germany two thousand years ago and more. One thousand years ago, Viking traders, not marauders, took their lightweight boats from the Baltic through the Russian rivers to Constantinople. Somewhere in Russia, someone shouted at them, "Who is your leader?" And their reply has resounded down through Scandinavian tradition. "We have no leaders. We are all equal." OK, they were equal looters, rapists, racists.

I don't think many historians face up to the delightful ironies of the Magna Carta. Eight hundred years ago, the robber barons of England pointed their swords at King John and said, "Sign that or else." They did not want rights for anybody but themselves. If anybody had suggested that they were achieving rights which would later on be used by tradespeople and peasants, God forbid, they might have added some qualifying clauses to make sure that these rights would be given to them and to them alone. But as it was, they got the right of trial by jury of their peers and the right of *habeas corpus* and a few other things.

Three and four hundred years later, the rising middle classes claimed these rights also, and after several centuries of jailings and torturings,

---

7. Marshall (1908–1993) was a Supreme Court Justice, the first African American to hold the position, who served from 1967 to 1991. Having begun his career as a lawyer for the NAACP, Marshall was a champion of civil rights during his tenure on the Court. The speech Seeger references, given to commemorate the United States Constitution's bicentennial in 1987, garnered some controversy for Marshall's statements suggesting that the Constitution was an imperfect document which had, among other things, allowed for the subjugation of some Americans, and which thus required ongoing adjustment.

got them. A couple hundred years later [Thomas] Jefferson put them into the Bill of Rights and 200 years later young lawyers fought successfully for these rights to be applied to the grandchildren of slaves in Alabama and Mississippi.

I never really appreciated these rights myself until the House Un-American Activities Committee tried to put me in jail in the 1950s. And in the '60s one of my children was standing on the sidewalk in Mexico City, watching a student demonstration, when the police opened up with their guns and later she was in jail for six months with no right of *habeas corpus*, no right of a speedy trial, and so on. Most of Latin America, I think, could learn something from North European traditions.

Give a hand to the Dutch, also. When Peter Stuyvesant tried to rule New Amsterdam with an iron hand, it was an English Quaker who foiled him and ended up sailing all the way to Amsterdam and coming back with a piece of paper which said that he had the right to worship God in his own manner. You might want to sometime learn the whole story by visiting the Bowne House in Flushing [Queens, New York].

Well, I'm getting off the subject. What I think I intended to say in the beginning was that I will celebrate some of the better parts of the Constitution, like the Bill of Rights, like the fact that the method of amending it was built in so securely that the various amendments are some of the best parts of it and have overruled gradually some of the worst parts.

Some of the checks and balances are so subtle, they are worth studying in detail, such as the president being the civilian head of the Army, but not being able to wage war unless the House of Representatives granted him the power. And this one particular item may be the thing which may bring down the racists and militarists who have been so powerful in Washington during the last few years.

I have to admit that, partly because it was so ingenious, the Constitution has kept one ruling class in power[8] for 200 years and thwarted the attempts of revolutionists to overturn the rule of this class. It has been my lifetime belief that the rule of this class must be overturned or else, in the long run, there is not only no hope for the United States but no hope for the human race, as some people become more and more and more powerful through their accumulations of billions and soon to be trillions of dollars. At age 68, I don't think bombs and bullets will do it, nor do I think words alone will do it. Songs won't do it. Pictures might have a better chance. I look forward to the videotape revolution, with hundreds of thousands of tapes flying around the world, making connections between human beings of all sizes, shapes and colors. And

---

8. "Precisely because it was somewhat flexible and responsive to pressure, and rich men could bounce back into power the minute that pressure was relieved—rich, white men." —P. S.

in the end, what will save this world will not be our words nor any other mean of communication, but it will be our deeds.

Sincerely,
Pete Seeger

"One Helluva Fine Man," 1995

Letter to the Parole Board Director of the New York State Department of Corrections, dated October 4, 1995; found in Seeger files

Dear Sir,

I write you to testify that Elder Ben Monroe (89A7357)[9] is in my opinion not only rehabilitated but is one of helluva fine man, and will be of great help to society. The sooner he is paroled, the better.

Sincerely,
Pete Seeger

"The Freedom to Discover and Destroy," c. 2000

Letter to the editor of *Scientific American* magazine; found in Seeger files

Dear Editor,

If we believe in basing our actions upon logic and observation, would it not be wise for the scientists of the world to try and agree what are the most dangerous areas of knowledge, and thus help the human race reduce the problems which our children and their children will face? Some say the problems are insolvable. Here is their logic:

1. How can we have a technological society without research?
2. How can we have research without researching dangerous areas?
3. How can one research a dangerous area without uncovering dangerous information?
4. How can one uncover dangerous information without it sooner or later falling into the hands of insane people like Hitler?
5. How then can the end of the world be prevented?

I write today because it seems to me that work can be done on all these five levels, and it would be a mistake to think that a solution will be found on any one level alone, unless at the end the entire human

---

9. Elder Ben Monroe was an inmate at Sing Sing Prison, where Seeger met him while giving a concert. He graduated from a seminary program offered to inmates, becoming an ordained minister. He was paroled soon after this letter was written.

race, facing up to the danger, achieves the tenuous peace of the conference table, while we all discuss our options.

Is your magazine concerned with such matters, or does it say, "These are questions for others to solve"? But wouldn't that be like the churchgoing housewife who prays, "God, please bring peace to the world. All I can do is take care of my family and my kitchen"?

We have observed that the human race includes not only generous and thoughtful people, but selfish and power-hungry people—and hence now also angry and insane people. So, logic tells us that sooner or later these latter types will use science and technology to destroy the world. You think not? Why? Because they haven't yet?

What the whole world needs to do is face up to the contradiction that the freedom to discover, which has given us modern folks the freedom to prosper, to travel, to learn and discover more, has also given us the freedom to destroy ourselves and our children. How can we limit one without limiting the other?

Sincerely,
Pete Seeger

"E-lim-inate the Negative," 2007

Letter to former President Bill Clinton, dated
March 9, 2007; found in Seeger files

Dear President Bill Clinton,

I write to apologize—deeply apologize—for injecting a negative note when we met briefly at Harry [Bealfonte]'s[10] birthday party[11]—an otherwise wonderfully positive occasion. I should have remembered Johnny Mercer's old song:

> *You want to ac-cent-u-ate the positive,*
> *E-lim-inate the negative,*
> *Latch-on to the affirmative*
> *Steer clear of Mister In Between*

---

10. Belafonte (b. 1927) has had an illustrious career as a singer/entertainer and in movies. Throughout his career, he has also been a political activist, campaigning internationally for civil rights.
11. As Seeger recalls the incident five years later: "Around ten o'clock, ex-president Clinton came in. I said to him, 'President Clinton, I would have given my life for you if you had supported Lani Guinier. Why didn't you?' His face dropped—'Pete, I couldn't do it. Ted Kennedy was against it and ...' and then he noticed a camera was on, pushed past me and just put on a big smile. And then the word came down, please destroy that footage." Guinier was a law professor Clinton nominated to be Assistant Attorney General for Civil Rights in 1993, but then asked to withdraw from consideration after conservatives charged that her support for proportional representation amounted to "anti-Constitutional" views on voting.

I've told Jim Brown, whose film crew may have caught the inter-change, to destroy the footage.

And I'll say now, as I should have said then, congratulations for having survived the presidency in good health, and able (as President Carter has shown) to do good things impossible to do when you were in the White House.

I will say: I'm with Granny D.[12] It's a scandal and a shame that so few people vote. I'm for IRV.[13]

But you keep on. Stay well. (At 88 I'm losing my brain.)

Pete Seeger

12. Doris "Granny D" Haddock (1910–2010) was a political activist, famous for walking across the United States in 2000, at the age of 90, in support of campaign finance reform.
13. Instant-runoff voting (IRV) is an alternative voting system, whereby voters rank their choices for office instead of merely selecting the one candidate they most like.

Part 4
Looking Back and
Looking Forward

20

Philosophical Musings and Utopian Visions

"Dear Fellow Humans," 1963

From *Seventeen* magazine, November 1963

I usually mistrust older people's giving advice to younger, because while often their advice is very good (the values of foresight, temperance, persistence, etc.), they forget that younger people usually know one of the most important things of all: the value of enthusiasm and enjoyment of life.

Twenty-five years ago Franklin Roosevelt spoke to my generation. "Youth: Hold fast to your dreams," he said. In other words, don't give up on your ideals of peace, freedom, justice, truth—the way so many adults do. When you come down to it, more people die from discouragement than from any disease. And why do people get discouraged? Because they feel that life's a joyless struggle; because they feel they're on a dead-end street.

So here are a few of my own recipes for avoiding this kind of discouragement. They may or may not apply to you. Only you can decide.

1. It's better to take a job you want at less pay than a job you don't want for more pay. But you can learn from any job.
2. It's okay to suffer intense temporary discomforts in order to reach a longer-range goal. But make sure it is only temporary.
3. Debts can be chains, best used when they can haul you to new heights, rather than entangle your legs. It's the same with possessions: "Man doesn't possess possessions; they possess us."
4. Travel while you are young and still are free of responsibilities.

See what a big, broad, beautiful land we have here, then maybe a foreign land or two. See that there are honest, hard-working people in every corner of the globe, all quite certain that their own way of living, their local geography, their music, etc., is the most beautiful.

5. Keep your health. It's easy while you are young. But our fine, tempting, modern civilization can erode it easily too. Many a man or woman has finally worked himself into a position in which he could do something and then found he no longer had the health to do it or enjoy it.

5½. In view of the fact that good health and energy don't last forever, it's worth doing some things earlier than later. When my wife and I were about thirty and very broke, we built our own house, inch by inch, on a mountainside. Glad we did: doubt we'd have energy enough to do it now. And I've known too many people who put off such projects "until we have the money" or "until we have the time"—and if they eventually did get the money or the time, they no longer had the energy.

6. A happy sex life may take years to achieve, but it's worth it in the long run. Worth the time, the thought—or rather, the thoughtfulness—and, often, the waiting.

7. A few short ones. Prestige is much overrated. The celebrity business is for the birds. Respectability is nice, but consider: whom do you most want to respect you? Money is like air or water. You need a certain amount to live. Beyond that, who wants to be a dog in the manger?

And now I'll stop before I rattle on any longer, like any old graybeard. All the foregoing applies to the one central thing I mentioned at the beginning: how to keep discouragement from withering the priceless enthusiasm which most young people have.

…Well, here's hoping all the foregoing will help you avoid a few dead-end streets (we all hit some), and here's hoping enough of your dreams come true to keep you optimistic about the rest. We've all got a lot to learn. And don't let your studies interfere with your education.

Sincerely,
Pete Seeger

"There Are No Old, Bold Pilots," 1992

From *The Ageless Spirit,* Ballantine Books, 1992

In sailing we have a saying: "There are old pilots and there are bold pilots, but there are no old, bold pilots." So I think one should praise old people because they managed to get old. You don't manage to get old if you're too careless or reckless. And, you know the old joke: growing old is a lot better than the alternative.

When I reflect on where I am, I just feel blessed. I have good health and energy and a family that has stuck by me, even when they disagreed with me. And I have a large family. I lived with my grandparents as a child, and I had in-laws living near us when our children were small. Now I'm a grandfather in a three-generation household, and I have a lot of brothers and sisters and nephews and nieces. Also, I was able to make a living all my life doing something I loved. Think how many people have had to scramble just to pay the rent all their lives. My kids never went hungry. Oh, we pinched pennies, but that's the way things should be when you think of the people in this world who don't have a penny to their name—it's kind of immoral not to pinch pennies in a way.

I'm an old grandpa now. When I go out singing, I don't have much of a voice, but larger audiences than ever come to listen. I used to sing in Pittsburgh for a hundred people here, or two hundred there, but Arlo Guthrie and I went back and sang for 50,000 in a local park. So there are advantages to being a grandpa.

Another advantage is that you gain a bit of insight, a little more wisdom. That's one of the by-products of living a long time. I do know that I am more suspicious than ever, though, about words. We used to have a little sign hung up on this sloop club here where we're talking and it said, "In trying to persuade others, setting a good example is not the best thing; it is the only thing." And it's signed "Albert Schweitzer."[1] There's an old Southern saying, "I wish his 'do so' would match his 'say so.'" But, you know, I don't do as good a job of it as I wish I could. I still talk too much and don't act enough. Somebody, I don't know who, said, "Words lie halfway between thought and action, and too often substitute for both."

I guess I've gradually come to the opinion that everything's connected more closely than I realized. You can't really solve the problem of poverty on earth unless you can also solve the problem of pollution on earth. And vice versa. My guess is we won't solve the problem of racism and sexism and a whole lot of other things until each of us, individually, realizes how much we depend on others—sometimes those near and dear to us, sometimes those faraway and unknown. It gets you to thinking about eternity, about the spiritual, about the ways we are connected to one another.

---

1. Schweitzer (1875–1965) was a theologian and philosopher who received the Nobel Peace Prize in 1952 for his contributions to ethical philosophy and his charitable work as a missionary in Africa.

These days, I look upon God as everything. Some people say, "Oh, God is in everything." Well, that's our difference of opinion. If I was able enough to look through an electron microscope, to see something one-millionth of an inch in size, they'd say, "That's God's handiwork." But I'd say, "That *is* God." If I was able to look at the screens of a radar telescope to see something five billion light years away, I'd be looking at God there too. They say, "Well, that's the handiwork of God." Well, okay, that's our difference of opinion. And consider that five billion miles away is a long ways, but it's nothing compared to infinity. I really believe that God is infinite.

The late great mathematician and philosopher Alfred North White-head said that religion is the ideal of education throughout the ages because it inculcates duty and reverence. I think that's a good defini-tion of religion—duty and reverence. He says, "Duty arises from our potential control over the course of events, and reverence arises from the perception that the present includes the complete sum of existence, that great amplitude of time, forward and backward, which is eternity." If that can't make you reverent, I don't know what would. We live in a web of interconnections. If I slap my hands together and I disturb some atoms, they're going to disturb other atoms and they're going to push others and, in effect, have influence for all eternity to come. That can make you reverent.

I try very hard to see the world as a whole, and I try to remind myself as much as possible that you can accomplish more with good deeds than bad deeds. The USA would like to have influence throughout the world, but we could have far more influence throughout the world right now if we had not spent three trillion dollars or more on guns and bombs in the last few decades. And they have plans for spend-ing another trillion in the next few years with fancy, new, high-tech weapons in the sky and so on. But we wouldn't have needed any of these high-tech weapons if we'd spent half that amount of money on schools and colleges and training institutions throughout the entire world, because how are the billions of people in the world going to get out from behind the eight ball? True, they need food, but food is a temporary thing, as you know. Remember the old Chinese saying, "Give a man a fish, you can feed him, but teach him how to fish and he'll feed himself a long time." And so, if there was one wish I could have, I guess it would be for the world to learn this lesson, which it seems it still hasn't learned yet. The leaders of the world are saying, "Well, the way we solve this problem is to get rid of those people." That's their solution. But Abe Lincoln said it much better: "It's good to get rid of an enemy, but the best way to get rid of the enemy is to make him your friend." The important thing is, of course, the long human chain we are a part of; if we don't do it right, this chain's going to be broken in too many places. The world may keep on turning, but it may not have any human beings on it, or maybe not any life at all. I think we have to face up to this possibility.

Growing up is about becoming responsible, about lending ourselves and our talents and our energies to the great chain that connects us all.

...This is, of course, the world's best advice to any old person: You don't give up simply because you're not as good at it as you might have been; you still have fun with it. And this goes for almost anything. You do have to recognize limitations, or else you literally won't live long. Don't try and repeat your successes of youth; the aim is to have fun. And within your limitations you *can* have a lot of fun.

...I myself stay active doing a wide variety of things, some intellectual, others physical. I do an average of about three hours a week working in the woods around my house, because we burn four or five cords of stove wood every year. It's good exercise and kind of nice to be out in the woods, listening to the birds and seeing the leaves and the beauties of nature. It's also a time to reflect. In many ways those are the most satisfactory hours of my week. I get away from the telephone and just get to think. In fact, more often than not, the ideas I get for music or songs will come during those hours because in the day there's just too many things going on.

I'm just an old do-it-yourselfer, you know. I think there is a limit to specialization, and I take great pleasure in learning how to do new things. Now, there are times, I'll admit, when I'll be glad to let somebody else do things for me. I was very glad to have an expert doctor repair my knee when I foolishly tore the ligament in it; otherwise, I'd have been on crutches the rest of my life. But by and large, I love to see people in the world trying to do more things and not just watching other experts do it. My father puts it in a good way: "Judge the musicality of a nation not by the presence of virtuosos, but by the general level of people who like to make music." It's kind of the equivalent of what W. E. B. DuBois, the great black scholar, said: "I'd count the wealth of a nation not by the presence of millionaires, but by the absence of poverty."

My father told me there was a graveyard in Tombstone, Arizona, with a little wooden cross over some cowboy's grave and somebody had scrawled on it, "He done his damnedest." And really, that's all we can do in this world: We do our best wherever we are to be a strong link in the chain. If we can be a strong link, we should know how lucky we are, even though the links to come never knew our name, don't know where or when we lived. But in the future, assuming there is a future, they'll know that they would not be there if it hadn't been for a lot of links that came before.

"Good Science Can Be Bad Science," 1989

Dated June 1989; found in Seeger files

"There is nothing good or bad in all this world, Horatio, but that thinking makes it so," said Hamlet. And we are taught that science is neutral; only "what is done with it" is good or bad.

Like most people my age, I'm alive today thanks to medical science. I would not be able to read this page without optical science, nor hear well without the modern miracle of hearing aids. I say this to try to be fair. Because now I must say I believe that a certain religious belief of scientists is a main danger to the future of life on earth, and I know it is offensive to question another person's religious belief.

My father, an old scholar, wrestled with this problem in the last years of his long life, and got me to tangling with it. He put it this way: Scientists pride themselves on making decisions only on a logical basis, on advancing science one more step by strictly sticking to the evidence. Yet at some point in their life, every scientist made a religious decision, a value judgment, unsupported by any evidence, obvious or arcane.

A religious decision? Impossible!

No, said my father; every scientist decided it was a good thing to have an uninhibited, ever-increasing store of empirical information. Yet, he said, if a world were destroyed by the misuse of this knowledge, could we say that it is maybe a good thing to have been a scientist? "Of course," he continued with a wry smile, "I have to admit that if one followed my line of reasoning, one would end up saying that the church committee which told Galileo to shut up was right."

My father died without finding an answer, but I think there is a solution to this contradiction: scientists, and all of us, should recognize that a line can be drawn between good science and bad science, and much of our life's effort should be in trying to agree on the line between the two.

The common definition of bad science is science which proceeds with sloppy evidence, which ends with unsupportable conclusions. Lysenko's attempts to ignore eighty years of genetic research is a good example.[2] Many physical scientists say that the social scientists are bad scientists because their evidence is too difficult to evaluate; it depends on too many variables. Social scientists, from Marx on down, spend their lives trying to define words, without finding agreement.

There is another kind of bad science, though, not so agreed upon. Science that ignores its necessary sequence in the life of our planet is

---

2. Trofim Lysenko (1898–1976) was a Soviet agricultural scientist whose anti-Mendelian theories in crop genetics earned him the support of Joseph Stalin, despite his unorthodox research methods. However, in the years following Stalin's death, Lysenko's methods and theories came under attack from mainstream scientists and he was discredited.

bad science. In early times we could ignore an invention which had not been thoroughly tested. "Let life's experience verify it." And of course in everyday life we often marry, take on jobs, have children, without thinking through a sequence logically.

But in scientific endeavors one tries to plan a sequence of steps to follow. A project without a proper sequence is a badly planned project, from the assembly of materials to the testing of a product. Thalidomide[3] and the Dalkon Shield[4] are recent examples of ignoring proper sequence. Marketing came before sufficient testing. Haste made waste. Science out of sequence is bad science.

And considering the life of our planet today, it must be obvious that world science is ignoring proper sequence in developing certain kinds of knowledge before developing a stable world society able to use this knowledge safely.

To say that all knowledge is equally dangerous is a cop-out. Parents withhold certain knowledge from small children till they can handle it safely. We keep the contents of medical cabinets out of reach. I keep my chain saw hung up high, but keep screwdrivers in a kitchen drawer.

Einstein is supposed to have said near the end of his life, "Ach, mankind is not ready for it." Would the next thing be to say that E = MC[2] was bad science? Perhaps. Subsequent development of the [Atomic] Bomb was.

You say that good results can come unexpectedly from bad things? Of course they do, just as surely as the path to hell is paved with good intentions. Genghis Kahn's disciplined murderers brought the violin to Europe and perhaps pasta·as well. But as Charles Lamb[5] pointed out, eventually we learn that we don't have to burn down houses to get roast pig.

I've never met Jeremy Rifkin,[6] but from what I've read, he seems to have his own particular brand of tunnel vision. We should suspect all tunnel vision, whether of chemists, musicians, or housewives. Nevertheless I think he's got on to something in alerting us all to the dangers of recombinant DNA. What would Hitler have done with this

---

3. Thalidomide is a drug that acts as a sedative and as an antiemetic, combating nausea. The drug was widely prescribed to pregnant mothers during the 1950s to alleviate nausea associated with morning sickness but was soon discovered to cause birth defects in children whose mothers had taken the drug. Tens of thousands of children were affected, and the drug was banned from sale for a number of years in the United States.
4. The Dalkon Shield was an intrauterine contraceptive device possessing a design flaw that allowed bacteria to travel through the device and enter a woman's typically sterile uterus. This intrusion often caused infection, sometimes rendering the user incapable of conceiving a child or, in other cases, producing birth defects in children born to mothers who had used the device.
5. Lamb (1775–1834) was an English writer who produced a wide variety of works, including poetry, nonfiction essays, and Shakespeare's plays, adapted into children's stories.
6. Rifkin (b. 1945) is an economist and political activist, known for his environmentalism and controversial environmental advocacy.

knowledge? And there are little Hitlers throughout the world today, probably in every country.

Won't there always be? Of course not. Always is a long time. Will it take 100 years or 10,000 years to solve this particular problem? What's that compared to 16 billion years before the next visit of the Nemesis Comet, or 5 billion years before the sun puts an end to the watery planet. We do know one thing for sure, as Las Vegas experts know: accidents will happen. That will remind us not to be too hasty.

Until experimenters with recombinant DNA go any further, they should consider how to determine where science out of sequence begins.

And to say, "If I didn't discover it someone else would," should go in the book next to, "If I didn't rob this bank somebody else would." And, "If I didn't rape this woman somebody else would."

No, all science is not out of sequence. Admittedly, finding the right sequence will take a lot of arguing. But only lazy people, bad scientists, will shy away from such arguments. So it is I make so bold as to try and get these few pages printed.

Science is neutral? I have a right to think science is bad when it puts us in danger of our lives, just as I have a right to consider cooking bad which makes us unhealthy even though the dish is tasty, or a tool bad when it tempts people to do bad things. A bulldozer might be a good thing some places, but several times the mountainside where I live has been severely damaged by bulldozers in the hands of careless people. A carcinogen is considered bad over a population as a whole, over a period of time, even though it kills only a small percentage of persons each year. When will scientists be willing to discuss this?

"We'll Disagree on So Many Things," 1997

Draft of a piece published in *250 Ways To Make America Better,*
Villard, 1999. Dated September 4, 1997; found in Seeger files

150 years ago the slave owner's mansion could be an island of comfort surrounded by a large plantation worked by sweating slaves. It didn't last. In the modern world, it will be impossible for USA to be an island of affluence in a world of poverty. It can't last.

To make America better we have to make the world better. Higher wages. That means unions, the right to speak your mind. Literacy. Stable populations, not more population explosion. That means women's rights.

I'll be 80 years old in 1999, so like most folks my age, I tend to be pessimistic. But if there is a human race still here in a hundred years, I'm convinced it will not be because of any one big organization—big church, big government, big political party, big corporation or slogan, or even big UN [United Nations]. Big organizations attract power-hungry people. It will be here because of tens of millions of little organizations, throughout the world. We'll disagree on so many things it'll be hilarious. Save this. Stop that.

But we will agree on a few main things, like, it's better to talk than shoot. Right? And bombs always kill innocent people, whether in Oklahoma City or Hiroshima. Likewise chemical and bacteriological warfare, land mines. And when words fail (they will), we'll use sports, the arts, good food. One woman told me, "Don't forget hot tubs."

And our country with its wonderful 225-year-old traditions of independence, and cooperation, and a few priceless laws like our Bill of Rights—"Congress shall make no laws respecting an establishment of freedom of religion, etc."—we can help lead the way.

In a frontier community folks have to cooperate. In every neighborhood, in every city of the world now, we have to learn how to cooperate again.

"The Teaspoon Brigade," 2008

Foreword to the revised edition of David Dunaway's *How Can I Keep From Singing?: The Ballad of Pete Seeger,* Villard, 2008

Consider: The Agricultural Revolution took thousands of years. The Industrial Revolution took hundreds of years. The Information Revolution is taking only decades. If we use the brains God gave us, we can perhaps now bring about the Non-violent Revolution. If we don't, this could be the last century for the human race.

Who knows, who knows? Technology may save us if it doesn't wipe us out first. In any case, the next few years will be the most exciting years any of us have ever known.

Maybe there's room to retell my parable of the Teaspoon Brigade. Imagine a big seesaw. One end is on the ground, held down by a bushel basket half full of rocks. The other end of the seesaw is up in the air with a bushel basket on it one-quarter full of sand. Some of us have teaspoons and are trying to fill it. Most people are scoffing. "It's leaking out as fast as you put it in."

But we say, "No." We're watching closely, and it's a little more full than it was. And we're getting more and more people with teaspoons. One of these days that whole seesaw will go *zoop!* in the opposite direction. People will say, "Gee, how did it happen so suddenly?"

Us and all our little teaspoons over thousands of years.

Keep in mind that we have to keep using our teaspoons, because the basket does leak. Are you in the teaspoon brigade?

"Optimistic in an Upside-Down Way," 2009

From *Where Have All the Flowers Gone,* Revised
Edition, W. W. Norton & Company, 2009

As the world crisis deepens, many are pessimistic: the rich are still getting richer; billions of people are in terrible poverty; oceans are rising; precious resources are getting gobbled up; populations still exploding. When will the human race straighten up and fly right?

God only knows what the future will be. But I find myself getting a little more optimistic. Why? Because at last people worldwide are realizing that unless there is some sort of world peace, there'll be no world at all. We've had a lot of narrow escapes already. U. S. General Curtis LeMay tried his best to start WWIII. [President Dwight] Eisenhower's people thwarted him in 1954. Kennedy stopped him in 1962.[7] But Murphy's Law says that if an accident can happen, sooner or later it will. In the USSR in 1984, Colonel Stanislav Petrov did not press a nuclear button when computers mistakenly lit up. Now there are chemical and biological weapons that could wipe us all off the face of the earth. Murphy's Law says that, "If anything can go wrong, sooner or later, it will."

But yes, I feel, in an upside-down way, a little more optimistic. Why? Because everywhere in our country, and throughout the world, there are more and more good little things happening. Little organizations. Little political groups, little religious groups, little scientific groups, little cultural groups. Little groups, like the Hudson River Sloop *Clearwater,* which are partly scientific, partly political, partly cultural. And all these little organizations realize that they have to reach out and co-exist in some way.

Songs can help. That's why this book has been put together. Sad songs, funny songs, old songs, new songs.

. . . Now, as I pencil these lines, close to age 90, in bed with my foot up in the air in a sling, I know I'm lucky to be alive. Lucky that Sing Out Corporation (the nonprofit publisher of this book and *Sing Out!* magazine) is alive and kicking. And hoping that this book [*Where Have All the Flowers Gone*] can be part of the worldwide effort to bring this world together, as we learn the art and science of human relationships.

Then, someday, the great art and science of war and military weaponry will be something our great-grandchildren's children will read about, like cannibalism.

As Woody Guthrie said in his first (mimeographed) songbook: "This songbook got an ironclad copyright, number 586139772405318962

---

7. LeMay (1906–1990) was a U.S. Air Force general who presided over the bombing campaign in the Pacific theater in World War II, and subsequently built up the power of the Strategic Air Command, essentially readying it to wage nuclear war.

and anyone caught singing one of these songs will be—a good friend of mine, 'cause that's why I wrote it."

And why I wrote this for you.

Old Pete

"Not a Sustainable Worldview," 2002

Introduction to a reading by Barbara Kingsolver,[8]
dated May 2, 2002; found in Seeger files

Barbara Kingsolver and I have things in common, even though we just met for the first time a few minutes ago.

We've both used the arts to move people to action. We've both gotten more than our share of hate mail, and even death threats.

I wish it could be otherwise. The hate wounds us deeply.

Barbara Kingsolver was one of the lone voices in America to look at the aftermath of September 11th as a true world citizen. She had the courage to say what many of us thought—and time has proved her right.

We've learned a lot about terrorism, and a lot about Afghanistan. Now that we've bombed it, American schoolchildren actually can point to it on a map!

We've also learned that our own money, spent at the gas pump filling up our gas-guzzling SUVs, paid for the attacks on the World Trade Center.

We've learned that many of the caves in which the Taliban were hiding had been dug by farmers long ago, clawing their way through soil and rock in search of a rapidly vanishing water table. The Middle East is an object lesson in the consequences of overpopulation and poor land stewardship. But instead of planting trees, we used American tax dollars to arm and train the *Mujahideen*[9] in fortified cave complexes.

We've learned that our own CIA created Osama Bin Laden, and many more like him. That America built Bin Laden's training bases.

And we learned that America, land of the free, is not as well-loved as we had all presumed.

Why is that?

Because all people everywhere can recognize hypocrisy and cynicism. The great democracy dropping bombs on children. Maybe we are

---

8. Kingsolver (b. 1955) is a novelist whose books have been noted for their social commentary and activist spirit. She wrote a controversial essay shortly after the September 11, 2001, terrorist attacks, in which she argued against the usefulness of a retaliatory strike and noted that the United States had previously and frequently wreaked similar destruction on other nations, presumably engendering the same sense of rage and indignation.

9. *Mujahideen* are Muslims who engage in jihad, a religiously informed struggle against perceived oppression of Muslim peoples and ideas.

despised because our government has not looked at the world through Barbara Kingsolver's eyes. It has not seen the world through the eyes of a biologist who is also a mother. Apparently our government sees the world simply as a business opportunity, and views nations as competitors, to be dominated or even obliterated in the search for competitive advantage. A world of the Self and the Other, in which the Other doesn't need to be treated with love and respect.

This will not prove to be a sustainable worldview. Our government must represent us—we, the people. Not just big oil and other special interests. It must recognize that the United States, as the most powerful nation on Earth has inherited a moral obligation to the people of the world. We must lead by example. We must assume that our vision of egalitarian democracy and civil society applies to people of all nations, colors and faiths, and not just to certain segments of the population within our national boundaries.

We need to practice what we preach. Maybe we can do that simply by seeing the world through the eyes of a biologist and a mother—Barbara Kingsolver.

"The Right Questions," 2004

From Seeger's regular "Appleseeds" column in *Sing Out!* magazine, no. 48.2, Summer 2004

Friends, it looks like this is my last "Appleseeds" column.[10] Doctors and pills have failed to bring my memory back and I can't remember names, words. But, I feel more optimistic about my country and the world as I see women and men in thousands of communities working with young people to solve some local problems. And I feel optimistic about *Sing Out!* magazine as its present staff and directors are steadily improving it and reaching out to more and more people.

Any last words? Keep on learning from people like Woody Guthrie, Malvina Reynolds and others like them throughout the world. People who keep a sense of humor in spite of all the crazy things going on, people who can use words honestly and economically, and yet remember the old saying: "Well done is better than well said."

We can help bring the peoples of this world together in spite of powerful fools in powerful places. We can help by finding the right questions to ask at the right time.

---

10. In fact (as the next entry shows), Seeger continued to write his "Appleseeds" column. As we go to press, he still continues to contribute from time to time to *Sing Out!* and other publications.

"First Things First," 2007

From Seeger's regular "Appleseeds" column in
Sing Out! magazine, no. 51.1, Spring 2007

I can't type much any more, but I've found someone who can read my handwriting and can type, and I've decided I'll try and pick up this column again, if only to urge folks not to give up. I can no longer write songs—words and tunes don't come easy now. But I'm fascinated that this little magazine is still keeping pace with what old John Lomax started a little over a hundred years ago: (John Lomax put out the first book of cowboy songs in 1908. His son, Alan, encouraged Leadbelly, Woody, Josh White and Burl Ives. And helped me.) that a good song can be put together by someone who perhaps hardly knew how to read and write. Now the songs can be spread by modern means of communication and can bring joy, and yes, hope, to millions who are almost ready to give up.

...Today, I think, we must use the most sophisticated technology we have to get back to a point where we will not need it so much. We once hoped the pen would be mightier than the sword. I once hoped the guitar would be mightier than the bomb. Today the TV camera, and that silly little screen which at present wastes the lives of the immature, may be our best hope. It can leap the language barrier. Hooray for the DVD revolution and for the Internet revolution!

"Like Another Sunrise," 1972

From *The Incompleat Folksinger,* Simon and Schuster, 1972

In each of my concerts there are some old songs which you and I have sung together many times before, but which can always stand another singing. Like another sunrise, or another kiss, this also is an act of reaffirmation.

Our songs are, like you and me, the product of a long, long human chain, and even the strangest ones are distantly related to each other, as are we all. Each of us can be proud to be a link in this chain. Let's hope there are many more links to come.

No: Let's make damn sure there are more links to come.

Rob & Sam - I just found another filing cabinet you should check out. It's upstairs in the barn, in the last room on the right, at the foot of the bed.

old Pete

Index